Psychological, Philosophical and Sociological Foundations of Education

J. C. Aggarwal

SHIPRA

(2022, 21,18, 16, 12, First Published 2010)

Rs. 1600

ISBN: 978-81-7541-825-7

2026 Impression

Psychological, Philosophical and Sociological Foundations of Education

Published by:
SHIPRA PUBLICATIONS
LG 18-19, Pankaj Central Market,
I.P. Ext., Patparganj, Delhi 110092, India
Ph.: +91 1147322068; 96500 28065, 9810522367
Email: info@shiprapublication.com
www.shiprapublication.com

Preface

The book is prepared in accordance with the curriculum of a variety of diplomas and degrees in education. It covers the emerging concerns in education presented by the changing philosophical, psychological and sociological perspective.

The volume follows an easy-to-understand approach as well as language.

The content is organized into thirty-seven chapters in three units as indicated below:

Unit I:	Educational Psychology as the Foundation of Education	15 Chapters
Unit II:	Philosophical Foundation of Education	12 Chapters
Unit III:	Sociological Foundation of Education	10 Chapters

The author is grateful to all the authors and publishers whose publications he has made use of in preparing this book.

J.C. Aggarwal

Contents

UNIT II
PHILOSOPHICAL FOUNDATION OF EDUCATION

UNIT I : EDUCATIONAL PSYCHOLOGY AS THE FOUNDATION OF EDUCATION

1

Meaning, Definition and Significance of Educational Psychology

MEANING AND DEFINITION OF EDUCATIONAL PSYCHOLOGY

Educational psychology is the applied branch of psychology in an educational setting. In simple words, it implies the application of principles and practices of psychology to the various dimensions of education with a view to modify the behaviour in an educational environment so that he may amicably adjust himself with the society with maximum confidence, satisfaction and security.

Important definitions are given below so as to understand the true meaning of educational psychology in its various facets:

1. *The Encyclopaedia of Educational Research* states, "Educational psychology is the study of the learner and of the learning-teaching process in its various (branches) directed towards helping the child come to terms with society with a maximum of security and satisfaction".

2. *Stephen* regards educational psychology as "the systematic study of the educational growth and development of a child".

3. *Judd* considers educational psychology as "the science which explains the changes that take place in the individuals as they pass through the various stages of development".

4. According to *Skinner*, "Educational psychology is that branch of psychology which deals with teaching and learning". He further observes, "Educational psychology covers the entire range and behaviour of the personality as related to education".

5. *Crow* and *Crow* put it as, "Educational psychology describes and explains the learning experiences of an individual from birth through old age".

6. *E.A. Peel* considers educational psychology as the "Science of Education".

7. In the words of *Anderson*, "While general psychology is a pure science, educational psychology is its application in the field of education with the aim of socialising an individual and modifying his behaviour".

8. In the words of *Trow*, "Educational psychology is the study of psychological aspects of educational situation".

9. According to *Walter B. Kolesnik*, "Educational psychology is the study of those facts and principles of psychology which help to explain and improve the process of education".

Summing up: A perusal of the above definitions would indicate that the definitions given by Anderson Kolesnik and '*The Encyclopaedia of Educational Research*' provide the true meaning of educational psychology. Other definitions, by and large, put emphasis on 'Study' but do not emphatically state the ultimate aim of studying. A mere study of the behaviour of the learner is not enough unless it is related to the modification of the behaviour towards desired ends.

From these it is concluded that educational psychology is that applied branch of psychology which studies the experiences and behaviours of the learners in relation to educational environment which is mainly provided by the teacher. Therefore, educational psychology becomes a psychology of teaching and learning. Teaching and learning are the main processes of education and the learner is a key figure in the process.

NATURE OF EDUCATIONAL PSYCHOLOGY

Following points bring out the nature of educational psychology. Some of the points overlap:

1. Educational psychology is an applied science.
2. Educational psychology is a social science.
3. Educational psychology is a positive science.
4. Educational psychology is a specific science.
5. Educational psychology is a developing and growing science.
6. Educational psychology is an academic discipline.
7. Educational psychology is not as exact as natural and physical sciences.

SCOPE OF EDUCATIONAL PSYCHOLOGY

Scope of educational psychology is as vast as the scope of education itself. Gates and others have very aptly remarked, "The boundaries of educational psychology are uncertain and changing". The exposition of 'Information Technology' (IT) has been exercising a far-reaching influence on the scope of educational psychology. New and novel situations need new and novel approaches to educational matters. Nevertheless, we may mention the most significant areas of the scope of educational psychology.

Classification I: Broad Areas

1. *Learner: Growth and Development.*
   (a) Heredity and environment affecting the learner.
   (b) General growth and development of the learner at different stages of education.
   (c) Emotional, intellectual and social development of the learner.
   (d) Individual differences of the learners.
   (e) Learner's aptitudes, interests and intelligence
2. *Learning*
   (a) Concept of learning.
   (b) Process of learning.
   (c) Primary and concomitant learning.
   (d) Domains of learning: Cognitive, Affective and Psychomotor.

(e) Factors affecting learning.
(f) Transfer of training.
(g) Learning situations.
(h) Forgetting.
(i) Remembering.
(j) Learning span.
(k) Theories of learning.
(l) Practices of learning.

3. *Personality and Adjustment*
(a) Emotions.
(b) Mental health of the learner.
(c) Mental health of the teacher.
(d) Character development.
(e) Social interaction.

4. *Evaluation and Measurement*
(i) Meaning of the concepts of evaluation and measurement.
(ii) Basic principles of evaluation and measurement.
(iii) Measurement of aptitudes, attitudes and intelligence.
(iv) Measurement of learning.
(v) Measures of adjustment.
(vi) Applications of the results of measurement and evaluation.

5. *Techniques and Methods in Educational Psychology*
(a) Scientific study of educational problems.
(b) Statistical techniques.
(c) Implications of research for the classroom teacher.

Classification II

(1)	(2)	(3)	(4)	(5)	(6)
The Learner (Pupil)	The Learning Experiences	The Learning Environment or Situation	The Learning Process	The Teaching Situation	Evaluation of Learning Experience

1. *The Learner*: This includes the study of growth and development of the individual in various aspects of his personality – physical, mental, social and emotional.

This includes the study of the abilities, needs of motivational forces and anxiety of the individual learner as well as the difference that exist among different individuals.

2. *Learning Experiences*: This includes providing activities and subjects according to the maturity level of the students.

3. *The Learning Situation*: In the learning situation, educational psychology studies such factors as classroom management and discipline, techniques and aids which facilitate learning, methods of teaching, evaluation techniques and practices, guidance and counselling.

4. *The Learning Process*: In the learning process, educational psychology deals with the nature of learning and how it takes place. It considers the various theoretical view points as well as experimental evidences to explain the role and nature of reinforcement, forgetting, problem solving, transfer of training and the learning of concepts, skills and attitudes.

5. *The Teaching Situation*: Effectiveness of educational psychology becomes relevant only when its methods and findings become a part of educational practices when the teachers apply psychological methods.

6. *Evaluation of Learning Experiences*: In recent years, evaluation of learning experiences has assumed great significant in the subject-matter of psychology.

'When to Teach', 'What to Teach', and 'How to Teach'—Questions of Educational Psychology

Educational psychologists are more concerned with the answer of these questions. The first question refers to the developmental processes that gradually mature as the child grows up. Similarly the problem of what to teach is important because of its close relationship with the process of maturation. Certain types of learning can be useful to the child only when he has matured sufficiently in certain faculties. We cannot think of teaching mathematics to a three year child, though he may be taught to count simple things. The problem of how to teach is equally important because there are ways and means of teaching which can make the education of a child more effective, meaningful and useful.

SIGNIFICANCE OF EDUCATIONAL PSYCHOLOGY TO TEACHERS

The work of the teacher is like that of a gardener to a great extent. The gardener needs the knowledge of the plant life. The teacher also needs the knowledge of the learner. It is the duty of the gardener to ensure that all the plants grow and yield good flowers and fruits and he can do so when he is well-acquainted with all the details about them. The objective of the teacher is to ensure that all the learners under his care and charge develop into happy and healthy personalities and he can do so only when he knows how the learners develop and behave. This knowledge is provided to the teacher by educational psychology.

The work of the teacher may also be compared to that of an artist who must know his material thoroughly if he wants to produce a fine piece of art. What will happen to the artist if he starts his work without fully understanding the kind of material he has to work with. The teacher as an artist, is not only required to know the subject-matter but also to know the child's nature and the techniques of moulding his behaviour in accordance with the objectives.

The work of the teacher assume all the more significance and needs more delicacy and expertness than that of the gardener and the artist as here, human beings are involved.

R.A. Davis in '*Applicability and Applications of Psychology with Particular Reference to Classroom Learning*' (1943) has pointed out the significance of educational psychology as, "Psychology has made a distinct contribution to education through its analysis of pupil potentialities and differences as revealed by means of various types of psychological tests. It has also contributed directly to the knowledge of pupil growth and maturation during the school years".

G.M. Blair in '*The Psychological Interpretation of Teaching*' (1947) has stated the importance of educational psychology to the teacher in these words, "Modern teacher, if he is to succeed with his work should be a specialist who understands children, how they grow, develop, learn and adjust. He should be diagnostician, who can discover special difficulties of children and at the same time possesses the requisite skill for carrying forward the necessary remedial work. He should also be performing important educational and vocational guidance functions. No person untrained in the methods of psychology can possibly fulfil the obligations and tasks which are the responsibilities of the teacher".

Principles and practices of educational psychology are needed by the teacher on account of the following considerations:

1. *Knowledge of John and Latin* (*Knowledge of the Learner and the Subject-matter*) *Equally Necessary*: Sir John Adams has put it thus in his book '*New Teaching*'. The verbs of teaching govern two accusatives, one of the person and another of the thing as, 'the master taught John Latin'." He says that there are two definite subjects—John, the student and Latin the subject which are governed by the verb taught". Now the teacher must understand both John as well as Latin if he wants to make 'teaching' effective. Educational psychology helps him in understanding 'John'. He may be a great scholar of Latin but he will not succeed in teaching Latin to John if he has no knowledge of the mental set up of John. Acquisition of knowledge is now no more the main object of education but it is still very significant in the process of education. Acquisition of knowledge is also a sort of modification in the behaviour of the child. For this purpose the educator will have to consider the mental process of the child and not only the quality of knowledge which he is going to put into the living mind.

2. *Knowledge of Individual Differences*: No two persons are exactly alike. There is individual difference. Pupils always differ in their level of intelligence, aptitudes, likes and dislikes and in other propensities and potentialities. Different minds are to be trained by the teacher. There are gifted, backward, retarded, talented and handicapped children. All of them should not be treated in the same manner. Knowledge of educational psychology helps the teacher to cater to individual differences of children.

3. *Educational Psychology and Process of Learning*: Teaching and learning go side by side. All education depends upon the learning of new responses and the capacity of a human child to learn new responses. Educational psychology discusses the nature of learning theories and types of learning for different age levels and situations. Therefore, knowledge of educational psychology becomes essential to a teacher to study all these problems.

4. *Knowledge of Educational Psychology Helpful in Providing a Scientific Attitude to the Teachers*: The knowledge of psychology can make the teacher more scientific in his educational practices and consequently he will be more objective and methodical in his work.

5. *Educational Psychology Useful in the Methods of Teaching*: Educational psychology has discovered many secrets about mental forces. Recent researches made in the field of educational psychology give us valuable suggestions for better methods of teaching and memorising, for making desirable habits and eradicating anti-social tendencies. Educational psychology tells us how significant play and recreation are for the children and how play-way and project methods turn the work of learning into an interesting play.

6. *Educational Psychology Helpful in Changing the Outlook and Attitude of the Teacher Towards His Pupils*: The knowledge of psychology can change the outlook and attitude of the teacher towards children by understanding them adequately.

7. *Educational Psychology Helping the Teacher in His Own Mental Development*: The study of educational psychology can help the teacher to understand himself. He will realise his own merits and weaknesses and make attempts to overcome his weaknesses.

8. *Educational Psychology and Nervous System*: The entire education depends on the function of the brain and nervous system. It becomes essential for a teacher to study the nervous system which controls human behaviour. He must have the knowledge of sensory organs which are the gateways of knowledge.

9. *Educational Psychology and Play*: Play is a natural tendency having great educational potentials. Knowledge of educational psychology helps the teacher to provide for a variety of activities for children.

10. *Educational Psychology Measurements are very Useful for the Teacher*: Educational psychology has made many strides in this respect quite recently. It has produced many reliable tests and instruments of mental measurement. These are proving to be extremely useful in the field of education. We can quite easily measure mental capacities, basic intelligence, temperamental attitudes and special inclinations of children and base educational programmes on these findings. These measurements show that all the children differ and that every child is a unique being. The teacher can know that children with I.Q. below 90 cannot do well in medical, engineering, administrative or other similar vocations. But he knows that such young ones are not doomed if they cannot do well in intellectual callings. He can easily explore some other fields where such children can also flourish.

11. *Character Development*: Educational psychology helps a lot to the formation and development of character. The teacher comes to know the methods he should adopt in inculcating suitable character traits, and moral principles among the children.

12. *Educational Psychology and Productive Activities*: A great stress is being laid these days on work experience and socially useful productive work. Educational psychology helps the teacher to know how various activities in these fields can be used for the fulfilment of the basic needs of children.

13. *Educational Psychology Useful in Guidance and Counselling*: Students need various types of guidance and counselling. A teacher with the knowledge of educational psychology can render very useful service.

14. *Educational Psychology Useful to the Teacher in Realisation of the Aims of Education*: The main aim of education is the harmonious and all-round development of the educand. Development comes from within and the inner potentialities must be understood and approached for the desired modification in the development of the child. The knowledge of educational psychology helps the teacher to understand the inner potentialities which underlie the behaviour of the child.

IMPORTANCE OF EDUCATIONAL PSYCHOLOGY TO DIFFERENT SECTIONS

Educational psychology, being functional in its character is very helpful to all sections of society engaged in pursuing different dimensions of education at all levels of education, i.e., formal, non-formal and informal.

Educational psychology is of great importance to parents, teachers, guidance workers, career masters, and psychoanalysts etc.

According to *W.A. Kelly* (1941), educational psychology is helpful in the following ways:

1. It provides a knowledge of the nature of the child.
2. It gives understanding of the nature, aims and purposes of education.
3. It gives understanding of the scientific methods and procedures which have been used in arriving at the facts and principles of educational psychology.
4. It presents the principles and techniques of learning and teaching.
5. It gives training in methods of measuring abilities and achievement in school subjects.
6. It provides a knowledge of the growth and development of children.
7. It assists in the better adjustment of children and helps to prevent maladjustment.
8. It helps to understand the significance and control of emotions.
9. It gives an understanding of the principles and techniques of correct training.

IMPORTANCE OF EDUCATIONAL PSYCHOLOGY TO PARENTS

An elementary knowledge of educational psychology would prove very useful to the parents who are undoubtedly the first teachers in the following manners:

1. The knowledge of educational psychology points out to the parents that they should show reasonable amount of love and affection to their children. They should bear in mind the maxim, "Love the child and the child will love you. Hate the child and he will hate you".
2. It helps the parents to understand the process of development and growth of their children.
3. Educational psychology acquaints the parents with the emotional, mental and physical needs of the children.
4. Educational psychology impresses upon the parents of the necessity of providing wholesome environment to the children so that they lead a happy life and are free of anxiety.

5. Educational psychology enables the parents to know that they should not take resource to repression and punishment which adversely affect the mental health of children.

6. Educational psychology enables the parents to observe keenly the behaviour of children. It enables them to control their habits.

7. It helps the parents to understand themselves, their roles and responsibilities towards their children.

2

Human Growth and Development: Significance, Characteristics and Principles/Stages—Educational Implications

SIGNIFICANCE OF CHILD DEVELOPMENT

Children constitute a nation's future human resources. It is, therefore, very important that their welfare receives the highest importance.

India's commitment to the cause of children is as old as its civilisation. The child is believed to be a gift of God. He must be nurtured with care and affection within the family and the society.

The development of the child should receive all the more attention in Indian scenario as here child population constitutes nearly 34 per cent of the total population (nearly 15 per cent up to the age of 6 years and 19 per cent between 6 and 14 years of age). This is the most crucial and vulnerable period of life. The foundations of future are laid at this stage. Naturally, the foundation must be stable and strong.

The great Indian economist Amartya Sen reminds us, 'You reap what you sow and you don't reap what you do not sow". Now it is the time to sow properly the future of this great Indian nation by investing properly in children.

On account of the paramount importance of child development, the UNO adopted the Convention on the Rights of the Child (CRC) on November 20, 1989. India ratified this Convention in 1992.

The Convention recognises that the child, for the full and harmonious development of his or her personality, should grow up in a family environment, in an atmosphere of happiness, love and understanding.

Article 28 of CRC recognises the right of the child to education.

Article 29 states that the education of the child, shall be directed to the development of the child's personality, talents, mental and physical abilities to their fullest potential.

The Convention proclaims that childhood is entitled to special care and assistance.

SOME PROMINENT EDUCATORS AND THINKERS ON THE DEVELOPMENT AND EDUCATION OF CHILDREN

A. Indian Thinkers

It is the highest duty of parents, teachers and relatives to adorn children with good education, noble character, refined manners and amiable temper.

—*Swami Dayanand (1825-1883), 'Satyarth Prakash'*

No one was ever really taught. Each of us has to teach himself. You can supply the growing seed with the materials for the making up of its body, bringing to it the earth, the water, the air that it wants. And there your work stops. So with the education of the child.

—*Swami Vivekanand (1863-1902), 'The Complete Works of Swami Vivekanand, Vol. V'*

To say good words, give wise advice to a child has very little effect, if one does not show by one's loving example the truth of what one teaches.

—*Sri Aurobindo (1872-1950), 'The Supramental Manifestation', 1952*

I now clearly see the mistake is to judge boys by the standard of grown-ups, children are living beings—more living than grown up people. The child learns so easily because it has a natural gift. But adults, because they are tyrants, ignore natural gifts and say that children must learn through the process as themselves. This is one of man's most cruel, most wasteful mistakes.

—*Rabindranath Tagore (1861-1941), 'Personality'*

By education, I mean an all-round drawing out of the best in child and man—body, mind and spirit. I would develop in the child his hands, his brain and his soul. —*Mahatma Gandhi (1869-1948), 'Basic Education'*

Heaven is in the happiness of the child.

—*Gijubhai Badheka (1885-1939), Education in Primary School in Hindi*

Unfortunately in our schools we look upon children as mere raw stuff on which we can impose our unjust views through our powerful wills. We must liberate the young from the blind despotism of the old. We must not destroy his right and power of self-direction.

—*Dr. Sarvapalli Radhakrishnan (1888-1975), 'Occasional Speeches and Writings, 1956'.*

In the training of our teachers for various kinds of schools, they should be provided with the technique of such competent observation as will enable them to understand their pupils and direct their educational work in the light of this understanding. —*Dr. Zakir Hussain (1897-1969), 'Educational Reconstruction, 1958'*

B. Western Thinkers

Let our maxim be to follow the laws of nature in all things.

If the teacher's skill cannot make any impression, his blows will have no effect. —*John Comenius (1592-1670), known for his publication 'Great Didactic'.*

Begin by making a careful study of your scholars (Children).
—Jean Jacques 'Rousseau' (1712-1778)

I wish to psychologise education.

Teach him (child) nothing by words that you teach him by things themselves. *—John Heinrich Pestalozzi (1746-1827)*

Play is the highest phase of child development. It is the purest, most spiritual activity of man at this stage. It gives, therefore, joy, freedom, contentment, inner and outer rest, peace with the world. *—Fredrich Froebel (1782-1852)*

The secret of education lies in respecting the child.
—Ralph Waldo Emerson (1802-1882)

The pupil is immature and helpless and he must not be given a long rope with which he may hang himself. *—W.C. Bagley (1874-1946)*

Education must begin with a psychological insight into the child's capacities and interests. The curriculum must grow out of child's interests, experiences, impulses and needs. *—John Dewey (1857-1950)*

Child is a body which grows and a soul which develops—these two forms—physical and psychic, have one eternal form, life itself. We must neither mar nor stifle the mysterious powers which lie between these two forms of growth. The school must permit the free, natural manifestations of the child.
—Maria, Montessori (*1870-1952*)

MEANING OF HUMAN DEVELOPMENT

The primary aim of education is the development of the whole child (Fig. 2.1) which implies well-balanced personality; aesthetically sound, culturally defined, emotionally stable, mentally alert, morally upright, physically strong, socially efficient, spiritually enlightened, vocationally self-sufficient and internationally liberal. It is, therefore, very important to understand the meaning of development, its very dimensions, factors influencing development and the role of the teacher and the school in this task.

In the words of *A. Angyal*, "Development cannot be considered in terms of the mind alone but rather in terms of the individual as a whole in relationship with his experience with others". *J.E. Anderson* explains development as, "Development does not consist merely of adding inches to one's height or improving one's ability. Instead development is a complex process of integrating many structures and functions".

In the words of *E.B. Hurlock*, "Development means a progressive series of change that occur in an orderly predictable pattern as a result of maturation and experience".

DISTINCTION BETWEEN GROWTH AND DEVELOPMENT

The terms growth and developments are often used interchangeably but they are conceptually different. According to *L.D. Crow* and *A. Crow* (1962), growth refers to structural and physiological changes whereas development is concerned with growth as well as those changes in behaviour which result from environment. Usually growth contributes to development but not always.

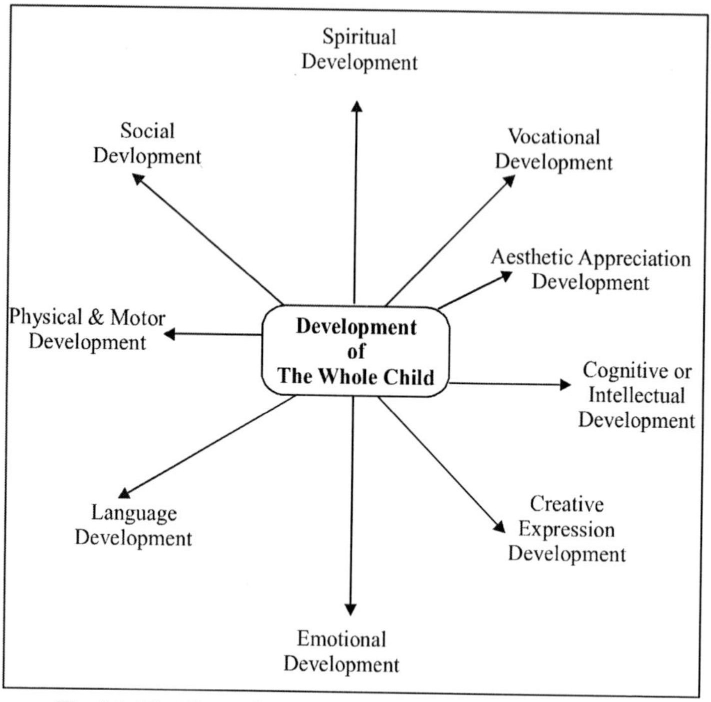

Fig. 2.1: The Figure Illustrates the Various Aspects/Patterns of the Development of the Learner

In general growth refers change in size and body—bones, muscles etc.

Maturity involves qualitative change.

Development involves a series of progressive, orderly and meaningful changes leading to the goals of maturity.

As the child grows, his mind and body mature and he is able to function at a higher level. Development is a product of maturation and learning.

	Growth		*Development*
1.	The term growth generally refers to an increase in size, length, height and weight.	1.	It refers to overall changes in the quality or character rather than quantitative aspects.
2.	Growth is one of the parts of development.	2.	It includes growth also.
3.	Growth describes the changes that take place in a particular aspect of the body and behaviour of an organisation.	3.	Development refers to the changes in the organism as a whole.

(*Contd.*)

Growth	Development
4. Growth does not continue throughout life. It stops when maturity is attained.	4. Development is continuous and goes from womb to tomb.
5. Growth may or may not lead to development. A child may grow in terms of weight by becoming fat but this growth may not result in any functional improvement, i.e., qualitative change or development.	5. Development is possible without growth as we notice that some children may not gain in terms of height or weight or size but they do experience functional improvement or development in intellectual, social, emotional aspects.

CHARACTERISTICS AND PRINCIPLES OF DEVELOPMENT

Following are the general principles of growth and development of individuals:

1. *The Principle of Individual Differences*: There are individual differences in the development of children. The difference is mostly in the intellectual capacity of all human beings. Difference in special aptitudes is most marked among children. This is caused by differences in heredity, endowments and environment.

2. *Principle of Continuous Growth and Development Process*: The growth and development starts from the moment of conception of the individual in the mother's womb and continues till he reaches his grave. It is a continuous stream of development. Development proceeds by stages but it is a continuous process. Changes in the patterns of body and behaviour take place throughout life. Emergence of each type of behaviour is dependent on the development that has gone before.

3. *Principle of Uneven Tempo of Growth and Development*: Growth and development though is continuous, yet its rate of development is in fits and starts and not uniform at all times. In the earlier stages it is quick, but slows down in later years of infancy. Again at the state of puberty, there is a sudden rise in the growth and development.

4. *Principle of Uniformity of Development Pattern*: Although development has individual differences, yet it follows a definite sequence common to the off-springs of human beings. The outstanding example is that off-springs develop their head first and other parts of the body later on. Motor and language development in human off-springs has a definite sequence.

5. *Principle of Development from General to Specific Responses*: If we examine the different developmental aspects of the child we will find that general activity precedes specific activity in all his/her actions. The movements of the child are of general nature in the beginning but later on they become specific.

6. *Principle of Interrelation*: It has been observed that the growth and development in various aspects like physical, mental, social, etc. are inter-related and interdependent. Growth and development of the child in one aspect leads to the development in other aspects as well. It has also been observed

that children who are highly intelligent, generally have a robust health, whereas children with lower intelligence have weak health and regress in their emotional and social development.

7. *Principle of Developmental Direction*: There are two important principles of development: (a) Cephalo-cadal, and (b) Proximo-distal.

By cephalo-cadal development we mean that it has a longitudinal axis, i.e., that human development is from head to foot. This implies that control of the body as well as improvement in the structure itself, develops first in the head and progresses later to parts further from head. Another example of this aspect of development is that a child can lift his head by his neck before he can do so by lifting his chest.

The proximo-distal tendency means that child develops from the centre of the body, i.e., the spinal chord to the periphery of the body, i.e., fingers. In the beginning, the child is able to control his large fundamental muscles and smaller muscles later on. The outstanding example is that the control over fingers comes after control over the arm and the hand.

8. *Principle of Integration*: This principle implies that the development of the child is both from general to specific and specific to general. The child while busy in his specific activities arrives at a general rule. Again he gives a tryout of his general rule on certain specific activities. Thus, the development of the child integrates both general and specific activities.

9. *Principle of Predictability of Development*: We know that every child develops in his own way and develops nearly constantly. It is with this presumption that we can also predict his future range of development. This prediction is only possible in the case of children of average or normal development. We shall not be able to predict in the case of abnormal or highly intelligent children.

10. *Principle of Spiral and Non-Linear Development*: This principle implies that the development of the child is not in a straight line (linear) but it is in the form of a cork-screw (spiral). He advances in his development in one period but takes rest in the following period. This enables him to consolidate his development.

11. *The Principle of Struggle*: While the child is developing up towards maturity there are conflicting impulses and demands. The child struggles against these in his striving for maturity.

12. *The Principle of Indigenous Motivation*: As the child matures in his capacities of doing, thinking and feeling, he has an impulse to put them to use and he does it wholeheartedly. This has been described by *Jersild* as 'Indigenous Motivation'.

13. *The Principle of Anticipation*: The child in his/her process of development also uses his capacity of self-repair. He modifies his behaviour and even habits keeping in view what he is going 'to become' in future. Thus, he consciously anticipates his future direction of development.

14. *The Principle of Interaction between Heredity and Environment*: The development of the child is a product of both. This is true at all times and stages of his development.

EDUCATIONAL IMPLICATIONS OF THE PRINCIPLES OF DEVELOPMENT

A knowledge of principles of growth and development will enlighten the parents and teachers on the potentialities of their children. They should, therefore, provide suitable opportunities for the maximum development of their children. For planning and implementing suitable programmes for the all-round development of children, following guidelines may be taken into consideration:

1. *Need for Paying Attention to Individual Differences of the Learners*: The parents and teachers should keep in view that there are individual variations in the rates of growth and every child develops in a unique way. Hence they should pay individual attention to every child. It stipulates the provision of diversified courses and provision of all activities according to needs and interests of various stages of growth.

2. *Need for Developing Motivation*: Teachers should organise teaching-learning programmes, procedures and practices according to the maturational levels of children.

3. *Need for a Pragmatic Outlook*: Every stage of growth has its possibilities and limitations. Teachers and parents should not place undue demands on the child. Such demands lead to mental tension for the child.

4. *Need for Correlation*: Teachers should keep in mind that children develop on the principle of interrelatedness of development growth. It is, therefore, necessary for them to search for the principle of correlation.

5. *Influence of Heredity and Environment*: Parents and teachers should keep in view that it is difficult to change the heredity of the child but environment can be modified.

6. *Emphasis on Doing*: 'Doing' helps in the development of mental, physical and social skills.

7. *Creativity Aspect*: Children are creative and they need assistance and guidance to develop their creativity.

8. *Individual Attention*: Each child needs attention and a neglected child in the home or in the class loses interest in work and play.

9. *Different Modes of Teaching-Learning*: Singing songs and learning rhymes, drawing pictures and reading stories help the child's mind to grow at the pre-primary, primary and middle stages.

10. *Recognition Aspect*: For proper development, all children need adequate praise and recognition for their work.

11. *Satisfaction of Curiosity*: Children are curious to learn and respond with interest to new things.

12. *Reasonable Repetition*: Children learn through repetition; of course excessive repetition tends to kill interest.

13. *Need-Satisfaction at Each Stage*: Each stage in the development of an individual has developmental needs peculiar to it and these must be taken note of.

14. *Observation*: Observation of children leads to better understanding on the part of parents and teachers.

15. *Clarity*: When parents and teachers speak clearly, use appropriate words and adopt a proper style and manner, children are likely to do the same.

16. *Healthy Environment*: Children need an environment which promotes initiative and trust.

17. *Consistency and Firmness*: Consistency, firmness, love and patience on the part of parents and teachers will go a long way in the wholesome development of children.

18. *Human Relations*: Children need close, loving and sensitive relationships with the adults who are charged with the responsibility of looking after them. The feeling of being wanted and loved in the children is vital to their inner development. Children need a sense of security which should be provided by parents and teachers. Anger and violence are damaging to the inner development of the children. Healthy relationships established in the earlier stages of life help to set the pattern of future development.

INTERRELATIONSHIPS AND INTERDEPENDENCE OF VARIOUS PATTERNS OF DEVELOPMENT

It has been observed that the growth and development in various aspects like cognitive, emotional, language, motor, physical and social is inter-related and interdependent. Development in one aspect of the child leads to the development in other aspects as well. As observed by *Pestalozzi*, "Education is the natural, harmonious and progressive development of man's innate powers". *Gandhiji* wrote: "By education, I mean an all-round drawing out of the best in child and man—body, mind and spirit". Education, therefore, has to develop all these in such a way that the development is balanced and harmonious. While taking measures for the all-round development, it must be remembered that all the aspects of development are inter-related and interdependent.

An individual is one 'whole'. He cannot be compartmentalised. All parts of the individual need equal attention. It is very difficult to decide whether it is the hand or the head or any other part which needs more attention at the cost of the other.

Interrelationships of Physical Development and Other Aspects of Development

'Healthy mind in a healthy body' is an old adage and it is true to the core. Appropriate physical development makes valuable contribution to other aspects of development. When a child is physically weak, he cannot devote necessary attention to the cognitive aspect. A physically weak individual may remain emotionally disturbed. Likewise he may not be able to participate in social interactions. His language and motor development may also suffer. A physically unhealthy person, other things being equal, is unable to perform effectively his duties to himself, to the community and to the God. He cannot offer his prayer properly.

Interrelationship of Emotional Development and Physical Development and Other Aspects of Development

A child under emotional strain is likely to be physically unhealthy and socially inefficient. An emotionally unstable individual is not able to acquire cognitive abilities. His motor development may remain stunted.

Interrelationship and Interdependence of Motor Development with Other Aspects of Development

Motor development is closely related to physical development, creative and productive activities. As observed by A.I. Gates, "The acquisition of motor skills is of value not only from the point of view of the personal satisfactions that accrue from competence in self-help and independence of adult aid, but also from the point of view of good social relations with others".

Interrelationship of Social Development with other Aspects of Development

Social development is dependent upon language development, physical development, cognitive development and motor development. Social development leads to development of other aspects. Likewise if an individual does not mix up with others, he may feel lonely. Loneliness may lead to emotional disturbance which may create difficulties in cognitive and language development.

Interrelationship of Cognitive Development with Other Aspects of Development

Without cognitive development, an individual may remain ignorant and indifferent to other aspects of development. He may be termed as a 'snob'. He may not be able to appreciate and understand social relationships. Undue emphasis on cognitive development may ignore emotional side of an individual's personality. His health may also be adversely affected.

To sum up, for the harmonious and total development of an individual, it is absolutely necessary to pay due attention to each aspect of the development as all aspects are interrelated and interdependent.

Fig. 2.2 illustrates the interdependence of various aspects of development.

Fig. 2.3 illustrates the interrelationship of cognitive development with other aspects of development.

Likewise are the interrelations of other aspects of development.

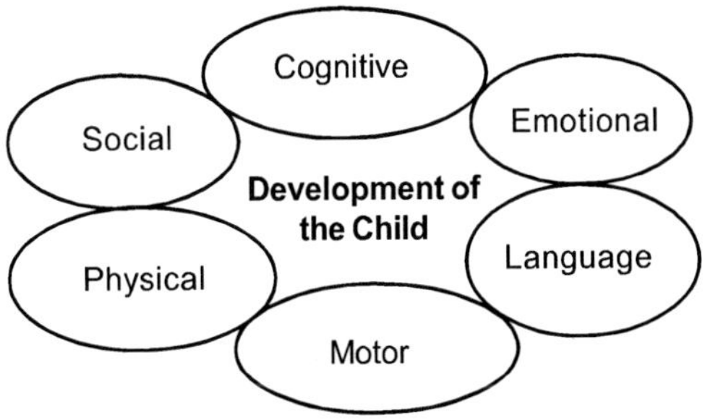

Fig. 2.2: Interdependence of Various Aspects of Development

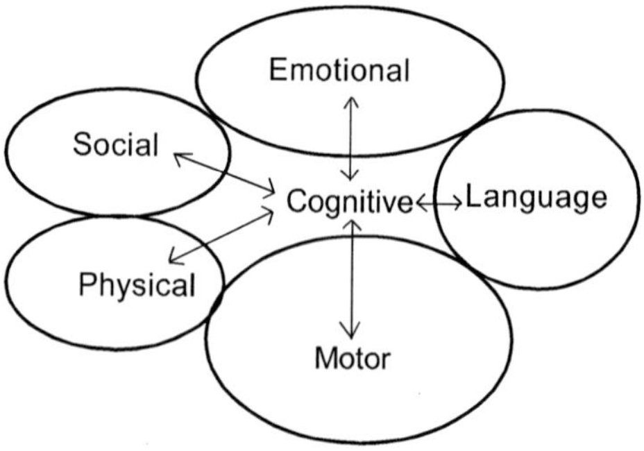

Fig. 2.3: Interrelationship of Cognitive Development with Other Aspects of Developments

DIFFERENT STAGES OF DEVELOPMENT AND IMPLICATIONS

Strictly speaking there is no sharp line of demarcation between one stage of growth and development and the other. Nevertheless each stage has certain specific characteristics which must be kept in view while upbringing and teaching children. There is no doubt that the entire development is usually influenced by two important factors, i.e., (i) Heredity and (ii) Environment. Each stage has its own problems of development.

Scholars and thinkers differ as regards the ages of various stages of development. Here the generally acceptable stages of development are given:

Table 2.1: Generally Acceptable Stages of Development

Age Groups	*Stage of Development*	*Schooling Stage*
Birth to 2 years	Infancy	
2 years to 6 years	Early childhood	Pre-primary (Nursery/Kindergarten etc.)
6 years to 14 years	Later childhood	Primary/Elementary
14 years to 18 years	Adolescence	Secondary and Senior Secondary
18 years to 40 years	Young adulthood	
40 years to 65 years	Mature adulthood	
Over 65 years	Aged adulthood	

Infancy (from Birth to 2 years)

Characteristics: The period is marked by rapid physical growth.

Importance: Modern researches have established that the period of infancy is the foundation on which the future development of the child depends.

Highlighting its importance *Ruth Strang* of Columbia University remarked "During the first two years of his life he lays the foundation for his future".

Dr. F. Goodenough, a prominent child psychologist is of the view, that "One-half of an individual's mental structure has been attained by the age of three years".

Educational Implications: 1. The Montessori approach seems to be the ideal approach.

2. The environment in the family should be of affection and love. The child should have the feeling that everybody in the family loves him.

3. Freedom should be given to the child in his movements.

Early Childhood (from 2 Years to 6 Years)

Characteristics: This is the most important and impressionistic period of child's life. He learns his first lesson of citizenship in the home and the school. He develops the instinct of curiosity. He loves make-believe plays.

Educational Implications: This period of a child's life is of great educational significance. It has been correctly held by *Watson* that "the scope and intensity of learning during this period exceeds that of any other period of development". The following points should be kept in view both by parents and teachers while planning the education of the child at this stage.

1. Provision of Healthy Environment.
2. Rational Treatment.
3. Satisfaction of Curiosity.
4. Learning by Doing.
5. Dynamic Methods of Teaching.

Education may be imparted to children with the help of the Montessori Method which is based on sound psychological principles required for this stage.

These methods provide opportunities for the child to develop his five senses as well.

Play-way spirit should permeate all learning activities.

Later Childhood (from 6 to 12 years)

Characteristics: Bodily proportions change. Generally boys are considered superior in games requiring physical strength while girls are superior to boys on the use of fine muscles and in acquiring skills like drawing, painting, sewing etc. According to *Watson*, "A derivative of anger, annoyance becomes more prominent in later childhood. There is rapid intellectual advancement".

Educational Implications: He develops his basic outlook, values and ideas. We, as parents, teachers and social workers have an important role to play.

The school authorities have a special responsibility towards the development of the child.

1. Child's individuality should be respected.
2. It should be kept in mind that each child is unique.
3. Co-curricular activities should be organised.
4. Group competitions may be arranged.
5. Games should be regularly organised.
6. Creative talent should be developed.

Adolescence (from 14 to 18 years)

Chief Characteristics: (i) There is an outburst of various aspects of development; (ii) It is the period of opposite pattern; (iii) It is the period of preparation for living well in society; (iv) The period is marked by far-reaching sex changes.

Educational Implications: (i) Compulsory physical exercises and games; (ii) Monthly health check-up; (iii) Provision of good library; (iv) Organisation of clubs; (v) Guidance services; (vi) Rational approach by the teacher; (vii) Meeting fears of inadequacy; (viii) No discrimination; (ix) Excursions and educational tours.

(*Discussed in detail separately*)

Significance of the Knowledge of the Growth and Development Process to the Teachers

A knowledge of development patterns at each stage is essential for psychological, practical and scientific reasons. Proper acquaintance with the pattern of human development would enable the teacher to know to a considerable extent at what age what behavioural changes occur and when these patterns are usually replaced by more mature patterns. This is important as too much is expected from students and if they do not show such results, they develop a feeling of inadequacy. A knowledge of development pattern enables the teachers to adjust the teaching-learning process according to the needs and interests of the students. The teachers come to know when students need special guidance.

Deviation from normal behaviour becomes a cause of anxiety for the teachers as when the pattern of development is normal, one stage leads them effectively into the next.

3

Heredity (Nature) and Environment (Nurture): Development and Educational Implications

INTRODUCTION

There are extreme views regarding the influence of heredity and environment on the development of an individual. However, the fact is that the functioning of heredity and environment is similar to that of two eyes, two hands, two feet, two legs, etc. on the development of a person. Each one is complementary and supplementary to the other. Sometimes one plays a more dominant role and the other relatively less. For the balanced and harmonious development of an individual, a balance and harmonious interaction between heredity and environment is essential. Of course, each has its limitations. There is a limit to which each can influence the development of the individual. The role of the home and the school is to ensure that optimum use is made of these limits.

MEANING OF HEREDITY

O.B. Douglas and *B.F. Holland* define heredity as "One's heredity consists of all the structures, physical characteristics, functions or capacities derived from parents, other ancestry or species."

According to *R.S. Woodworth*, "Heredity covers all the factors that are present in the individual when he begins life not at birth, but at the time of conception about nine months before birth."

Every child comes into this world with certain physical and mental characteristics which he got from his parents and ancestors.

He is born with a body and mind which developed from the fertilised ovum. His limbs and organs grow from the same. Some of his mental tendencies are also based on the same. This is all on account of heredity.

It is seen that a cat gives birth to a kitten, a dog to a puppy and a human being to a human being. It is on account of this factor we say that the class of dogs will give birth to puppies or that like begets like. Still, we find a lot of variation among cats or dogs or human beings even if they are born of the same parents. Why does this happen? We shall make a brief study of this phenomenon.

PRINCIPLES OF HEREDITY: HOW HEREDITY OPERATES

1. *Like Tends to Beget Like*: Black-coloured parents generally have black children, tall parents tall children, bright parents bright children and so on.

This holds good of all other characteristics and racial differences. "Nature sees to it that each species or genus breeds true to type, save where there are laws governing occasional deviations."

2. *Principle of Variance*: Only certain traits follow hereditary laws. Common observation shows that although like tends to beget like, yet the resemblances of parents and their off-springs are never perfect. Black-eyed children may be born to brown-eyed parents. Even the two twins are not exactly alike.

3. *Principle of Convergence of Two Life Streams*: A portion of inheritance comes from the maternal side and the remaining portion is contributed by the paternal side, i.e., the child's maternal and paternal lines, contribute about fifty per cent each of his inheritance. More specifically, it is generally assumed that 1/2 comes from parents, 1/4 from his grandparents, 1/8 from his great grandparents and so on from all the other more remote ancestors.

4. *Principle of Chance*: Chance plays an important role, making any absolute prediction almost impossible. This is on account of several reasons: (i) The paring of the chromosomes is in the state of flux; (ii) cell to which the set of maternal or paternal chromosomes go during the reduction division; (iii) the particular cell which unites with another in the maternal and paternal lines; (iv) the pattern of genes in any chromosome; (v) genes carried in any particular chromosome; (vi) crossing over of genes from one paired chromosome to another; (vii) how dominant and recessive traits will be distributed according to the three to one ratio as per Gregor Mendel's Law (1866), especially if there are less than four children in the family and (viii) determination of sex.

5. *Principle of Dominant and Recessive Traits*: Some traits are dominant while others are recessive causing apparent exceptions to the principle of *like produces like*. The union of the best traits of the father with the best traits of the mother produces talented children. Therefore, a talented father or mother must be the offspring of the best combination of the determiners in the germ cells of his or her parents. But such gifted parents may carry on the determiners of genes which are average. There are many chances that when they produce a child, their average traits combine and a child of average calibre may be the result.

CHART SHOWING THE CONTRIBUTION OF HEREDITY ON PERSONALITY DEVELOPMENT

Structural Influences (Tendencies Towards a Structure)	*Behaviour Influences (Tendency to Behave)*
(a) Bodily weight	(1) Nature response (Reacting quickly or slowly)
(b) Bodily structure (Skeletal etc.)	(2) Sensory response (Sense of touch etc.)
(c) Sex	(3) Operation of the Vegetative System (Reproductory System etc.)
(d) Appearance (Skin, colour etc.)	(4) Functioning of the endocrine system
(e) Internal Structure (Size of the heart etc.)	

ENVIRONMENT

Meaning of Environment

In a broad sense, environment means cultural, economic, intellectual, moral, physical, political, religious and social factors which influence the development of the individual. All these factors influence and mould the behaviour of a person from time to time. Two individuals born with the same biological heritage differ because of differing environments. Sometimes it is said that environment is nothing but a process under suitable conditions to change the shape of raw material just as a potter does while making toys of mud. But this analogy is not exactly applicable to a human being who is an animate one. He is not only influenced by the environment but also influences the environment. Environment includes the home, the neighbourhood, the peers, the school and a host of other agencies. No individual is the same at maturity as he was born. The environment changes him. Everything that influences the child apart from himself what he inherits from his parents and ancestors is his environment. In this context we may note the following definitions of environment.

E.G. Boring, *H.S. Longeld* and *H.P.* define environment as "The environment is everything that affects the individual except his genes."

O.B. Douglas and *B.F. Holland* (1947) define environment as "a word which describes, in the aggregate, all of the extrinsic (external) forces influences and conditions, which affect the life, nature, behaviour and the growth, development and maturation of living organisms."

R.S. Woodworth and *D.G. Marques* (1948) state: "Environment covers all the outside factors that have acted on the individual since he began life."

HEREDITARIANS' ARGUMENTS AND STUDIES

Heredity is All in All: According to *A.E. Wiggam* (quoted by *G.W. Allport*, 1948), "Nearly all the misery and nearly all the happiness in the world are due not to environment. The difference among men are due to differences in the germ cells with which they are born."

Study of Family Histories of Some Famous and Notorious Families: 1. *Francis Galton* (1869), a great hereditarian, studied the family histories of 977 famous persons of various western countries. Almost all of them were discovered to be belonging to great families. The results of the study led him to believe that their greatness was due to their heredity.

2. Later, *Karl Pearson* also made research on the same lines and reached the same conclusions.

3. The most interesting study in this connection is that of a *Jukes family*, quite notorious. The research was conducted by *Dugdale* (1877). *Jukes* was a fisherman. His son happened to marry a woman from a very degenerate family. The study was extended to many generations. According to the report of *Dugdale*, he studied 28,309 individuals of the family. Out of them only 350 men and women were normal. The remaining 92 per cent were all criminals, beggars, paupers, prostitutes or diseased ones.

4. Quite similar to this study is the research of *H.H. Goddard* (1912). He studied a house as notorious as *Kalikak* family. Kalikak was a soldier. He married a feeble-minded woman. Later he married in a good family. 480 individuals descended from his first wife and 496 from the second. Out of all the 480 descendants of the first wife none came to prominence. They were mostly feeble-minded, criminals, sexual perverts and drunkards. Out of the latter one there were many famous doctors, teachers, tradesmen, lawyers and administrators.

Study of Siblings and Twins: Results of such investigations have been given in the earlier part of this chapter.

The Study of Hybrids: The hereditarians say that the hybrids are a clear proof of the importance of heredity. The offspring of a mare, crossed with a donkey, lies in the same parental environment as a normal horse before birth. But the issue is a mule, quite different from horse in every respect and it is never a normal horse. The apparent difference is due to heredity.

CRITICISM OF HEREDITARIANS' POINT OF VIEW

The environmentalists criticise this view. They say that the 977 famous persons of Francis Galton were famous not because they were born of famous parents but because they were provided selected environment by the great families. Similarly, the Jukes and the Kalikaks were degenerated because they had Jukes and Kalikaks around them to breed them. A beggar Juke could not provide good conditions of life to his young ones. A prostitute Juke was a very bad model for her daughter and she was sure to be influenced by her and to be allowed into the valley of sin and darkness. A criminal Kalikak could not protect his children from bad influence while he was shut in jail. The wants and needs of life naturally dragged the innocent children to the same paths which had led the elder Kalikaks to jail. The young Jukes and Kalikaks simply imitated the behaviour of their elders. Their needs were seldom satisfied and they were seldom provided with desirable schooling and guidance. Their degeneration was inevitable.

As regards siblings they say that they too are brought up in the same house under the same roof, in the same circumstances and influences. Therefore, they are apt to be similar to some extent. In the case of identical twins, even, some remarkable differences which occur after separation of a long time, have been quoted.

In the case of hybrids they say that different species combine and therefore the differences are natural.

ENVIRONMENTALISTS' POINT OF VIEW

Environment is All in All: J.B. Watson (1925) considered environment all in all in human development. He wrote: "There is no such thing as inheritance of capacity, talent, temperament, mental constitution and characteristics. There is nothing from within to develop. You do not need anything else in the way of raw material to make a man, be that man a genius, a cultured gentleman, a rowdy or a thug."

SOME STUDIES ON ENVIRONMENT

1. *Wolf Children*: In the early nineteen twenties some hunters found two children from a cave of wolves in a jungle. One of them was about eleven years old and the other about seven. It seemed as if the children had been carried away one by one by the female wolf when they were young babies and instead of being eaten up, they were reared up in the cave. The social environment turned them into wild beasts. They howled and crawled like beasts. They could not stand erect. Their limbs were crooked. But they could crawl very swiftly just like wolves. Their jaws had been deformed and disfigured. They ate raw meat and felt restless in the presence of men. They sipped water.

They were taken to a hospital. After some days a priest took them home. He made great efforts to reclaim them. He taught them how to eat and drink. He trained them in wearing clothes. At first they resisted but after some months they began to wear clothes. He trained them how to walk erect and he succeeded soon. Meanwhile the younger child died. But the behaviour of the elder one was modified and he looked like a human being.

The environmentalists say that it was purely environment that turned the children into beasts and again it was environment which brought them back to human form and behaviour.

2. *Story of Monster*: If the eggs of fish or birds are tempered with during the incubation period monsters are born. If the young fish embryos are placed in an ice-box before their eyes are formed some of the young fish hatched out produce only one eye located in the centre of the forehead. In some experiments the eggs of fish treated with magnesium chloride or electric current are hatched as strikingly different off-springs. The environmentalists say that it is environment that works wonders.

3. *Study of Twins*: Environmentalists also studied the twins. Norman made many studies of this kind. He found that twins reared apart did differ in I.Q., weight and other traits, mental as well as physical.

4. *Bloom's Studies*: F.A. Fredenburg has explained the effect of environment thus, "Obviously, there was no genetically based structure of personality but rather a dynamic formation growing out of environmental influences.

5. *Elkins Study*: Elkins (1959), a historian, sees slavery as exerting a crushing blow upon the personality not dissimilar in its effect from that of the concentration camps of Nazi Germany. He maintains that both were closed systems which produced personality changes in the individual. A high degree of dependence was introduced in both systems. There was a total acceptance of the plantation owner as a father-figure among Negro slaves so much the same way as prisoners of war accepted the Nazi S S guards."

6. *East Tennessee Children's Survey*: Caster Lockceler (1942) compared the intelligence of East Tennessee children over a ten-year period. During this time the schools in the area had improved their circulating libraries, the training of their teachers, the availability of free textbooks and so on. It was found that the average child had gained ten points in I.Q. or nearly one point per year during the ten-year period.

RELATIVE CONTRIBUTION OF HEREDITY AND ENVIRONMENT ON GROWTH AND DEVELOPMENT

Heredity in the Environment

In the words of H.J. Butchar (1968), "It should be realised at once that hardly any observable quality, physical or mental, can be ascribed to the influence of heredity alone or environment alone. Even where a particular observable aspect of behaviour has been shown to be directly influenced by a gene or a single genetic unit (such cases are rare in the study of human beings), this is no guarantee in itself that the observable is not also substantially dependent on variations in the environment. This principle is illustrated by a finding of Hogben about the fly Drosophila, in which he established that "two distinct genetics mutations affect the number of facets in the fly's eye."

According to T.P. Nunn, "The fundamental truth is that it (the child) is a centre of creative energy which uses endowment and environment as its medium; so that the elements it receives from nature and nurture do not themselves make it what it is, except insofar as they are the basis of the free activity which is the essential fact of its existence."

The much-mentioned slogan 'heredity *versus* environment' is misconception. We should talk of 'heredity in the environment'. Both heredity and environment are essential for development. Hence any trait of the individual is the 'product' of heredity and environment. The individual does not equal heredity + environment but equals heredity × environment, i.e., O (Organism or individual) = H (Heredity) × E (Environment). Heredity sets the probable biological limit, whereas environment determines the level up to which the development is possible. Every development is due to an interaction of heredity and environment.

Personality may be compared to a rectangle. Heredity makes the base while environment the altitude. A rectangle cannot exist without either of the two.

Environment | Personality | Personality | Environment

Heredity | Heredity

Personality = Heredity × Environment

Sometimes heredity plays a major role in the development of personality and sometimes environment. However, both play their roles. In case both the base, i.e., the heredity and the altitude, i.e., the environment are inferior, we shall have Jukes and Kalikaks as off-springs. (Anti-social and misfit individuals)

INFLUENCE OF HEREDITY AND ENVIRONMENT

		Heredity	Environment
1.	*In the area of physical growth and development*	Height, bodily frames and structure of the bodily organs are probably determined by the growth potentials in the genes; the structure of the nervous system also is probably determined genetically. The limits of sensorimotor development are set genetically, and these limits vary widely. Thus, the great differences in the motor skills and athletic abilities of children, youth and adults are caused, largely by heredity.	All hereditary influences can be distorted by abnormal environment. However, physical health and survival itself depends on good care. Good medical skills, including public health practices, and good nutrition are essential. Deficiencies and deprivation inflict huge penalties on the human body.
2.	*In mental growth and development*	The evidence indicates that children are born with a very wide range of general mental potential and with different potentialities for music, painting, the other arts, public speaking, and so forth, for which limits are set genetically.	Good environments are needed for developing abilities to levels close to capacity levels.
3.	*In mental and emotional health and personality*	People seem to be born with physical structures—nervous system, glands and organs on which emotional stability depends, and they differ greatly in their potential stability as a result; that is some people are much more disposed by heredity to mental instability than others.	If children are raised in a healthful home where the blood or foster parents live in love and harmony and are kind and supportive to the children, there is a high probability that the children will have good mental and emotional health and thus good personality development. In protective environments, fewer in the population will become mentally and emotionally ill than in severe and insulting environment.
4.	*In attitudes, beliefs and values*	Position in life depends a great deal on capacities, which are set, to a considerable extent by inheritance.	Attitudes, beliefs, and values develop largely from the culture in which one is born, and are influenced greatly by ego, or personal involvement.

EDUCATIONAL IMPLICATIONS OF THE ROLE OF HEREDITY AND ENVIRONMENT

The problem is very important for education. If heredity is everything, if we get a ready-made personality by birth and it is to develop according to its own inborn tendencies which are already there in the little child and if all the influences of environment are meaningless, then why to establish so many schools and other institutions for the reform and guidance of children. On the other hand, if it is all nurture that is to count, then why should we tolerate anybody less than Gandhi or Nehru in calibre. In the words of *Woodworth*: "Shall the gardener pin his hope on careful cultivation of the soil or on selection of the best seed?" Both the schools have their own claims and arguments. Let us discuss the same.

The parents, the teachers and the community have to play a significant role in providing rich environment in all its facets. As teachers we have to have a greater faith in the force of environment though the force of heredity cannot be totally ignored. Education can eliminate those influences and circumstances which inhibit and stunt the full growth and development of inherited traits and capacities and encourage and provide for those which favour it. Scientific educational principles require that the inherited inclinations, capacities and interests of every child should be studied early and every facility should be provided in the environment to develop all that is best in him as an individual. Educational institutions should provide suitable opportunities for every individual to unfold his latent powers. A rich and fruitful environment must be provided to draw out the best in child and man—body, mind and soul. Individual differences of children must be found out and necessary conditions created for their optimum development.

4

Individual Differences: Types and Educational Implications

SIGNIFICANCE OF INDIVIDUAL DIFFERENCES AMONG CHILDREN

Teaching-learning process to be effective and inspirational must take into consideration the individual differences of the learners. The focus should be on the ability of the learners. There cannot be child-centred education without realising the differences and similarities among learners. At the same time, it must be appreciated that there cannot be, in general, individualised instruction in normal schools of the formal system of education. In Chapters 10 and 15, we have discussed teaching-learning strategies relating to learner centred techniques of exceptional children. In this chapter we are primarily concerned with individual differences in general and their classroom implications.

The following description of individual differences has been very beautifully given by Rita Malhotra, Director of a Guidance Centre in New Delhi in '*Journal of Indian Education*' (Volume XXII, February 2002, No. 4).

"Millions and millions of persons have been born and have died.
But no two persons were identical.
Billions and billions of persons will be born and will die.
But no two persons will be identical.
Trillions and trillions of leaves grow and fade away.
But no two leaves are identical.
Nature is perfectly imperfect.
Universe is designed to coexist with imperfections and individual differences."

This description equally applies to individual differences of learners.

Individual differences play the most dominating role in the development of the individuality of the child. It is of utmost importance to study the significances of individual differences.

H.C. Mckown has given a very vivid description of individual differences, "In the whole world there are probably no two things alike—no two trees, no two leaves, flowers, blades of grass, rocks, drops, clouds, animals, houses, pianos, books, baseballs or photographs, even though at first glance they appear to be identical. Similarly no two human beings are alike, they differ physically in size, weight, height, colour of eyes and hair, texture of skin—and in a thousand other details as well as in thousands of details of mental, social and spiritual life". Not only this, an individual reacts to the same situation in different manners at different times. Mass procedures, no matter, how well-intentioned, fail to accomplish the desired results in educational programmes, unless they are supplemented by adequate attention to the individual needs of the learner. In the words of Charles E. Skinner, "Today we think of individual differences as including any measurable aspect of the total personality." Differences in children may be slight, moderate or extreme.

TYPES OF INDIVIDUAL DIFFERENCES

Following are the important types of individual differences:

1. *Differences in Physique*: This means tall or short, thin or fat, fair or black, normal or handicapped, etc.

2. *Differences in Health*: It means healthy or ill, weak or strong.

3. *Differences in Intelligence*: Here the range is very wide—from almost nil intelligence to 140 or above. On the basis of one's I.Q., one can be classified to fall in any of the idiot to genius categories.

4. *Differences with Reference to Achievements*: Pupils differ in achievements in school subjects and their efficiency in vocation.

5. *Differences in Affective Factors*: There are differences in attitude towards ideas, subjects, things and people, etc. Likewise differences in interests.

6. *Differences in Motor Ability*: This means control over muscles. The performance of some in some mechanical task is superior and the performance of others is inferior.

7. *Sex Differences*: Sex differences operate in different ways.

8. *Differences with Reference to Learning Ability and Speed of Learning*: This is evident from daily example. Take a class-room. Some boys learn things quickly—other take days to learn it and some do not learn at all.

9. *Differences with Reference to Race and Nationality*: Many studies lead us to conclude that people belonging to different races and nationalities differ in respect of nature, physical and mental traits, interests and personality, etc. It can be intelligence also.

10. *Personality Differences*: Many classifications of personality differences are made. According to Hipprocrates, people are of four types: (a) sanguine, (b) choleric, (c) melancholic, (d) phlegmatic.

According to Jung, people can be classified into three types: (a) Introverts, (b) Extroverts, (c) Ambiverts.

Terman has classified people on the basis of intelligence into nine categories—from genius to idiot.

11. *Differences with Respect to Development*: It includes social development, emotional development which includes emotional maturity, emotional stability, etc.

INDIVIDUAL DIFFERENCES: READINESS

On account of differences in ability and in previous experiences all children are not at the same readiness (preparation for action) for learning when they enter school or when they learn a new topic or unit in the same subject or when they are promoted to the next class. This makes difference in the new situation because of differences in basic concept formation and the level of knowledge required as foundation on which to build a new lesson.

Thorndike has propounded the Law of Readiness. The law states, "When any conduction unit is not in readiness to conduct, for it to conduct is annoying. When any conduction unit is in readiness to conduct, for it not to do so is annoying."

The law is indicative of learner's state to participate in the learning process. According to Thorndike, readiness is preparation for action. Readiness does not come automatically with maturation. It is a law of preparatory adjustment, not a law about growth. Thorndike termed the neurons and synapses involved in the establishment of a specific bond or connection, a conduction unit. According to this law, for a conduction unit ready to conduct, to do, is satisfying and for it not to do so is annoying.

Educational Implications of Readiness. The teacher should prepare the minds of the students to be ready to accept their knowledge, skill and aptitudes. For this, he should provide suitable opportunities for those experiences in which students can spontaneously participate. In other words, he should arouse their capacity to link the experiences with their everyday life. 'Simple to complex' is the important maxim. Aptitude tests may be given to the students to find out their readiness to learn.

EDUCATIONAL IMPLICATIONS OF INDIVIDUAL DIFFERENCES

Some students go faster than others and such students may be given double promotion or separate streams formed or some additional work given to them so that their progress is not retarded due to slow learners. Similarly, steps will have to be taken to ensure that the slow learners also make satisfactory progress commensurate with their capacity and ability to work.

A deaf, dumb, blind, undersized, oversized, too fat or too lean learner needs guidance in the selection of such a vocation where his physical defect may not be a handicap and he may be able to earn his living in an honourable manner. Such students need special educational courses. Ordinary schools fail to do justice to them.

There are some students whose parents are very dominating with the result that their children develop inferiority complex. Too lenient parents allow their children to be freelancers and such children suffer from other complexes and develop bad habits. Children of the rich and the poor have altogether different situations to be faced with.

The problems are as numerous as the learners.

The programme of guidance is not confined to the selection of subjects, schools, vocations, etc. All children need guidance in every aspect of their harmonious development. They need guidance in fields, such as, recreation, moral and religious, social adjustments, cultural pursuits, physical development, etc.

Democratically, all individuals are equal but physically and psychologically all individuals are unequal and in other words each individual is different from the other. All the same, all are agreed that equal opportunity or equality of opportunity must be provided to every individual for drawing out the best that an individual has so that an individual achieves optimum development. It has been aptly stated by Benjamin S. Bloom, an American educator, "A society which places such great value on education and schooling that it requires the individual to attend school for a long period of time must find the means to make education attractive and meaningful to the individual learner." This implies that education should be individual-centred. But in spite of the loud talk on child-centred or individual-centred education, it is observed that there is very little practical action in this regard.

Undoubtedly, all the students need guidance in one or the other aspect, some need more guidance and others less. Without proper guidance the superior child may go astray, the average one may become backward and the backward may be lost to the society altogether.

MEETING NEEDS OF INDIVIDUAL DIFFERENCES: TEACHING STRATEGIES AND CLASS-ROOM MEASURES

In view of the individual differences, it is quite clear that the same curriculum, same methods of teaching and same discipline and in some cases even the same educational institution will not serve the individual needs of children. Ideally speaking each student needs a particular setting and individual instruction with a lot of group interaction. This, however, is not feasible in normal classroom routine. At the same time individual differences of children must be catered to. There are nine broad areas, in which a lot of work could be done to take into consideration individual differences. These are:

1. Streaming of students, i.e., making ability groups.
2. Curriculum planning, i.e., providing advanced and ordinary curriculum in different disciplines.
3. Disciplinary treatment.
4. Guidance and counselling.
5. Special schools for the handicapped children.
6. Combining individualised, group and class instruction.
7. Using maxims of teaching and mnemonics.
8. Using team teaching.
9. Taking up projects where possible.

GENERAL GUIDELINES FOR MEETING INDIVIDUAL DIFFERENCES

1. Courses should be selective to meet the needs of individual students.
2. Opportunities for acquiring manual and mechanical skills should be provided.
3. A wide range of pupil experiences may be provided in the school.
4. Remedial instruction should be made available to such students who need it.
5. Courses should be organised in such a way as bright pupils can learn at their own speed and slow pupils follow their own speed.
6. Guidance regarding co-curricular activities should be provided.
7. Counselling should be given to students.
8. Assignments should be adapted to the needs of students.

9. Special care should be taken to accept the under-achieving child as a unique individual. His particular needs should be immediately attended to.

10. Efforts may be made to re-establish child's confidence in himself.

11. The teacher should seek the co-operation of other teachers and the parents of the under-achievers.

12. In case of deep-rooted emotional problems which lie at the root of under-achievement, referral may be made to a child guidance clinic after taking the parents into confidence.

13. Students should be taught to recognise their handicaps, and counselled in methods to overcome or compensate for them.

14. Some programme of parents' education may be taken up as many problems of the students result from unsatisfactory home conditions.

15. School programme should take into account the needs of those students who are not likely to go to college and those who would join college.

16. The school programme, administration and management should be made flexible enough to allow for adjustment to individual differences.

SUMMING UP

In the end it must be stressed that there is a limit to which individual differences of students can be accommodated in the normal class-room teaching. This is possible to some extent when the number of students in a particular class or section is small. In larger classes, it is not feasible to meet with all the individual differences. There must be some sort of flexible environment like the Dalton Plan. Additional time, i.e., other than the normal class time schedule is needed to cater to the specific individual learning needs of the students.

5

Physical Development Pattern and Educational Implications

GENERAL PHYSICAL DEVELOPMENT PATTERN

In the words of R.M. Liebbert, Rita Wicks Poulos and Gloria Strauss Marmor: "Viewed in its larger perspective, bodily growth occurs through approximately the first twenty years of life in humans. It is generally felt to be fruitful to divide this overall growth period into three major sub-divisions—infancy and early childhood (up to about the fifth year of life), middle and late childhood (up to about age twelve), and adolescence (up to about age twenty). Growth is more rapid and more likely to show spurts during both the infancy—early childhood period and the adolescent period than during middle childhood".

Although there are wide individual differences among children, yet physical growth and development seems to follow to some extent a general pattern. This general pattern of development and growth may be summarised as under.

1. *Changes in Height and Weight*: The Table 5.1 illustrates increase in height and weight at different ages.

On an average, at birth a baby is about 56 cm. in height and between 4 and 5 kg. in weight, boys being slightly taller and heavier. During the first two years, there is rapid increase in both height and weight. There is a steady and slower growth from the third year till the onset of puberty. By five years the height of the child, approximately increases by 80 per cent and he acquires almost 3½ times his birth weight. During the period of adolescence we again find a sudden increase in both height and weight. Girls reach puberty about a year or two earlier than boys do. Therefore, at the age of 12, they are found slightly taller and heavier than boys. But they are again surpassed by the boys at about the age of 14. By the end of adolescence, the young men are generally higher and heavier than the young women. Generally both men and women get their maximum height and weight up to the end of adolescence. But there is much variation in weight as it is more susceptible to environmental influences. Therefore, it is no surprise to note the sudden increase or decrease in weight in later years after attaining maturity.

Weight of the brain increases rapidly in the early years of life. By the time the child completes the age of four his brain gains almost 80 per cent of its final weight, another 10 per cent being added by the time he completes his eight years. By the 20th year, the brain gains almost all its weight.

2. *Changes in Body Proportions*: There are changes not only in the size of the body of the child but also marked changes in the proportion of the different parts of the body. For instance, the head constitutes about one-fourth of the height of the body at birth. The size of the head is relatively much larger than the arms and legs. As the child grows older, the proportion of the head decreases. By the end of adolescence, head becomes one-eighth of the body. The other parts of the body, legs, arms, etc. also change in proportion.

Table 5.1: Mean Height and Weight of Male and Female Children (All-India)

Age Group	*Mean Height (cm.)*		*Mean Weight (kg.)*	
	Male	*Female*	*Male*	*Female*
3 months	56.2	55.0	4.5	4.2
4-6 months	62.7	60.9	6.7	5.6
7-9 months	64.9	64.4	6.9	6.2
10-12 months	69.5	66.7	7.4	6.6
1 year	73.9	72.5	8.4	7.8
2 years	81.6	80.1	10.1	9.6
3 years	88.8	87.2	11.8	11.2
4 years	96.0	94.5	13.5	12.9
5 years	102.1	101.4	14.8	14.5
6 years	108.5	107.4	16.3	16.0
7 years	113.9	112.8	18.0	17.6
8 years	119.3	118.2	19.7	19.4
9 years	123.7	122.9	21.5	21.3
10 years	128.4	128.4	23.5	23.6
11 years	133.4	133.6	25.9	26.4
12 years	138.3	139.2	28.5	29.8
13 years	144.6	143.9	32.1	33.3
14 years	150.1	147.5	35.7	36.8
15 years	155.5	149.6	39.6	36.8
16 years	159.5	151.0	43.2	41.1
17 years	161.4	151.5	45.7	42.4
18 years	163.1	151.7	47.4	42.4
19 years	163.5	151.7	48.1	42.4
20 years	164.1	151.7	49.2	43.5

Source: Growth and Physical Development of Children. All India—Indian Council of Medical Research, New Delhi, 1968.

3. *Bones*: Most of the bones at birth are soft. The child's bones contain relatively a great amount of water and smaller quantity of mineral matter than those of an adult. More blood flows through their bones than through the bones of adults. They are, therefore, more pliable.

4. *Teeth*: Teeth begin to appear in a systematic order after the age of six months. On an average, around seven months of age, the first two front teeth in the lower jaw erupt and are followed by four molars, one on both sides of the front teeth on both jaws. By the time the baby is 2 to 2½ years old, it will

have twenty teeth. Girls show more advanced teeth growth than the boys, except in the case of wisdom teeth, where boys are usually ahead of the girls.

5. *Nervous System*: There is a marked growth of nervous system during the pre-natal period and the first four years after birth. Before birth, the development primarily consists of increase in the number and size of nerves. After the age of four years, the growth of the nervous system proceeds at a relatively slow rate.

6. *Muscular System*: Muscles at the time of birth are more delicate and less firmly attached to the bones than those of adult muscles. The movements of the muscles are random and uncoordinated. Gradually muscles get changed in shape, size and composition and become firmer and stronger.

7. *Circulatory and Respiratory System*: In early childhood, lungs as well as heart are very small but gradually they grow in volume and height. The veins and arteries do not follow the same growth pattern as that of the heart and lungs. They grow rapidly prior to adolescence but show little growth during adolescence.

8. *Digestive System*: The young child has a small tubular-shaped stomach as compared with the bag like shape stomach of the adult. A young child needs more feeding in the earlier years.

9. *Lymphatic System*: It is concerned with the elimination of waste and destruction of bacteria in the body. From birth onward this system shows the sign of rapid development until it reaches its maximum between the age of eleven and twelve years. After 12 years of age, it decreases rapidly.

10. *Reproductive System*: The development of sex organs is very slow during early childhood but picks up speed as the child advances towards adolescence.

CHARACTERISTICS OF PHYSICAL DEVELOPMENT PATTERN AND NEEDS OF CHILDREN

A. From 5 to 8 years

	Physical Characteristics	*Needs*
1.	Average increase in height of about 5 cms.	Adequate sleep for 10 to 12 hours.
2.	Girls mature faster than boys.	Frequent periods of rest and recreation.
3.	Legs lengthen rapidly.	Active play and large space for play.
4.	Nose and throat difficulties are frequent.	Guidance in eating and health protection.
5.	Tend to take more food than their stomach can hold.	Preventive measures against childhood diseases like measles.
6.	Show resistance taking a bath.	Proper dress according to weather.
7.	Average gain in health.	Care of teeth, etc.
8.	Gradual improvement in speed, steadiness of movement and accuracy.	Varied play activities.

B. From 9 to 12 years

Physical Characteristics	*Needs*
1. Children are extremely active.	Careful eye examination.
2. Relatively free from disease.	Correction of postures.
3. Relatively healthy and sturdy.	Frequent change of physical activity.
4. Choosy about food but eat a great deal.	Independence in caring for physical needs.
5. Girls increase steadily in physical skills.	Adequate nutrition.
6. Girls usually have less stamina than boys.	Supervision of strenuous physical activities.
7. Interested in competitive games which require skill.	do
8. More easily fatigued after physical activity.	do

C. Physical Development at the Adolescent Stage (Discussed Separately)

GROWTH AND DEVELOPMENT RATE, GROWTH AND DEVELOPMENT CURVE: CHARACTERISTICS AND STAGES

Growth and development rate is rhythmic and regular. It comes in cycle of waves, "periods" or "phases" of growth. This growth rate is not haphazard and random. According to W.H. Krogman, "The child outgrows in obedience to certain biological laws."

According to studies, there are four distinct periods or phases or rates of growth. Two periods are characterised by slow growth and Development and two by rapid growth and development.

Growth and Development Rate at Different Stages in Different Parts and Organs of the Body: From birth to two years growth rate is rapid. This is followed by a period of slow growth up to the time of puberty or sexual maturity which usually takes place between the eighth and eleven years. Onwards till fifteen or sixteen years, rate of growth is rapid and it is followed by a period of fairly abrupt tapering of the growth up to the time of maturity.

(i) The '*body size*' category which includes the skeleton, muscles and internal organs shows more rapid growth during the infancy—early childhood period, and the adolescent period than during middle childhood.

(ii) The '*lymphatic system*' (thymus, lymph nodes, and intestinal lymphoid mass) reaches an adult level by seven years of age and is even larger during pre-adolescence before it declines.

(iii) Similarly, the '*neural system*' (head, brain and spinal cord) is almost fully developed by the age of six. In contrast, the '*reproductive organs*' grow very slowly until adolescence at which point they undergo rapid growth.

Table 5.2: Rhythmetic Sequence in the Physical Development Pattern

Age	*1-2 years*	*2-11 years*	*12 to 16 years*	*17-18 years*
Rate	Rapid	Slow	Rapid	Slow

The Physical Growth and Development Curve

For weight and height curve reflects a steady increase during childhood. The rate is rapid at first and it slows down.

Physical growth follows a cephalocaudal direction, i.e. the rate of growth is faster at the head in initial stages until this area is well-developed. Growth rate then becomes more rapid towards the lower parts of the body. (*See* Fig. 5.1).

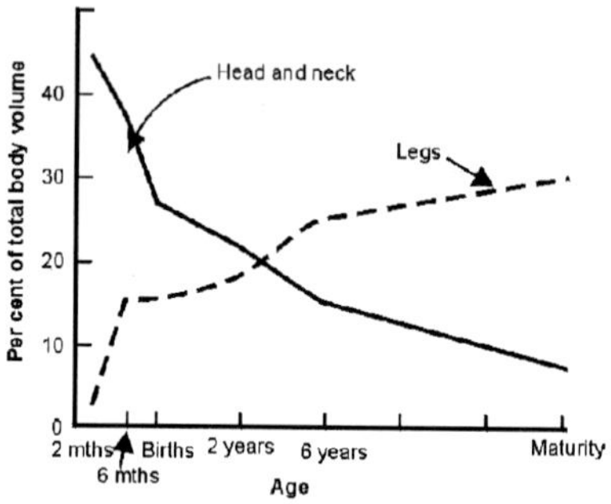

Fig. 5.1: Growth in Relative Volume of the Cephalo and Caudal Parts of the Human Body. (Data from Arey, L.B., "*Development Anatomy*", 1934)

The growth rate of heart beat declines rather sharply during the first two years of postnatal life and then continues a less precipitous decline with further development. (Fig. 5.2).

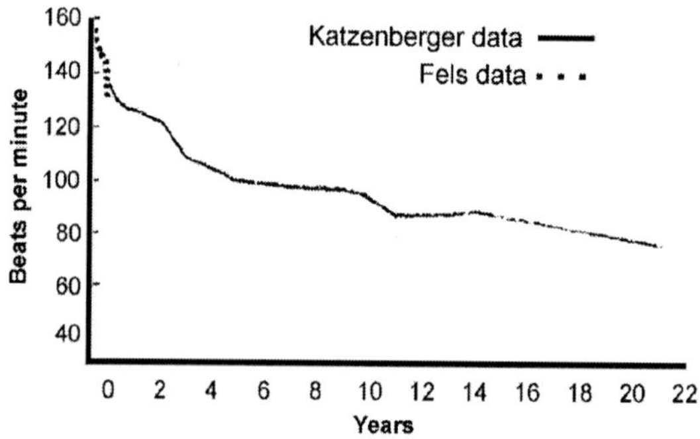

Fig. 5.2: Heart rate at Various Developmental Levels

The general development of motor behaviour is reflected in Fig. 5.3.

COMMON CAUSES OF DELAYED MOTOR AND PHYSICAL DEVELOPMENT

1. Poor physical conditions caused by illness, malnutrition, etc.
2. Lack of opportunities to develop manual skills.
3. Nagging, scolding and ridiculing of the child by parents and teachers when he does not succeed in an activity.

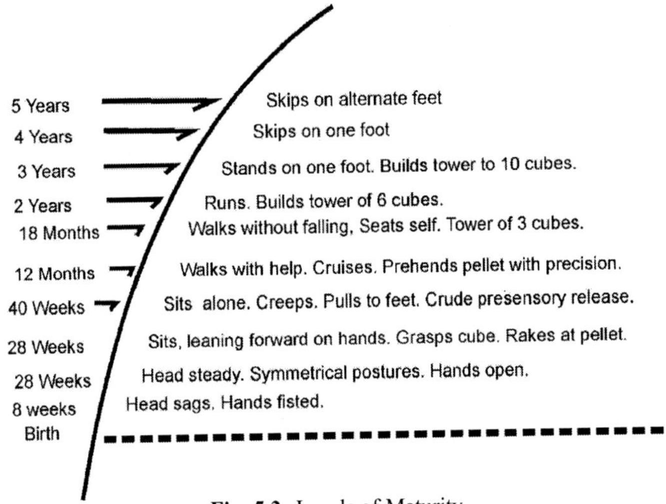

Fig. 5.3: Levels of Maturity

FACTORS AFFECTING THE PATTERN OF PHYSICAL GROWTH AND DEVELOPMENT

1. The traits and characteristics inherited at the time of conception.
2. The physical as well as mental health of the mother during pregnancy.
3. Nutrition received by the embryo within the womb of the mother.
4. Conditions and care at the time of delivery.
5. Normal or abnormal delivery.
6. Single birth or multiple births.
7. Care of the baby and its mother.
8. Presence or absence of physical defects.
9. Presence or absence of illness and disease.
10. Proper or improper medical care.
11. Nutrition received by the child after birth.
12. The living conditions physical, social and cultural.
13. The opportunities for recreation, self-expression, play and exercise.
14. Adequate or inadequate rest and sleep.
15. Emotional and social adjustment of the child.

SUMMARY: IMPORTANT CHARACTERISTICS OF PHYSICAL DEVELOPMENT PATTERN

1. It is very rapid during infancy (from birth to three years).

2. Period of pre-childhood (4 to 6 years) is the period of fixation, i.e., what is acquired in infancy is fixed or stabilised.

3. Period of early childhood (7 to 9 years) shows again a period of growth and development but the speed is slow in comparison to infancy.

4. Later childhood (10 to 12 years) is again a period of fixation.

5. The first three years of adolescence are marked as the years of rapid growth and development. This is followed by a period of slow growth.

6. All the sensory and motor organs of the child's body are in the process of growth.
7. The urge for motor activities like walking, running, jumping, catching, throwing, etc., is at its peak.
8. Muscular development takes place rapidly.
9. In the middle and late childhood, coordination of hands and fingers becomes possible.
10. Children take delight in strenuous physical activities.
11. Children enjoy movement.
12. There is an urge among children to participate in activities which involve speaking, seeing and manipulating.

EDUCATIONAL IMPLICATIONS OF THE PHYSICAL DEVELOPMENT OF THE CHILDREN FOR THE TEACHER

A knowledge of the process of physical development of the children would serve the teacher him in the following ways:

1. The teacher comes to know about the specific needs of children. Consequently he can plan his programmes and help them in their emotional and social adjustments also.
2. Physical welfare of the children is an integral part of the development of the whole child. It is, therefore, very important for the teacher to know the details in this regard.
3. Physical growth and development exercise a great influence on the development of other aspects like intellectual and social development, etc.
4. Knowledge of the pattern of physical growth and development helps the teacher to arrange school programmes like co-curricular activities.

ORGANISATION OF PHYSICAL DEVELOPMENT PROGRAMME

A programme of physical growth and development is not confined to the playground but should pervade the class-room and in fact the entire school programme. Physical development in the class-room may take the following forms:

1. Direct instruction emphasising the necessity of having a good physique.
2. Suggestions regarding the maintenance of good health.
3. Emphasis on right postures.
4. Provision of good seating and lighting arrangements in the class-room.
5. Provision of nutritious diet.
6. Regular medical check-up and follow-up.
7. Free and guided play activities.
8. Activities involving handling of tools and materials.
9. Exercise and morning walk.
10. Yogic exercises.
11. Preparing charts and models.
12. Proper postures.
13. Games and sports.
14. Opportunities of skipping, hopping, jumping, throwing, grasping, etc.
15. Excursions.
16. Community cleanliness programmes.

6

Social Development Pattern and Educational Implications

MEANING OF SOCIAL DEVELOPMENT PATTERN

Social development pattern means the development of an individual in such a way that he becomes an efficient and useful member of the society to which he belongs. He conforms to the culture of the society of which he is a member. An individual, by nature, is a human being who cannot live in isolation. He is compelled by biological, psychological and social needs to live in a group or society. The process of the development of such qualities which bring desirable changes in the social behaviour of an individual is referred to as social development or socialisation of the child.

Important definitions of social development throwing light on its various dimensions are given below:

1. *E.B. Hurlock* notes: "Social development means the attaining of maturity in social setting".

2. *Freeman and Showel* write: "Social development is the process of learning to conform to group standards".

3. *H.E. Garret* is of the view that "Socialisation or social development is the process whereby the biological individual is converted into a human person".

4. *Herbart Sorenson* thinks that, "By social growth and development we mean increasing ability to get along well with oneself and others".

5. *James Drever* states: "Socialisation (social development) is a process by which the individual is adapted to his social environment (by attaining social conformity), and becomes a recognised, cooperating and efficient member of it".

6. *L.D. Crow and A. Crow* write: "Social development means acquisition or the ability to behave in accordance with social expectations".

7. *Freeman and Showel*: Social development is the process by which a person acquires the necessary knowledge, skills and disposition that make him an acceptable member of his own group".

CHARACTERISTICS OF SOCIAL DEVELOPMENT PATTERN

1. Social development begins with the infant's first contact with other people.

2. Social development continues throughout life.

3. Social development is the net result of the child's constant interaction with his social environment.

4. Social development helps in learning and acquiring social qualities of character.

5. Social development enables the child to adjust himself to his social environment and to maintain social relationships.

SOCIAL DEVELOPMENT PATTERN AT VARIOUS STAGES

A. Social Development Pattern or Behaviour of the Pre-School Child

The child at this stage is ready to expand his social contacts. By the age of two years, he can obey certain commands given to him. He calls attention of other persons to objects he feels interested in. He is more or less self-centred. The pre-school child is active. A pre-school child has usually one or two friends. He plays with them only for short intervals. Race, caste, colour or sex or social and economic status have no effect in the selection of friends at this stage. Nursery school experiences contribute in acquiring acceptable social habits.

B. Social Development Pattern or Behaviour of the Primary School Child (6 to 10 years)

By the time a child enters school he wants to have many friends. At this stage he is not satisfied just by the company of his parents. He is interested in the play activities of his group, of the same age and sex. However, quarrels are also common among friends. Boys of this stage tend to be more aggressive. Girls more frequently engage in bickering. Bullying and teasing are more common. Children are interested in group activities and team work. Team games become more interesting than individual work. Social behaviour of the child is greatly influenced by the social environment in which he lives.

C. Social Development Pattern or Behaviour of the Child During the Middle School Stage (10 to 12 years)

1. The period is marked by a greater degree of social awareness.
2. There is a great expansion of child's social world.
3. A child tries to be independent of his parents and other elders.
4. A child becomes an active member of a 'peer group'.
5. There is a sort of segregation among boys and girls of the same age.
6. The child enters the peak of 'gang age'. There is increasing loyalty towards his own gang and conflict with other gangs. The gang life develops many good as well as bad social qualities in the child.

D. Social Development Pattern or Behaviour During Adolescence

(Discussed Separately)

Note: It is not possible to divide the social behaviour pattern at clear-cut stages or ages. Patterns overlap.

Social Development Pattern at Different Ages

Age/Ages	*Social Development Pattern*
First month	A child cannot differentiate between human voices and other voices.
Second month	Begins to recognise the sounds of human being and to give smiles to others.
Third month	Recognises the mother and begins to feel unhappy on separation.
Fourth month	Shows selective attention to the human face and feels happy in company.
Fifth month	Reacts to smiling and scolding. Differentiates between friendly and angry voices.
Sixth month	Recognises familiar faces with a smile and shows definite expression of fear of strangers.
Eighth and ninth month	Attempts to imitate the speech, simple acts and gestures of others.
Tenth to twelfth month	Plays with his image and even kisses it as if it were another person.
At twelfth month	Can refrain from doing things in response to 'no-no' or some other form of request.
One year	Emotional aspects like fear, shyness are seen and social behaviour is linked with these.
1½ years—2 years	Likes to play with toys alone (Solitary social behaviour)
3 to 6 years	Likes to play with others (Social play behaviour), three to six friends. Friends are generally changed.
6 to 8 years	Plays with small groups.
8 to 10 years	Begins to identify the sex difference.
10 to 12 years	Begins to participate in competitive games. Membership of friends increases.
Adolescence period	Discussed separately.

FACTORS AFFECTING THE SOCIAL DEVELOPMENT OF THE CHILD

1. *Culture*: A child's social behaviour is regulated by the culture of the society in which he lives. The ways of behaving by the people of one generation, pass on from generation to generation. Our *Sanskaras* shape our outlook and finally personality. There are two ways in which the behaviour patterns of culture are transmitted to the next generation. (a) Directly and formally as in educational programmes at various stages of education, and (b) Informally through interactions between parents and their children which occur in the course of bringing up children. These interactions include the parent's expression of attitudes, beliefs, interests and values, etc. some of the informal social development takes place through interactions with relatives, neighbours, peer groups and teachers and other groups of the society.

2. *The Family*: Among the various social groups, the family makes the first and the most significant influence on the social development of the child. It provides the hereditary transmission of basic potential for his development.

It also provides environmental conditions and personal relationship. Parent-child relations have various dimensions of interaction. As such, they remain basic for social development of the child. Parent-child relationships determine behavioural adjustment of the child in the family.

Religion: Like home, religion has long been regarded as a primary social institution. Earlier religion played a dominant role in the social development of the child.

3. *Peer Groups*: The child is introduced to the social world outside his family, mainly for play purposes. The peer groups satisfy various needs of the children like acceptance, achievement, affection, approval, belongingness, fame, recognition, expression of thought and opinion etc. According to A.T. Jershid (1947), peer association is a meaningful process through which the child changes with his age group into youth and adulthood.

4. *School*: The school life plays an important role in the social development of the child. Its curriculum, co-curricular activities and teacher's influence have a great bearing on the social development of the child.

5. *Community and Neighbourhood*: The environment prevailing in the community has a great influence on the social development of the child.

6. *Mass Media*: Agencies like cinema, newspapers, radio and television, etc., also play a vital role in bringing about social changes in children.

7. *Bodily Structure and Health*: A healthy child has more ability and strength to make himself adjusted in the challenging social setting. A child with poor health or any physical deformity or defect develops feelings of inferiority as well as insecurity in social settings.

8. *Intelligence*: The more intelligent a person is, the more chances of his social adjustment.

9. *Emotional Development*: Emotional development of the child bears a positive correlation with his social development. Emotional adjustability is one of the very important elements of social adjustment.

10. *Physical Health of the Individual*: A healthy child with normal physique is likely to develop more self-confidence than the unhealthy child with not normal physique.

HINDRANCES IN THE SOCIAL DEVELOPMENT OF THE CHILD

1. Social evils like untouchability and caste prejudices, etc.
2. Co-education according to conservative view.
3. Language barriers.
4. Miscellaneous factors like income, occupation and religion of the family.

ROLE OF THE SCHOOL IN THE SOCIAL DEVELOPMENT OF THE CHILD

The role of the school has considerably changed in the rapidly changing civilisations. The traditional role of imparting the basic skills of the three R's is now no longer considered to be adequate to meet the present challenge. The present day school has also to perform some of the functions of the family. It must develop certain desirable moral attitudes and good social habits among students. It is through co-curricular and extra-curricular activities that the task of socialisation can be achieved more successfully. In India today we find that the number of first generation learners in schools and colleges is swelling up. They come from varied backgrounds. Some of them come from deprived homes. It is only the sympathetic understanding and sincere desire of the teacher to act positively in an unprejudicial manner that can help in these situations.

Class in the Process of Social Development

Class provides innumerable opportunities to the children to move and mix with students belonging to different strata of society. This is the beginning of the socialisation of the child for his future life. Here children get many chances to mix without any distinction of caste, colour or creed. The children who are selfish or self-centred learn to adjust their behaviour in terms of class norms. The teachers are expected to be vigilant to ensure that the students do not think in terms of untouchability, caste distinctions and other prejudices.

TEACHER'S ROLE IN THE SOCIAL DEVELOPMENT OF THE CHILD

A teacher's role is very vital in the social development of the child. In recent years, the role of the teacher in functional terms has been gradually decreasing on account of the influence of the electronic and print media. At the pre-school stage and at the elementary stage, teacher's influence on the development of character and personality is of great significance. There is no doubt that, the role of the teachers in the social development of the child is still of great significance.

Following are the important suggestions for the social development of the child which the teachers should always keep in mind:

1. The teachers should demonstrate democratic outlook.
2. Teachers and parents may encourage the children to mix with inter-caste rather than intra-caste and inter-regional rather intra-regional groups.
3. The teachers should respect the personality of children.
4. The mechanism of praise and blame, reward and punishment should be carefully used to socialise the children.
5. The teacher should not show any discrimination. He must ensure a safe and healthy social environment in which the children may imbibe desirable values of freedom, equality, integrity, honesty, patriotism, etc.
6. Community activities like camps, common meals, social service, etc., should be frequently organised.
7. There should be close cooperation between the teachers and parents on matters relating to proper socialisation of the children.
8. Adequate stress may be laid on group activities.
9. Exhibitions on "Know Our Country" may be organised from time to time.
10. Stories depicting self-sacrifice made by great men for the cause of general good may be told to children so that they are motivated to rise above petty gains and work for the betterment of the humanity.
11. With proper guidance and responsibilities, the students' council can build up a sense of shared responsibility among children.

12. Proper socialisation of children very much necessitates that the ideology of the common school system is allowed to function in letter and spirit in India.

13. Children may be taken from time to time to public places like museums, courts, places of historical importance, etc.

14. People engaged in different economic activities or vocations may be invited to school for giving a faithful and pragmatic description of what they do and how useful their work is to the nation. This will enable the children to be acquainted with those around them in the society. This will also develop vocational socialisation in children.

15. Work experience should be introduced in schools. This will enable the children to have first hand experiences of the activities pursued in farms and factories.

16. Children should be acquainted with the social events like the celebration of the birthdays of great personalities.

17. The school or college programme should be full of numerous co-curricular and curricular activities in which children meet, cooperate and learn from each other's personalities.

18. Children should be told about the socially accepted institutions in their society.

19. The introduction of common school dress, common lunch, etc., in the schools and colleges will prevent children of poor and lower middle classes from facing humiliation due to the inflated ego of the children of the well-to-do families who take pleasure in showing off their wealth and status through costly clothes.

CONCLUDING OBSERVATIONS

The task of social development of the child is not an easy one. The educational thinkers point out very emphatically that certain conditions in the learning-teaching situation must be created and made available in the school so that it may become an effective instrument of social development. These conditions are: (i) A democratic social climate in the school; (ii) Effective interpersonal relationships; (iii) Motivated learning situations; (iv) Group methods of teaching; (v) Social discipline; (vi) School-community inter-relationships; (vii) Student participation and involvement in the school management; (viii) A rich programme of co-curricular activities; (ix) Equal treatment to children irrespective of caste or status etc. considerations; (x) Emphasis on egalitarian ideals and values.

7

Emotional Development Pattern and Educational Implications

SIGNIFICANCE OF EMOTIONAL DEVELOPMENT PATTERN

Emotional development pattern plays an important role in the personal and social development of an individual. An individual with stable emotional pattern leads a happy, healthy and peaceful life. He is at ease with himself and his surroundings. On the other hand an individual who is emotionally disturbed becomes a problem for himself as well as for others. Continuous emotional disturbance affects the individual's growth and development. Therefore, the development of emotions is extremely important for the harmonious development of the personality of an individual. Emotions influence all the aspects of an individual's personality. Proper training and education will go a long way to enable the young people to control their emotions and obtain mental balance and stability. Emotions are the prime motive forces of thought and conduct and their control is very important. It has been rightly said, "To keep one's emotions under control and be able to conceal them is considered a mark of strong character".

MEANING OF EMOTIONAL DEVELOPMENT

With a view to understand the meaning of emotional development it is necessary to know the meaning of emotions as they are the prime movers of emotional development.

Etymology: The word emotion is derived from the Latin word '*Emovere*' which means to 'stir up', 'to agitate' or 'to excite'.

Kimbel Young notes: "Emotion is the all-round state of the organism marked by increased bodily activity and strong feelings directed to some subject".

According to *Crow and Crow*, an emotion "is an affective experience that accompanies generalised inner adjustment and mental and psychological stirred up states in the individual, and that shows itself in his own behaviour. By making use of this explanation R.S. Woodworth (1945) has defined emotion in this way. "Emotion is a *moved or stirred up* state of feeling that is the way it appears to the individual himself. It is a disturbed muscular and glandular activity—that is the way it appears to an external observer".

William McDougall (1949) says: "An instinct is an inherited or innate psycho-physical disposition which determines its possessor to perceive and to pay attention to objects of a certain class, to experience an emotional excitement of a particular quality upon perceiving such an object, and to act in regard to it in a particular manner, or, at least, to experience an impulse to such an action". This statement gives us the nature of emotions as well. According to McDougall, an instinctive behaviour has three aspects:

(i) Cognitive or knowing or perceptual aspect.
(ii) Affection or feeling or emotional effect.
(iii) Cognitive or doing or striving or executive, active or behaviour aspect.

Let us take an example. A child sees a bull coming towards him. He experiences an instinctive fear and undergoes the above three processes. Firstly, he perceives the bull, secondly he experiences an emotion of fear and thirdly he tries to run away. It is, therefore, concluded that an emotion is an affective experience that one undergoes during an instinctive excitement.

McDougall discovered 14 basic instincts and pointed out that each and every emotion, whatever it may be, is the product of some instinctive behaviour.

The instincts in their alphabetical order with their associated emotions are listed as under:

Sl. No.	*Instinct*	*Emotion Accompanying an Instinct*
1.	Acquisition	Feeling of ownership
2.	Appeal	Distress
3.	Construction	Feeling of creativeness
4.	Curiosity	Wonder
5.	Flight or Escape	Fear
6.	Food seeking	Appetite
7.	Gregariousness	Feeling of loneliness
8.	Laughter	Amusement
9.	Parental	Tenderness, Love
10.	Pugnacity or Combat	Anger
11.	Repulsion	Disgust
12.	Sex mating	Lust
13.	Submission	Negative feeling

CHIEF CHARACTERISTICS OF EMOTIONS

1. The emotional experiences are associated with some instincts or biological drives.

2. Emotions, in general, are the product of perception.

3. The core of an emotion is feeling which is essentially linked with some sort of urge or impulse act to do. There is only a difference of degree between feeling and emotion.

4. Every emotional experience involves several physical and psychological changes in the organism. Some of these changes like the bulge of the eyes, the flush of the face, the flow of tears, the pulse rate, etc., are easily observable. There are also internal physiological changes like circulation of blood, the impact on the digestive system and the changes in the functioning of some glands, etc.

5. Emotions are frequent.

6. Emotions are expressed in relation to the concrete objects or situations.

7. Emotions are temporary.

8. Emotional expressions in early childhood are intense irrespective of the intensity of the stimulus.

9. Small children fail to hide their emotions and express them indirectly through different activities like crying, nail-biting, thumb-sucking and speech difficulties.

10. Emotions are prevalent in every living organism.

11. Emotions are present at all stages of development and can be aroused in young as well as in old.

12. Emotions differ from person to person.

13. Same emotion can be aroused by a number of different stimuli—objects or situations.

14. Emotions rise abruptly but die slowly.

15. Emotions are subject to displacement. The anger aroused on account of one stimuli gets transferred to other situations. The anger caused by the rebuking of the officer to his subordinate may be transferred in beating the children at home.

16. One emotion may give rise to a number of likewise emotions.

POSITIVE AND NEGATIVE EFFECTS OF EMOTIONS

Positive Effects of Emotions

1. Emotions provide energy to an individual to face a particular situation.
2. Emotions work as motivators of our behaviour.
3. Emotions influence our adjustment in the society.

Negative Effects of Emotions

1. Highly emotional conditions disturb the mental equilibrium of an individual.
2. Highly emotional conditions disturb the reasoning and thinking of an individual.

UNDERSTANDING EMOTIONS OF ANGER, FEAR, LOVE AND JEALOUSY

Emotion	Signs	Contributory Factors	Values	Methods of Dealing
1. *Anger*	(i) Extreme rage (ii) Resentment (iii) Irritation (iv) Feeling of fear, grief, jealousy	1. Unnecessary interference in the child's daily affairs 2. Assignment of tasks be-yond his capacity 3. Imagined or real favouri - tism shown by parents and teachers	1. Sometimes performance of brave tasks 2. Development of insight 3. Change in the attitude of parents	1. Understanding the causes of anger 2. Minimising provocations 3. Restraints on the part of elders 4. Changing the programme
2. *Fear*	(i) Trembling (ii) Crying (iii) Running away	1. Sight of an abnormal object and animal 2. Loud sound or flash of light etc. 3. Strict discipline 4. Unfamiliar persons or things 5. Fear of darkness 6. Fear of being alone 7. Fear of ghosts 8. Failure in examination or in some important task	1. Safe-guards against harm 2. Developing cautious approach 3. Hard work 4. Punctuality 5. Change in the outlook of elders	1. Narration of examples set by others 2. Encouraging children to face situations boldly 3. Showing love 4. Sympathetic approach 5. Appropriate discipline

(Contd.)

Emotion	Signs	Contributory Factors	Values	Methods of Dealing
3. *Love*	1. Happiness 2. Belongings 3. Feeling of creativeness	1. Caring 2. Protecting 3. Feeling 4. Fondling 5. Smiling	1. Mutual love 2. Admiration 3. Change in the attitude 4. Enthusiasm	1. Feeling of acceptance. Giving suitable tasks
4. *Jealousy*	(i) Kicking (ii) Biting (iii) Pinching (iv) Scratching (v) Bed-wetting (vi) Thumb sucking (vii) Refusal to eat	1. Feeling of getting less attention 2. Comparison with the performance of others.	May lead to hard work	1. Showing affection 2. Fair treatment 3. Avioding undue competition

EMOTIONAL BEHAVIOUR PATTERN AT DIFFERENT STAGES

A. Emotional Behaviour Pattern of the New Born Infant

According to J.B. Watson (1919), the new born infant, displays three primary 'emotion', 'love' in response to strolling, 'fear' in response to loud noises and loss of support and 'anger' in response to physical restraint. Watson believed that all other emotional responses were built upon these primary emotions through the conditioning process.

B. Emotional Development Pattern During Infancy

In the words of Hurlock, "At birth and shortly afterwards, the first sign of emotional behaviour is general excitement to strong stimulation. There are no indications of clearly definite emotional patterns that can be recognised and identified as specific emotional states".

C. Common Emotional Pattern in Babyhood

	Emotion	*Stimuli that Give Rise*	*Response*
1.	Affection	Playing with the baby. Taking care of the baby. Providing toys.	Expresses by hugging and kissing
2.	Anger	(i) Interference with the movements of the baby (ii) Thwarting of some wish (iii) Not being able to do what he sets out to do	1. Screaming 2. Kicking 3. Waving the arms
3.	Curiosity	Anything new or unusual	Expression of curiosity through facial expression, *i.e.*, opening the mouth
4.	Fear	1. Loud noises 2. Strange persons 3. Objects 4. Dark rooms 5. Animals	1. Attempting to withdraw 2. Crying 3. Temporary holding of breath 4. Stopping the activity
5.	Joy	Physical well-being	(i) Smiling (ii) Laughing (iii) Moving arms and legs

D. Common Emotional Pattern During Early Childhood

	Emotion	*Stimuli that Give Rise to*	*Response*
1.	Anger	Conflict over play things. Thwarting of wishes. Attack from another child.	Temper tantrums. Crying. Screaming. Stamping. Kicking. Jumping up and down. Striking

(*Contd.*)

	Emotion	*Stimuli that Give Rise to*	*Response*
2.	Attention	Loves people, things, pets or objects that give him pleasure	Expresses his affection physically or verbally
3.	Curiosity	New things or persons	Sensorimotor exploration. Asking questions
4.	Fear	Unpleasant experiences. Frightening scenes on T.V. etc.	Panic, running away, hiding, crying
5.	Grief	Loss of something that the child loves	Crying, losing interest in normal activities including eating
6.	Jealousy	Parental attitude towards different children, usually new sibling	Open expression, bed-wetting, pretending to be ill showing naughtiness
7.	Joy	Physical well-being. Acquiring new objects. Playing pranks with others.	Expression of smile. Clapping hands. Jumping. Hugging the person or object.

E. Emotional Pattern during Late Childhood

According to E.B. Hurlock, following are the chief characteristics of the emotional pattern:

1. Emotional expressions are pleasant ones.
2. The child laughs uproariously.
3. The child displays a release of pent-up animal spirits.
4. Emotional expressions are immature by adult standards.
5. Children who are popular tend to be less anxious and jealous than those who are less popular.
6. In order to win social approval, the child tries to curb the forms of expression that are socially unacceptable.
7. As he grows older, he begins to express his anger through moodiness and sulkiness.
8. Girls are likely to express more fears, worries and feelings of affection than boys.
9. Girls often dissolve expressions of anxiety and fears into tears.

Nevertheless all emotions are not of a pleasant sort. Several outbursts of temper occur.

F. Emotional Pattern During Adolescence (Discussed Separately)

CLASSIFICATION OF EMOTIONAL PATTERN

1. Aggressive *vs*. Submissive emotional pattern.
2. Normal *vs*. Abnormal emotional pattern.
3. Pleasant *vs*. Unpleasant emotional pattern.
4. Stable *vs*. Unstable emotional pattern.

COMPARISON BETWEEN THE EMOTIONAL PATTERN OF CHILDHOOD AND ADULTHOOD

	Childhood	*Adulthood*
1.	Too much intensity.	Comparatively less intensity.
2.	Short duration of emotions.	Long duration of emotions.
3.	Emotions transitory in nature.	Emotions marked by greater degree of stability.
4.	Easy detection of emotions.	Difficult to detect emotions.
5.	Intensity of feelings rules over reasoning.	Emotional response relatively guided by reason.

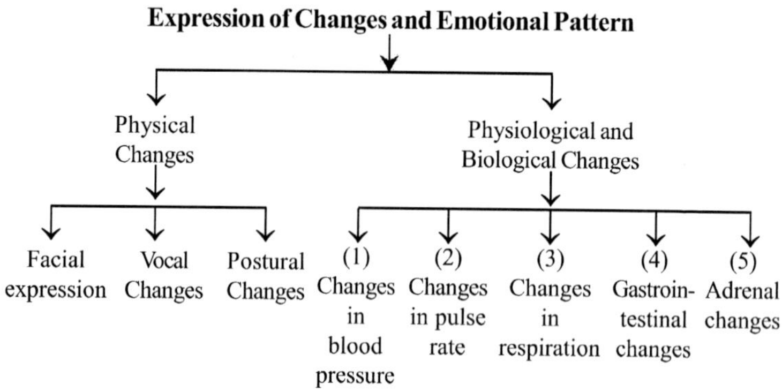

FACTORS AT HOME AND SCHOOL WHICH DISTURB THE EMOTIONAL DEVELOPMENT OF CHILDREN

Some of the important factors which disturb the emotions of children in school are:

1. Lack of security.
2. Economic disparities.
3. Faulty methods of teaching.
4. Fearful atmosphere in school.
5. Emotionally unbalanced teacher.
6. Traditional concept of discipline.
7. Poor physical conditions in schools.
8. Disregard of individual differences.
9. Lack of co-curricular activities.
10. Lack of sex education.
11. Faulty examination system.
12. Faulty curriculum.

TRAINING, SUBLIMATING AND MODIFYING EMOTIONS

1. *Redirection*: An emotion is dynamic in nature and cannot be suppressed totally. It cannot be destroyed. It is just like a tumultuous stream which cannot be obstructed permanently without giving some outlet. But as we can harness

a wild stream by building a dam against it and giving new channels to the powerful waters, quite in the same way, emotional waves can also be re-channelled for the advantage of the organism itself and for the whole society to which he belongs. Let us take the example of 'anger'. It is a furious emotion. It exists in its wild form in every organism. We have simply to tame and redirect it to broad and beneficial channels for the benefit of the person and the society.

2. *Sublimation*: Sublimating is also a sort of redirection with this difference only that in the former case the emotion does not lose its original form while in the latter case it is so much elevated that it changes its form. It assumes nobler and higher form. Lust is transformed into love for fine arts or social services or devotion to some deity. *Anger* turns to be *zeal and enthusiasm. Fear* takes the form of *anxiety for the betterment* of mankind.

3. *Catharsis*: Intensity of emotions is dangerous for health especially when they do not find expression. Even their expression in original form is very costly for the mind and the body. Therefore, catharsis of pent-up emotions is necessary for the well-being of the organism. Play and extra-curricular activities are very useful devices for this purpose.

4. *Inhibition*: Human life is very complex in the present civilisation. We need to control our emotions at every step. Redirection, sublimation and catharsis are not always possible and at every moment. Often we have suppressed our emotions for a short time or for a long time. It can be done with the help of strong will. But we should know that inhibition should not be permanent and we should give some outlet to the pent-up emotions in some form as soon as possible.

ROLE OF THE SCHOOL AND THE TEACHER IN THE EMOTIONAL DEVELOPMENT OF THE CHILD

School is expected to provide a purified, constructive and creative environment to children and teachers can play an important role in this. A teacher should not merely preach the significance of the emotional control, but he should also teach emotional control by personal example. The teacher should be patient and sympathetic towards the expression of the children's emotions. He should not be harsh, otherwise repression and inhibition would emerge and consequently conflicts would arise which may lead to neurotic and psychotic disorders in the children. He should rather sublimate the emotions of children by presenting suitable opportunities and situations for their healthy expression. Scientific methods of teaching and organisation of co-curricular activities would promote the emotional development of the child in the right direction. Undue reliance on codes of ethics, standards and ideals of society, etc. leads to emotional disturbances in children in the long run, particularly when they find their superior themselves transgressing them. "Example is better than precept" is a famous saying.

Important Ways for the Emotional Development of Children

1. *Providing Emotional Security*: When the child enters the school for the first time he finds quite a new world for him over there. He was just like a

prince in the domain of his home. His likes and dislikes had great significance. He felt himself secure physically as well as emotionally. He had a sense of belongingness and his feeling of self-assertion was also satisfied adequately. But everything is changed in the school. He has little significance and voice in the matters over there to start with. All the other children appear to him well-knit and well-adjusted in their own groups while he stands aloof. Sometimes he is ridiculed by the fellow students. All these things make him very uneasy emotionally. If the teacher is also indifferent to him or he proves to be a bit harsh for him, he loses his emotional balance. The teacher should be very careful of this situation. He should try to make the shift from home to school very agreeable for the newcomers. He should see that the newcomer may not feel the change adversely. There may be a welcome committee comprising some pupils under the guidance of a teacher to help the newcomers in desirable adjustment.

2. *Equal Treatment Irrespective of Income*: Poverty is not a bad thing in itself but sometimes it happens to be the cause of emotional disturbance for some pupils in certain situations. At home the poor child was quite contended and happy in his limited world. But when poor children come across rich ones in the school, they find colossal differences between themselves and their rich classmates as regards their clothes, their modes of life, their meals and pocket allowances. Some of them may develop jealousy, worry and inferiority complex if they cannot make proper adjustment with hard realities. Sometimes the teachers aggravate the situation when they happen to be quite partial and do not treat the poor children at par with the rich ones. Heavy financial demands may also disturb the poor children emotionally as they are often unable to meet the same easily.

The school is responsible to the poor students as much as to the rich ones. Resources of poor students should be studied individually with their education. Simple living should be a guiding principle in all the educational institutions.

3. *Dynamic Methods of Teaching*: Faulty methods of teaching do not develop motivation in the children. Therefore, lessons become a drudgery. The children begin to hate the very process of education. There is always tension in their minds. Learning is no more a joyful activity for them.

The improvement of the methods of teaching can go a long way in bringing back emotional security for many children. Educational work can easily be turned into play and then it will be interesting, joyful and at the same time more instructive.

4. *Role of Love in Schools*: In most of the traditional schools teaching is based on fear. Children know that they will be caned if they are not successful in studies. They get heavy home task which is often impossible to complete without help and guidance which is not always available at home. They sleep at night with the 'dreams of canes'. They wake up in the morning with fear and constant worry. Under such circumstances emotional tranquillity is hardly possible.

There is a famous saying, "Love the child and the child will love you. Hate the child and he will hate you". Love should be the basis of all work.

5. *Balanced Emotional Behaviour of the Teacher*: Some teachers themselves need emotional stability. Emotionally unbalanced teachers prove contagious for the innocent children. They themselves become a prey to inferiority complex, persistent worries or over-excited emotions. They are generally irritable and provocative. For the balanced emotional development of children, teachers themselves should be emotionally developed.

6. *Due Regard to Individual Differences*: All children differ mentally, emotionally and physically. But we provide little individual attention to the children in schools. Some of them are backward in studies, while some of them are very superior. But they are dragged on the same lines. The backward lag behind still more. This leads to emotional disturbance.

7. *Creative and Democratic Concept of Discipline*: Traditional methods of discipline are faulty. Sometimes schools are just like jails and some teachers are like jailors. Such discipline is negative. It may serve the purpose superficially but in reality the things are far from being satisfactory. There should be positive devices of discipline. Discipline should be creative and constructive. Children should be made responsible for handling their own affairs as far as it is possible.

8. *Provision of Co-curricular Activities*: All the children and especially adolescents need provision for the expression of their pent-up emotions and for redirection of their emotional behaviour. In the absence of such provision, emotional stability is not possible. Various co-curricular activities organised properly can solve this problem quite satisfactorily.

9. *Provision of Sex Education*: During adolescent period lack of information about sex causes emotional disturbance. Teacher should provide necessary information about the sex matters and problems. There should be no shyness and this work should be done seriously.

10. *Continuous and Comprehensive Evaluation*: The present system of examination is faulty. Chance factor counts much in this system. It does not measure the all-round development of the child and causes disturbance. Evaluation should be made continuous and objective.

11. *Healthy Physical Conditions in the Schools*: Poor physical conditions in the school bring fatigue and boredom to the children. They are very soon fed up with the school and its activities. Lack of creational activities is also responsible for emotional disturbance. The school authorities should be careful in this respect also.

12. *Rich and Varied Curriculum*: The curriculum in schools should relate to the real life of children. Learning in schools should be related to the modern needs of children.

Summing up

Whenever, a slight deviation from normal emotional behaviour pattern in children is noticed, steps must be taken to find out the reasons and corrective measures adopted. It must be kept in view that a lot of patience is needed on the part of the teachers in this regard.

8

Cognitive Development Pattern and Educational Implications: Piaget's Theory

MEANING OF COGNITIVE OR MENTAL OR INTELLECTUAL DEVELOPMENT

Cognitive development pattern implies the development of the mental abilities and capacities which help the learner to adjust his behaviour to the ever changing environmental conditions. According to *J.S. Bruner* (1964), "Intellectual development is the capacity to deal with several choices at the same time".

Cognitive development is not merely acquiring knowledge and adding to it. Knowledge must be accompanied by understanding and wisdom otherwise it is barren.

Cognitive development is inherent in the development of those basic skills which help us in getting to know the environment. The formulation of all awareness of the environment rests on the proper development of the five senses, i.e., touch, taste, smell, hearing and sight. While the senses are the 'gateways' to all experiences in the environment, the child learns from these experiences and develops an understanding of the world around him with the assistance of certain skills which are 'observation', 'memory', 'classification', 'sequential thinking', 'reasoning' and 'problem solving'. Thus all these elements help in the development of cognitive behaviour.

PROCESS OF COGNITIVE DEVELOPMENT PATTERN

The process of cognitive development implies the progressive changes in the mental process which go on from birth to death. Mental process is an activity on the part of the organism which is of a psychological nature or involved in the mind. There are mental tests to evaluate a specific ability or performance. Cognitive development includes various aspects, such as, development of concepts, perception, language, memory, reasoning, thinking, imagination and intelligence.

Various Elements of Cognitive Development

(1) Intelligence and Cognitive Development
(2) Sensation and Perception Pattern
(3) Concept Formation
(4) Language Development
(5) Memory Development
(6) Creativity
(7) Problem Solving

1. *Intelligence and Mental Development*: The results of intelligence tests show that mental or intellectual growth is rapid in infancy, moderate in childhood and slow in youth.

2. *Sensation and Perception Pattern During Various Stages*: Both sensation and perception are considered important aspects of mental development. The elementary impressions are gathered by sense organs. Impression take the form of perception when they are interpreted and some definite meanings are attached to them.

Through experience, child's sensations become perceptions and he is able to give meaning to it. Child's sensory equipment becomes mature at the age of five. He shows great interest in seeing, hearing, touching, smelling and tasting. However, child's sensations do not automatically assume meaning. During his early childhood, the child is more likely to misrepresent things and objects because of lack of experience. For example, when viewed from a distance, a train may appear to a child as a toy train. But gradually child's perceptions become more and more accurate through right kinds of experiences. By the time a child enters the school, he has gained enough experience. Yet he needs assistance and guidance to improve his ability to perceive by having first hand experiences and observations of objects, persons and situations around him. Gradually he develops a proper perception of space, time, form, movement and distance.

Perception patterns become more organised and refined when an individual passes through the years to his adolescence. Now they tend to become more definite, detailed and rich. At this stage they need not be associated necessarily with objects. They are beginning to be influenced by his beliefs, ideals, opinions, etc.

3. *Concept Formation*: Another important aspect of the child's mental development is the formation of concept. A concept is the generalised meaning that is attached to an object or idea. It is the result of one's perceptual experiences. It involves both discrimination and generalisation. Discrimination begins sometimes after the child tries to generalise his perceptual experiences and he begins to acquire concepts. Experience is an important factor in concept formulation. In the early childhood, a child tries to develop various concepts from the concrete experiences in the form of actual objects.

Normally, concept formation proceeds from concrete to abstract, from vague to clear and from inexact to exact, depending on the type of experiences a child receives. The child has a very poor concept of time. As stated by *Crow and Crow*, "Time as such means little to the young child. He cannot distinguish among 'to-day', 'tomorrow', and 'next week' except as they represent words rather than actual duration of time".

In later years, various experiences provided by reading, lecturing and movies, etc., help in concept formation.

Generally, concepts may be broadened, and developed. They may even take a new shape. Wrong concepts can be altogether abandoned.

Gradually as a result of learning and maturation, child's concepts become clear, definite and specific.

4. *Development of Language*: The development of language contributes

to the mental growth and development of the child. Important aspects of language development are speech, vocabulary and length of responses, etc.

5. *Development of Memory*: Memory is also an important element of mental development. There is little memory at birth but it gradually increases with maturation and experience. This has been explained by *Hurlock and Schwartz* in these words: "Memory of an impressionistic kind appears in the first half of the year and instances of the true remembrance appear by the end of first year. During the first year memory is only aroused by sensory stimuli. With the learning of speech the child is able to remember ideationally by the end of the second year. During the first and second years the memory is stronger for persons and objects than for situation. In pre-childhood from 3 to 6 years, situations become significant factors in the child memory. By 3 years the child can recount the story heard a few days ago and he can also give information about past experiences".

A child has a good memory in the earlier stages but this memory is generally a rote memory. His memorisation is without reasoning. He seldom uses logic and insight in memorisation. A child can cram and reproduce the matter easily. The memory tends to function more logically during later childhood and adolescence. A selection process of remembering and forgetting begins to operate. After that memory tends to decrease.

Memory depends upon person to person. It is generally affected by health and situation of the child. The stimuli which are associated with a kind of memory significantly influence, its remembrances or forgetting.

6. *Creativity*: It may be stressed that creativity is the most single ability which is at the root of human progress. Like many other activities, it can be developed at a young age.

In a general sense, creativity is the ability to think in novel ways which result in some new and original solution.

7. *Problem Solving*: All thinking and reasoning involve meeting difficulties, facing complex situations and finding out solutions. An individual is beset with all these since childhood. Thinking and reasoning powers are used in problem solving and these begin to grow as early as two and a half or three years of age. Gradually the ability to reason grows.

FACTORS AFFECTING COGNITIVE DEVELOPMENT PATTERN

1. *Heredity*: Cognitive development of an individual is greatly affected by the interaction between inherited intelligence and the individual's experience.

2. *Physical Growth*: There is a strong relation between physical growth and cognitive development. A healthy person is likely to have a better intelligence than a person who has a poor physique.

3. *Physical Environment*: Physical environment like fresh air, sufficient light and ample space has a great bearing on cognitive development.

4. *Family Environment*: The kind of discussions held in the family, type of reading material like books and magazines read by the family affect the cognitive development.

5. *Socio-economic Status of the Family*: Parents of high socio-economic group have better access to send their children to good schools.

6. *School Environment*: The methods of teaching, availability of good reading material in the library, attitudes of teachers and school discipline, etc. affect cognitive development.

It is concluded that cognitive development is the result of a large number of factors. It is not an automatic process. It is a gradual and painstaking process.

COGNITIVE DEVELOPMENT CURVE

Learning Curve: It is observed that children are able to learn more difficult things as they grow older (see Fig. 8.1).

Steepness of the cognitive ability curve during middle childhood and adolescence is illustrated in Figures 8.2 and 8.3.

Cognitive Development is indicated by growth in vocabulary (see Fig. 8.4).

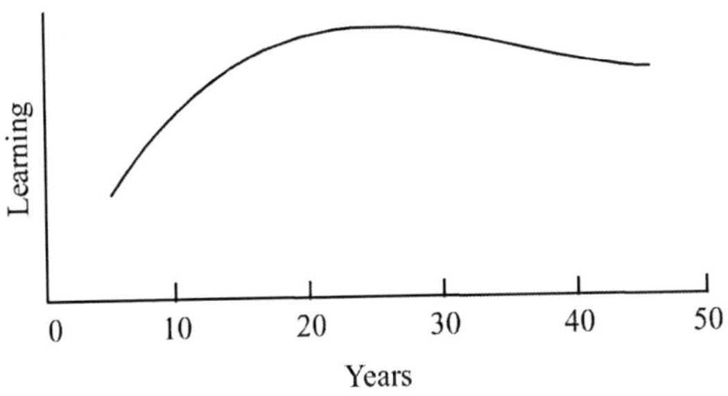

Fig. 8.1: Cognitive Growth Curve (Learning Growth Curve)

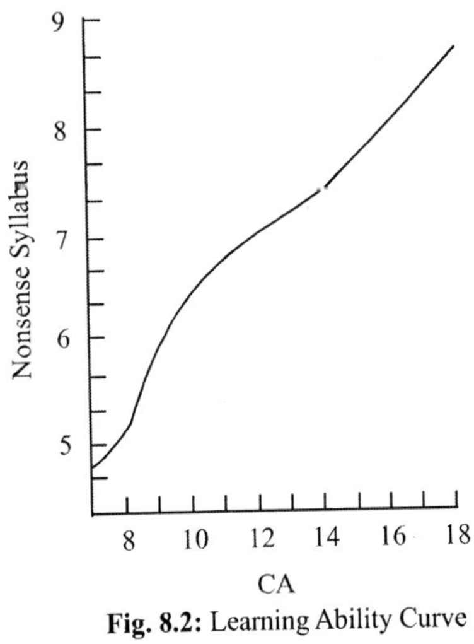

Fig. 8.2: Learning Ability Curve During Middle Childhood

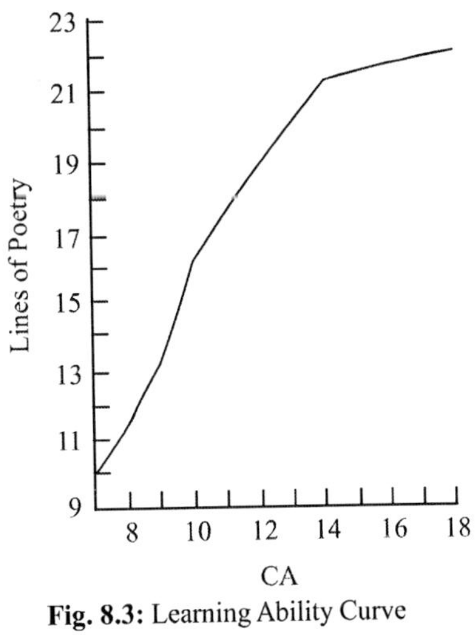

Fig. 8.3: Learning Ability Curve During Adolescence

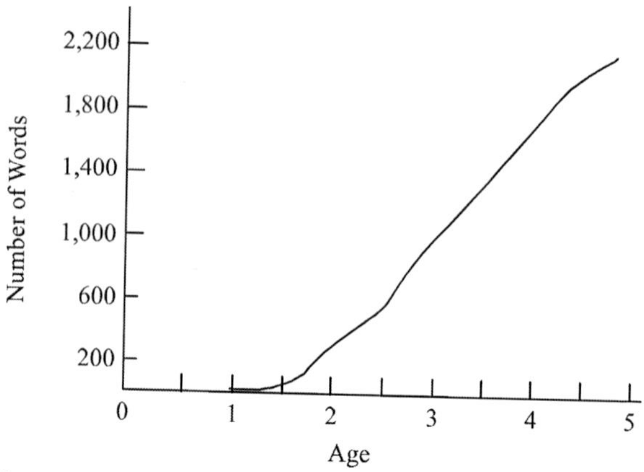

Fig. 8.4: Vocabulary Development Curve During Early Childhood

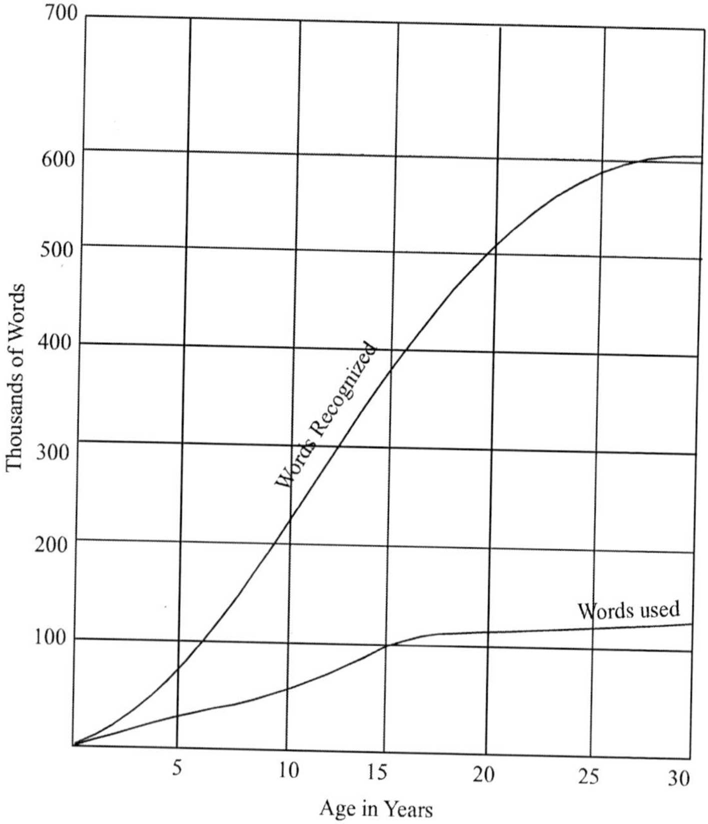

Fig. 8.5: Cognitive Development

JEAN PIAGET'S THEORY OF COGNITIVE DEVELOPMENT PATTERN (MENTAL OR INTELLECTUAL DEVELOPMENT)

Brief Life Sketch of Jean Piaget (1896-1980)

Piaget is regarded as one of the pioneers in psychological investigation of children although he neither undertook formal study nor passed any examination in psychology. He was a biologist by training. At an early age of 22, he obtained his Doctorate Degree in Zoology on Mollusks of Valias. He worked on child development for more than 50 years and produced enormous literature on Development Psychology. He read Philosophy, Psychology and Sociology etc. He pursued clinical research at the Alfred Binnet Laboratory at Paris. By observing, dissecting and experimenting with children, he developed his educational theory regarding cognitive development or learning by children. His work as a Professor of Child Psychology at the University of Geneva (Switzerland) made him famous throughout the world.

Piaget began his study of child development with the observation of his own three children. From this beginning, his investigations were gradually extended to other children. These investigations resulted in the publication of a large number of papers and books which are often quoted by eminent psychologist and other thinkers on education.

Cognitive Development Pattern at Various Stages

The most detailed description of the development of cognition has been provided by Jean Piaget. Piaget divides cognitive process development into 4 stages or 4 major periods:

(i) Sensorimotor,
(ii) Pre-operational,
(iii) Concrete Operational, and
(iv) Formal Operational.

Piaget asserts that all children progress through all these stages in a fixed order. According to his theory, human intellect is constructed over time as the individual experiences progressively more complex interactions with the environment.

Two Processes: In Piaget's system, two processes—Organisation and Adaptation—actively operate during each of the four stages.

Organisation is the process by which different elements within a system maintain communication, e.g., we have a tendency to organise basic sensory information (such as, images and other experiences) in order to form more complex ideas and thought.

Adaptation consists of complementary processes of assimilation and accommodation. These two processes are the basis for Cognitive Growth.

Assimilation: 'Assimilation' implies incorporation of something from the environment. New ideas, concepts and stimuli are taken in and incorporated into one's 'existing set of schemes'. A scheme is the organised pattern of behaviour which the child develops when he is engaged in any activity. For example, when a child is engaged in sucking, there is a certain pattern of movements of the cheeks, lips and hands. When a child is confronted with a new object, he will try to understand the new object by applying his old scheme to it. He grasps it and adapts himself to a new object by assimilating it. His old scheme does not change in the process.

Accommodation: 'Accommodation' involves modification or change of some elements of an old scheme or learning a new scheme which is more appropriate for the new object. A baby who has already got a scheme of sucking mother's breast accommodates to the object placed in the mouth—finger, nipple, pencil, a toy—depending on its shape, form and the size. The baby develops a new scheme or a modified scheme. This is called 'accommodation'.

Thus a baby assimilates when he understands and perceives the new in the light of his old perceptions. A baby forms a new scheme when he modifies or changes his old perception to suit the new. This implies adjusting or accommodating. In this way a baby forms new structures or new schemes and consequently develops cognivity.

A. Cognitive Development at the Sensorimotor Stage (Birth to Two Years)

There are six steps at this stage.

Step I: During the first month of life, the babies are unaware of themselves and of the object around them, e.g., they do not realise that the bottle they suck and the bottle they grasp are one and the same thing. The infant has a lack of what Piaget calls object permanence.

Step II: During first four months, babies motor activities become more coordinated. They begin to look at the thing which is being grasped.

Step III: Between 4 to 8 months, the infants attempt to control and manipulate the objects which are often conical. They may hear an interesting noise but since they do not know what caused it, they try to make the noise recur by repeating whatever they were doing when they heard the noise. The baby at this stage also realises that objects exist when they are out of sight.

Step IV: During 8 to 12 months, thinking gives way to more instrumental activity. The child has achieved object permanence. He has developed some internal image of the object to help him recall it and its location—he displays sense of space and time—but the child is limited intellectually.

Step V: 12 to 14 months: The child is able to locate the hidden toys. Piaget sees much of the cognitive growth as the formulation of increasingly complex hypotheses in the light of the experiences.

Step VI: 18 to 24 months: During this period the child can infer what the moving hand holds. This last stage is important because it represents the beginning of the child's ability to represent mentally objects that are no longer physically present. In essence, it is the start of abstract thought.

B. Cognitive Development Patterns at the Pre-Operational Stage (2-7 Years)

1. The major advance made during this period is the ability to represent the external world mentally by means of arbitrary symbols that stand for objects.
2. This is the period in which language develops and begins to reflect the child's cognitive abilities and limitations.
3. The pre-operational period is transitional period.

4. The perspective of the child on the world is expanding rapidly, but the child is still confused in the use of physical concepts and in evaluation of cause and effect.

5. During this phase, the child makes appropriate generalisations and attributes his feelings to inanimate objects—assuming, for example, that clouds 'cry' to make rain.

6. Alternate perspectives are not imaged by the child. This is also known as stage of proportional thought.

7. The child cannot do abstract thinking.

8. The child does not think of operations. He is thus a static thinker.

9. The child's thinking is for a very short duration.

C. Cognitive Development Pattern at the Concrete Operational Stage (7-11 Years)

This period (Concrete operational stage) is characterised by the emergence of operations, such as, conservation. Conservation is Piaget's term for the idea that a property or attribute of an object remains the same despite some transformation that changes the appearance of the object. Piaget found that when a child at pre-operational stage is shown two identical balls of clay and then sees one rolled into a saucer he may claim that the saucer contains less clay because it is thinner than the ball. The child is taking only one aspect (shape) into account. The child does not know that this saucer has taken shape from the same ball.

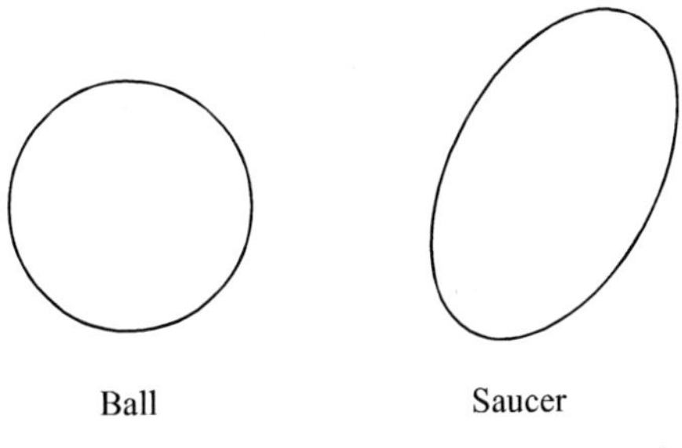

At about age 7, the child grasps the solution to conservation problems by developing three concepts that characterise concrete operations. The first is *compensation*—sausage is thinner but that change is balanced by its increase in length. The second is *reversibility*—if you role sausage back, you get the same ball you started with. The third is *identity*—nothing has been added to or subtracted from the clay, so the sausage and the ball contain same amount of clay.

Children at the level of concrete operations are able to consider two aspects of a problem simultaneously. In their social interpretations, they consider not only what they are saying but also listen to others.

The child performs operations: combining, separating, multiplying, repeating, dividing and substituting etc.

He begins to analyse. He is aware of variables. He classifies.

D. Cognitive Development at Formal Operations Stage (11-15 Years or Adulthood)

Here the youth begins and the nature of thought undergoes a change. The complex abstract and mature logic of adult begins to manifest itself during adolescence with the systematic analysis, exploration and solution of problems.

During this period, thinking is purely abstract and hypothetical. Piaget has been most concerned with the capacity to reason with respect to problems, concepts of geometry, language, space, time, number, order etc.

During the teenage years young people realise that thoughts are private and that no one else knows what they are thinking. They value friendship and sincerity and spend much time trying to discern real motives. The adult is more sensitive to the discrepancy between reality and ideals. Teenager has knowledge of the rules and his knowledge is different from that of small children.

Lastly, during this period (Formal operations), the crystallisation of personality development takes place. Forming of social and ideational position is closely linked with the acquisition of moral values.

At this stage, the individual has reached his intellectual maturity.

Problems Related to Cognitive Development

1. Poor environmental stimulation.
2. Poor hereditary environment.
3. Lack of proper attention, assimilation etc. on the part of the learners.
4. Defective teaching-learning material.
5. Low level of learner's intelligence.

EDUCATIONAL IMPLICATIONS OF PIAGET'S THEORY OF COGNITIVE DEVELOPMENT AND THE ROLE OF THE SCHOOL AND TEACHER

1. The child is learning by *himself*, the teacher occupies a secondary position. The child *discovers* things actively. Infants explore the world. Knowledge should not be imposed.

2. It is the duty of the school, teachers and parents to provide materials to children to sharpen their interests. Let the child explore and solve the problems. The classroom in early grades might be arranged in a series of counters stocked with intriguing materials to arouse children's curiosity. Children should be allowed to manipulate things and see results.

3. Instruction should be geared to the level of the child. As the level of the child changes at each stage, the level of instruction or exploratory activities should also change.

4. The knowledge of cognitive stages of growth of a child does help the teacher in more than one way. The teacher should be sensitive to understand the child's actions and be guided by his spontaneous interests.

5. Social interactions have a great educational value for Piaget. Positive social actions, therefore, should be encouraged.

6. Cognitive behaviour skills of the teacher have the following dimensions.

   (a) *Knowledge*: Imparting information.

(b) *Comprehension*: Making the content clear.
(c) *Application*: Enabling the learners understand the use of theoretical statements in real situations.
(d) *Analysis*: Enabling the students to breakdown material into its constituent parts for comparison etc.
(e) *Synthesis*: Enabling the students to combine elements in components to form new structured wholes.
(f) *Evaluation*: Enabling the learners to make judgements (quantitative and qualitative) about the extent to which material satisfies criteria.

Following activities should prove useful in developing proper cognitive development pattern:

(i) Story making, telling, writing and listening.
(ii) Picture competition.
(iii) Essay writing involving imagination.
(iv) Assembling of parts of some dismantled object.
(v) Modelling.
(vi) Quiz questions.
(vii) Debates and elocution contests.
(viii) Problem-solving opportunities.

9

Adolescence: Meaning, Characteristics, Problems and Educational Implications

MEANING AND DEFINITION OF ADOLESCENCE

The term adolescence is derived from a Latin word '*adolescence*' meaning 'to grow', 'to mature'. Now this term primarily implies to emerge or to 'achieve identity'. It is very difficult to define exactly the period of life which constitutes adolescence. No sharp chronological boundaries may be fixed to this period. Generally speaking, it covers a period of seven or eight years, normally from 12 to 18 or 20 with large variations in many cases. Some children may manifest traits of its advent as early as the 10th year while others may manifest it till the fifteenth or sixteenth year. Twelve or thirteen may be considered as the normal period for boys in India and even for girls when adolescence begins.

Adolescence is best defined in relation to puberty. This is the period which begins with puberty and ends with the general cessation of physical growth; it emerges from the later childhood stage and merges into adulthood.

According to *G.R. Medinnus and R.C. Johnson*, "Adolescence begins when signs of sexual maturity begin to occur in both physical and social development and ends when the individual has assumed adult roles and is concerned in most ways as an adult by his reference group".

A.T. Jersild observes, "Adolescence is that span of years during which boys and girls move from childhood to adulthood mentally, emotionally, socially and physically".

According to *Dorthy Rogers*, adolescence is "a process rather than a period, a process of achieving the attitudes and beliefs needed for effective participation in society".

The Hadow Report in England has described this stage as, "There is a tide which begins to rise in the veins of youth at the age of eleven or twelve. It is called by the name of adolescence. If the tide can be taken as flood, and a new voyage began in the stream and along the flow of its current, we think it will move on to fortune".

WHO defines adolescence both in terms of age (spanning the ages between 10 and 19 years) and in terms of a phase of life marked by special attributes. These attributes include:

- Rapid physical growth and development
- Physical, social and psychological maturity, but not all at the same time

- Sexual maturity and the onset of sexual activity
- Experimentation
- Development of adult mental processes and adult identity
- Transition from total socio-economic dependence to relative independence

To distinguish adolescents from other similar (and sometimes overlapping) age groupings, which, however, differ in these special characteristics, WHO has also defined youth and young people.

- Youth—persons between 15 and 24 years
- Young people—persons between 10 and 24 years.

GENERAL CHARACTERISTICS OF THE PERIOD OF ADOLESCENCE

1. The adolescent is a combination of opposites. Sometimes he is an altruist and sometimes a miser. On the one hand, he behaves like a child in many ways and on the other hand he likes to be treated as an adult. He wants to have the privileges of adulthood but does not want to undertake its obligations and responsibilities.
2. The adolescent lacks experience though he may exhibit a 'know-it-all' attitude.
3. He regards himself as more suited than the adults and grown-ups to frame rules, laws, codes and morals which will be just and true.
4. He is intensely emotional. He fluctuates between two extremes. He may be active and happy at one time and moody and dull at another.
5. He is seeking his own place in the life around him.
6. There is a strong tendency of self-assertion which is prominent owing to the new orientation which sets in life.
7. The adolescent wants to free himself from bondage. There is a tendency to revolt against authority.
8. The growth of intelligence reaches its maximum during this period.
9. The adolescent is extremely passionate for expressing his own opinions and appreciation.
10. A group of adolescents set to practical work with great zeal and works patiently.
11. He responds more readily to the influence of the teacher than of the parents.
12. There is unlimited admiration for some adult whom he considers to be outstanding. An adolescent is essentially a hero-worshipper.
13. There is lot of interest in and need on physical attractions and good grooming.
14. Girls are more interested in boys than boys are in girls; of course both are interested in the opposite sex.
15. In extreme cases, homosexuality (associated with the same sex) develops.
16. An adolescent exhibits exuberant imagination. This period is characterised as a period of day-dreams.
17. He wants to form small groups or gangs.

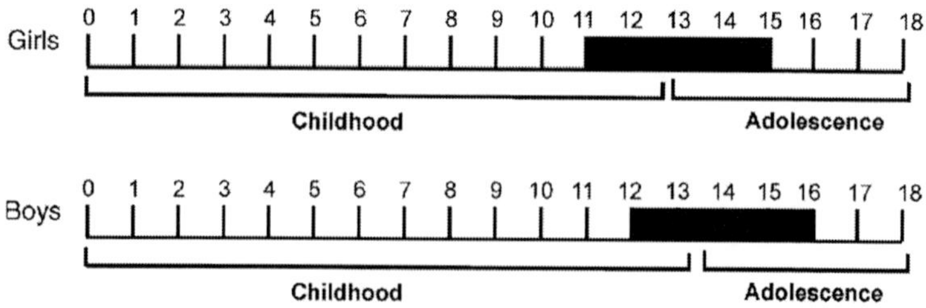

Fig. 9.1: Puberty Overlaps the End of Childhood and the Beginning of Adolsescence

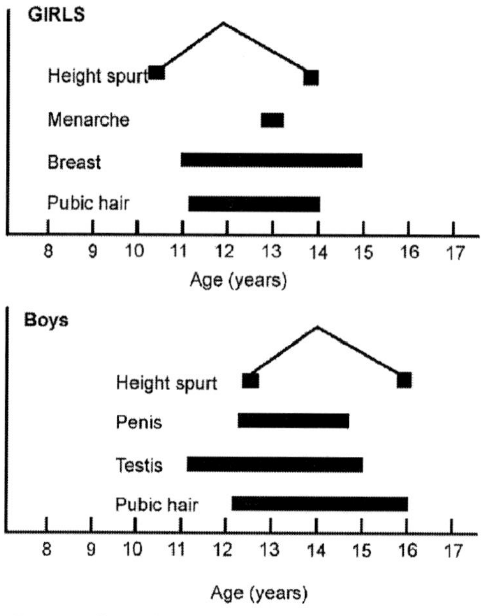

Fig. 9.2: Pattern of Development of Secondary Sex Characteristics in Boys and Girls

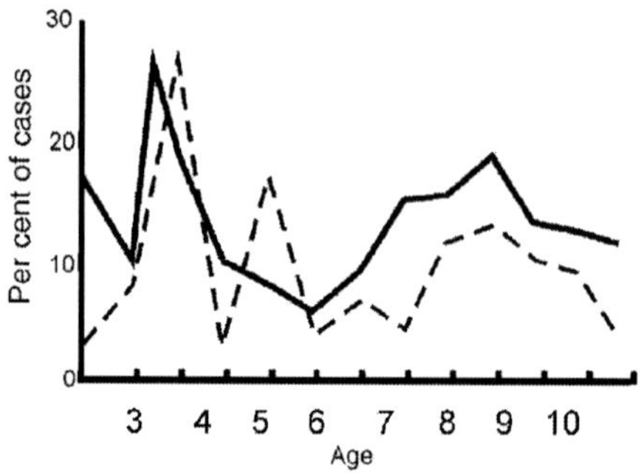

Fig. 9.3: Irritability Tends to Increase Early in Puberty and then to Decline

SPECIFIC NEEDS OF ADOLESCENCE WITH SPECIAL REFERENCE TO INDIAN ADOLESCENTS

Although in many respects, several needs of adolescent stage are similar to the needs of the other stages but they are quite different in the matter of intensity and forcefulness. These needs are interrelated. The following chart illustrates the specific needs of the adolescence.

Significant Specific Needs of the Adolescence

(1) *Physical Needs*

1. Need for enough nutrition for physical development.
2. Need for outlets for the utilisation of abundant energy.
3. Need for acquaintance with body development aspects.
4. Need for sex.
5. Need for security.
6. Need for adventurers life.

(2) *Emotional and Psychological Needs*

1. Need for satisfaction of heightened emotions.
2. Need for recognition of self-identification.
3. Need for the satisfaction of arousal of sexual emotions.
4. Need for development of confidence.

(5) *Social Needs*

1. Need for acceptance in the society.
2. Need for suitable peers.
3. Need for adjustment in the group and society.
4. Need for equal treatment.

(3) *Intellectual Needs*

1. Need for the satisfaction of heightened curiosity.
2. Need for independent thinking.

(4) *Moral Needs*

1. Need for search for values.
2. Need for equality.
3. Need for sound mind

(6) *Vocational Needs*

1. Need for practical experience.
2. Need for appropriate vocational guidance.

The interrelatedness of the various aspects of the development of the personality of the adolescent may be illustrated as under:

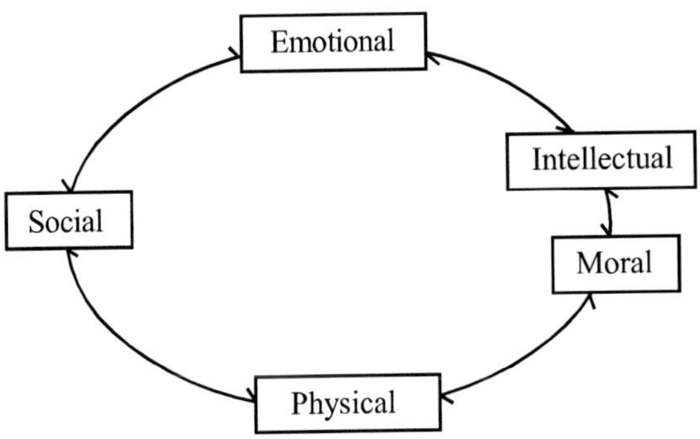

Fig. 9.4: Interrelatedness of the Various Aspects of the Development of the Adolescent

PHYSICAL NEEDS OF THE ADOLESCENTS AND THEIR SATISFACTION

Hall has very emphatically observed, "A ton of knowledge, bought at the expense of an ounce of health which is the most ancient and precious form of wealth and worth costs more than its value". Similar views have been expressed by Carlyle when he writes, "We manufacture clever devils by the thousand because health is not the object of party politics". Great seer Swami Vivekananda has also stressed the importance of well-built bodies when he remarks, "What India needs today is not the Bhagwad Gita but the football field". Our schools must give due importance to this aspect of education. W.M. Ryburn remarked: "We need in Indian Education—a general philosophy of physical education—we need a conception of education in which physical education takes its rightful place and in which its vital importance is recognised".

A properly directed physical development programme should result in health, happiness, efficiency and character.

Meaning of Physical Education and Development

Physical education relating to physical development is that field of education which deals with muscle activities and their related responses. Physical development includes the following aspects:

(i) It is growth of nervous system.
(ii) It is growth of muscles.
(iii) It is functioning of glands.
(iv) It is change in height and weight which people normally observe.
(v) It is development of sex.

Physical development and growth include the physical as well as psycho-motor changes in an individual. Physical development also includes qualities like courage, endurance and self-control.

Physical Development at the Adolescent Stage

At the adolescent stage, marked changes take place in the following domains:

(i) Height and weight.
(ii) Bodily proportions.
(iii) Change in voice.
(iv) Increase in motor performance.
(v) Sexual changes.

Sexual Changes: Sexual changes are very prominent during the period of adolescence.

(A) *Primary Sex Features*

1. Boys develop their sex organs.
2. Sex glands—the gonads—start producing sperms. Boys may suffer from night dreams.
3. The growth of sex glands among girls is not visible. The first menstrual flow is indicative of their sexual growth.

(B) *Secondary Sex Features*

These features are not related to sex organs but are indicative of sexual maturation which is a part of adolescence. These are different in the case of males and females. Among the males the features are:

(a) Growth of pubic hair around the sex organ.
(b) Hair in the armpit, legs, arms and the chest.
(c) The growth of beard, and
(d) The tone of voice deepens.

Among the girls the growth of sex organs is not visible. Other changes are:

(a) The development of breasts.
(b) Increase in the width of hips.
(c) A rounded appearance of body and limbs.
(d) Growth of pubic hair, and
(e) A shrill voice.

Sexual identity includes the expression of sexual needs and feelings and the acceptance or rejection of sex.

Adolescence period is the onset of puberty. Puberty implies a series of physical changes that make the organism capable of reproduction.

Puberty leads to sexual activity, erotic fantasy, experimentation and masturbation.

The period of puberty is a difficult one for most of the adults.

Educational Implications of Physical Growth and Development

A programme of physical growth and development is not confined to the playground but should pervade the classroom and in fact the entire school programme. Physical development in the classroom may take the following forms:

1. Direct instruction emphasising the necessity of having a good physique may be given.
2. Suggestions regarding the maintenance of good health are very helpful.
3. Emphasis on right postures should be laid.
4. Provision of good seating and lighting arrangements in the classroom, thereby impressing upon them the importance of studying under healthy surroundings should be made.
5. Providing ample opportunities to the children for physical activity should be given its due importance.
6. Medical examination of school children by the school doctor should be made at suitable intervals.
7. Physical exercise for every child should be compulsory in the school.
8. Various activities promoting physical development should be well-planned and children should be encouraged to take part in these activities.
9. Activities like woodwork, spinning and weaving, bookbinding, gardening etc. may be introduced in the school as a group project. Such activities will lead to motor development as well as promote cooperation, and emotional adjustment among students.
10. At this stage students also have sexual development. It is necessary for us to impart them sex education.

11. Teachers should be conversant with norms of motor development of the child.

12. A variety of co-curricular activities should be introduced to provide outlets for the development of emotions and instincts which have a close link with physical growth and development.

Summing Up: Montaigne has very aptly remarked, "Physical education does neither train up the soul nor body, but the whole man". Froebel rightly stated, "Early education must deal directly with the physical development and influence the spiritual development through the exercise of senses".

EMOTIONAL DEVELOPMENTAL NEEDS AND THEIR SATISFACTION

Meaning and Need for Emotional Development

Emotional development is one of the major aspects of adolescence growth and development. Not only adolescent's physical growth and development is linked with his emotional make-up but his aesthetic, intellectual, moral and social development is also controlled by his emotional development. To keep one's emotions under control and be able to conceal them is considered a mark of strong and balanced personality. Therefore, adolescents must be trained to control their emotions and achieve a mental balance and stability which will lead to individual happiness and social efficiency.

The term emotion is derived from the Latin word '*emovere*' which means to 'stir', 'to agitate', 'to move' or 'to excite'.

Woodworth, by making use of this explanation has defined emotion in the following way: "Emotion is a 'moved' or 'stirred-up' state of an organism. It is a stirred-up state of feeling that is the way it appears to the individual himself. It is a disturbed muscular and glandular activity—that is the way it appears to an external observer".

Crow and Crow have defined emotion in the following way: An emotion "is an effective experience that accompanies generalised inner adjustment and mental and psychological stirred-up states in the individual, and that shows itself in his overt behaviour."

According to *Kimball Young*, "Emotion is the aroused psychological state of the organism marked by increased bodily activity and strong feelings directed to some subject.

How Emotions Work

All of us observe a large number of persons and objects in the world. We have some feelings for them in our mental make-up. Sometimes our feelings become strong either in favour or against the object or individual or an occasion. This disturbs our mental balance. This disturbance is known as Emotion. It not only disturbs our mind, but the entire organism. It is expressed in various movements and expressions of body and it tries to adjust to face the situation.

Features of Emotions

1. We have emotions due to our intensity of feeling. The depth of intensity differs from individual to individual.

2. The expression of emotions is universal in nature, i.e., it is found in all living beings.
3. Every individual has his own outlet of emotions in his own way.
4. Expressions of emotions are related to a person, object, idea or work.
5. Sometimes the expression of emotions leads to the loss of thinking power.
6. Emotional expression is related to our instinct.
7. Emotions persist for sometime and then they disappear.
8. Expression of emotions leads to changes in our behaviour.
9. Emotions rise abruptly but die slowly.

EDUCATIONAL IMPLICATIONS OF SATISFYING THE EMOTIONAL AND PSYCHOLOGICAL NEEDS OF THE ADOLESCENTS

A suitable educational programme needs to be developed to enable the adolescents to control their emotions and obtain a mental balance and stability which will mark for individual happiness and social efficiency.

Emotions can be suitably modified by the following mechanisms:

(i) Redirection
(ii) Sublimation
(iii) Catharsis
(iv) Inhibition
(Already Discussed)

Factors in School Environment Which Disturb the Emotional Development of the Adolescents

Some of the important factors which disturb the emotions of adolescents in school are:

1. Lack of security.
2. Economic disparities.
3. Faulty methods of teaching.
4. Fearful atmosphere in school.
5. Emotionally unbalanced teacher.
6. Traditionally concept of discipline.
7. Poor physical conditions in schools.
8. Disregard of individual differences.
9. Lack of co-curricular activities.
10. Lack of sex education.
11. Faulty examination system.
12. Faulty curriculum.

Role of the School and the Teacher in Satisfying the Needs of the Emotional Development of the Adolescent

Following are the ways for meeting the needs of the adolescents:

1. Providing equal treatment irrespective of considerations of wealth, status or gender of the adolescents.
2. Using dynamic and progressive methods of teaching-learning.
3. Love and affection on the part of the teacher to be made the basis of work.
4. Balanced emotional behaviour of the teacher himself.

5. Creative and democratic classroom and school discipline.
6. Healthy physical conditions in the school.
7. Due regard to individual differences of the adolescents.
8. Due regard to the individuality of the adolescents.
9. Adequate provision for a variety of co-curricular activities.
10. Provision of sex education.
11. Rich and varied curriculum.

SOCIAL DEVELOPMENT NEEDS OF THE ADOLESCENTS AND THEIR SATISFACTION

Meaning of Social Development

Educators have defined social development in a number of ways.

Freeman and Showel observe, "Social development is the process of learning and conforming to group standards, morals and traditions and becoming imbued with a sense of oneness, inter-communication and co-operation".

H.E. Garret states, "Socialisation or social development is the process whereby the biological individual is converted into a human person".

E.B. Hurlock thinks, "Social development means the attaining of maturity in social relationships".

Herbert Sorenson writes, "By social growth and development we mean increasing ability to get along well with oneself and others".

Thus social development refers to the process of development by which a child acquires the necessary attitudes, skills and values that make him an acceptable member of the group to which he belongs.

Characteristics of Social Development During Adolescence

Following are the important characteristics of social development during adolescence:

1. Adolescence is marked with too much sex consciousness resulting in sexual social relationships.

2. During adolescence loyalty becomes very much pronounced and adolescents are in a mood to sacrifice their selfish interests for the greater cause of the group, society and nation.

3. Adolescence stage is often marked with increased friendly relationships.

4. Emotional behaviour of the adolescent dominates his social characteristics and qualities.

5. There is too much diversity in the adolescents regarding their social interests.

To sum up, we may say that the adolescence is a period of maximum social awareness, increasing and intimate social relationships.

Factors Affecting Social Development of the Adolescents

Important factors are given below:

1. *Personal Factors*: These include: (i) Physical strength and health, (ii) Level of intelligence, (iii) Emotional set up.

2. *Environmental Factors*: These comprise: (1) Family environment, (2) Social and physical environment of the school, (3) Peer group relationships

and gang influence, (4) Community environment, (5) Social clubs, (6) Mass media.

According to *T.P. Joseph*, an adolescent wants a friend 'someone to be trusted', 'someone to talk', 'someone who is dependable'.

Harrocks and Benimoff observe regarding the peer influence on the adolescence as, "The peer group is the adolescent's real world, providing him a stage upon which to try himself and others'.

Role of the School in the Social Development or Satisfaction of the Social Needs of the Adolescence

The function of the school has considerably changed in the rapidly changing civilisations. The traditional function of imparting the basic skills of the three R's is now no longer considered to be adequate to meet the present challenge. The present day school has also to perform some of the functions of the family. It must develop certain desirable social habits. It is through co-curricular and extra-curricular activities that the task of social development can be achieved more successfully. It is only the sympathetic understanding and sincere desire of the teacher to act positively in an unprejudicial manner that can help.

***Class in the Process of Socialisation*:** Class provides innumerable opportunities to the adolescents to move and mix with other groups. This is the beginning of the social development of the child. Here children get many chances to mix without any distinction of caste, colour or creed. The teachers are expected to be vigilant to ensure that the students do not think in terms of untouchability, caste distinction and other prejudices.

***Role of the Teacher in Social Development of the Adolescent*:** A teacher can play a vital role in the social development of adolescent under his change. He exerts a great influence upon the development of the personality of the adolescent.

Following are the important suggestions for the social development of the adolescent:

1. Adolescents may be taken from time to time to public places like museums, courts and places of historical importance etc. to observe social interaction.
2. People engaged in different economic activities or vocations may be invited to school for giving a description of what they do and how useful their work is to the nation. This will enable the adolescents to be acquainted with those around them in the society.
3. Work experience will enable the adolescents to have first hand experiences of the activities pursued in farms and factories.
4. Adolescents should be acquainted with the social events like the celebration of the birthdays of leaders.
5. The school programme should be full of numerous co-curricular and curricular activities in which adolescents meet, cooperate and learn from each other's personality.
6. The introduction of common school dress, common lunch, etc., in the schools will present adolescents of poor and lower middle classes from facing inferiority complex due to the ego of the children of the well-to-do families.

7. Teachers and parents may encourage the adolescent to mix in intercaste and regional groups.

8. The teachers and the parents should respect the personality of adolescents.

9. The mechanism of praise and blame, reward and punishment should be carefully used for the social development of the adolescents.

10. Appropriate social education may be provided to the parents so that they understand the significance of the social development of the adolescents.

11. The teachers should demonstrate democratic outlook.

12. Community activities like camps, common meals, social services etc., should be frequently organised.

13. There should be a close cooperation between the teachers and parents on matters relating to the proper social development of the adolescents.

14. Adequate stress may be laid on group activities.

15. Stories depicting self-sacrifices made by great men for the cause of general good may be told to adolescents so that they are motivated to rise above petty gains and work for the betterment of the humanity.

16. The teachers should not show any discrimination. They must ensure a safe and healthy social development in which the adolescents may imbibe desirable values of freedom, equality, integrity, honesty, patriotism etc.

***Concluding Remarks*:** The task of social development of the adolescent is not an easy one. The educational thinkers point out very emphatically that certain conditions in the learning-teaching situation must be created and made available in the school so that it may become an effective instrument of social development. These conditions are: (i) A democratic social climate in the school; (ii) Effective interpersonal relationships; (iii) Motivated learning situations; (iv) Group methods of teaching; (v) Social discipline; (vi) School-community inter-relationships; (vii) Student participation and involvement in the school management; (viii) A rich programme of co-curricular activities.

INTELLECTUAL/MENTAL NEEDS OF THE ADOLESCENTS AND THEIR SATISFACTION

Meaning of Intellectual Development: Mental or intellectual development implies the growth and development of those abilities and capacities of the adolescents that enable them to accomplish a task that needs complex cognitive abilities and enable them to adjust their behaviour to the ever changing environmental conditions. Cognitive abilities include abilities like sensation, perception, imagination, memory, reasoning, understanding, generalisation, interpretation, problem-solving and decision-making etc. In fact most parts of the school programmes relate to mental developments.

Main Characteristics of the Mental Development of the Adolescents: The adolescents learn to reason and seek answer to 'how' and 'why' of every thing rationally and scientifically. Power of critical thinking and observation is much developed. They are more creative and inquisitive. They are almost critical of everything. They develop a lot of imagination. This becomes the beginning of the artist, inventor, philosopher, poet and writer etc. in the adolescent. An adolescent tends to become a day-dreamer.

Factors Affecting Intellectual Development: Intellectual development of the adolescent in the school is affected by curricular and co-curricular programme, teaching-learning environment, and the role of the teachers.

Measures for the Satisfaction of Intellectual Needs or Intellectual Development of the Adolescents: Among the important factors are:

(i) Provision of rich curriculum.
(ii) Provision of streaming.
(iii) Provision of varied activities like debates and discussions.
(iv) Provision of socialised teaching.
(v) Project work related to subjects.
(vi) Subject related educational tours.
(vii) Library and reading room facilities.
(viii) Problem solving teaching-learning.
(ix) Challenging questions.
(x) Exploratory activities.

MORAL DEVELOPMENT OR SATISFACTION OF THE MORAL NEEDS OF THE ADOLESCENTS

Meaning of Moral Development: By morality we mean conformity to the moral code of the social group. The term comes from the Latin word '*mores*', meaning manners, customs or folkways. To act in a moral way means to act in conformity to group standards of conduct. Morality also includes a sense of right or wrong—a behaviour which has to do with the conscience of the individual. Moral behaviour is learnt. Moral standards vary from group to group depending upon what has been accepted by the group as the socially approved behaviour. True morality comes from within the individual. It is internal in nature and not imposed by external authority. Immoral behaviour is that behaviour which is unfavourable to the group.

Bowley and others are of the view that a person of moral character has the following qualities: (i) Self-control, (ii) Reliability, (iii) Persistence in action, (iv) Industrious, (v) Feeling of responsibility, (vi) Consciousness.

Several thinkers equate morality with character.

B.N. Jha has stated that character is "a mental factor of the individual, which determines his social behaviour. It is a mental organisation which lies at the back of all his connotations".

A person of character has the following characteristics in his behaviour:

(a) He is firm and not impulsive in his behaviour.

(b) He is not dominated by others in his actions.

(c) He has a strong sense of self-respect and is governed by his self-regarding sentiment.

(d) He is intelligent and cheerful in his behaviour.

(e) He is hard working and faces difficulties with courage and optimism.

(f) He is idealistic in his approach. His inner and outer self is dominated by some ideals.

Most Crucial Areas of Concern: An overview, based on the secondary data available, confirms the need for a separate focus on the health, education, employment and protection of human rights of adolescents. Reproductive health, in particular, represents the most critical area where an emphasis on the special needs and concerns of adolescents is required. In India, given its predominantly patriarchal set up, ideology of son preference, incidence of early marriage and high rates of maternal mortality, a strong focus on the needs of adolescent girls is warranted. However, both sexes are vulnerable to problems such as those of drug abuse, HIV/AIDS and other infections and sexual abuse.

MAJOR INTERESTS, GOALS AND VALUES OF INDIAN ADOLESCENTS

There is a lack of reliable and scientific data on this issue. However, it must be accepted that on account of the influence of electronic media, Indian adolescent cannot remain unaffected by globalisation. Nevertheless, following interests, goals and values of Indian adolescent are discernible although it is very difficult to generalise as there are several sub-groups on account of the vastness of the country and its plural culture.

I. Interests

1. *Recreational Interests*: (i) Interest in folk dance; (ii) Television watching; (iii) Celebrating birthdays and attending parties; (iv) Folk dance and music; (v) Pop dance and singing; (vi) Watching movies; (vii) Reading comics and sensational literature; (viii) Travelling; (ix) Interest in pen-friendship; (x) Interest in television games; (xi) Watching and Listening Cricket commentaries; (xii) Playing cards; (xiii) Trends towards for fun gambling; (xiv) Interest in smoking as a fashion symbol; (xv) Trends towards use of drug and pills; (xvi) Interest in fine arts; (xvii) Exchanging jokes; (xviii) Interest in drinking, it being status symbol.

2. *Religious Interests*: (i) Usually sceptical of religious beliefs; (ii) Disinterest in the observance of religious rites and ceremonies; (iii) Indifference to formal religion.

3. *Social Interest*: (i) Attending group parties; (ii) Mixing with the opposite sex; (iii) Interest in global matters; (iv) Demonstrating self-identity in the group; (v) Group loyalty.

4. *Vocational Interests*: (a) Interest in professions related to Commerce; (b) Interest in information technology and especially computers; (c) Declining.

5. *Miscellaneous Interests*: (i) Conversation in groups; (ii) Interest in beautification of the body; (iii) Interest in new things; (iv) Trend towards foreign studies; (v) Trend towards settling in foreign lands; (vi) Heightened sex interest.

II. Goals

(i) Becoming rich over night, (ii) Getting power and exercising influence, (iii) Capturing political power, (iv) Occupying higher posts, (v) Becoming independent of joint family and having nuclear family.

III. Values

(1) Re-examination of traditional beliefs and customs and acquiring new ones, (2) Emancipation from home and becoming independent, (3) Knowing everything attitude, (4) Growing gulf between the values of parents and adults;

(5) Critical attitude, (6) Indifference to respect for elders, (7) Declining faith in the leaders of all shades.

IMPORTANT PROBLEMS AND ISSUES INVOLVED IN THE PROPER DEVELOPMENT OF INDIAN ADOLESCENTS

1. *Serious Problem of 10-14 Year Group*: Since adolescents comprise a major part of the reproductive age group, addressing their needs will be critical in determining India's population. An analysis within the age group itself indicates that proportion of 10-14 year olds is greater than the 15-19 year group.

2. *Problem of Gender Discrimination*: Any programme for adolescents must recognise the problem of gender discrimination of the adolescents.

3. *Problem of Under Nutrition*: If India wishes to achieve the goals of 'Health for All' and adequate 'Nutrition for All', it must attend to the problem of under nutrition among adolescent girls. A sizeable number of adolescent girls are actually malnourished. This will increase the risk of difficulty to child birth.

4. *Problem of Poor Understanding of Reproductive Health*: A poor understanding of reproductive health and sexual issues creates several problems in this area.

5. *Problems of High Level of Pre-marital Sexual Activity, Mainly Among Young Adolescent Males*: In this regard, following trends are noticed:

(i) The magnitude of adolescent sexual activity is significant, and is higher in boys than girls. There is also under-reporting of non-marital relationships by adolescent girls due to fear of social disapproval.

(ii) Men are more likely to be sexually active and at an earlier age than girls, and attitudes on premarital sexual activity is greater among boys than girls.

(iii) Parents and teachers play a minor role in giving information, and are usually reluctant to impart such information. The majority of information on sexual and reproductive issues is obtained from peers (which can sometimes be misleading and inaccurate).

(iv) Commercial sex workers usually serve as partners for first-time sexual encounters.

(v) Contraceptive use is low and rarely used in first-time sexual encounters, including with commercial sex workers. Contraceptive awareness is usually about sterilisation, which is unsuitable for most adolescents. Knowledge of HIV/AIDS, safe sex and preventive behaviour (like use of condoms) is low, across all ages and education levels.

(vi) Knowledge of sexual and reproductive issues is extremely poor. In some studies, 50 percent of female adolescents did not know about menstruation, and the limited knowledge was based on social factors (such as, not being permitted to cook) than the actual physiological changes.

(vii) There is considerable interest among adolescent boys for information on reproductive health.

(viii) Education did not increase knowledge of sex and reproduction.

(ix) The educational system does not adequately meet the needs for imparting sex education.

(x) Sexual and reproductive decision-making by adolescents is constrained by age and gender factors. Adolescent women have little choice on whom and when to marry, and are usually not in a position to negotiate contraceptive use. This varies slightly with age, with an older wife more likely to make such decisions.

(xi) There is a huge unmet demand for adolescent health facilities, information and counselling services.

6. *Unwanted Pregnancies and Abortions*: There is a lack of knowledge of appropriate use of contraceptives. Son preference is another reason.

7. *Maternal Mortality*: This is on account of the fact that the body has not yet reached full maturity. Marriage age is very low.

8. *Sexually Transmitted Diseases (STD), including HIV/AIDS*: Young people between the ages of 10 and 25 years make up 50 per cent of all new infections.

9. *Drug Abuse*: In India, it is estimated that a substantial number of drug users are in the age group of 12 to 18.

10. *Violence against Women, Sexual Abuse and Trafficking of Girls*: Available data indicate that a high incidence of rape occurs in the 10-16 year age group.

11. *Gender Difference in Literacy and Education*: The gross enrolment ratio (GER) for girls including adolescent girls lags behind boys. Likewise drop-out rates in the case of adolescent girls are higher than boys.

12. *High Incidence of Unemployment among Adolescents*: Overall, the unemployment rates are almost three times as high for adolescents as that among aged 15 and above.

(*Source*: Adapted from '*Adolescents in India: A Profile*'. UNFPA 2000).

Dr. Tapisha G. Kumar, in a write-up in '*The Hindustan Times*' (Nov-27, 2000) under the caption 'Wonder Years' detailed the following facts regarding Indian adolescents.

(1) *Depression Leading to Suicide*: Every year, suicide is one of the most leading causes of death among them. Each year, 15 to 25 per cent of high school students seriously consider taking this course with depression being the prime motive.

(2) *Alcohol and Tobacco Abuse*: Alcohol and tobacco abuse is very common among 2.5 to 3 per cent of children between 15 to 20 years of age.

(3) *Sex Encounter*: In Delhi alone, 15 per cent of children in the age group 15 to 20 have already had their first sexual encounter.

(4) *HIV Infections*: Sex encounter combined with the lack of awareness at this stage has also increased the possibility of HIV (Human Immunodeficiency Virus) infections. India has currently an HIV infection rate of 1.7 per 1000 of which more than 40 per cent is concentrated around teenagers.

(5) *Emotional Stress*: Family pressures to study and perform better indirectly result in emotional stress for a teenager.

(6) *Improper Company*: Hanging around with improper friends may also lead to drug abuse, HIV and early pregnancy.

(7) *Miscellaneous Issues*: Teenagers face numerous issues ranging from pubertal changes, pimples, obesity, short height and changes in body structure,

to medical problems like asthma, diabetes, thyroid disorders, eating disorders (anorexia) and bed wetting.

SUGGESTIVE MEASURES FOR MEETING THE NEEDS OF INDIAN ADOLESCENTS

1. *Adolescent Clinic*: Dr. Kumar suggests special adolescent clinics. 'Adolescent medicine' a new branch of medical science, might just be the sweet pill in teen's life'.

2. *National Policy*: There should be a national policy that facilitates establishing adolescent care clinics in hospitals and health centres across the country.

(For other measures see earlier part of this Chapter)

10

Learning: Types and Factors of Learning

MEANING OF LEARNING: DEFINITION, CHARACTERISTICS AND GOALS

Learning is a term used for a relatively permanent change in behaviour or response as a result of practice, training for experience. As a result of learning some change takes place in the individual; now he can do what he could not do earlier. The outcomes of learning from learning activities may be attitudes, skills, social competence and abstract and creating thinking. Learning is an enrichment of experience.

Schools are set up for children and thus learning occupies the central place in the school programme.

Following definitions of learning would help us to have a comprehensive view of learning.

1. For *Boaz*, "Learning is a process by which the individual acquires various habits, knowledge and attitudes that are necessary to meet the demand of life in general."

2. *Commins and Fagin* define learning in these words, "Learning as a sequence of mental events or conditions leading to changes in the learner?"

3. In the words of *Crow and Crow*, "Learning involves the acquisition of habits, knowledge and attitudes."

4. *Encyclopaedia of Educational Research* reads, "Learning refers to the growth of interests, knowledge and skills and to transfer of these to new situations."

5. *Gates* defines learning in these words, "Learning is the modification of behaviour through experience and training."

6. In the views of *Gooch*, "Learning as we measure it is more or less a permanent change in behaviour which occurs under the motivational conditions of practice."

7. In the words of *Hilgard*, "Learning is the process by which an activity originates or is changed through reacting to an encountered situation, provided that the characteristics of the change in activity cannot be explained on the basis of native tendencies, maturation or temporary states of organism."

8. According to *Hunder and Hilgard*, "Learning is the process by which behaviour (in the broader sense) is originated or changed through training procedures (whether in the natural environment or in the laboratory)".

9. According to *Munn*, "To learn is to modify behaviour and experience."

10. *Peal, E.A.* states, "Learning is a change in the individual following upon changes in the environment".

11. *Skinner* views are: "Learning as acquisition and retention."

12. *Travers J.F.* writes, "Learning is a process that results in the modification of behaviour."

13. According to *Wordsworth, R.S.*, "Any activity can be called learning so far as it develops the individual (in any respect, good or bad) and makes his behaviour and experience different from what that would otherwise have been."

Characteristics and Nature of Learning

1. Learning is acquiring new behaviour.
2. Learning is adjustment in behaviour.
3. Learning is change in behaviour.
4. Learning is doing.
5. Learning is a life-long process.
6. Learning is pre-planned.
7. Learning is purposeful.
8. Learning and maturation have positive connection.
9. Learning is related to environment.
10. Learning and intelligence are correlated.
11. Learning exposes 'new vistas' of knowledge.
12. Learning is universal, i.e., both human beings and animals learn. Of course, human beings have a rational will of their own. They are, thus in a position to get the maximum from the environment.
13. Learning is organising experience.
14. Learning affects the behaviour of the learner.
15. Learning is both individual and social.
16. Learning is affected by physiological, psychological and environmental factors.
17. Learning involves psychological, motor and affective activities.

Goals in Learning: Following are the broad categories:

1. Acquisition of knowledge. This includes (a) Perception, (b) Conception, and (c) Association learning.
2. Acquisition of skills.
3. Acquisition of attitudes, ideals and values.

MAJOR DOMAINS OF LEARNING

There are three major domains of learning as given below:

	Domain	*Nature of the Domain*
1.	Cognitive Domain	It is related to knowing or intellectual abilities.
2.	Affective Domain	It is concerned with emotions, feelings and values.
3.	Psychomotor Domain	It relates to learning of skills.

Major Areas in the Three Domains

Knowledge Domain	*Affective Domain*	*Psychomotor Domain*
1. Knowledge 2. Comprehension It relates to student's ability of giving: (a) Meaning of a concept, definition or principle (b) Interpretation, i.e., seeing interrelations (c) Extrapolation, i.e., drawing conclusions 3. Application 4. Analysis 5. Synthesis 6. Evaluation The highest form of learning is problem solving. The measurement in the cognitive domain as compared with the affective domain is easy and specific.	(a) Receiving (b) Responding (c) Valuing (d) Organisation (1) Learning in the affective domain influences attitudes/feelings and values (2) The measurement of learning in the affective domain as compared with the cognitive domain is less specific and difficult.	(i) Gross body movements (ii) Coordinated movements (iii) Non-verbal communication (iv) Speech behaviour or (1) Initiation (2) Manipulation (3) Precision (4) Articulation (5) Naturalisation (mechanisation and internalisation). Articulation implies coordination of action performed with efficiency in terms of time, speed and case. Naturalisation implies performance in skill with natural case and almost without conscious effort so that it is like a habit.

LEARNING PROCESS

Aspects of the Learning Process: Learning process in general includes the following:

(i) Acquisition of new experiences.

(ii) Retention of old experiences in the form of impressions, engrams or skills.

(iii) Development and modification of experience.

(iv) Growth and increase in these experiences.

(v) Creation of new experiences.

(vi) Synthesis and organisation of the old and the new experiences, resulting in a novel pattern called learning.

Fagin (1958) states that learning is a sequence of mental events or conditions leading to changes in the learner. As a sequence of events, the learning process is as under:

1. The individual has needs and is therefore in a state of readiness to respond. These are antecedent conditions within the learner.

2. He meets a learning situation or problem. A new interpretation is required

because previously learned responses are not adequate for reaching the goal and satisfying his need. He encounters something new or unexpected, and searches for a different response.

3. He interprets the situation with reference to his goals, and tries a response or responses which seem to satisfy his need. The way he perceives the situation and the response he makes depends both on his 'readiness' and on external conditions of the situation.

4. If his response leads to desired goals or satisfaction, he will tend to interpret and respond to similar future situations in the same way. If not, he keeps on trying and reinterpreting until satisfying consequences are attained. The learning process is this whole sequence!

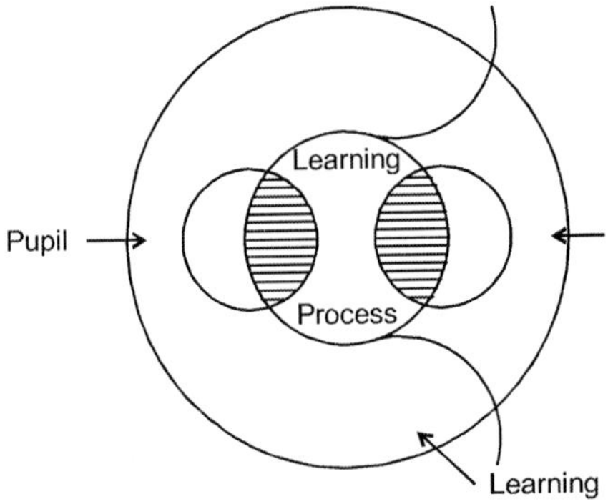

Fig. 10.1: Learning Process and Teacher-Taught Interaction

Four Aspects of the Learning Process in the Classroom

Learning cannot be visualised without teaching. They are inter-related. One cannot exist without the other. To have a proper perspective of the learning process, we must consider it in the teaching-learning situation: teacher, student, learning and the interaction. The teacher creates the learning situation. The process is the interaction between student and teacher. Teaching and learning relationship or interaction may be explained with the help of a diagram.

1. *The Teacher*: The teacher has to be an 'inducer of change'. The teacher has to understand the significance of creating rapport in the class.

2. *The Environment*: The teacher at the very outset must set the stage or environment the effective study of the pupils.

(i) A definite place of study.
(ii) Favourable physical conditions for learning such as proper light, adequate space and ventilation, etc.
(iii) A definite time schedule for study—what to study, when to study and how to study.
(iv) A clear idea of the purpose of study.

3. *The Child as a Learner*: A wise teacher takes note of the following:

(i) Individual differences in learning and an individual approach which may, however, differ from child to child or within the same child when his learning takes place under different situations and conditions.

(ii) Setting up goals or standards not beyond the capacity of the learner.

(iii) Keeping in view that the previous experience of the learner is fundamental in the process of learning.

(iv) Awareness of the fact that knowledge of one's own performance, mistakes and information of successful result helps in learning.

(v) Knowing that the active participation by the learner is essential in learning.

(vi) Realising that motivation is a powerful influence in determining effective learning.

(vii) Realising that a motivated learner can acquire knowledge and understanding more quickly than one who is not motivated.

(viii) Keeping in view that excessive motivation may sometimes be less effective in some kinds of learning. In some instances it may result in 'pushing' the child too much disregarding his abilities.

(ix) Knowing that learning depends on the mental set or the mood of the learner. The teacher has to find out whether the learner is ready for the task or not. If not, what are the ways and means to make him ready for the purpose.

(x) Believing that emotion of the learner is a powerful factor in learning and the teacher must learn how to use this to his greatest advantage. In this respect the good interpersonal relationships in the classroom as well as in the school should not be neglected by the teachers.

(xi) Having faith that good study habits of the individual also promote learning.

4. *Subject Matter and Its Presentation*: In the course of formal and informal teaching, a resourceful teacher plans and directs pupil experiences which lead to effective learning. The study of the learning process enables the teacher to make the following deductions, with the help of which he tries to affect purposeful learning in pupils.

1. by following certain well-tried principles and maxims of teaching to guide the pupils learning activities;
2. by considering the maturity and the capacity of the learner;
3. by employing fruitful motivational devices;
4. by directing and modifying perception of the learner;
5. by using practices most effectively;
6. by removing emotional disturbances; and
7. by directing teaching towards transfer.

Factors Influencing Learning

Health of the Child	*Personal Factors*	*Environmental Factors*	*Relationships with*	*Media Influence*	*Methods of Learning*	*Methods of Teaching*	*Maxims of Teaching*
(1)	(2)	(3)	(4)	(5)	(6)	(7)	(8)
1. Physical develop ment 2. Postures 3. General health	1. Sensation and perception 2. Fatigue and boredom 3. Maturation 4. Emotional condition 5. Needs 6. Intelligence 7. Motivation 8. Attention 9. Aptitude 10. Attitude	1. Natural surroundings 2. Social surroundings 3. Cultural surroundings 4. Home environment 5. Class-room environment 6. School environment 7. Political environment	1. Teachers 2. Parents 3. Peers	1. Print Media 2. Non-print Media	1. Whole vs. Part Learning 2. Mediating Method 3. Space vs. Un spaced Method 4. Recitals 5. Memory Systems 6. Laws of Association	1. Lecturing 2. Demonstration 3. Individual Practical work 4. Individual work in work-shop 5. Field trips 6. Projects 7. Discussion 8. Conference, Seminar etc. 9. Assignments 10. Tutorial (Individual) 11. Programmed Instruction 12. Teaching Machines 13. Electronic Media 14. Audio-visual Aids	1. From known to unknown 2. Easy to difficult 3. Simple to com pact 4. Concrete to abs tract 5. Indefinite to de finite 6. Particular to ge neral 7. Empirical to ra tional 8. Deductivein-ductive 9. Psychological to logical

GENERAL PRINCIPLES OF EFFECTIVE LEARNING

1. Different types of learning experiences should be provided to satisfy the needs of each and every learner as notable 'differences' exist between individuals.

2. Learning experiences should be provided for natural integration of feeling, doing and thinking as the learner is a living 'organism', a unitary integrated whole.

3. Rich learning experiences should be provided to meet the needs of the learner as he always seeks to maintain equilibrium or balance by satisfying his needs.

4. The setting of learning should be purposive or goal-oriented as the learner is a goal seeking organism to satisfy his needs.

5. The learning situations should provide freedom to make creative contribution as the learner is an active, behaving and exploring individual.

6. While providing learning experiences for the learner, family background and individuality of the learner should be taken into account as the learner is a social being and needs social environment.

7. The learner needs sympathy and guidance for his personality development as he is quite immature.

8. Learning activities should be based on cooperative group work so as to develop the socialised personality of the learner.

9. Bright students can learn things quickly than the dull ones.

10. A motivated pupil learns more readily than one who is not motivated.

11. Learning through reward or success motivation is more effective than punishment or failure.

12. Learning goals should be neither too high nor too low.

13. The personality of a teacher is a great contributory factor in teaching-learning.

14. Active participation of the learner is more effective than passive reception.

15. Meaningful materials and meaningful tasks are learned more quickly.

16. Moderate practice and repetition is very useful for durable learning.

17. Effective audio-visual aids contribute to make learning effective and inspirational.

18. Transfer of learning will be better if learner himself discovers relationship between new and old tasks.

19. Optimal learning takes place when appropriate teaching strategies are adopted.

ELEMENTS IN THE TEACHING-LEARNING PROCESS: IMPLICATIONS OF LEARNING FOR THE CLASSROOM TEACHER

The teacher would make learning effective, if he attends to the following elements carefully.

1. *Who is to Learn or Whom to Teach*? The child is to learn and therefore his interests, abilities and aptitudes have to be taken note of. It must be remembered that he is an active being. Individual differences have to be attended to.

2. *Who is to Teach or from Whom to Learn*? The teacher is to teach. He should, therefore, present a good model of teaching.

3. *Why to Teach or Why to Learn*? Education should not be taken in terms of traditional 3 R's, i.e. reading, writing and arithmetic, but in terms of 7 R's, i.e. reading, writing, arithmetic, recreation, rights, responsibilities and relationships.

4. *What to Teach or What to Learn*? This includes the acquisition of the knowledge, skills and behaviour.

5. *How to Teach*? The teacher must be well-versed with the technology of teaching.

6. *How to Learn*? The teacher and the learner must fully understand that learning takes place through mutual cooperation. A learner learns maximum when he is motivated. The teacher, therefore, has to provide motivational situations so that the learner is at his best. He has to be fully conversant with learning theories and teaching strategies.

7. *What to Teach or When to Learn*? This is concerned with creating motivational situations for the learner.

8. *Where to Teach or Where to Learn*? The school should not be taken as the only place of imparting or receiving education. It is one of the agencies of education; of course, the most important one.

KINDS/TYPES OF LEARNING: PRIME AND CONCOMITANT LEARNING

It is very difficult to classify learning into clear-cut categories because one category overlaps the other.

Chart Showing Broad Kinds of Learning

(1) Prime or Conscious Learning
(2) Concomitant or Unconscious Learning
(3) Developmental Learning
(4) General Learning
(5) Hierarchical Learning

Prime and Concomitant Learning: As a matter of fact, there are only two broad categories of learning, i.e., Prime learning and Concomitant learning.

Prime learning is deliberate, formal as well as non-formal, purposeful and systematised. It includes all types of learning except concomitant learning. All aspects of the entire instructional programme, i.e., curriculum, textbooks, methods of teaching and evaluation etc. are related to prime learning. Most of the changes in behaviour take place through prime learning.

Concomitant learning is that learning which comes in a casual manner without any direct intention to learn but on some occasions it becomes very powerful. Concomitant learning in a broad sense takes place under the indirect influence of the home, the school and the society. Students learn so many things in the school in a casual manner. It is sometimes called incidental learning. We are reminded of the learning of King Robert Bruce from the efforts of a spider. After making several unsuccessful attempts, ultimately it achieved its objective.

The King, who had been unsuccessful in defeating his enemies, picked up courage like the spider again and succeeded. It was not deliberate learning.

It is said that a student gets one-fourth of his learning from his teacher (Prime learning), another fourth from his intellect (Prime learning), another fourth from his fellow students (Prime learning) and the rest (Concomitant learning) through his general experience in various situations.

MAKING LEARNING EFFECTIVE: ROLE OF THE SCHOOL AND THE TEACHERS

Learning is influenced by various conditions of life at home and school. As far as home conditions are considered, i.e., heredity and other influences of the home, very little can be done by the school to modify these. However, schools can ensure that students are given adequate opportunities to develop their hereditary endowment.

The schools should take the following steps to promote learning in the learners to their optimum levels.

1. *Healthy Physical Conditions in the School*: Unsuitable furniture in the class-room (i.e., desks and chairs and blackboards etc.), bad ventilation, over crowding etc. affect the rate of learning and the general response of the learners.

Teachers' health, voice and speech etc. also affect learning.

Therefore, all possible attempts should be made to provide healthy physical environment.

2. *Stimulation and the Role of the Teacher*: Best learning takes place when the teacher is successful in arousing the interest of the student. "The guidance of the teacher is mainly a matter of giving the right kind of stimulus to help him to learn the right things in the right way," writes Ryburn.

3. *Goals Set Before the Pupils*: A definite goal should be set before each child according to the standard expected of him. Immediate goals should be set before small children and distant goals for older ones. It must be remembered that the goals should be very clear and the children must understand these goals.

Complacency in the pupils should be avoided and in no case the pupil should feel that there is nothing more which he should learn and that there is no scope for improvement. *R. Strang* writes: "A little learning is a dangerous thing insofar as it may make a child content with what he has accomplished. The child's felt need for a skill is decreased once he has obtained enough proficiency to accomplish his immediate purpose. It is important, therefore, that as soon as the child begins to acquire skills, he should set for himself suitable specific standards of accuracy and precision."

4. *Association of Things*: Thorndike points out that things which we want to go together should be put together. Many different things should be brought together as a part of one process. Then it becomes easier to make the students understand their connection. We have discussed at various places that things can be associated in a number of ways.

5. *Guidance and Instruction*: Suitable guidance should be given to the students in selecting the best response to the environment. Demonstration is very helpful to teach various skills.

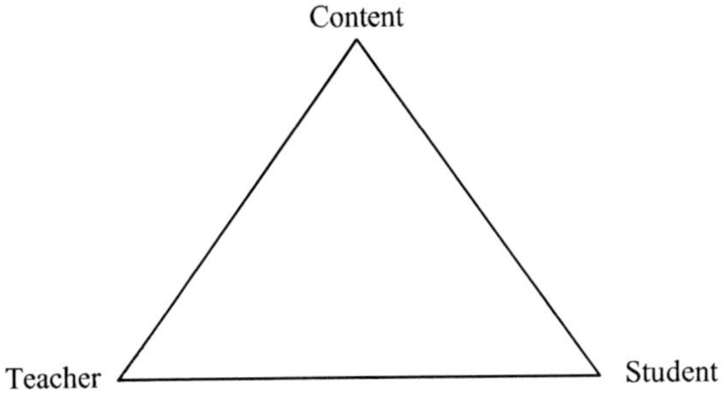

Fig. 10.2: Condition related to Content, Teacher and Student

6. *Emotional Conditions*: Children should be praised when they show good results. This gives them encouragement to show all the more better results and they develop confidence, hope, self-reliance and self-respect. Sympathetic attitude on the part of the teachers gives stimulus and a sense of security to the students. We should discard our habits of fault-finding. This develops fear and feelings of insecurity and of inferiority.

7. *Result of a Total Situation*: Learning is affected by the whole situation. It is not always possible to estimate the result of one individual factor. Learning is fruitful and permanent if the total situation is related to life.

In fact total situation includes all the factors that we have enumerated above. Learning is influenced both by heredity and environment. There is a lot that can be done by the teachers to facilitate learning.

Summing Up

Internal classroom factors which affect learning and improvement are: (1) Goals or Purposes, (2) Motivation, (3) Interest, (4) Attention, (5) Drill or Practice, (6) Boredom or Fatigue, (7) Aptitude, (8) Attitude, (9) Emotional factors—Instincts, (10) Speed, Accuracy and Retention, (11) Age, (12) Learning activities provided by the teacher, (13) Testing, (14) Guidance.

11

Motivation

MEANING OF MOTIVATION

The word motivation has been derived from the Latin word '*Motum*' which means to 'move', 'motor' and 'motion'. Motivation is an internal force which accelerates a response or behaviour. Some learners learn the same subject matter or task more efficiently than others, some find it more rewarding and interesting than others; and some enjoy it more than others. At any given time learners vary in the extent to which they are willing to direct their energies to the attainment of goals, due to difference in motivation.

The difference in their performance can be due to differences either in their abilities or in their willingness to perform as best as possible. The performance of an individual is considered as a product function of two different variables as follows:

1. A learner's ability/capacity to perform the work;
2. A learner's willingness to use his ability to perform the work.

In algebric terms, if P stands for performance in learning, C stands for capacity to learn and M stands for willingness to use capacity to learn, then P may be expressed as follows:

Thus, given the ability, it is the willingness of the learners which determines whether they will be more efficient or less. Similarly, given the willingness, it is the ability of learners which determines whether they will be more efficient or less.

$$\text{Performance} = \text{Capacity to learn} \times \text{Willingness to use capacity to learn}$$
$$P = C \times M$$

Thus, given the ability, it is the willingness of the learners which determines whether they will be more efficient or less. Similarly, given the willingness, it is the ability of learners which determines whether they will be more efficient or less.

How to make learners performance more or better is an issue that requires an understanding of what motivates learners to do so.

The following definitions throw adequate light on the meaning of motivation:

1. *Arun Monappa and Mirza S. Saiyadain*: "Motivation is propensity or the level of desire of an individual to behave in a certain manner at a certain time and in a certain situation."

2. *C.W. Goods*: "Motivation is the process of sustaining and regulating activity."

3. *D.O. Hebb*: "The term motivation refers (i) to existence of an organised phase sequence, (ii) to its direction and content, (iii) to its persistence in given direction or stability of content."

4. *F.G. McDonald*: "Motivation is an energy change within the person characterised by affective arousal and anticipatory goal relations."

5. *T.W. Atkinson*: "The term motivation refers to the arousal of tendency to act to produce one or more effects."

Sources of Motivation

Motivation has the following four sources:

1. Needs, 2. Drives, 3. Incentives, 4. Motives.

Motives: Psychologists do not agree on the meaning of the term 'motives'. These have been defined as follows:

1. *E.C. Murray*: Motive is an internal factor that arouses, directs and integrates a person's behaviour.

2. *Alice Crow*: Motives can be regarded as those internal conditions or forces that tend to impel an individual towards certain goals.

3. *Shoffer and Others*: Motive is a tendency to an activity initiated by a drive and concluded by the adjustment.

4. *M.C. Dougall*: Motive is a condition, physiological and psychological, within the individual that disposes it to act in certain ways.

5. *All Port*: A motive is any internal condition in the person that induces action or thought.

6. *Arun Monappa and Mirza S. Saiyadain*: Motivation is propensity or the level of desire of an individual to behave in a certain manner at a certain time and in a certain situation.

7. *Bernard*: Motivation is the stimulation of actions towards a particular objective where previously there was little or no attraction to that goal.

8. *Goods*: Motivation is the process of arousing, sustaining and regulating activity.

9. *Harold Koontz and Cyril O'Donnell*: Motivation refers to the drive and effort to satisfy a want or goal.

10. *Guilford*: A motive is any particular internal factor or condition that tends to initiate and sustain activity.

11. *Lovell*: Motivation is defined more formally as psycho-physiological or internal process initiated by some need which leads to activity which will satisfy that need.

12. *Skinner*: Motivation in school learning involves arousing, persisting, sustaining and directing desirable behaviour.

13. *Gates*: Motives are conditions—Psychological and physiological with the organism that dispose it to act in a certain way.

14. *Blair*: Arising from our needs motives are the energies which give direction and purpose in behaviour.

Motives are expressions of a person's needs and hence they are personal and internal. Need here means something within an individual that prompts him to action. Motives or needs are 'whys' of behaviour. Motives are the primary energisers of behaviour which prompt people to action. Motives give direction to human behaviour because they are directed towards achievement of certain 'goals'.

Types of Motives

We can divide motives in various ways:

A. *Primary Motives and Secondary Motives*

Primary Motives are the biological or physiological motives. The examples of such motives are: hunger, thirst, sex, sleep, rest, etc. These motives ensure the preservation of life for the individual and for his race. An important feature of these motives is that they are inborn and *innate*.

Secondary Motives are psychological and social motives. Examples of such motives are: need for security, achievement, gaining status and recognition, etc. These motives are acquired like other forms of learning behaviour, when we are trying to satisfy our needs.

B. *Innate and Acquired Motives*

Innate motives are known as physiological motives and are associated with the birth of the individual. Examples are: hunger, thirst, sleep, sex, etc.

Acquired motives are learnt motives. Examples are: habit, interest, etc.

C. *Natural and Artificial Motives*

Natural motives are present in the individual by birth. Examples are play, prestige, etc.

Artificial motives are complementary motives to natural motives. Examples are: reward, punishment, etc.

Thus motivation refers to the process by which human needs direct and control the behaviour of a human being. Motivation may also be defined as the process which inspires the people at work to contribute to the best of their capability for the achievement of organisational objectives. In other words, motivation may be defined as the process of stimulating people to action to accomplish desired goals. In simple terms, creation of a will to work or to work more or better is motivation.

Nature and Characteristics of Motivation

The characteristics of motives highlight the nature of motivation.

1. *Personal and Internal*: Motives are personal, internal and invisible because, these are expressions of a person's needs. Motives are the energising forces within us. Motivation is a psychological phenomenon which arises from the feeling of needs and wants of learners.

2. *Different from Learner to Learner*: Motives differ from learner to learner because every learner has his own set of needs at a particular point of time.

3. *Different from Time to Time*: Motives energising us differ from time to time. Motives come and go. A motive need not have the same energy potential at all points of time.

4. *Different Behaviour from Same Motive*: One motive may result in many different behaviours.

5. *Same Behaviour from Different Motives*: The same behaviour may result from different motives. That is why a motive cannot be identified from any specific behaviour.

6. *Continuous Process*: Motivation is a continuous process because human needs are unlimited and fulfilment of one set of needs gives rise to another set of needs.

7. *Pervasive Function*: Motivation is required in all types of organisations (commercial, educational, social, religious, political, small or large) and at all levels. However, its ways, methods, forms and types may differ at different levels.

8. *Behaviour for Estimating Motives*: Repeated behaviour can be used as an estimate of learner motives. It is possible to get repeated observations of one learner's behaviour and then make an estimate of the cause of that behaviour.

9. *Operate in Harmony or in Conflict*: Motives can operate in harmony or in conflict. For example, a learner may want to get high marks in school while also wanting to help his father in the business.

10. *Interact with the Environment*: Motives interact with the environment.

11. *Causes Goal-Directed Behaviour*: Motives cause goal directed behaviour.

PROCESS AND IMPORTANCE OF MOTIVATION

Process of Motivation

The elements of the process of motivation are:

(1) Motives, (2) Behaviour, (3) Goal, (4) Feedback. The process of motivation has been shown below:

1. *Motive*: Motives prompt learners to action. Motives determine the general direction of learner's behaviour.

2. *Behaviour*: Behaviour is a series of activities of an individual. It is generally motivated by a desire to achieve a goal.

3. *Goal*: Motives are directed towards goals. Goals are the ends which provide satisfaction of human wants.

4. *Feedback*: Feedback may be in the form of reduction or increase in tension.

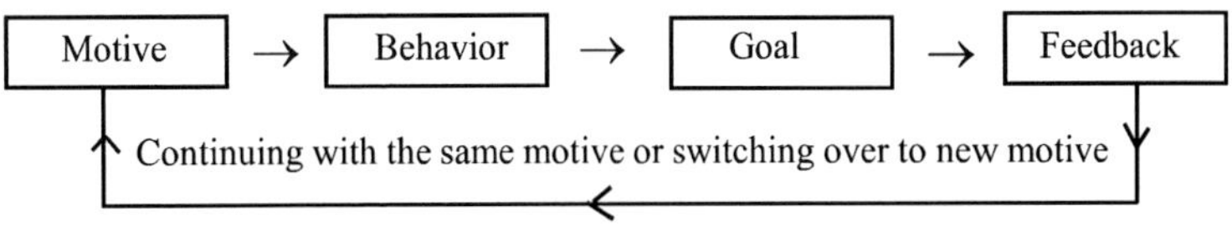

Importance of Motivation

Motivation is the core of learning. The importance of motivation arises from the benefits which flow from it. These benefits are shown below:

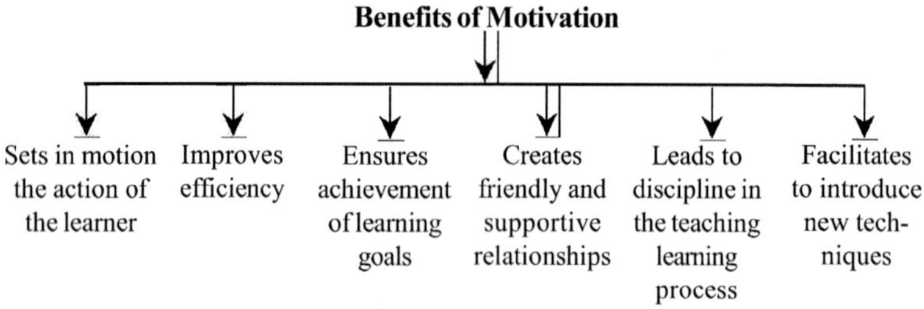

Fig. 11.1: Importance of Motivation

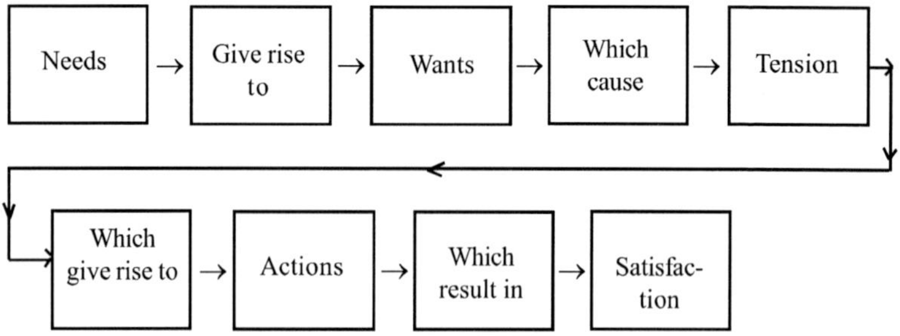

Fig. 11.2: Motivational Cycle: Needs—Satisfaction Chain

MASLOW'S NEED—THEORY OF MOTIVATION

To get work done with the cooperation of learners for the attainment of learning objectives every teacher must study the behaviour of learner. To determine their needs and provide an environment in which appropriate incentives are available for their need satisfaction. Human needs serve as driving force in human behaviour.

Abraham Maslow explained how needs influence human behaviour through his 'Need Hierarchy Theory of Motivation' in 1943.

Table 11.1: Five Types of Human Needs

Need	*Meaning*	*Examples*
1. Physiological needs	These needs relate to the survival and maintenance of human life.	Need for food, clothing, shelter, air, water.
2. Safety needs or Security needs	These needs relate to the economic and physical security.	Security of source of income, personal security, provision for old-age insurance against risks.

(*Contd.*)

Need	*Meaning*	*Examples*
3. Social or Affiliation or Acceptance Needs	These needs relate to social interaction. They are the desires to belong and to be socially accepted, to love and be loved, as a social animal. Socialising is one of those reasons why many individuals (especially older people) go to work, and why people generally work better in small groups where they can develop affiliations that are important to them.	Need for love, affection, affiliation, acceptance belongingness.
4. Esteem or Ego Needs	These needs relate to the awareness of self-importance and recognition from others.	Need for self-image, self-confidence, self-respect, status, recognition prestige, attention, and respect from others.
5. Self-Actualisation or Self-fulfilment needs	These needs relate to self-fulfilment, are the desires to realize one's own full creative potential through creativity, self-expression and self-development to become what one is capable of becoming.	Need to grow, sense of fulfilment, maximum self-development, personal achievement.

Hierarchy of Human Needs

Maslow proposed that human needs can be arranged in a particular order (i.e., hierarchy) of their importance or prepotency) from the lower to the higher level needs. Physiological needs are placed at the lowest level of hierarchy of needs. Then safety needs, social needs and esteem needs are positioned in ascending order. Self-actualisation needs are placed at the highest level of hierarchy of needs. (Fig. 11.3)

Merits of Maslow's Need Hierarchy

Following are the merits of Maslow's Need Hierarchy:

1. It is simple to understand and has an intuitive appeal.
2. It recognises the spectrum of human needs and indicates how humans are motivated in their work behaviour.
3. Its basic proposition that deprivation of a need dominates behaviours, seems to be quite sound.
4. It provides some guidance to teachers and educational administrators.
   (a) Identification of unfulfilled needs among the various learners.

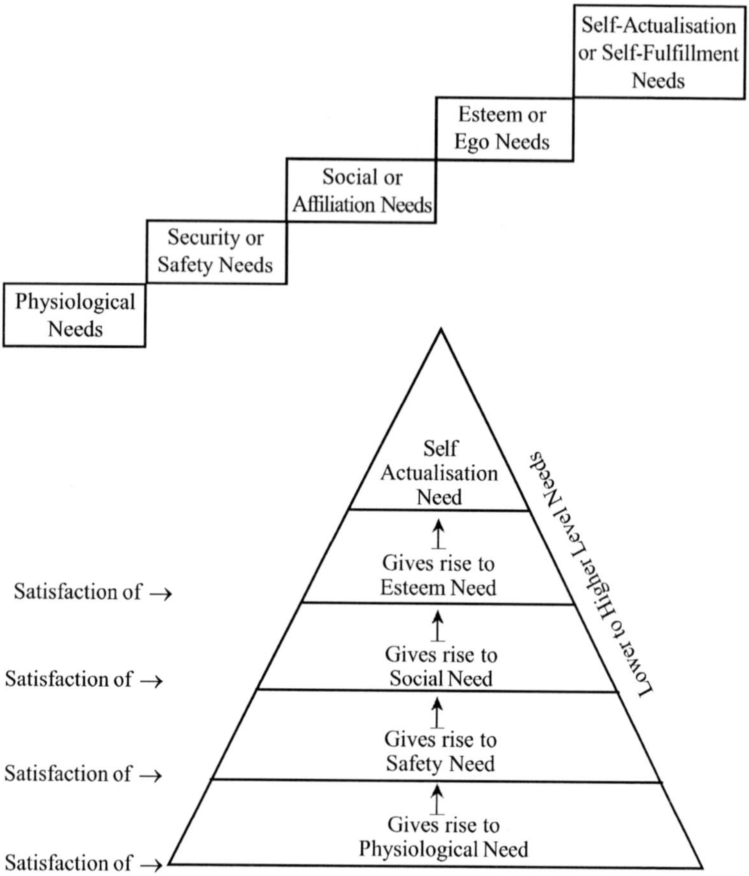

Fig. 11.3: Maslow's Hierarchy of Needs

(b) Designing of measures to satisfy unsatisfied needs as a means of motivation.

(c) Designing of measures to arouse new higher level needs.

Criticisms of Maslow's Theory

Maslow's theory is subject to the following criticisms:

1. It is not amenable for empirical validation on account of complexity of developing meaningful measures for various needs.

2. The hierarchy appears to be rigid. The learners need not necessarily follow a step-by-step way of meeting their needs for example—

(a) Some learners may not be aware of esteem and self-actualisation needs. For example, for majority learning of underdeveloped countries, higher level esteem and self-actualisation needs have no meaning.

(b) A learner may go in for higher level needs before complete satisfaction of lower level needs.

3. It is doubtful whether Self-actualisation is a need or not. It may be merely a philosophical and ethical aspiration based on wishes and dreams of what one should be than on what one can be or one is.

4. There is a direct link between needs and motivation. Different learners may adopt different practices to fulfil the same type of needs. Different types of needs may be gratified by similar methods.

5. It fails to clarify the complexity of human needs and motivation since the learners differ:

(a) in awareness of their needs;

(b) in the extent and depth of their needs;

(c) in their willingness to fulfil their needs;

(d) in their ability to fulfil their needs;

(e) in ordering their needs on a preference scale;

(f) in choosing ways and means to fulfil their needs;

(g) in the degree of gratification which they desire from meeting their needs.

For example, for some learners need for self-esteem seems to be more prominent than that of love. There are also creative learners in whom the drive for creativeness seems to be more important. In certain learners the level of motivation may be permanently lower.

6. Need may not necessarily be the only factor which influences a learner's behaviour at a particular point of time. There may be other factors which may affect the behaviour at that time.

7. It is also doubtful—

(i) Whether deprivation of a need dominates behaviour at all. It may not motivate the learner in a unidirectional positive manner. It may even lead to his depression, diversion, frustration and inaction.

(ii) Whether relative gratification of needs at a particular level drives the learners to move to next higher level needs.

(iii) Whether a satisfied need motivates a learner. He may remain at that level and continue to seek need fulfilment in a routine manner. Several needs recur in cycles, short or long, and hence satisfaction could not be a permanent or one time affair.

(iv) One need is satisfied at one time. The phenomenon of multiple motivation is of great practical importance in understanding the behaviour of the learner. A learner's behaviour at any time is mostly guided by multiplicity of motives.

Intrinsic and Extrinsic Motivation

Intrinsic Motivation: It comes into display when the resolution of tension is to be found in mastering the learning task itself. The material learned provides its own reward. For example, the student who studies the construction of model dams diligently so that he can make a model, is experiencing a king of intrinsic motivation.

Extrinsic Motivation: It occurs when a student pursues a learning task for reasons which are external. If a student engages in construction of model dams because he thinks it will please his father, who is an ex-engineer, this becomes a case of extrinsic motivation. Motivation is probably a function of an interactive situation where reward for a particular action acts as an incentive. Some of the common forms of extrinsic motivation are:

(a) Purposive goals
(b) Knowledge of results
(c) Punishments and rewards
(d) Praise and blame
(e) Rivalry

TECHNIQUES OF ENHANCING LEARNER'S MOTIVATION

The teaching-learning process aims at maximum learning in a minimum period of time. It is, therefore, necessary that children should be properly motivated and the teacher should be conversant with important ways of motivating children.

1. *Child-Centred Approach*: The child is the focal point in the learning process. The teachers, therefore, should keep in view the needs, interests and aptitudes of children while planning for their education.

2. *Law of Association*: The child is easily motivated to learn new knowledge if he thinks that he knows all that is required as a base for new learning. This enables him to master new facts and acquire knowledge.

3. *Progressive Methods of Teaching*: The teacher should use new methods like the Montessori Methods, the K.G. Method, the Project Method and the Dalton Plan as methods of teaching. These methods are child-centred and based on important psychological principles.

4. *Use of Teaching-Learning Aids*: The teacher should introduce various aids and devices of teaching, for example, audio-visual aids, radio, television, etc. to create interest in learning. These will motivate children in grasping and digesting new learning.

5. *Element of Success*: The teacher should divide new learning into smaller and smaller tasks and assign them to the different students of the class. Children will complete them in a short period of time and will have a feeling of success. It is this feeling of success, which will motivate them for future achievement and success.

6. *Learning by Doing*: Children are active by nature. They want to do something with their hands. Let this need of the children be satisfied. A satisfied child is always a well-motivated child.

7. *Sense of Achievement in the Child*: The teacher should keep an eye on the progress of every child. He should maintain a proper record of the same. He should inform his pupils about the success achieved by them, after two or three months. This will develop a sense of achievement among the pupils. This will also lead to achievement – motivation.

8. *Group Work*: Children like group life. They may be divided into various groups. Group work leads to quicker, better and easier learning.

9. *Value of Learning*: The teacher should highlight the value of learning among his pupils. They should realise that 'knowledge is power' and can be helpful in life and will make them successful.

10. *Ego-Involvement*: The personality of the child should be given its due recognition.

11. *Healthy Environment*: A healthy class-room environment in itself is a great motivating force.

12. *Constructive and Creative Discipline*: The teacher's attitude towards his children should be sympathetic but firm.

13. *Stimulus Variation and the Teacher*: It has been generally observed that children are not able to attend to one thing for a very long period. The effectiveness of the teaching-learning process in such a situation depends to a great extent on the stimulus variations used by the teacher behaviour. Some of the common teacher behaviours in the class-room which fall under variation are:

(a) Teacher movement
(b) Teacher gestures
(c) Changes in speech pattern
(d) Changes in sensory focus
(e) Changes in postures

14. *Reinforcement*: *Praise and Blame*: These may be classified as:

(a) *Positive Verbal Reinforcement*: Following a pupil's answer, the teacher verbally indicates pleasures at the pupil's response by the use of words like 'Good', 'Fair', 'Excellent', 'Correct', etc.
(b) *Positive Non-Verbal Reinforcement*: These include:
Nods and smiles.
Teacher's friendly movements towards pupils.
Teacher's friendly look.

12

Memory and Forgetting

SIGNIFICANCE OF MEMORY

There is no doubt that memory is one of the best friends, guides and philosophers of an individual. Memory enables a person to be efficient, both individually and socially. Memory enables us to remember and recall important facts, ideas, names etc. One of the important functions of school instruction is, therefore, to encourage the students develop good and sharp memory to use in school life for the purpose of examination and evaluation etc. and also to meet out-of-school life problems successfully.

MEANING OF MEMORY

Memory may be defined as the function of the mind by virtue of which it records, retains and processes ideas.

According to Woodworth, four main elements of memory are: learning (acquisition), retention, recall and recognition.

Learning: It is the process of establishing association of the ideas in mind.

Retention: It is the process of relegation of the past experience in the sub-conscious mind of the individual in the form of a mental experience.

Recall: It is bringing again to mind the past experience on the basis of association of ideas.

Recall is of two types: (1) Spontaneous and (2) Deliberate. In spontaneous recall we make no effort to recall but the experience or ideas just flow. In deliberate recall, we make an effort to recall something.

Recall is dependent on association of ideas. This association of ideas is dependent on these laws: (i) Law of Similarity, (ii) Law of Contrast, (iii) Law of Contiguity, (iv) Law of Regency, (v) Law of Frequency, (vi) Law of Primacy, and (vii) Law of Vividness.

Recognition: It is the capacity to recognise or express knowledge of all—seeing a thing that has been seen earlier.

DEFINITIONS OF MEMORY

Some of the important definitions of memory are given below. These illustrate the various elements involved in memory.

1. James Drever in *Dictionary of Psychology* has defined memory as "The

characteristic of living organisms in virtue of what they experience leaves behind effects which modify future experience and behaviour."

2. Woodworth and Marquis say, "Memory consists in recalling what has been previously learnt."

3. Stout defines memory as the "ideal revival", i.e. to revive the things, objects or experiences in the same order and form.

4. Ross defines memory as "a new experience determined by the disposition laid down by previous experiences and the relation between the two being clearly apprehended."

5. J.A. Adams—Memory is the "learning capacity for responding, and its persistence over time is measured by the retention test. Memory is the state of a subject that gives the capability for correct occurrence of a criterion response. There is an initial acquisition session in which the subject makes a discriminative response to a stimulus, followed by a period of time called the retentional interval when the criterion response does not occur."

MEMORY SYSTEM

Information from the environment arrives through the senses and is held briefly in a sensory store (the sensory register) of relatively large capacity. Some of this incoming information, once it is identified and categorised, can be passed along to the short-term store and then to the long-term store.

Short-term Store: It is assumed to be a temporary working memory with a quite limited capacity. In a sense, this is a record of the current contents of consciousness.

Long-term Store: It is conceived of as a permanent repository of information. This memory store contains essentially, our knowledge of the world, and its capacity is assumed to be very great. Once material has been transferred to long-term store, there seems to be very little—if any loss of information.

As material is acquired, it presumably passes through the sensory register and into the short-term store. Control process such as rehearsal permits the transfer of this material to long-term store, from which it may be subsequently retrieved. Actually, although not indicated in this diagram, long-term store enters the picture in a number of different ways. First, information from long-term store is necessary to permit pattern recognition and identification of raw sensory information held in the sensory register. Second, information that has been sufficiently rehearsed or organised is thought to be transferred to long-term store. Finally, the very control processes that are assumed to govern the movement of the information through the system must be represented in some way (as rules) in long-term store (see Fig. 12.1).

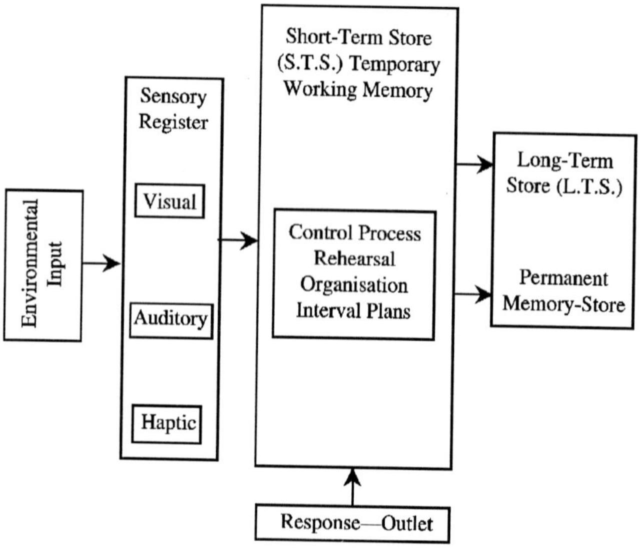

Movement of Information within Memory System

Fig. 12.1: An Overview of Memory System

KINDS AND TYPES OF MEMORY

Kinds and Types of Memory: Classification I

- Immediate Memory
- Permanent Memory

Kinds and Types of Memory: Classification II

- Short-Term Memory
- Long Term Memory

Kinds andTypes of Memory: Classification III

- Personal Memory
- Impersonal Memory

Kinds and Types of Memory: Classification IV

Active Memory

Positive Memory

Kinds and Types of Memory: Classification V

Rote Memory

Logical Memory

Immediate and Permanent Memory: The span of immediate memory is very wide. An example of immediate memory is memory near the examination. When things or ideas etc. are recalled after sometime, it is called long-term memory or permanent memory. Immediate memory is also called Short Term Memory (STM) and Permanent Memory as Long Term Memory (LTM).

(ii) *Personal and Impersonal Memory*: When personal experiences are recalled, it is called personal memory and when dry facts are recalled, it is called impersonal memory.

(iii) *Active and Passive Memory*: When effort is made to remember things, it is active memory and when things come to mind automatically, it is passive memory.

(iv) *Rote Memory/Logical Memory*: In rote memory, there is no understanding of things, and when things are learnt by insight, it is logical memory.

FACTORS CONTRIBUTING TO GOOD MEMORY

Factors Contributing to Good Memory: Classification I

(1) Factors Relating to the Learner

(2) Factors Relating to Different Types of Material

(3) Factors Relating to Retention or Retention as Affected by Original learning

General Factors Contributing to Good Memory: Classification II

(1) Health of the Learner

(2) Attentiveness of the Learner

(3) Distinct and Vivid Impressions

(4) Repetition Insight

1. Factors in the Learner:

These are as under:

(i) Age of the learner.
(ii) Intelligence of the learner.
(iii) Mental state of the learner.
(iv) Physical state of the learner.
(v) Health of the learner.
(vi) Attitude of the learner.

2. Factors Relating to the Subject Matter or Types of Materials to be Learnt

(i) Meaningful of the material.
(ii) Pleasantness of the material.

3. Factors in Retention or Retention as Affected by Original Learning

(a) *Will to Remember*: The mental set with which the material is learnt enhances retention. When one is motivated to learn, this leads to better attention and better retention.

(b) *Recitation increases* the amount retained.

(c) Materials learnt by *distributed practice* are better retained than those learnt by massed practice.

(d) *Associations Also Help Retain Better*: Most of us remember while learning arithmetic problems of simple fraction. We associate the technique with the word 'BODMAS' and this leads to better retention of the procedure of simplification.

(e) Material learnt by the *whole method* is better retained than that learnt by the part method. But relative efficiency of the whole method also depends upon the nature of the material learnt.

(f) *Over-learnt* material is better retained. Over-learning is the term applied to learning beyond the stage where the material can be said to have been learnt.

SIGNS OF GOOD MEMORY

Psychologists identify five signs of good memory.

1. *Rapidity*: The first sign of good memory is rapidity, i.e., how quickly the learner recalls his experiences. How little time the learner takes in recalling his experience is denoted by rapidity.

2. *Accuracy*: This implies the exactness with which a past experience is recalled. There may be rapidity in memory but accuracy may be missing. A good memory must possess these elements simultaneously.

3. *Length of Time*: This element denotes the time for which one can retain the past experiences and recalls them accurately. One individual may be able to retain and recall only a small quantity of the experience while another is able to retain and recall a large quantity of the experience. The latter has relatively a good memory.

4. *Quantity of Experience*: Some persons are able to recall whatever they learn while others can recall only a little.

5. *Promptness*: It implies the ease and spontaneity with which experience is recalled.

6. *Serviceableness*: It refers to the recall of right experience at the right time at the right place and in the right manner.

METHODS OF MEASUREMENT OF RETENTION

Recall Method or Reproduction Method

For instance, the learner may learn a list of 40 words and after 8 hours he is able to recall or reproduce only 20 words. Thus his recall store is 20 out of 40 words or 50 per cent.

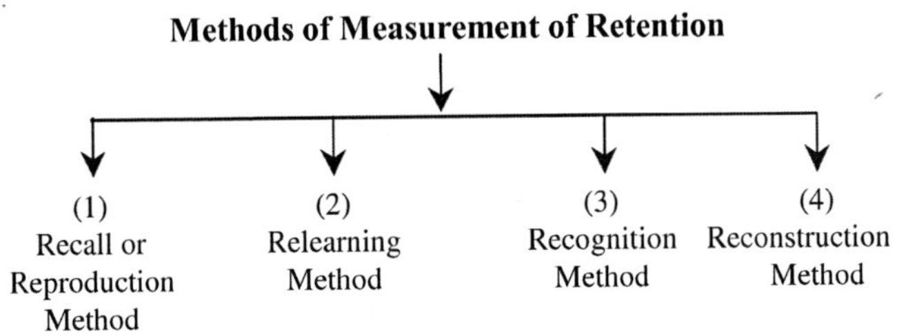

Relearning or Saving Method: In this method we first calculate the number of trials taken to learn the material in the beginning and then note down the saving of trials on relearning it after some lapse of time. For example, if the subject takes 10 trials to recite a whole poem correctly, and only takes 6 trials to master the same after 2 days, his saving score would be:

$$\frac{10-6}{10}=\frac{4}{10} \text{ or } 40\%$$

Recognition Method: In a typical recognition test, the learner's ability to recognise items he has just studied is tested by showing him the study items together with new items and asking the learner to identify the study items.

Method of Reconstruction: In this method, the learner first learns material in a serial order and then the items of the learning material are mixed up and shuffled. Then the learner is required to rearrange the items in their proper sequence.

GENERAL CHARACTERISTICS OF CHILDREN'S MEMORY AND ADULT'S MEMORY

Children's Memory	*Adult's Memory*
1. Children commit to memory without any logic.	1. Adults have a logical memory. They observe facts intelligently and organise them logically in their mental make up. This makes assimilation of facts possible.

(*Contd.*)

Children's Memory	Adult's Memory
2. Children have a mechanical memory. It is by mechanical repetition that they remember facts.	2. Adults have an understanding memory.
3. Children learn more quickly and retain their impressions in a better way about concrete things.	3. Adults have better memory of concrete things as well as abstract ideas.
4. Memory of children is short-lived. They are not able to retain it for long.	4. Adults have relatively a long-lived memory.
5. Children's memory is passive.	5. Adults have an active memory.
6. Children recall facts spontaneously. Past experiences are recalled without any effort.	6. They have to make a conscious and deliberate effort to recall facts.

ECONOMICAL METHODS OF MEMORISING

Following are the important economical methods of memorising.

1. *Principle of Association*: The law of association is very helpful in memorisation.

2. *Law of Exercise and Intelligent Repetition*: Repetition and its quality affects memorising. Several psychological experiments have shown that the items repeated more often are remembered longer than those repeated less. However, repetition should be with understanding.

3. *Spaced Repetition*: The material to be committed to memory should be repeated at intervals with periods of rest. This will save the learner from fatigue. Effort-rest-Effort will lead to better memorisation.

4. *Use of Progressive Methods of Teaching-Learning*: The project method and the problem method are very helpful in making the matter interesting. Students assimilate easily and retain for a longer period.

5. *Use of Modern Technology*: A variety of aids should be used in the teaching-learning process to make the students motivated in the lesson. They help in enhancing the concentration of the students.

6. *Whole or Part Method*: There are two methods of memorising any content of learning which are known as the *Whole method* and the *Part method*. We may give an example of a poem which the child wants to memorise.

According to the *whole method* the child may read the whole poem again and again from the beginning to the end and thus memorise it.

According to the *part method*, the poem may be divided into smaller units and the child may try to memorise each part intelligently until the skill related to that learning has been fully acquired.

THE WHOLE METHOD AND PART METHOD

The Whole Method: Advantages

1. The parts are combined into one and give a meaning to the child.
2. If the child has learnt some content material by heart, this method works.

***Limitations*:** This method does not operate if the subject matter for memorisation is too long and difficult.

The Part Method

Advantages

1. It works well when the subject matter of learning is short.
2. It gives better results if the learner is young and the subject matter is difficult.

Limitations

1. The structure of the entire poem is not clear to the child till the end of the learning.
2. The child finds it difficult to link the parts of the poem into the whole poem.
3. It is psychologically unsound.

Latest Researches

1. Aveling came to the conclusion that nearly one-fifth of the time of learning can be economised with the wise use of the whole method.
2. Pyne and Syner came to the conclusion that the whole method is more effective when the poem has about 240 lines.

The Part Progressive Method or Mediating Method

A modification of the Whole method is suggested which is known as Part Progressive or Mediating Method. The outlines are as follows:

1. The difficult words or phrases may be mastered or understood before hand and then the whole method may be employed.
2. The learner should make a cautious approach while making use of the whole method.
3. The poem may be sub-divided into three units. The child may combine 1 and 2 and later on combine 2 and 3 and finally 1, 2 and 3.

The Recitation Method

Features

1. In this method, the learner first reads the matter once or twice and then recites and recalls that matter without looking at the matter.
2. The learner evaluates himself from time to time and notes down those points which he has not been able to recall.
3. Small children really recite their lessons in a sing-song manner with a rhythm.

Advantages of the Method

1. The learner is able to constantly evaluate himself and find out his limitations.
2. This leads to concentrated attention as the weak links in his learning are strengthened.
3. The child is able to find out his own mistakes and thus explores new avenues of further improvement.

4. The learner comes to have a sense of achievement leading to further effort.

5. It saves the efforts of the teacher in the learning process.

6. In case of small children the rhyme and rhythm help to fix up words in the mind and enable the child to enjoy the music. This enjoyment leads to retention and memorisation.

7. The subject matter is learnt as it to be used. Little transfer is necessary in the later reproduction.

Spaced and Unspaced Methods of Learning

Spaced or Distributed Method of Learning: In this type of learning the child is not required to memorise the entire subject-matter in one continuous sitting. After learning for some time some rest is given to the child. The principle of 'work and rest' is followed.

If the child has to memorise a poem, he at the initial stage is advised to go on repeating it for many times. After repetition, he takes rest for some time. After rest the child again repeats the poem and takes rest. In this way with repeated intervals of work and rest he will be able to have mastery over the poem or any other assigned work.

Unspaced or Spaced Method: The child has to memorise the assigned work in one sitting without any interval or rest. The learning goes on continuously without any interruption till it is mastered.

Suggestions: Many experimental studies have been conducted to assess the relative values of these two methods. It has been found that:

1. In-short lessons unspaced method of leaning may be followed.

2. In giving lessons spaced method of learning should be followed. One suggested modification is that it is better to distribute the hours of work in the sittings of the child and also introduce the periods of rest in between these sittings. This helps in removing the monotony caused by long periods of study. Rest keeps away the fatigue element and the attention also does not flag. The child feels fresh after a period of rest and his interest is kept alive.

Improvement of Development of Memory: Suggestions

Memory may be improved by following the techniques as give below:

1. *Law of Exercise and Intelligent Repetition*: Repetition and its quality affects memorising. Several psychological experiments have shown that the items repeated more often are remembered longer than those repeated less. However, repetition should be with understanding.

2. *Spaced Repetition*: The material to be committed to memory should be repeated at intervals with periods of rest. This will save the learner from fatigue. Effort-rest-effort-will lead to better memorisation.

3. *Use of Modern Technology*: A variety of aids should be used in the teaching-learning process to make the students motivated in the lesson. They help in enhancing the concentration of the students.

4. *Use of Progressive Methods of Teaching-Learning*: The project method and the problem method are very helpful in making the matter interesting. Students assimilate easily and retain for a longer period.

5. *Interest*: For proper memorising, interest in the topic or subject is essential. There is a popular saying 'you can take the horse to water for drinking but you cannot make him drink unless he is interested in drinking'. Similar is the case with the children.

6. *Motivation in Learning*: Motivation creates interest and produces the right condition for memorisation.

7. *Will*: Will to learn a topic or subject enhances interest and motivation and thereby it leads to better retention.

8. *Association*: The law of association is very helpful in memorisation.

9. *Over-learning*: Over-learning implies practice that continues after a perfect recall has been established. Over-learning leads to better retention. However, over-learning should be moderate. Expensive over-learning will lead to boredom. Under-learning hinders retention.

10. *Use of Mnemonics*: Mnemonics devices are useful in retaining several types of material. Through this device, information in the brain is deliberately transformed into meaningful system to improve memory. For instance, aims of education may be memorised with the aid of 7 R's. 7 R's denote Reading, Writing, Arithmetic, Rights, Responsibilities and Recreation.

Three A's may represent Age, Ability and Aptitude of students while referring to individual differences.

Four H's may denote four aims of education: Development of Head, Hand, Heart and Health.

11. *Meaningful Organisation of the Subject Matter*: One of the most effective methods to improve memory or retention which teachers can use is the meaningful organisation of the subject-matter. Approach should be logical-cum-psychological.

12. *Formation of Clear Concept*: Efforts should be made to improve memory with the help of illustrations, and various types of audio-visual aids.

13. *Principle of Learning by Doing*: Learning experiences acquired through doing are remembered for a longer period.

14. *Overall Classroom Environment*: It includes proper physical conditions and the attitude of the teacher.

Conclusion

1. It is difficult to specify which method is the best one. It may be pointed out that a single method cannot work on all occasions.
2. The abilities of the child also determine the success of the method.
3. The quantum of work also determines the methods to be adopted.
4. Environment also plays an important role in learning.
5. The will of the child determines the efficiency and effectiveness of learning.

Latest Research: Gates conducted an experiment with sixteen non-sense syllables and live short biographical materials accounting for about 170 words. He used two methods: (a) Reading and re-reading of the subject-matter by one group of students. (b) Another group was asked to follow the recitation method. Gates came to the conclusion that recitation method proved to be better than the reading and re-reading method.

Suggestion: It may be pointed out that the child should devote three-fifths of the period of study to recitation. This method will help both in the immediate and delayed recall.

FORGETTING

Meaning of Forgetting

Following are a few definition of forgetting which throw light on the concept of forgetting.

Adams—"True learning is judicious forgetting".

James Drever—"Forgetting means failure at any time to recall an experience when attempting to do so, or to perform an action previously learned".

Num—"Forgetting is failing to retain or able to recall what has been acquired".

Munn—"Forgetting is the loss permanent or temporary of the ability to recall or recognise something learned earlier".

NATURE AND CHARACTERISTICS OF FORGETTING

1. Forgetting is a process of fading with the passage of time.
2. Forgetting occurs when memories of the same type interfere with each other.
3. Forgetting is attributed to change in traces in the brain.
4. Forgetting is not losing something but rather is more like being unable to find it.
5. Forgetting is influenced by motivation.
6. Forgetting is caused by lack of proper organisation and systematisation of the learned material.
7. Forgetting takes place on account of change of stimulating conditions.

Summing up: Forgetting's nature requires more than one explanation.

CURVES OF FORGETTING

Following two curves based on Ebbinghaus illustrate the amount of forgetting with time to lapse. (Nonsense syllabus—meaningless words like Nof, bdf and cem etc.)

Table 12.1: Time Lapsed and Percentage of Amount Forgotten

Time Lapsed	*Percentage of Amount Forgotten*
20 minutes	47%
One day	66%
Two days	72%
Six days	75%
Thirtyone days	79%

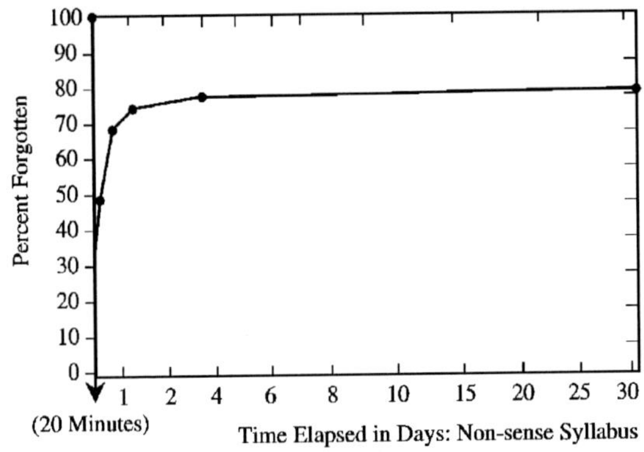

Fig. 12.2: Time Elapsed in Forgetting

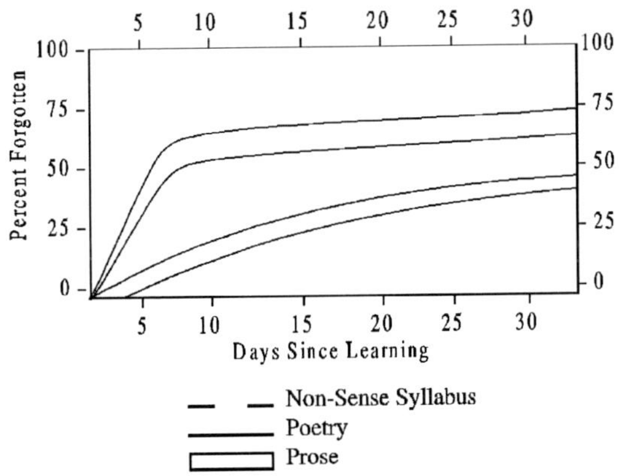

Fig. 12.3: Different Types of Forgetting

TYPES OF FORGETTING

Types of Forgetting: Classification I

- Natural Forgetting or Passive Forgetting
- Unnatural or Morbid Forgetting or Active Forgetting

Types of Forgetting: Classification II

- General Forgetting
- Specific Forgetting

Types of Forgetting: Classification III

- Physical or Organic Forgetting
- Psychological Forgetting

CAUSES AND MINIMISING FORGETFULNESS

Causes of Forgetting

1. Lack of interest in work.
2. Disuse of activity.
3. Lapse of time.
4. Lack of integration and synthesis. This may be due to:
   (i) Interference of another activity.
   (ii) Continued experience of various kinds, all serious in nature.
   (iii) No time for rest after serious activity for integration and synthesis.
5. Emotional disturbance.
6. Fatigue.
7. Morbid forgetfulness on account of unpleasant and painful experiences.

Minimising Forgetfulness

1. *Vividness*: Vivid impressions backed by illustrations and aids are better retained.

2. *Organisation of the Learning Material*: Material which is properly related and organised is easily retained than the material which is unrelated and disconnected.

3. *Recapitulation and Review*: The lesson or experience needs to be recapitulated or reviewed.

4. *Nature of Learning Material*: Meaningful material is better retained than material which is confusing.

5. *Distributed Learning*: Retention is definitely better if the learning material is spread over suitable sittings.

6. *Over-learning*: Studies have shown that an over-learned lesson is better retained than one barely learned. Of course, extreme is always bad.

13

Intelligence

MEANING OF INTELLIGENCE

Intelligence has been viewed differently by scholars. More than one hundred definitions of intelligence are found in the psychological literature. However, in general, intelligence is considered as the global capacity of an individual to think rationally, to act purposefully and to deal effectively with the environment. All the discoveries and inventions of the world are usually attributed to persons of high intelligence.

Here some of the most prominent definition of intelligence are given. These definition throw meaningful light on the meaning, nature and development of intelligence.

1. *Binet* describes intelligence as: (1) the tendency of thought to take and maintain a definite direction, (2) the capacity to make adaptations for the purpose of attaining a desired end, and (3) the power of self-criticism.

2. *Colvin* defines it as capacity to learn.

3. *Burt* calls it the power of readjustment to relatively novel situations by organising new psycho-physical co-ordination.

4. *Stern* defines intelligence as the general mental adaptability to new problems and conditions of life.

5. *William James* calls it the ability to adjust oneself successfully to a relatively novel situation.

6. *William McDougall* states "an intelligent action as one which seems to show that the creature has profited by prior experience of similar situations, that it somehow brings to bear its previous experience in the guidance of its present action; intelligence is the capacity to improve upon native tendency in the light of past experience."

7. *Thorndike* defines it as, "We may define intelligence in general as the power of good responses from the point of view of truth or fact."

8. *Terman* writes: "An individual is intelligent in proportion as he is able to carry on abstract thinking."

9. *Num* regards it as the "flexibility of the mind to meet new situations."

10. *Boynton* states, "Intelligence is an inherited capacity of the individual which is manifested through his ability to adapt to and reconstruct the factors of his environment in accordance with the most fundamental needs of himself and his group."

11. *Johnson* thinks that intelligence stands for an "ability to solve the general

run of human problems to adjust to new situations and in short the ability to think."

12. *Spearman* thinks intelligence in terms of two abilities, e.g., general ability or '*g*' and specific ability or '*s*'. Both kinds of abilities work in every performance. His '*g*' is the common factor which will colour every response, and his '*s*' is independent in every process. A scientist has two kinds of abilities, general as well as one specific for science. A musician has two kinds of abilities, general as well as specific, for music in this case. In the measurement of the intelligence of a person, both of these abilities should be taken into consideration.

13. *Vat Wagenen* treats intelligence as "capacity to learn and to adjust to relatively new and changing conditions."

14. *Freeman* writes, "Intelligence is represented in behaviour by the capacity of the individual to adjust himself to new situations to solve new problems to learn."

15. *Thurstone* stresses the "factorial analysis" theory which recognises intelligence as consisting of several abilities, seven of which have been identified:

(i) number facility, (ii) word fluency, (iii) visualising, (iv) memory, (v) perceptual speech, (vi) induction, and (vii) verbal reasoning.

16. *Terman's* definition of Intelligence is on the following pattern—

(i) Ability to carry on abstract thinking. This means, it cannot be manifested at the level of perception whereas in fact intelligence is involved in perceptual tasks.

(ii) Capacity for abstract thinking, like all other abilities, involves factors specific to itself as well as intelligence.

This definition does not state that the abstract thinking is to be directed or relevant to a question or to some end.

Definitions: Classification of Intelligence

Broadly speaking there are three types of definitions regarding the meaning and development of intelligence.

(i) One group of definitions emphasises that intelligence is the ability to adjust, or adapt oneself to one's total environment or to limited aspects thereof—Burt, William James, McDougall, Goddard.

It is the capacity to organise one's behaviour pattern so as to act more effectively and more appropriately in novel situations. Thus, the more intelligent person could be one who can more easily and more extensively vary his behaviour as changing conditions demand.

(ii) The second type of definition states that intelligence is the ability to learn. Colvin is the propounder of this definition.

(iii) The third type of definition states that it is the ability to carry on abstract thinking—Binet, Terman and Freeman.

However, it would be very difficult to separate all these definitions into three clear-cut categories.

A definition of intelligence as the capacity to behave appropriately and effectively in new situations and a definition that intelligence is the ability to learn are in fact two aspects of the same process. Similarly, ability to carry on abstract thinking contributes to a person's ability to adjust or adapt to changing or new situations.

Wechsler's definition seems to combine and extend the three types of definitions. He states: "Intelligence is the aggregate global capacity of the individual to act purposefully, to think rationally and to deal effectively with his environment".

G.D. Stoddard offers the following definition: "Intelligence is the ability to undertake activities that are characterised by: 1. Difficulty, 2. Complexity, 3. Abstractness, 4. Economy, 5. Adaptiveness to a goal, 6. Social value, and 7. The emergence of originals and to maintain such activities under conditions that demand a concentration of energy and a resistance to emotional force."

OPERATIONAL DEFINITION AND MEANING OF INTELLIGENCE

Since theoretical discussions do not lead us to some precise nature of intelligence, Vernon states: "Intelligence is what intelligence tests measure".

Some argue, "We can measure electricity without being able to define its precise nature. But we can put electricity to use and measure it. So we can use and measure intelligence".

Now going into the discussion of these various definitions of intelligence, it may be said that intelligence is an ability to "see the right thing at the right moment in the right way." It is a general capacity to understand and meet with the situations that life may present, successfully. To quote Principal R.R. Kumria: "Call it practical wisdom; call it common sense; call it genius; it is just the same in different names and grades".

INTELLIGENCE AND SCHOLARS OF ANCIENT INDIA

Kautilya defines it as the ability to work.

According to Visnusarma, it is the power which enables human beings to control the world.

The *Brahmasutra* tells us that intelligence is the gift of God and it is fixed at birth.

The *Agnipurana* prescribes diet for infants to help the growth of their intelligence.

Types of Intelligence Accordance to Ancient View

Agadha buddhi or intelligence that cannot be measured or superior intelligence.

Mohabuddhi or great intelligence, *malin buddhi* or dull intelligence.

Sthira buddhi or calm intelligence.

Alpa buddhi or little intelligence.

In ancient India, intelligence was measured through conversation, physical features, gestures, gait, speech, changes in the eye and facial expression.

KINDS OF INTELLIGENCE AND A FEW GENERALISATIONS

Kinds of Intelligence

Thurstone has suggested three broad categories of intelligence:

1. *Abstract Intelligence*: He defined this as the "ability to understand and manage ideas and symbols, such as, words, number, chemical or physical formulas, legal decisions, scientific principles and the like. ..." In the case of students this is very close to what is called scholastic aptitude.
2. *Mechanical Intelligence*: This includes, "The ability to clean, to understand and manage things and mechanisms, such as, a knife, a gun, a moving machine, an automobile, a boat, a lathe..."
3. *Social Intelligence*: "This is the ability to understand and manage men and women, boys and girls to act wisely in human relations".

A Few Generalisations about Intelligence

Usually scholars, executives in business and Government, and scientists possess high abstract intelligence.

Mechanics, builders, expert carpenters and plumbers possess high mechanical intelligence.

High social intelligence is found in politicians, sales people and leaders in society.

A successful civil engineer presumably possesses high abstract as well as high mechanical intelligence; the successful criminal lawyer possesses abstract as well as social intelligence.

Distribution of Intelligence

The majority of the school children, say about 60%, are found in the I.Q. interval 90—110 and are referred to as 'Normal' or 'Average'.

Intelligence and Sex Differences: Generally speaking, the research studies show that the average scores of the sexes are strikingly similar.

Intelligence and Race Differences: Every racial and cultural group contains some gifted children. Franz Boas states, "If we were to select the most intelligent, imaginative, energetic and emotionally stable type of mankind, all races would be represented".

DEVELOPMENT OF INTELLIGENCE AND MENTAL TESTING

Intelligence cannot be increased or decreased. The amount of intelligence that a person possesses is inherited and fixed. The amount though fixed does not reveal itself at the start of life. With the growth of the child, the amount inherited by a child also grows. The general belief is that the growth of intelligence stops and it reaches its limit at the age of sixteen or seventeen. It is true that a man of forty knows more than a boy of sixteen. But this does not mean that the amount of intelligence possessed by him has increased. This may be due to his experience. As regards his intelligence, his position remains the same.

The growth of intelligence of certain children may be checked on account of certain unfavourable circumstances and when these are removed, intelligence begins to grow and functions normally.

An intelligent person has the ability to adjust himself to the changing circumstances with ease, efficiency and speed. He has the capacity to assimilate ideas very quickly and clearly. He can cope with new situations very successfully. All the inventions of the world can be attributed to persons of intelligence.

The unintelligent or the dullard individuals fail to think of new situations. They are always guided by others. They lack originality.

Are all persons equally intelligent? Are all the students fit for school instruction? Are all students capable of pursuing the same course? Are all students fit for all occupations? Is it proper to educate all students in the same way?

These and various such questions have been engaging the attention of the psychologists for the past hundred years or so. Many attempts have been made to measure intelligence possessed by individuals so that necessary arrangements may be made to give them training according to their intelligence. Thanks to the ceaseless efforts of various psychologists whose standardised tests are available which can be used to measure intelligence.

Psychological Testing

Anne Anastasi observes: "Psychological testing is a relatively young branch of one of the youngest of the sciences".

One of the first problems, which stimulated the development of psychological tests, was the identification of the feeble-minded. French physician *Esqurioi* was the first person to write a two-volume work in 1938 in which over one hundred pages were devoted to feeble-mindedness.

Another French physician who made a valuable contribution was *Seguin* who in 1837 established the first school devoted to the education of mentally defective children. In 1848 he migrated to America where his ideas gained recognition.

The general aim of the early experimental psychologists of the nineteenth century was the formulation of generalised description of human behaviour and not the measurement of individual differences. Many of the early experimental psychologists received their training in a laboratory founded by *Wundt* at Leipzig in 1879.

Sir Francis Galton, an English biologist, was primarily responsible for launching the testing movement on its course. In 1882, an anthropometric laboratory was established by him in South Kensington Museum, London. In this laboratory individuals could be measured in certain physical traits by the payment of a small fee. Galton himself devised most of the simple tests. Galton also paved the way for the application of rating scale and questionnaire methods etc. One of his disciples, Karl Pearson carried forward his work.

James McKeen Cattell of America occupies a prominent position in the development of psychological testing. He used the term "mental test" in an article in 1890. The article related a series of tests which were being administered annually to college students in the efforts to determine their intellectual level. Cattell like Galton felt that a measure of intellectual functions could be obtained through tests of sensory discrimination and reaction time.

Among others the names of *Jastrow, Krae Pelin* and *Ferrai* may also be mentioned.

The early experiments of Wundt were all concerned with sensory discrimination and motor ability. His worthy pupil Cattell did much useful work in America. However, the credit of scientific mental testing goes to Binet and Simon. The names of Terman and Cyril Burt may also be mentioned who did very useful work in mental testing.

In India, Dr. V.V. Kamat, Dr. C.H. Rice, Pt. L.S. Jha, Prof. S. Jalota and Principal R.R. Kumria have contributed a lot to psychological testing.

Landmarks in the Development of Testing

1826	Robert Owen's rating scale
1842	Seguin's form boards
1905	Binet-Simon scale
1908	Goddard translation of Binet's scale
1909	Court is practice test in arithmetic
1910	Thorndike handwriting scale
1911	Healy and Fernald performance test
1912	Hillegas composition scale
1913	Buckingham spelling scale
1915	Yerkes point scale
1916	Stanford revision of the Binet-Simon scale
1917	Army Group tests, Stenquist assembly tests
1919	Sea-shore tests of musical ability
1921	Rorschach test
1927	Strong vocational interest inventory
1933	Hildreth readiness tests
1935	Murray apperception test
1938	Thurstone primary abilities test

MEASUREMENT OF INTELLIGENCE

Intelligence is measured through a complicated process. It involves a comparison and establishment of a relationship between C.A. (Chronological Age) and M.A. (Mengal Age). This relationship is expressed by the term I.Q. (Intelligence Quotient). When the mental age is divided by the chronological age and the quotient is multiplied by 100, the result is I.Q.

$$\text{I.Q.} = \frac{\text{M.A.}}{\text{C.A.}} \times 100$$

BASIC CONCEPTS INVOLVED IN INTELLIGENCE AND INTELLIGENCE TESTING

1. *Chronological Age*: This refers to the age in years, months, hours. This is counted from the time and date of the birth of an individual. It is symbolically expressed as C.A.

2. *Mental Age* (*M.A.*): Binet was the first psychologist to introduce the concept of mental age. He gave a better footing and credibility to the

intelligence test results. Alfred Binet was a French psychologist and an Education Officer. He is known as the father of Modern Psychological Testing. He was assisted by Simon and as such his intelligence test is known as Binet-Simon Test of Intelligence. The then French Government was faced with the problem of separating mentally retarded children from the normal ones. The job was assigned to Binet. It took about 15 years to complete the job. The year 1905 is a great landmark in the history of intelligence testing.

Menal age refers to '*Mental Maturity*' of a person. Corresponding to his level of performance in an intelligence test—irrespective of his C.A. If a person of C.A. 7 years old is able to score satisfactorily on a test meant for a child of C.A. 10, then the mental age (henceforth referred as M.A.) of the former is 10. Mental age can also be defined as an expression of the extent of development achieved by the individual stated in terms of the performance that can be expected at any given age".

And when the score of a given intelligence tests are put into M.A. scores—we have with us what is known as Age Scale. Maximum mental age is 19 or 20.

3. *Basal Age*: Basal age is that age of the child with reference to his chronological age where he can solve all questions in a given test. Mental age cannot be calculated directly. It is basal age which helps in the calculation of mental age.

This concept of basal age may be explained with the help of an example. There is a child with C.A. 6. He solves all questions in a test meant for child of C.A. 7. He also does the same for a child of C.A. 8 and then his efficiency declines, i.e., he solves only 2 questions out of 6 questions in a test meant for a child of C.A. 9. The basal age of a child with C.A. 6 is 8 years. His mental age will be

Mental age = Basal age + partial credit
= 8 years + 4 months

The child has an M.A. of $8\frac{1}{3}$ years

CLASSIFICATION OF INDIVIDUAL ON THE BASIS OF I.Q.

Terman's Classification

A. On the basis of I.Q., Terman gives the following classification on American testees:

Near genius or genius	Above 140
Very superior intelligence	120—140
Superior intelligence	110—120
Normal or average intelligence	90—110
Dullness	80—90
Borderline cases	70—80

Definite feeble-mindedness which has been further classified as under:

Morons	50—70
Imbeciles	25—50
Idiots	below 25

B. Classification of Indian Children

The Bombay-Karnataka Revision Tests: Dr. V.V. Kamat revised Binet's scale to suit Indian conditions and administered intelligence tests to 1,074 children and adolescents of all ages from 2 to 20 of both sexes. The locality selected for the experiment was the town of Dharwar in the Bombay Presidency. The children selected were fairly representative of the general population of Indian children.

Dr. V.V. Kamat classifies Indian children as under:

Class	*Range of I.Q.s*
Near genius or genius	140 and above
Extraordinary	130—139.9
Very superior	120—129.9
Superior	110—119.9
Average or normal	99—109.9
Backward	80—98.9
Very backward	70—79.9
Borderline	60—69.9
Morons	40—59.9
Imbeciles	20—39.9
Idiots	Below 20

IMPORTANT USES OF INTELLIGENCE TESTS IN EVALUATION

Intelligence tests are very useful for the following purposes:

1. *Knowing Individual Differences among Learners*: Dr. V.V. Kamat has classified Indian children as above:

2. *Grouping in the Class*: Sometimes grouping in the class is done on the basis of intelligence test results.

3. *Classroom Teaching*: Intelligence tests enable the teacher to know the general mental level of the students and accordingly he adopts his teaching techniques.

4. *Identification of Slow Learners and the Gifted*: Intelligence tests help to identify learners in their capacity to learn. Accordingly enrichment programmes are provided to the gifted and compensatory/remedial education to the slow learners.

5. *Selection to Courses*: Different subjects require different degrees of intelligence. Some call for a higher order of intelligence and the others of a lower order.

A nation-wide study in the U.S.A. gave the following Median I.Q. of the high school students in different courses:

Course	*Median I.Q.*
Technical	114.00
Scientific	108.00
Academic	106.00
Commerce	104.00
Trade	92.00

(*Contd.*)

Course	*Median I.Q.*
Technical	114.00
Scientific	108.00
Academic	106.00
Commerce	104.00
Trade	92.00

This implies that children of high I.Q. are superior in abstract thinking than those of low I.Q.

5. *Selection in Occupations*: Burt draws up the following provisional scheme for occupational classification according to the degree of intelligence occupations require:

S.No.	*Occupation*	*I.Q. Require*
1.	Higher professional and administrative work—Lawyer, physician, architect, teacher (University and Secondary level)	150
2.	Lower professional technical and executive work	130 to 150
3.	Clerical and highly skilled work—shorthand, typist, bank clerk, salesman, electrician, nurse	115 to 130
4.	Skilled work—tailor, dressmaker, carpenter, cashier, printer	100 to 115
5.	Semi-skilled repetitive work—barber, welder, miner, painter, banker	85 to 100
6.	Unskilled repetitive work—manual labour	70 to 85
7.	Casual labour—simplest routine work	50 to 75

6. *Promotion*: Intelligence tests are used for the promotion of students to the next class.

7. *Selection of Students to a School*: In good schools, there is always rush for admission. All the applicants though eligible for admission cannot be admitted. It then becomes necessary to adopt some additional methods of selection. Intelligence tests help to meet out this difficulty to a considerable extent. By administering these tests, authorities pick out the innately brighter boys.

8. *The Discovery of Unusual Cases*: The lack of intelligence may be the main cause of abnormal behaviour. The intelligence tests help to find out cases of abnormal behaviour.

9. *Intelligence and Success in College*: Gates and others think that an I.Q. of at least 120 is needed to do acceptable college work in a first class college with an average expenditure of time and energy.

10. *Help in Diagnosis of Backwardness*: Ordinary scholastic examinations fail to discover 'educable abilities'. The failure of a child in the examination is no indication that he lacks intelligence. This failure may be on account of defective methods of teaching or it may be due to some temperamental or physical obstacles which might have stood in the way of the child. There may not be any fault with the intelligence of the child only it has not been allowed to work itself out.

11. *Award of Scholarship*: Various public scholarships are awarded on the basis of the results secured through intelligence tests. The Government of India selects some students for the award of scholarships for studying in Public Schools on the basis of the intelligence and achievement tests.

12. *Evaluation of Methods and Materials of Instruction*: Intelligence Tests are helpful in evaluating the results of the experiments conducted by a school in the relative importance of the different methods of instruction i.e., achievement obtained with different text-books or with a certain text-book as contrasted with extensive reading material not confined to any one book.

13. *Assessment of Teacher's Work*: When the achievement of the pupils in a subject does not correspond to the scores of intelligence tests, it gives indication to the fact that the subject has not been properly taught by the teacher and properly understood by the students.

Limitations of Intelligence Tests

It would be a great mistake to think that these tests are all in all in measuring the various aspects of the learner's personality. Intelligence is one of the factors. Too much reliance cannot be made on this evaluation tool. It is to be used in conjunction with other tools. Following are the important limitations of intelligence tests:

1. Intelligence tests seek to measure intelligence which in itself is not a clear concept. Psychologists differ radically on the meaning and nature of intelligence.
2. Intelligence tests fail to measure the depth, strength, weakness and quality of an individual relating to his emotional stability.
3. Intelligence tests fail to evaluate the ethical, moral and spiritual qualities of an individual.
4. Intelligence test do not take into account the environmental factors. The test may include items/material with which the children of socio-economic groups have more experience than those of weaker sections.
5. Use of intelligence tests need a good deal of care and caution on the part of the test administrator/user.

14

Personality

In simple language by personality, we mean the totality of everything about an individual—his emotional, ethical, mental, physical, social and spiritual make-up. It includes an individual's appearance, emotionality, sociability, intelligence, character and moral traits.

The term 'personality' is derived from a Latin word '*Persona*' which means the mask worn by a Roman actor. In this sense personality means the individual as seen by others. Personality thus implies the cover-up of the real person. One actor plays several roles. In other words, personality is taken to refer to the outward aspect of the individual which actually does not mean anything except in theatre.

COMPLEX NATURE OF PERSONALITY AND DEFINITIONS OF PERSONALITY

As observed by Murphy (1947), "We do not believe that anyone today can seriously understand to say that he knows what personality is." Present situation also seems to be very unclear, although no topic in the field of psychology is more fascinating than personality. Volumes have been written on the topic, yet we are unable to say clearly what personality is.

Earlier in 1937, G.W. Allport, who had done a good deal of research on personality, mentioned fifty-three definitions of personality in his book "*Personality: A Psychological Interpretation*". Since then how many definitions have been added is any body's guess!

Following are some of the definitions of personality:

1. According to R.B. Cattell, "Personality is that which permits a prediction of what a person will do in a given situation."

2. In the words of L.J. Cronbach, "Character is not really a cumulation of separate habits and ideas, character is embedded in the total structure of personality."

3. J.F. Dashiell, states: "Personality is the sum total of behaviour trends manifested in social adjustments."

4. In the opinion of J.P. Guilford: 'An individual's personality is his unique pattern of traits".

5. Healy William describes personality as "an integrated system of habitual adjustment to environment particularly to social environment.

6. Kurt Lewin, considers personality as "a dynamic totality of systems."

7. Mortem Prince thinks personality as "the sum total of biological innate dispositions, impulses, tendencies, aptitudes and instincts of the individual and the dispositions and tendencies acquired by experience."

8. In the words of R.M. Ogsten, "Personality is the expression of man's inner life, character is the expression of what he does or achieves."

9. According to G.W. Allport, "Personality is the dynamic organisation within the individual of those psycho-physical systems that determine his unique adjustment to the environment."

10. Woodworth gives the following definition, "Personality is the '*total*' quality of an individual's behaviour as it is revealed in his characteristics habits of thought and expression, his attitudes and interests, his manner of acting and his personal philosophy of life.

11. Eysenck's definition of personality is as follows, "Personality is the more or less stable and enduring organisation of a person's character, temperament, intellect and physique, which determine his unique adjustment to environment.

12. S.R. Maddi, an American psychologist in his work, '*Personality Theories—A Comparative Analysis*' (1976), one of the latest analysis has defined personality as, "Personality is the stable set of characteristics and tendencies that determine those commonalities and differences in the psychological behaviour (thoughts, feelings and action) of people that have continuity in time and that may or may not be easily understood in terms of the social and biological pressure of the immediate situation alone."

Evaluation of Definitions

A perusal of the above definitions would indicate that the definition given by Eysenck (H.J.) seems to be quite functional and operational. It has the following merits.

First. It takes into consideration a balanced view of the conative behaviour or will, affective behaviour based on emotions and cognitive behaviour—intellect or intelligence. Thus this definition attempts to give a complete picture of human behaviour by involving all of its three aspects—Conative, Cognition and affective.

Second. It accords appropriate consideration to the physiological aspect of the personality of an individual.

Third. It emphasises the need to integrate the behaviourist characteristics.

Fourth. It makes personality somewhat assessable and measurable.

However, this definition has one important weakness. It may not be stable in the sense that some circumstances may bring about radical changes in the character and other aspects of an individual. The world is moving so fast that in the span of life of an individual, he may be required to change his behaviour pattern altogether to adjust himself to the changed environment.

Some scholars consider Allport's definition to be comprehensive and clear. It lays stress on these characteristics of personality: (i) Dynamic nature, (ii) Heredity and environment, (iii) Wholeness.

CHARACTERISTICS AND NATURE OF PERSONALITY

From the definitions given above, following characteristics of personality emerge very clearly:

1. Personality is what one is.
2. Personality of each individual is unique.
3. Personality is dynamic and not static.

4. Personality functions as a unified whole.
5. Personality is the product of both heredity and environment.
6. Personality is through and through social.
7. Personality is continually adjusting itself to environment.
8. In rare cases personality influences the environment.
9. Personality is always striving for certain ends.
10. Personality is self-consciousness. We do not attribute personality to animals.
11. Personality is influenced by the school environment.
12. It is only through the study of personality of individual students, that the relative differences among them can be known and their personality developed to the optimum level.

BEHAVIOURAL PATTERNS OF PERSONALITY

The totality of a man's personality may be described as under:

1. The attitude of an individual with which he does some work.
2. The skill of an individual with which he does a job.
3. The way he acts.
4. The way he behaves.
5. The way he dresses.
6. The way he drinks and eats.
7. The way he sits and stands.
8. The way he speaks.
9. The way he walks and so on.

MARKS OF BALANCED DEVELOPMENT OF PERSONALITY

1. Good physical appearance.
2. Emotional stability.
3. High intellectual ability.
4. High degree of social adjustment.
5. High moral character.
6. Cool temperament.
7. Good directedness.
8. High adjustability.
9. Tremendous common sense, drive and pragmatic thinking.

Classification or Types of Personality

Following are the important types of personality:

Type	*Author*
1. Active and Inactive	Heymans
2. Active and Reflective	Jordan
3. Extrovert and Introvert	C.G. Ung
4. Masculine and Feminine	Apfelback
5. Romantic and Classical	Ostwald
6. Stable and Unstable	Trotler
7. Subjective and Objective	Binet
8. Tender minded and Tough minded	William James

Spranger's Six Types of Personality

1. *Aesthetic*: Lovers of beauty.
2. *Economic*: Inclined to hoard money.
3. *Political*: Interested in political affairs.
4. *Religious*: Believer in mysticism and engaged in religious activities.
5. *Social*: Interested in social affairs.
6. *Theoretical*: Theoretical in nature.

DEVELOPMENT OF PERSONALITY: BIOLOGICAL AND SOCIO-CULTURAL DETERMINANTS

↓

Biological Determinants
This is primarily determined by heredity. It includes:
(i) Physique of the individual
(ii) Chemique of the individual

Socio-Cultural Determinants *or* **Environmental Factors**

↓

Family Factors

Environmental Factors

↓

(1)	(2)	(3)	(4)	(5)	(6)
Neighbourhood	Per Group	School Enviornment	Cultural Environment	Social Environment	Political Environment

Physique: In physique are included such factors as the appearance, strength, body-build, bodily proportions, colouring and physical beauty of the individual. These factors have direct as well as indirect influence on the development of personality. Deformity handicaps the child both physically and psychologically. Fewer physically handicapped develop into normal personalities. Health and vigour are significant in early years since contacts and competitions among children are often on the physical level. Even in adult years, the man with a tough constitution is at an advantage in maintaining an aggressive attitude towards life and preserving his emotional balance.

Chemique: By chemique is meant the possible effects of the ductless glands on the personality development. Glands are small organs which change chemical substances from one form to another in the body.

Endocrine (Ductless Glands)

Meaning: The endocrine glands bring about chemical coordination by complex organic compounds called 'hormones'. Hormones are chemical regulators or chemical messengers of body. These are secreted in response to changes in the environment inside or outside the body. Hormones are secreted by specialised glands. These lack definite ducts for the transportation of their secretion but pour them directly into the blood. Therefore, these glands are called ductless glands or endocrine glands (glands of internal secretion).

Endocrine Glands in Man

Name of Gland	*Location*
1. Pituitary Gland	In head (on underside of fore brain)
2. Thyroid Gland	In neck-(across the front of wind pipe)
3. Parathyroids (4)	One at each of the outer corners of thyroid
4. Adrenals (2)	In abdominal—(across the upper end of each kidney)
5. Thymus	
6. Gonads or Sex Glands (Testes and ovaries)	In or below the pelvic cavity
7. Placenta	Pregnant uterus
8. Gastric and Intestinal mucosa	In the abdominal cavity (in the wall of stomach and intestine)
9. Kidney	In the abdominal cavity kidney cell

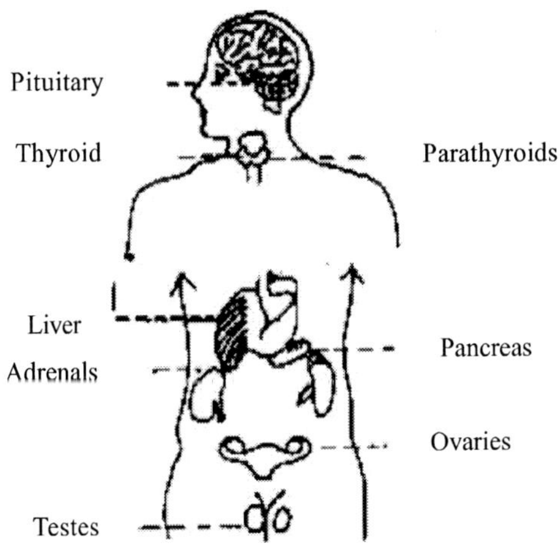

Fig.14.1: Location of Ductless Glands

Educational Implications of Endocrine and Ductless Glands

These glands have a direct bearing on the personality of an individual. Actually, there are the hormones secreted by these glands which play an important role. These hormones are circulated throughout the body and influence all those tissues on which the functioning of body system, emotional actions and even thoughts depend. As Murphy, Gardner (1968) has observed, "these harmones, ultimately may be regarded as bathing the nervous system, including the brain, and all the organs of the body in their own appropriate chemical juices."

If the thyroid gland is overactive, it results in nervousness, dizziness and difficulty in sleeping.

Sex glands or gonads are responsible for sex drive or urge. The effects of the sex glands on emotions, particularly personality and behaviour become specially significant when adolescence is reached.

The individuals with profound imbalance of ductless glands are rarely happy or well-adjusted. They suffer from apathy, anxiety, restlessness, fatigue, irritability, etc. It is not easy for certain bearded ladies and gents to remain good-natured and mentally serene when they are continuously exposed to ridicule, jest, and social isolation. This harsh and unfair treatment makes many of them morose, hypersensitive and depressed. So like other organs of the body, the ductless glands play an important part in bodily, mental and emotional, development and if defective, they may constitute an added burden contributing to abnormal behaviour.

The teacher can spot out those cases where the glands are not working properly and report those to a doctor. His duty does not finish here. He should follow up those cases and see to it that such children are getting due treatment.

The teacher must provide information to the adolescents on the functioning of sex glands as it is very essential for the mental health of the adolescent to be fully acquainted with this aspect. This will keep them on the track and they will not develop wrong notions.

There must be a periodical medical check-up in the school by a qualified doctor. Follow-up is equally important.

These glands do not function in isolation. If they are active normally, they give rise to a balanced personality. In case they are under-active or overactive, they may lead to personality problems and even abnormalities.

Family Factors

These are: (i) Discipline: Protection and rejection etc. (ii) Number of children, (iii) Value placed on the sex of the child, (iv) Step-parents, (v) Nuclear or joint family, (vi) Accommodation in the house, (vii) Parents' ambitions and interests, (viii) Economic, political, religious and social status of the family.

School Environment: This includes:

(i) Curriculum;
(ii) Technology of teaching;
(iii) Co-curricular activities;
(iv) Discipline—constructive, creative and social;
(v) Teachers' personality and their behaviour towards students;
(vi) General tone of the school; and
(vii) Physical environment.

BARRIERS IN THE DEVELOPMENT OF INTEGRATED PERSONALITY

- **Family Circumstances**
  - *Economic*
    - (i) Problem of unemployment or semi-employment
    - (ii) Low economic status
  - *Psychological*
    - (i) Over possessive parents
    - (ii) Unrealistic expectations from childrens
    - (iii) Faulty home discipline
    - (iv) Use of abusive language
    - (v) Lack of role model parents
    - (vi) Unequal parental treatment to siblings
    - (vii) Fear of insecurity
  - *Social*
    - (i) Loss of social status of the family
    - (ii) Broken homes
    - (iii) Fear of insecurity
    - (iv) Some anti-social stigma to the family
- **Personal**
  - Some physical defects
- **School**
  1. Unattractive school environment
  2. Unsuitable curriculum or wrong choice of subjects
  3. Lack of curricular activities
  4. Lack of discipline
- **Teachers**
  1. Unsympathetic teachers
  2. Emotinally unstable teachers
- **Peers**
  1. Undesirable interests and activities of peers
  2. Non-acceptance in the group

INTEGRATION OF PERSONALITY AND THE ROLE OF THE SCHOOL

Meaning of Integration of Personality

Just as a building is more than bricks, cement and wood; similarly, personality is more than basic elements or parts. Personality is formed because of the special relationship among its parts. Personality has an integrated structure. Any change in one part of the structure influences other parts.

Development of the following aspects of the personality must be fully integrated. Unbalanced development of any one of the aspects has an adverse impact on the total development of personality.

(i) Physical structure of the individual,
(ii) Emotional reactions,
(iii) Aspirations,
(iv) Aptitudes,
(v) Attitudes,
(vi) Interests,
(vii) Motivation,
(viii) Intellectual level—thinking, contemplation, reasoning, etc.

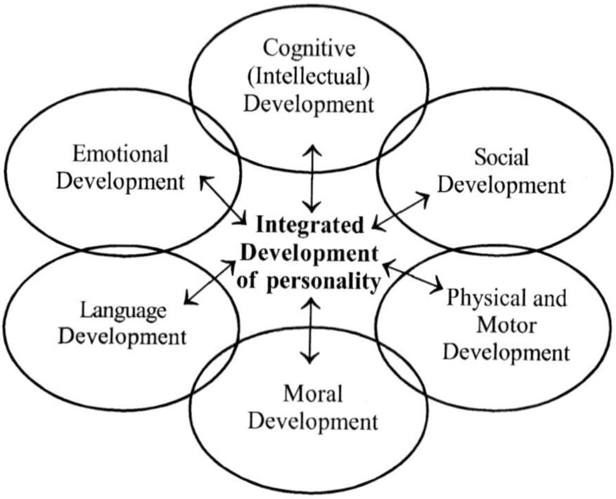

Fig. 14.2: Integrated Personality

Role of the School in the Development of Integrated Personality

An individual of a well-integrated personality is aesthetically refined, culturally rich, emotionally stable, intellectually sound, physically strong, politically wide-awake, religiously pious, socially efficient, spiritually enlightened and vocationally self-sufficient.

Role of the Teachers in Personality Development of the Students

1. Teacher as a 'Spiritual Preceptor' as in the Vedic Period.
2. Teacher as a 'Communicator and Provider of Knowledge'.
3. Teacher as a 'Living Facilitator'.
4. Teacher as a 'Gardener' or 'Directress' of Learning in the Naturalist Movement in Education.
5. Teacher as a 'Manager' of learning activity in the Pragmatic Philosophy of Education.
6. Teacher as an 'Ideal Person' in the Philosophy of Idealism.
7. Teacher as a 'Soldier' and 'Weapon' in Nazism and Communism.
8. Teacher as an 'Agent of Social Change' in the Democratic Philosophy.
9. Teacher as a 'Mediator' between the learner and the subject-matter.
10. Teacher as a 'Transmitter' of cultural heritage.

Chart: School Programmes for the Development of an Integrated Personality of the Learner

(1) Aesthetic Development	(2) Cognitive Development	(3) Emotional Development	(4) Ethical Development	(5) Language Development	(6) Physical Development	(7) Social Development	(8) Spiritual Development
1. Provision of attractive and beautiful physical development. 2. All-round Individual	1. Psychological methods of teaching–learning 2. Provision of varied instructional material 3. Satisfaction of the individual needs	1. Balanced personality of the teacher 2. Environment of love and affection 3. Appropriate disciplinary approach	1. Personal example of the teacher 2. Social Service activities	1. Correct modes of expression by the teacher. 2. Proper check on pronunciation of the students 3. Provision of rich language material	1. Regular physical exercise 2. School health programme 3. Medical inspection 4. Provision of games and sports	1. Stress on group work 2. Equal treatment irrespective of caste etc. 3. Organisation of camps etc. 4. Social service 5. School Self-government	1. Morning Assembly and talks on spiritual matters 2. Yogic training 3. Observance of silance.

11. Teacher as the 'Educational Media User.'
12. Teacher as the 'Spearhead' of change in the society.
13. Teacher as the 'Harbinger' of social change.

Character and Personality of the Teacher: Character and personality of the pupils cannot be developed if the teacher who is the model to be followed lacks character and personality. 'Example is better than precept' is an old saying and is absolutely true in the teaching profession. No amount of sermons from the teacher can make much headway. A teacher teaches not only by 'what he says and does' but very largely by 'what he is'.

'Man Know Thyself' is the advice of Yajnavalkya in India and by Socrates of Greece. The teachers must undergo a spiritual inner training. They should try to find out their own shortcomings and remove them. Ryburn has observed: "Self-analysis on the part of a teacher is a necessary equipment". Montessory stresses that "every teacher worth his salt must destroy these sins: pride, anger, sloth, sensuality and envy. He should be partly a doctor, partly a scientist and completely religious. He must acquire a moral alertness, patience, love and humility". Writing about the role of the teachers, Lauri has observed: "If a teacher has not an ideal aim, he had better to take to shopkeeping at once, he will there doubtless find an ideal within his capacity."

Summing up: There is a limit to the role of the school in the integrated development of the personality of the learner. In the ultimate analysis, it must be stressed that the overall environment of the society has a great bearing on the development of the personality of the learners. In this regard, a great responsibility lies on the role of the leaders, especially political and religious.

15

Suggestive Guidelines for Teachers for the Optimum Development and Education of the Students

These guidelines are to refresh the teachers, inspire them, encourage them and to give proper perspectives for coping with the challenges they face each day both in and out of the classroom. These need to be kept in mind while doing any work.

- Each child has the potential to bloom.
- The best way to develop children is to develop oneself.
- The best way to teach is to learn.
- Realise the dignity of your calling.
- Never threaten the learners.
- Obstacles present choices.
- Use of knowledge is as important as the knowledge itself.
- Curiosity is the seed of knowledge, it must be awakened in the learners.
- Anger is the logical expression of frustration.
- Don't just teach.
- Learn to balance yourself.
- The best example is experience.
- Let early education be a sort of amusement; you will then be able to find out the natural bent of the learners.
- Approach each day with humour.
- Love the learner and the learner will love you.
- Be at peace with yourself before endeavouring to bring peace to others.
- To be a teacher is to wear many hats.
- Children are most interested in those who are interested in them.
- Constant criticism of learners breads despair.
- Hardwork leads to greatness.
- Focus on solutions, not problems.
- A vision without action is but a dream.
- Repetition combined with understanding creates permanent memories.
- Consistent discipline is appreciated and honoured.
- Self-analysis and follow up would pay dividends.
- Manage your time.
- Be gentle, kind and soft but not confused.
- Have a true passion for your subject.
- When teachers turn the key of motivation, they will get much more mileage from the class.

— No matter how often the teacher uses the same brushes and paints, each canvas (student) will be different.
— The difference between memorising and learning is understanding.
— Behaviour is controlled by us, we are not controlled by behaviour.
— Avoid ego as it is the greatest obstacle to reality.
— Make no judgments before tests.
— No single test is an absolute measure of accomplishment.
— In anger and in peace, choose your words.
— Touch children's heart and you will be remembered.
— Touch a child's mind and you will be venerated.
— Students glean much more from actions than from your words.
— Knowledge is never a substitute for experience.
— When authority does not allow children to question anything, the children will question authority.
— It is wonderful when children learn that they can ask questions without fear.
— Interacting with all students during a lesson is the best way to find out how they are doing.
— Seek the promise of the future in the lessons of the past.
— Maturity is achieved when experience becomes the basis for decision.
— Always be positive.
— Courtesy costs nothing; it is the stepladder to respect.
— Self control is a function of self-discipline.
— Be strong and you can bend. Be rigid and you will break.
— Kindness is the one gift that all can afford and all can repay.
— Personality is the clothing, character is the soul.
— The ability to take responsibility is a true sign of strength.
— Community is the basic lesson of the classroom.
— A child can learn strength only from someone who is strong.
— The map of progress has no straight roads.
— When the quest for knowledge ceases, the mind and spirit die.
— Excitement is the bait on teacher hook. If you are to catch the students interest, excite their appetite.
— The great art of teaching consists of knowing how to occupy every moment of teaching-learning.
— A mother gives birth to the child, a teacher gives birth to the mind.
— Order in the classroom depends on self-discipline.
— A teacher who demonstrates character builds character.
— All children begin as children, adult perspective should not be imposed.
— Learning without thought is labour lost; thought without learning is perilous.
— The teacher who loves to learn is an exciting teacher.
— When one stops learning one stops growing.
— For teachers; it is better to get questions than answers.
— Teach students how to ask questions in a manner that leads to the answers.

— Let children learn by stimulating their natural sense of wonder in the world.
— The way to teach the value of life is to 'live' life.
— The mediocre teacher tells. The good teacher explains. The superior teacher demonstrates. The great teacher inspires.
— Welcome new ideas.
— Teach independence in conjunction with obedience.

A TO Z OF TEACHING COMPETENCIES AND SKILLS WHICH MAKE TEACHING-LEARNING EFFECTIVE

'A' is for alertness.

'B' is for business like attitude—keeping students and himself busy in worthwhile tasks.

'C' is for cooperative teaching-learning and clarity of the subject matter.

'D' is for devotion to work and discovering students' potential.

'E' is for enthusiasm expecting children to learn, and evaluating them properly.

'F' is for feedback for the guidance of the learner and the teacher himself.

'G' is for goal setting and achieving.

'H' is for hard work and honest work, humility and humour.

'I' is for involvement of children.

'J' is for judicious attitude, just action and judicious use of praise and blame.

'K' is for knowledge of the students, subject matter and oneself.

'L' is for linking learning with previous learning experience, with daily experience and life activities.

'M' is for motivation.

'N' is for need-based learning and creating novel situations for learning.

'O' is for objectivity and providing out-of-classroom learning experiences.

'P' is for patience and praising children when needed.

'Q' is for quiz-organising for monitoring learning process and appropriate technique of questioning.

'R' is for relationships and review.

'S' is for stimulation.

'T' is for tolerance and the technology of teaching-learning.

'U' is for unbiased attitude and unexpected encounters and situations and facing them efficiently.

'V' is for a variety of learning experiences.

'W' is for warmth for the students.

'X' is for x-ray of the teaching-learning process.

'Y' is for yearning and eagerness for the improvement of teaching-learning.

'Z' is for zeal for the optimum development of the learners.

UNIT II : PHILOSOPHICAL FOUNDATIONS OF EDUCATION

16

Basic Ideas in Education

SIGNIFICANCE OF EDUCATION

According to thinkers in ancient India, *Vidya* or knowledge or learning or education is the 'third eye' of man, which gives him an insight into all affairs and teaches him how to act; it leads us to our salvation; in the mundane sphere it leads us to all-round progress and prosperity. The illumination given to us by *Vidya* shatters illusion, removes difficulties and enables us to realise the true value of life. A person who does not possess the light of education, may be really described as blind. The correct insight, which men and women get from *Vidya*, naturally increases their power and efficiency. The uses of *Vidya* are too diverse to be enumerated exhaustively; it nourishes us like the mother; directs us to the proper path like the father; and gives us delight and comfort like the wife. It increases our fame; and makes us pure and more cultural. When we are in the solitude of a journey, or in a foreign country, it serves us as a valued companion.

According to a Sanskrit verse, education sharpens the intelligence makes our speech truthful, increases our fame, keeps us away from sin, delights us and spreads our name in all directions. It is like *Kalpavriksha*—a veritable desire-yielding tree.

The following verse is a common saying in India.

Swadesh pujayate raja
Vidyavan sarvatra pujyata

(A king is respected in his own kingdom while a learned man is worshipped everywhere).

The *Hindu law* givers observe that the very sight of a learned man is sacred.

The *Rig Veda*, the most ancient book in the world states, "Education is the source of all illumination".

The *Upanishadas* tell us, "Through education one enjoys the fruit of immortality".

Aristotle (384-322 BC), a famous Greek philosopher has said, "Educated men are as much superior to the uneducated as the living to the dead".

Diogenes (4th Century BC), a great cynic Greek philosopher writes, "Education is a controlling grace to the young, consolation to the old, wealth to the poor and ornament to the rich".

Epicetus (1st, 2nd Century A.D.), states "Only the educated are free".

Joseph Addison (1672-1719), an English essayist and poet believes, "What sculpture is to a block of marble, education is to human soul".

The Education Commission 1964-66, the first Commission in independent India which examined all the facets of education at all levels very aptly began its report with these words, "The destiny of India is now being shaped in her classrooms. This we believe, is no more rhetoric. In a world based on science and technology, it is education that determines the level of prosperity, welfare, and security of the people. On the quality and number of persons coming out of our schools and colleges will depend our success in the great enterprise of national reconstruction whose principle objective is to raise the standard of living of our people".

The National Policy on Education 1986 and as slightly modified in 1992 has also observed, "The country has reached a stage in its economic and technical development when a major effort must be made to derive the maximum benefit from the assets already created and to ensure that the fruits of change reach all sections. Education is the highway to that goal". Again it states, "In our national perception education is essentially for all. This is fundamental to our all-round development, material and spiritual. In sum, education is a unique investment in the present and the future".

DIVERGENT VIEWS ON THE MEANING OF EDUCATION

The word education has a very wide connotation. It is like a diamond which appears to be of a different colour when seen from a different angle. Like the concept of the proverbial elephant as described by blind men, an artist, a biologist, an economist, an educator, a philosopher, a political leader, a psychologist, and a sociologist etc. seems to have his own concept and meaning of education which are influenced by his own outlook of life.

ETYMOLOGICAL MEANING OF EDUCATION

Etymologically, the word 'education' is derived from the following Latin words which are briefly explained here:

(i) *Educare*. This means 'to raise', 'to nourish', 'to bring up'.
(ii) *Educere*. This implies 'to draw out', 'to lead out'.
(iii) *Educatum*. This denotes 'to train'.
(iv) *Educo*. 'e' meaning 'out of', and 'duco' meaning 'to lead', 'to lead out'.

Thus education means:

(i) to bring up
(ii) to draw out
(iii) to lead out
(iv) to nourish
(v) to raise
(vi) to train

A synthesis of the meaning of these terms implies that education is drawing out and leading out something from within the individual by bringing up, nourishing, raising and training him.

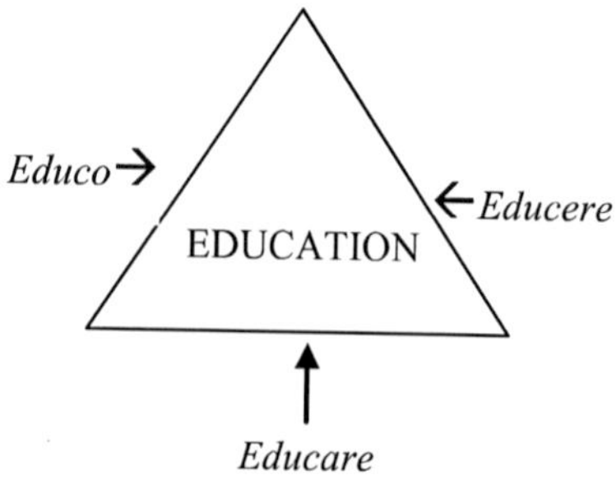

Fig. 16.1: Showing the Origin of the term Education (Derivation or Etymology of Education)

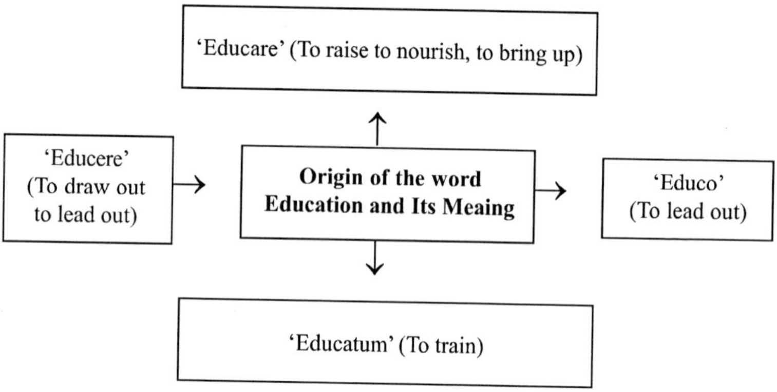

Fig. 16.2: Showing the Origin of the Word Education and Its Meaning

GREAT INDIAN AND WESTERN THINKERS ON THE MEANING OF EDUCATION

A. Views of Great Indian Thinkers on Education

1. *Yajnavalkya* (About 1600 B.C.). Bringing together of the individual and the Supreme.

2. *Chanakya/Kautilya/Vishnu Gupta* (4th Century B.C.). Training for the love of the country.

3. (*Swami*) *Sankaracharya* (788-820 A.D.). Realisation of the self and attainment of *Moksha* (Liberation).

4. (*Guru*) *Nanak Dev* (1469-1539). Enabling an individual to win victory over the five enemies – lust, anger, greed, infatuation and ego (*Kam, Krodh, Lobh, Moh, Ahankar*).

5. *Swami Dayananda* (1824-1893). Formation of character.

6. *Ramakrishna Paramhansa* (1836-1886). Purification of the mind and heart.

7. *Sen., Keshub Chander* (1838-1884). To develop morality.

8. *Gurudev Rabindranath Tagore* (1861-1941). Enabling the mind to find out the ultimate truth.

9. *Swami Vivekananda* (1863-1902). Manifestation of the perfection already in man.

10. (*Mahatma*) *M.K. Gandhi* (1869-1948). All-round drawing out of the best in the child and man—body, mind and spirit.

11. *Gijubhai Badheka* (1885-1939). Fashioning the emotion of the child.

12. *K.M. Munshi* (1887-1974). Making a young man an embodiment of the finest in his culture.

13. *Radhakrishnan Sarvapalli* (1888-1975). Training the intellect, refinement of the heart and discipline of the spirit.

14. *Zakir Hussain* (1897-1969). Helping the mind of the educand to realise absolute moral and intellectual value.

15. *J. Krishnamurti* (1895-1986). Understanding of oneself for it is within each one of us that the whole of existence is gathered.

B. Views of Great Western Thinkers in Education

1. *Socrates* (469-399 B.C.). Dispelling error and discovering truth.

2. *Plato* (427-347 B.C.). Developing the body and the soul of all the perfections which they are capable of.

3. *Quintilian* (38-86 A.D.). Character as the end of education.

4. *Erasmus, Desiderius* (1466-1536). Developing real wisdom.

5. *Montaigue, Michel Eyqueen De* (1533-1592). Cultivating manners, behaviour and judgement than bare and mere liberal learning.

6. *Comenius, John Amos* (1592-1670). Development of the whole man.

7. *Milton, John* (1608-1674). Fitting a man to perform justly, skilfully and magnanimously all the official, both private and public of peace and war.

8. *Locke, John* (1632-1704). Attainment of a sound mind in a sound body.

9. *Kant, Immanuel* (1724-1804). Man-making education.

10. *Rousseau, Jean Jacques* (1712-1878). Development from within.

11. *Pestalozzi, Johann Heinrich* (1746-1827). Natural, harmonious and progressive development of innate powers.

12. *Schiller, Fredrich* (1759-1805). Process of emotional development.

13. *Herbart, Johann Friedrich* (1776-1841). Developing morality.

14. *Froebel, Friedrich* (1782-1852). Leading and guiding for peace and unity with God.

15. *Mann, Horace* (1796-1859). Educating children in the great eternal principle of justice and might which underline the entire length of human existence.

16. *Emerson, Ralph Waldo* (1803-1883). Controlling the mind.

17. *Huxley, Thomas Henry* (1825-1895). Fashioning the will of the individual to enable him to move in harmony with nature.

18. *Parker, Francis Wayland* (1837-1902). Realisation of all the possibilities of human growth.

19. *Ruskin, John* (1819-1900). Developing physical health, manual and moral training.

20. *Spencer, Herbart* (1820-1903). Preparing for complete living.

21. *Tolstoy, Count Leo Nikolayevich* (1828-1910). Providing freedom in learning.
22. *Kilpatrick, William Heard* (1871-1925). Enabling the child full participation in the richest available group life.
23. *Nunn, T. Percy* (1870-1944). Complete development of the individuality of the child so that he can make an original contribution to human life according to the best of his capacity.
24. *Whitehead, Alfred Worth* (1861-1947). Assimilation of general ideas which could be applied to life.
25. *Santayana* (1863-1952). Providing liberal education to a minority and teaching the three R's to the masses.
26. *Tolstoy, Count Leo Nikolayevich* (1828-1910). Providing freedom in learning.
27. *Dewey, John* (1859-1952). Increasing social efficiency.

ANALYSIS OF SOME DEFINITIONS OF EDUCATION

1. One of the oldest treatises on education entitled *The Great Learning*, written around 2,500 years ago and attributed to Confucious, a great Chinese scholar and thinker sets out the meaning, the aim and the process of education in these words, "The great learning consists in manifesting the clear character, loving the people and abiding in the highest grid. Those who wish to make their wills sincere would first extend their knowledge. The extension of knowledge consists in the investigation of things; when things are investigated, knowledge is extended; when knowledge is extended, the will becomes sincere, when the will is sincere, the mind is rectified, when the mind is rectified, the personal life is cultivated; when the personal life is cultivated, the family will be regulated; when the family is regulated, the state will be in order, and when the state is in order there will be peace in the universe". Although this definition does not make clear the meaning of terms like 'will', knowledge and cultivated etc. yet it seems to be an operational one.

2. According to Nunn, "Education is the complete development of the individuality so that he can make an original contribution to human life to his best capacity". The individual is a sum total of various constituents and all these must be developed. Every individual is a unique one and as such the task of education is to cater to the individual needs. The development should take place to the maximum possible extent. This definition takes note of the needs of other human beings also.

3. Thomson says, "By education I mean the influence of the environment upon the individual to produce a permanent change in his habits of behaviour, of thought and of his attitude. Environment has various aspects—physical, social and cultural. Education should facilitate the task of adaptation of the child to his environment". The definition highlights the need for providing a suitable environment.

4. According to Redden, "Education is the deliberate and systematic influence extended by the mature person upon the immature through instruction, discipline and harmonious development of the physical, intellectual, aesthetic, social and spiritual powers of the human being according

to their essential hierarchy by and for the individual and social uses, and directed towards the union of the educand with the creator as the final end". The ultimate goal of life is the union of the individual with God. This union can take place only when the various capacities of the child are developed for the good of the individual as well as that of society.

This definition points out the three-fold function of the educator. One, for the development of powers of the individual. Two, for enabling the individual to become a useful member of the society. Three, for assisting the individual to be one with the Creator. In other words, education should liberate the individual. The objective of life as attainment of '*Moksha*' as advocated by ancient Indian seers is emphasised in this definition.

5. Aristotle's definition neglects the spirit and education is only in terms of creation of 'a sound mind in a sound body'.

6. Gandhiji observed, "By education I mean an all-round drawing out of the best in the child and man—body, mind and soul".

He has also stated, "True education is that which draws out and stimulates the spiritual, intellectual and physical faculties of the children".

The following points bring out the importance of the definition and meaning of education as given by Gandhiji.

Meaning of All-Round: Man is neither mere intellectual nor the gross animal body, nor the heart or soul alone. A proper and harmonious combination of all these is required for the making of the whole man.

Any programme of education that puts exclusive emphasis on one of these aspects of the human personality is against the basic principle of education.

Meaning of the term 'best in man': The best in man is related to three aspects: body, mind and spirit. No field should remain neglected. The best in man will include the harmonious development of all the three aspects or faculties of the child.

'Drawing out' and not 'Pouring in': has been stressed by Gandhiji. He wrote, "We have up to now concentrated on stuffing a child's mind with all kinds of information without even stimulating or developing them". He fully realised that nature has endowed children and youth with tremendous vitality. They have within them the springs of youth, joy and vigour. They have the God-given curiosity to wish to know things for themselves. The task of education is to use these powers. It would be wrong to suppress them. Their energy should be utilised and harnessed properly.

How can we draw out the best?: The best can be drawn out by touching the hearts of children. Gandhiji states, "If I was to be their real teacher and guardian, I must help them to solve the problems that faced them, and I must take along the right channel the surging aspirations of this youth".

Gandhiji further explained the concept of education in his book *Basic Education* as, "I hold that true education of the intellect can only come through a proper exercise and training of the bodily organs, e.g., hands, feet, eyes, ears, nose, etc. In other words an intelligent use of the organs in a child provides the best and quickest way of developing his intellect. But unless the development of the mind goes hand in hand with a corresponding awakening of the soul, the former alone would prove to be a poor lop-sided affair. By spiritual training I mean education of the heart. A proper and an all–round development of the mind, therefore, can take place only when it proceeds *pari passu* with education of the physical and spiritual faculties of the child. They constitute an indivisible whole".

For drawing out the best a suitable environment is needed in the family, the school, the community and the society.

FUNCTIONAL AND OPERATIONAL DEFINITION AND MEANING OF EDUCATION

By education we mean the natural, harmonious and progressive development of man's innate powers by drawing out the best in his body, mind and spirit so as to produce an individual who is culturally refined, emotionally stable, ethically sound, mentally alert, morally upright, physically strong, socially efficient, spiritually enlightened, vocationally self-sufficient and internationally liberal. This should be the end product of education. Any programme of education which puts exclusive emphasis on one of these aspects of the human personality will be considered as lop-sided and narrow. Broadly speaking, this functional and operational definition and meaning should guide us in planning and implementing our educational programmes.

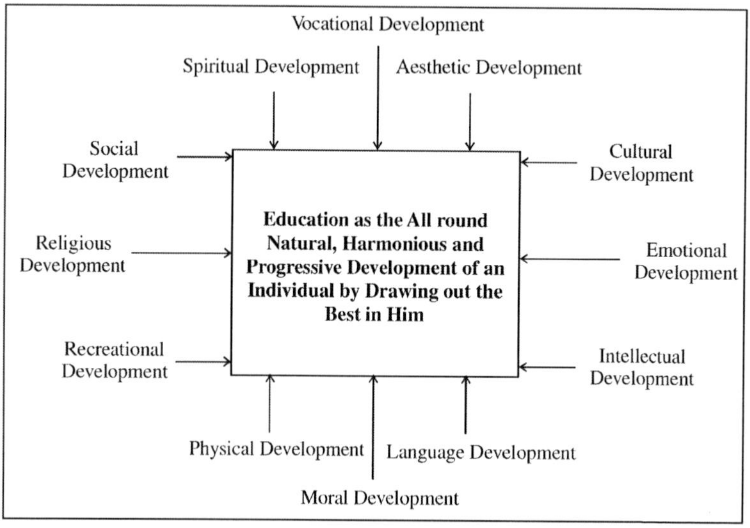

Fig. 16.3: Meaning of Education

SARCASTIC AND NEGATIVE VIEW OF EDUCATION

"We thought the students wanted education, but all that they wanted was a degree".

"We thought they wanted a degree, but all that they wanted was a job".

"We thought they wanted a job, but all that they wanted was work".

"We thought they wanted work, but all that they wanted was money".

"We thought they wanted money, but all they wanted was money through fair or foul means". —*Anon*

Education makes machines which act like men and produces men who act like machines. —*Erich Fromn*

A man who has never gone to schools may steal from a freight car, but if he has university education, he may steal the whole rail road. —*F.D. Roosevelt*

NATURE OF EDUCATION

There are several ways of explaining the nature of education. In this regard following points deserve consideration:

1. Retrospective and prospective nature of education.
2. Nature of education from a broader or wider point of view, i.e., wider or narrow meaning of education.
3. Type of education, i.e., whether formal, informal or non-formal.
4. Direct and indirect form of nature.
5. General characteristics of nature of education.

Classification of Education According to its Nature

- (1) Prospective and Retrospective Nature of Education
- (2) Broader or Narrow view of Nature of Education
- (3) Formal, Non-formal and Informal Nature of Education
- (4) Direct and Indirect Nature of Education
- (5) General Characteristics of Nature

RETROSPECTIVE AND PROSPECTIVE NATURE OF EDUCATION

Education is both retrospective and prospective. It is both conservative and progressive. Education transmits the culture of one generation to another. The rising generation has not only to be conveyed the activities and experiences of the past generation and asked to carry on those activities but it has to be asked to make necessary changes in these activities and experiences to meet the new situations with which it will meet. An integration of the old must take place with the new ones. It must be remembered that the communities live in the present on the past and for the future. This means that activities and experience in the present will guide the activities of the future. Thus education is continuous reorganisation and integration of activities and experiences. Education is a constructive agency for improving our society. Brown has stated, "Education brings changes in behaviour, and if its main functions are to remain mere transmission or enrichment of culture, it will fall short of its role in a dynamic society. Education must also provide situations at all age levels but within the maturity and ability of the individual to stimulate a creativeness of mind which can explore new horizons and bring the vision of the future into a living reality".

Education takes place when new ideas combine with the old. Something new is constructed by the synthesis of the two and this process goes on constantly and through life. Education is growth and growth never stops. We learn in terms of the old. An intelligent order, sequence and continuity is to be maintained as the new thing and best can be learnt in the context of the old one. Herbart's principle of 'appreciation' points out the same fact.

Child is active by nature. He plays and does so many things but these undifferentiated rich and practical experiences, do not lead to education unless they are guided and properly directed. So the experiences of the child should be given coherence, unity and organisation, and education is to be consciously and deliberately planned by providing rich and creative activities and experiences to children. The experiences of the child should be well-knit to give them meaning. Education is to bring about the growth of the educand through experience and activity. Every experience and activity leads to some sort of learning and enrichment of the mind of the learner. These in turn enter into combinations and thus increase the ability of the new learner to direct further noble activities and experiences.

CHIEF CHARACTERISTICS OF THE NATURE OF EDUCATION

Following are the chief characteristics of the nature of education:

1. *Education is Purposive, i.e.,* there is a definite purpose underlying all educational activities.
2. *Education is Deliberate, i.e.,* education involves care and guidance.
3. *Education is Planned, i.e.,* education is not haphazard. It is systematic.
4. *Education is Life-long, i.e.,* education starts from the time of conception and goes on till death—education from cradle to grave as is sometimes said.
5. *Education is Influence Exerted, i.e.,* the mature persons (parents, elders and teachers) influence the learners.
6. *Education is Balanced Development, i.e.,* education is concerned with the development of all faculties of the child.
7. *Education is Bi-polar, i.e.,* both the teacher and the pupil influence each other. Of course, the influence of the teacher is very prominent.
8. *Education is Tri-polar, i.e.,* education involves the teacher, the taught and the environment or the subject-matter.
9. *Education is Psychological as well as Social, i.e.,* the endowments or the capacities of the child—his needs, interests etc. must be interpreted in a social setting.
10. *Education is Growth, i.e.,* education modifies the behaviour of the child.

BROAD AND NARROW MEANING OF EDUCATION

Wider Meaning of Education

It is almost universally accepted that an individual educates himself so long as one breathes. Education of an individual begins from 'conception' and continues till 'cremation'. It goes on from 'womb' to 'tomb' or 'cradle' to 'grave'. Whatever broadens our horizon, deepens our insight, refines our emotions and stimulates our thought and feeling, educates us. It includes all influences, direct and indirect, formal and informal, deliberate or incidental, planned or unplanned. We learn whether we are conscious of this fact or not. Education includes all influences — cultural, domestic, economic, geographical, political, religious, social and spiritual.

According to William H. Kilpatrick, "From the broad point of view all life thoughtfully lived is education".

John Stuart Mill has stated the wider meaning of education in these words, "Not only does education include whatever we do for ourselves and whatever is done for us by others, for the express purpose of bringing us somewhat nearer to the perfection of our nature, it does more, in its largest acceptance, it comprehends even the indirect effects produced on character, and on human faculties, by things of which the direct purposes are quite different, by laws, by forms of government, by the industrial arts, by the modes of social life, nay even by physical facts not dependent on human will, by climate, soil and local position. Every environment, every surrounding, every activity helps to shape the human being. A human soul is in constant interaction with his environment. The interaction results in the modification of human behaviour or education".

R.C. Lodge explains the scope of education in his book *Philosophy of Education* which deserves careful consideration. "In the wider sense, all experience is said to be educative. The bite of a mosquito, the taste of watermelon, the experience of falling in love, of flying in an aeroplane, of being in a storm in a small boat—all such experiences have a direct educative effect on us. The child educates the parents, the pupil educates his teachers... Everything we say, think or do educates us no less than what is said or done to us by other beings, animate or inanimate. In the wider sense, life is education and education is life".

J.S. Mackenzie is of the view, "In the wider sense, it is a process that goes on throughout life and is promoted by almost every experience in life".

Dumvile writes, "Education in its widest sense includes all the influences which act upon an individual during his passage from cradle to grave".

The wider meaning of education includes all the meanings attached to formal, informal and non-formal education.

It is said that a pupil gets one-fourth of his education from his teacher, another fourth by his own intellectual efforts, another fourth from his fellow students and the rest in the course of time through life and experience.

The wider meaning of education includes the following:

1. The process of education is a lifelong process, from infancy to old age or from 'womb to grave'.

2. It includes experiences gained through the various formal and informal agencies of education. We learn from home, school, church, cinema, club, press, travel, friends, physical and social environments.

3. All experience is said to be educative.

4. We receive education many a time when we are not conscious of it.

Narrow Meaning of Education

To quote T. Raymont, "In the narrower sense in which the term is used in common speech and in legal enactments, education does not include self-culture and the general influence of one's surroundings, but only those special influences which are consciously and designedly brought to bear upon the younger by the adult population of the community, whether through the family, the church or the state".

J.S. Mill explains the narrow meaning of education as, "The culture which each generation purposefully gives to those who are to be its successors, in order to qualify them for at least keeping up, and if possible for raising the level of improvement which has been attained".

Prof. Drever explains the narrow meaning of education in these words, "Education is a process in which and by which knowledge, character and behaviour of the young are shaped and moulded".

G.H. Thompson's definition of education indicates the narrow view of education, "The influence of the environment on the individual with a view to producing a permanent change in the habits of behaviour, of thought and attitude".

Narrow meaning of education usually implies imparting information or giving instruction or schooling or training, or making people literate, or teaching or preparing for a trade or vocation.

A.N. Whitehead is right when he says, "A merely well-informed person is the most useless bore on God's earth".

Narrow education includes special and specific influences. Education in a narrower sense means a conscious and deliberate process, well-planned to modify the behaviour of the educand in desirable and socially approved channels and to bring about in the educand specific knowledge and skills. This point is explained as under:

1. Narrow type of education is imparted in planned institutions like schools.
2. It is limited to the teaching of ready-made material.
3. Education is regarded as synonymous with instruction.
4. It is a deliberate, conscious and systematic influence exerted by the mature person, i.e., the teacher, on the immature person, i.e., the child.
5. This type of education is intentional rather than incidental.
6. Knowledge is considered as the accumulated experience of the human race. It is more or less fixed.

WHAT EDUCATION IS NOT AND WHAT EDUCATION IS

1. *Literacy is Not Education*: Literacy is concerned with the traditional 3 R's, that is, reading, writing and arithmetic. It is related to acquiring knowledge of some subjects. Education, on the other hand, is related to 7 R's, that is, reading, writing, arithmetic, rights, responsibilities and their relationships and recreation.

Literacy is mainly concerned with theoretical knowledge which can be evaluated through different types of questions—essay type, short answer type and objective type. But education cannot be evaluated through these techniques. Education provides a way of life. It develops certain values. A person may possess high literacy and even high sounding degrees but he may be labelled uneducated if he lacks human qualities. Education is concerned with the development of character and personality.

2. *Education is not mere Schooling*: Education takes place within the four walls of the school and outside also. Education is not mere spending a few hours in the school and learning some subjects.

3. *Education is not information*: Information must lead to constructive thinking and wisdom.

4. *Education is not instruction*: Instruction is confined to classroom. Education is life-long and ends with death.

5. *Education is not indoctrination*: Indoctrination is confined to a particular belief but education is very broad and leads to broad mindedness.

6. *Education is not merely training of mind*: Education is concerned with the development of body, mind and soul.

FUNCTIONS OF EDUCATION

Education is expected to perform the following functions:

1. Individual development functions.
2. Social development functions.

Individual Development Functions of Education: These functions of education are:

(i) Maximum development of the innate or natural abilities and powers of individuals.
(ii) Development of character and personality of the individuals.
(iii) Preparing individuals for living present life amicably and happily.
(iv) Preparing individuals for taking up gainful employment/self-employment.
(v) Development of suitable leisure time pursuits.
(vi) Development of qualities of followership and leadership.
(vii) Development of emotions of individuals so that they are emotionally stable.

Social Development Functions of Education: These may be stated as:

(i) Development of skills of the individuals that help them to harness the natural resources of the country.
(ii) Development of community sense among the students.
(iii) Conservation of social heritage by providing suitable curriculum to the students.
(iv) Promotion of cultural heritage by broadening the outlook of students.
(v) Involvement of students in community service and welfare activities.
(vi) Development of ideals and values of emotional integration and national unity.
(vii) Development of social awareness.
(viii) Development of values of secularism, socialism and democracy.

CHARACTERISTICS OF THE PROCESS OF EDUCATION

1. *Education. A Tripolar and Multipolar Process*: Education is also regarded as a tripolar process involving the interaction of the personality of the educator on that of the educand in a social setting which affects the modification of the behaviour of the educand. The knowledge of the nature of the educand is at once very useful and essential. Similarly the educator also must thoroughly

understand himself—his assets and limitations and act accordingly in educating the educand. The social setting has to be presented by the educator to the educand in a simplified and purified manner. It must be remembered that the unconscious influence of the environment is subtle and pervasive.

The basic system of education as propounded by Gandhi emphasised three aspects (a) the student, (b) the craft, and (c) the environment—physical and social. Introducing the third element, i.e. the social environment. Dewey has emphasised the society as the source of the curriculum or subjects to be taught. Since all these three poles—the teacher, the pupil and curriculum are important, education is called a tripolar process.

2. *Education. A Deliberate Process*: The process of education is not only conscious but also deliberate. The educator is fully aware of the fact that his aim is to develop the personality of the child along definite lines through the modification of his behaviour.

3. *Education. A Sociological Process*: This implies that the educator must interpret and develop the endowments (capacities) of the child in a social setting. A child is a social being and as such must be educated in such a way that he becomes a useful member of the society.

4. *Education. A Psychological Process*: According to the psychological aspect of the process, the educator must understand the nature, interests, capacities and limitations of the child.

5. *Education. A Child-centred Process*: The modern educator considers the child as a 'hero' in the drama of education and assigns the central place to him. The subject-matter, the teacher and the environment are all for him and not he for them. The child-centred process signifies that the educator must study each child carefully and attend to his individual needs. Since the child is the focus, the school curriculum and environment must provide for his total growth taking into account all the essential areas: the aesthetic, the creative, the ethical, the linguistic, the manual, the mathematical, the physical, the scientific, the social and the spiritual.

6. *Education. A Life Long Process*: Education is a cradle-to-the-grave process, no longer a concentration on the early years. Every year, every month, every day and every minute, step by step a person learns. In the new world no one knows what the morrow will bring. And so every individual must equip himself in every moment of his life to meet the new challenges in life. Education at all stages must become self-education, so that with the tools of education acquired at school, the adult will continue his education throughout life with all the means at his disposal—the library, the reading room, camps, tours, mass media, clubs, institutions, etc. Life long education is acquired through formal, non-formal and informal means of education.

WHY, WHOM, WHO, WHERE, WHAT, HOW AND WHEN OF EDUCATION

1. *Why to Educate*? This includes aims of education. The educator and the educand must be clear about the aims of education so that efforts are made in the right direction. Aims of education depend upon a host of factors: political, economic, social, geographical, religious etc. In a nutshell, education must produce socially efficient individuals.

2. *Whom to Educate*? The educator must understand the educand, i.e., the child thoroughly—his aptitude, interest, temperaments etc. so that the 'best of him' is 'drawn out'.

3. *Who is to Educate*? The teacher is to educate and he must thoroughly understand himself also. He must rid himself of all the blemishes and remember 'Woe to the teacher who teaches one thing with the lips and carries another in the heart'.

4. *Where to Educate*? The child is to be educated in a school which must 'simplify', 'purify' and 'idealise' the environment. Likewise there are several other agencies that supplement school's work.

5. *What to Educate*? This leads to the contents of the curriculum which has been described as 'the environment in motion'. In a broader sense it includes all the courses, readings, associations and activities that go in the school—in the classroom, library, laboratory, workshop, playgrounds and in the numerous informal contacts between teachers and pupils.

6. *How to Educate*? This involves the knowledge and technique of various methods of teaching for making the teaching-learning process dynamic, effective and inspirational.

7. *When to Educate*? This is concerned with the different stages of the child so that 'motivational' aspects may be handled and attended to psychologically.

SCOPE OF EDUCATION

Scope of education is as vast as life itself. There is no aspect or dimension of life which is not covered under education. In fact all education is life and all life is education. Education is a life-long process. Education is formal, non-formal and informal. Likewise agencies of education are formal, non-formal and informal.

Every year, every month, every day, every moment, step by step we learn from every source.

Education is concerned with the aesthetic, cultural, ethical, intellectual, physical, religious, social, spiritual and vocational development of the individual.

Education has moved away from preparing pupils to fit into a particular society but it seeks to make them feel they belong to the larger world family.

17

Types of Education

THREE TYPES OF EDUCATION

Broadly speaking, there are three types of education although with the development of ICT (Information Communication Technology), the difference among these has been declining.

Three types of education are as under:

1. Formal Education
2. Informal Education
3. Non-formal Education

FORMAL EDUCATION

Formal education is imparted in an educational institution—a school or college. In ancient time in India, it was mostly imparted at the residence of the teacher. It is consciously and deliberately planned to bring about specific changes in the educand or the learner. As such it is synonymous with educational institutions. School is the most important agency of formal education.

Important characteristics of formal education are:

1. Planned education keeping in view some definite aim.
2. Education imparted through well-planned means or formal lessons.
3. Education having a definite course to be covered during a definite period.
4. A teaching-learning process with which the teacher and the learner are acquainted.
5. Education organised by some agency, say the Government or the private enterprise.
6. Education imparted in an institution having building/premises.
7. Education starting and ending at a particular age.
8. Education associated with a degree or certificate.
9. Education usually associated with some sort of mental strain on the teacher and the taught.

INFORMAL EDUCATION

Informal education takes into its orbit all indirect influences of the home and the society. The press, the libraries, the films and other such agencies are included as agencies of informal education. Their influence is subtle and imperceptible but at the same time very important and significant.

Important characteristics of informal education are:

1. Unconscious learning.
2. No fixed aim.
3. No fixed curriculum or methods of teaching etc.
4. No organised body or institution behind this process.
5. Life-long learning.
6. Natural outcome.

NON-FORMAL EDUCATION

This is an arrangement wherein flexibility is the key word. The system is an open one with regards to various aspects of education, i.e., admissions, curriculum, place of instruction, mode of instruction and the time and duration of instruction. Open university, open learning, the correspondence courses and distant education are the various examples of such a system.

Important characteristics of non-formal education are:

1. Flexibility in various aspects of education, i.e., admissions, place of education, curriculum, age, co-curricular activities, modes of teaching, evaluation etc.
2. Covering life span of an individual.
3. Guided by motivation of the individual for self-growth, self-renewal.
4. Diversified curriculum responsive to learner and environmental needs.
5. Process of sharing, exploring, analysing and judging with maximum participation of the learner.
6. Preparation for future needs.
7. Part-time education.

Some of the important definitions of non-formal education are:

1. *Bremwork*: "Non-formal education differs from formal education from the point of proximity to immediate action, work and the opportunity to put learning to use".
2. *Coombs*: "Non-formal education is one which is imparted through organisations and institutions outside the formal education institutions."
3. *Harbison*: "Non-formal education is the only means of filling the gap between the 'Schooled' and 'Unschooled population'."
4. *Henderson*: "Non formal education is far wider and more inclusive than schooling which imparts wider experience out of school".
5. *Mc-Call*: "Non-formal education is the entire range of learning experience outside the regular graded school system".
6. *Paulson*: "Non-formal education includes any structured, systematic, non-school educational and training activities of relatively short duration in which sponsoring agencies seek concrete behavioural changes in fairly distinct target population."

Main Characteristics of Non-formal Education

1. *Learner Centred-Education*: It is based on the needs of the learners.
2. *Life-long-Process*: It continues throughout life.

3. *Self-Education*: There is more emphasis on self-education.

4. *Boom for Drop-outs*: It provides suitable opportunities to those who on account of one or the other reason are unable to continue their formal education.

5. *Motivational*: It is motivated by individual growth.

6. *Community Need Based*: It takes note of the needs of the community and accordingly includes a variety of learning programmes.

7. *No Formal Qualifications Needed*: A large number of non-formal educational courses do not need minimum qualifications for entry.

8. *Multi-dimensional*: It provides a variety of opportunities to update one's knowledge and skills.

9. *Supplementary to Formal Education*: It supplements the system of formal education which is rather expensive.

10. *Multi-Agencies*: It is provided by part-time schools, open schools, adult education centres and voluntary agencies.

11. *Flexible System*: It is flexible in terms of hours of study, courses, examinations, duration, etc.

NON-FORMAL EDUCATION AND NATIONAL POLICY ON EDUCATION—NPE (1986 AND REVISED POLICY 1992)

The NPE has assigned an important place to non-formal education at the elementary stage of education and adult education. The programme of Non-formal education as envisaged in the policy in Part 5 is given below:

5.8 (*Revised Para*) *The Non-formal Education Programme, meant for school drop-outs, for children from habitations without schools, working children and girls who cannot attend whole day schools, will be strengthened and enlarged.*

5.8 (NPE, 1986) A large and systematic programme of non-formal education will be launched for school drop-outs, for children, from habitations without schools, working children and girls who cannot attend whole day schools.

5.9 (Revised Para) Modern technological aids will be used to improve the learning environment of NFE Centres. Talented and dedicated young men and women from the local community will be chosen to serve as instructors, and particular attention paid to their training. All necessary measures will be taken to ensure that the quality of non-formal education is comparable with the formal education. Steps will be taken to facilitate lateral entry into the formal system of children passing out of the non-formal system.

5.9 (NPE, 1986) Modern technological aids will be used to improve the learning environment of NFE centres. Talented and dedicated young men and women from the local community will be chosen to serve as instructors, and particular attention paid to their training. Steps will be taken to facilitate their entry into the formal system in deserving cases. All necessary measures will be taken to ensure that the quality of non-formal education is comparable with formal education.

5.10 Effective steps will be taken to provide a framework for the curriculum on the lines of the national core curriculum, but based on the needs of the learners and related to the local environment. Learning material of high quality will be developed and provided free of charge to all pupils. NFE programmes will provide participatory learning environment, and activities, such as, games and sports, cultural programmes, excursions, etc.

5.11 (*Revised Para*) *The Government will take overall responsibility for this vital sector. Voluntary agencies and Panchayati Raj institutions will take much of the responsibility of running NFE programmes. The provision of funds to these agencies will be adequate and timely.*

5.11 (NPE, 1986) Much of the work running of NFE centers will be done through voluntary agencies and panchayati raj institutions. The provision of funds to the agencies will be adequate and timely. The Government will take overall responsibility for this vital sector.

BROAD COMPARISON BETWEEN FORMAL AND NON-FORMAL EDUCATION

	Area	*Formal Education*	*Non-Formal Education*
1.	*Aims*	1. All-round development 2. To get a certificate or degree needed for a job or self-employment	(i) To increase knowledge and skills. (ii) To better qualifications. (iii) To pursue studies for self-satisfaction.
2.	*Place*	An educational institution—school or college—full time.	No specific place is important to learners—can be home, factory, farm, library, open space, etc.
3.	*Learners*	It caters to learners who are in a position to attend full time.	It caters to learners who cannot go to school or have dropped. It also includes learners who want to improve their qualifications by studying at home.
4.	*Age*	Usually prescribed ages.	Any age.
5.	*Grade*	Students are grouped into classes.	Usually no grouping.
6.	*Curriculum*	Rigid and fixed.	Curriculum not fixed.
7.	*Textbooks*	Prescribed textbooks	Usually no prescribed textbooks.
8.	*Examination*	Examination at regular intervals. Written tests. Essay and short answer-questions.	Normally no examination. Assignments.
9.	*Teachers*	Several teachers on full time basis.	Usually part time teachers.
10.	*Methods of Teaching*	Direct teaching methods, Face to face teaching, Lecturing.	Contact programmes, radio, T.V. Correspondence lesson, very little face to face teaching.

(*Contd.*)

	Area	*Formal Education*	*Non-Formal Education*
11.	*Status*	Usually high status.	Usually not considered at par with formal education.
12.	*Period*	It is limited to a period of 'being taught' as against a period of 'life' and 'work'. It is imparted in educational institutions.	It is lifelong with learning integrated with life and work. Life is upgraded and enriched by learning.
13.	*Points of Entry*	It has fixed points of entry and exit. Age of admission and entry qualifications are prescribed.	It has flexible points of entry and exit, re-entry and re-exit and so on throughout the life span of the individual.
14.	*Employment Function*	It is employment-oriented.	It is motivated by individual growth, self-renewal and maximising human potential.
15.	*Interaction*	It is usually imposed by 'giver' on the 'receiver' with little interaction between the two.	It is expected to be a process of sharing, explo-ring, analysing and judging together with participation of the learner.
16.	*Freedom*	It usually fosters an uncritical command obe-dience.	It develops an open-end critical and self-reliant awareness.
17.	*Access*	It works on the principle of weeding out 'failures'.	It works on the principle or universal success through universal learning satisfac-tion.
18.	*Status Quo*	It nurtures the status quo and discourages deviation.	It encourages healthy points of departure towards pro-gress.
19.	*Social Frame-work*	It works within a fixed social frame and hence gets quickly out of step with social change.	It anticipates and prepares for change for the future.
20.	*Environment*	Specially created environ-ment.	Normal Environment.
21.	*Agencies*	Usually full time insti-tutions. They are well-organised.	Usually part-time agencies. They are not well-orga-nised.
22.	*Rules and Regulations*	Rules and regulations are usually rigid.	Rules and regulations are usually flexible.

COMPARISON OF FORMAL AND INFORMAL EDUCATION

	Area	*Formal Education*	*Informal Education*
1.	*Objective*	There is some definite objective to be achieved.	There may or may not be any objective to be achieved.
2.	*Place of Study*	It is imparted in an institution.	There is no definite place. Even the home of the individual student may take the place of education.
3.	*Planning*	It is planned.	It has no definite planning.
4.	*Nature of Course*	There is a definite course to be covered during a definite period.	There is no such definite course and period.
5.	*Type of Lessons*	It is imparted through formal lessons or well-planned means.	It is not imparted through any formal lesson or well-planned means.
6.	*Awareness of the Process*	Both the teacher and the taught are aware of the process through which education is imparted.	The teacher and the taught are not conscious of the process.
7.	*Age*	It starts and ends at a particular age.	There is no age bar.
8.	*Mental Strain*	It puts mental strain both on the teacher and the taught.	Being natural, does not put strain or anybody.
9.	*Organisation*	It is organised by some agency—say the Government or non-governmental institutions.	There may not be any such organisation for the organisation of this type of education.
10.	*Evaluation*	Work of the learner is evaluated from time to time.	There is no evaluation.
11.	*Nature of Contact*	Normally teaching is done face to face.	Education may not be face to face.
12.	*Qualification of Teachers*	Persons who impart training are themselves trained.	No training is needed.
13.	*Time Schedule*	There is a fixed time-table to be followed.	No fixed time-table is followed.
14.	*Rules and Regulations*	There are definite rules and regulations.	There are no rules and regulations.

(*Contd.*)

	Area	*Formal Education*	*Informal Education*
15.	*Degree or Diplomas*	It involves granting of a degree or diploma.	No degree or diploma is awarded.
16.	*Discipline*	Students are expected to observe a definite type of discipline.	There is no such requirement.
17.	*Period of Schooling/ Stages/Classes*	Period of Schooling is fixed	It is a life long process. It has neither any end nor beginning. It continues for the whole life.

COMPARISON AMONG FORMAL, INFORMAL AND NON-FORMAL EDUCATION

	Area	*Formal Education*	*Informal Education*	*Non-formal Education*
1.	*Aim*	It has definite aims.	It has no definite aim.	It has mostly clear-cut aims.
2.	*Scope*	Its scope is definite.	Its scope is not definite.	Its scope is generally definite.
3.	*Duration*	It begins from school and goes up to university.	It is life long.	It can be life-long.
4.	*Entry Points*	It has fixed entry points.	It has no entry point.	Entry points are flexible.
5.	*Agencies*	It is provided usually in full time educational institutions.	It has no definite agencies.	It is normally available through part time institutions.
6.	*Organisation*	It is an organised and planned effort. There is usually a recognised organisation, which is more or less permanent.	There is no organisation for it.	Organisation may not be a permanent one. Ad-hoc organisations usually take up this work.
7.	*Time Schedule*	Its schedule is fixed.	It has no fixed schedule.	Schedule fixed as well as not fixed.
8.	*Conscious*	The teacher and the learners are aware of the process.	Unconscious process.	It is partly conscious.
9.	*Methodology*	Format, fixed and a variety of methods.	There is no set methodology.	Flexible approach is followed.

(*Contd.*)

	Area	*Formal Education*	*Informal Education*	*Non-formal Education*
10.	*Teachers*	Trained teachers impart education.	It can be obtained from any source.	Trained teachers/ instructors impart non-formal education.
11.	*Place*	It is confined to the four walls of educational institutions.	It can be acquired at any place.	It mostly takes place outside the four walls of educational institutes.
12.	*Environment*	Environment is more or less artificial.	Environment is natural.	Environment is artificial as well as natural.
13.	*Curriculum*	Curriculum is fixed.	There is no curriculum.	Curriculum is very flexible.
14.	*Discipline*	Discipline is normally strict.	Issue of discipline does not exist.	Discipline is rather flexible.
15.	*Resources Required*	Relatively higher resources are needed.	Resources are not needed.	Comparatively less resources are required.
16.	*Evaluation and Examination*	Examination are regularly held.	There is no examination.	Examination are not frequent.
17.	*Award of Certificates and Degrees*	Certificate and degrees form an integral part.	Certificate/degree is not given or received.	Certificate or degree may or may not be awarded.
18.	*Mental Stress*	It involves lot of mental stress.	No mental strain is involved.	Usually no mental strain is involved.
19.	*Motivation*	The teachers and learners are motivated.	Motivation is not involved.	Normally motivation on the part of the learners is quite high.
20.	*Interaction*	There is face to face interaction which is quite visible.	Interaction is incidental.	Interaction depends upon the situation.
21.	*Pass/Failure*	Students are labelled 'passed' or 'failure'.	Pass/Failure does not exist.	Normally it does not work on the principle of weeding, not failures.
22.	*Planning*	It is a planned system.	No planning is required.	Planning is flexible.

EXAMPLES OF DIFFERENT TYPES OF EDUCATION

	Types of Education	*Examples*
1.	Formal Education	School, College
2.	Non-formal	Radio, TV, Press etc.
3.	Informal	Social gatherings. Entire environment. Unconscious learning. Through imitation. Sitting on the table within a group. Street and market place.

NARROWING DOWN THE GAP BETWEEN DIFFERENT TYPES OF EDUCATION

The revolution in information and communication technology (ICT) and its use in the teaching-learning process has narrowed down the difference. The use of computers, radio and TV has introduced several elements of formal education into informal and non-formal education and vice versa. At one time radio and TV were used only for the purpose of non-formal education. Now they are being used in a planned way for formal education. In fact there is a special TV channel for this purpose. It is estimated that at the higher education level, nearly 10 per cent enrolment is through Distance Education/Open Education. New Slogans like 'Open Learning', 'University Without Walls', and 'Virtual University' are taking the place of formal education which at one time was confined to the 'four walls' of the school/ college. Use of Internet for educational purposes has become very popular. CDs on different subjects are available now. Students have the opportunities of pursuing their studies in their bedrooms. They can get University Degrees without visiting any place or even without coming into personal contact with the teachers. Students can complete their degrees without any prescribed schedule.

A BALANCED VIEW

We should try to avert the danger of education being isolated from the subject-matter of life experience. Hence one of the weightiest problems with which the philosophy of education has to cope with is of keeping a proper balance between the informal and the formal and the non-formal modes of education. Hence we should try to incorporate the good points of non-informal education as far as we can. The formal education makes it easier to bridge the gulf between the immature nature of the child and the demands of the society. The non-formal education helps to bridge the gulf between the education imparted in the school and the education needed to lead a successful life as a member of the community.

TRADITIONAL EDUCATION AND MODERN EDUCATION AT A GLANCE

	Aspect	*Traditional Education*	*Modern Education*
1.	*Aim*	Knowledge of 3 R's—Reading, Writing and Arithmetic, i.e., knowledge of subjects.	1. Training in 7 R's, i.e. Reading, Writing and Arithmetic, i.e., Teaching of subjects, Rights, Responsibilities and Relationship. 2. Development of total personality. 3. Social efficiency.
2.	*Function*	Broadly religious	Broadly social
3.	*Contents/Curriculum*	Subjects-centred	Subjects and experiences
4.	*Agencies*	Family, school and church etc.	School, several agencies, mass media.
5.	*Teacher*	Autocrat, policeman	Democrat, humanist.
6.	*School*	A Place for the pouring in of knowledge	1. Place for training in citizenship and democracy. Art of living together. 2. Idealised miniature society.
7.	*Child*	Like dumb-driven cattle, passive.	Human being. Active.
8.	*Individual differences*	Not recognised.	Utmost consideration to individual differences.
9.	*Methods of teaching.*	Bookish, memorisation, mechanical.	Dynamic and challenging. Question-answer. Project method, Discovery method, etc.
10.	*Courses*	Usually single track.	Diversified
11.	*Life experiences*	Very few	Related to life.
12.	*Media*	Mainly chalk and board.	New Media also.
13.	*Discipline*	Rule of the 'rod'	Self and social discipline.
14.	*Examination*	Rigid. Essay type.	Comprehensive and continuous, objective, tests, etc.
15.	*Chief concern*	Religious and spiritual	1. Sociological. 2. Several new concerns like environmental education and population education, etc. 3. New technologies.

EMERGING CONCERNS AND MODERN EDUCATION

The world has never changed so rapidly as in recent years. Eminent thinkers in the world began to contemplate in the 1990s on the emerging modern society and its impact on the modern education. UNESCO took the lead and in 1993 appointed an International Commission on Education for the 21st Century to consider the various dimensions of modern education. The Commission gave its report in 1996.

Major Issues Confronting the Society and Consequently Education

According to the Commission, modern education must take note of the following:

1. Tension between the global and local situations.
2. Tension between the universal and the individual.
3. Tension between tradition and modernity.
4. Tension between long term and short term considerations.
5. Tension, on the one hand the need for competition and on the other, concern for equality of opportunity.
6. Tension between the extraordinary expansion of knowledge and human beings capacity to assimilate it.
7. Tension between the spiritual and the material.

CHILD-CENTRED EDUCATION AND TEACHER-CENTRED EDUCATION

	Dimensions	*Child-Centred Education*	*Teacher-Centred Education*
1.	Goals	Goals set by the learner with assistance and the guidance by the teacher to meet the diverse needs as they evolve.	Goals set by the teacher in advance to meet the needs that he has anticipated.
2.	Approach	Discovery and experience approach to learning. Situations and resources provided by the teacher for the learner to generate, experience and discover ideas for himself.	Information and ideas put over to the child by the teacher.
3.	Homogeneity	Wide variety of activities at any one time. Various learners doing different activities suiting their needs at that point of time.	Same learning experiences for all students at any one time. All learners attend the same sessions and do the same things.
4.	Sequencing	Very flexible sequence. Sequence not determined in advance but according to the felt need of the learner. Similar items may be learned in different sequences by different learners.	Sequences or order fixed in advance. Sequences are determined according to the preferences of the teacher.

(*Contd.*)

	Dimensions	*Child-Centred Education*	*Teacher-Centred Education*
5.	Control	Decisions made by learners or jointly by the learners and the teacher. Hence joint control over the course.	Decisions made by the teacher and he maintains control over the course.
6.	Method	Wide variety of learning-teaching methods. Methods usually selected by the learners.	Relatively few teaching-learning methods. Methods selected by the teachers.
7.	Learner tutor relationship.	Very close, open, personal relationship.	Distant. Closed. Formal relationship.
8.	Group attitude	Trusting, supportive. Close relationships.	Not quite trusting. Not very supportive. Learners relatively distant from each other.
9.	Feelings	Full expression	Very restricted expression of feelings.
10.	Discipline	Free. Full of freedom.	Strict. Do's and Don'ts.

18

Aims and Objectives of Education

AIMS OF EDUCATION RELATED TO SOCIETY

A.K.C. Ottaway has rightly stated, "Education is an activity which goes on in a society and its aims and methods depend on the nature of the society in which it takes place". Likewise Clark has observed, "No writer on education, however, much he may strive after universality of thought can wholly shake himself free from the influence of time and space".

Aims are related to real situations of life. Education to be effective must meet the many-sided needs of the society. A child is not to be educated in a vacuum. He is a member of the society in which he lives and education must help him to become a useful member of that society.

Since, economic, physical, political, religious and social needs differ from place to place, from time to time and country to country, the educational aims also differ.

1. *Economic Factors*: Formal education is possible where production exceeds consumption. This may be the result of tremendous industrial development or favourable natural circumstances. This will depend upon fertility of soil, abundant mineral deposits and proper climatic conditions for work. Such conditions provide men with leisure to pursue education. Where there is a subsistence economy, it is a far cry to afford time for formal schooling. This is the reason why poorer and undeveloped countries have a minimum education for their children while industrially advanced countries afford to keep nearly all their children at school and for a longer time.

2. *Geographical Factors*: Educational system in ancient Greek States presents an interesting study. Education in Sparta aimed at developing physical strength, courage and endurance and obedience because the immediate aim was to train the Spartan youth as soldiers who could protect the state from foreign aggression. Athian education on the other hand was finer.

3. *Political Factors*: Political ideologies go a long way in determining the aims and the system of education. Different political ideologies like egalitarian or fascist communist or socialist and democratic will call for different systems of education.

The ruled nations had a different educational system than their rulers as they were being exploited by their rulers. The system of British education was implanted in this country from purely political motives.

4. *Religious Factors*: The influence of religion is very powerful as it

penetrates the emotional depth of human nature. The Brahmanic system of education, the Buddhist education and the early Mohammedan education were dominated by religion. Similarly in Europe, the Protestant countries were wedded to the education of the masses and the Catholic countries to the education of the classes.

5. *Social Factors*: Education reflects the social pattern of society. The tremendous explosion of science and technology has shaken the old leisurely outlook on life and has created intricate problems of social adjustment. A new emphasis has been placed on literacy. A growing interest is shown in reorganising the curricula at all stages. The new forces in the social structure of the Indian society have provided a fresh incentive for educationists to pattern the educational system.

Aim of Education in Primitive Societies

In ancient times men needed training in the use of bows and arrows for their safety. Their needs were simple and few. The process of production, consumption, distribution and exchange was quite simple. Thus, the educative needs were also simple and these could be met by a process of education which was also very simple.

Aim of Education in a Totalitarian State

The aims of education are determined by the political ideologies. J.F. Brown says, "Education in any country and at all periods reflects ideologies of the ruling class". There are many instances in the history of the world when persons with different ideologies from their rulers were threatened, sacked, and even assassinated. In Russia, the individual was to be trained in a way so as to become a Communist, in Germany a Nationalist Socialist and in Italy a Fascist. The aim of education is to force upon every individual an ideology which he must not question. The creed will be reflected in the curriculum, syllabi, methods, and techniques of education.

Aim of Education in Ancient India

Education in ancient India was in the hands of the Brahmans, and religion played an important role in the life of an individual. Indian education aimed at inculcating a spirit of piety and righteousness. Education constituted a real training for living life according to spiritual and moral values.

Aim of Education in Medieval India

The aim was religious and the educator was required to produce pious and religious minded people. Maktabs and Madarsas were the places where education was imparted. These institutions were generally run in mosques.

Aims of Education in British India

There was a radical change in the aims of education with the advent of British rule in India. Lord Macaulay laid down the aims of education in the Famous Minutes of 1835. The aim of the educational system was to train an army of individuals who could assist the Britishers in the administration of this country. Macaulay wanted an educational system which might bring about the cultural conquest of the people of India by the British.

Aims of Education in Free India

The ideals and values embodied in the Preamble to the Constitution of India are the guiding sources of educational aims in India. These may be expressed as under:

1. Development of democratic values.
2. Development of egalitarian values.
3. Development of secular values.
4. Development of values related to dignity of individual.
5. Development of values conducive to the unity of the country.
6. Development of the capacity of the individual to earn his livelihood.
7. Development of the capacity of an individual to increase national product.

General Aims of Education

1. Aesthetic aim.
2. Complete living aim.
3. Cultural aim.
4. Harmonious and all-round development aim.
5. Happiness aim.
6. Individual aim.
7. International understanding aim.
8. Knowledge aim.
9. Leisure aim.
10. Moral aim.
11. Physical health and well-being aim.
12. Political aim.
13. Religious aim.
14. Self-realisation aim.
15. Social aim.
16. Spiritual aim.
17. Vocational aim.

Summing up: Education to be effective cannot have a single aim. An ideal balance among various aims has to be struck.

INDIVIDUAL AIM AND SOCIAL AIM IN EDUCATION

Individual Aim in Education

The individual aim in education has found support from the following:

1. *Individual Aim and the Biologists*: Prof. G. Thompson has observed, "Education is for the individual: its function being to enable the individual to survive and live out his complete life".

2. *Individual Aim and the Naturalists*: In the words of Rousseau, the most ardent supporter of the individual aim in education, "Everything is good as it comes from the hands of the Author of Nature". Accordingly, he and others

who also think likewise advocate that education should be in accordance with the nature of the individual.

3. *Individual Aim and the Psychologists*: According to psychologists, each individual is a unique one and accordingly education should develop the innate powers of the individual.

4. *Individual Aim and the Spiritualists*: The Spiritualists are of the view that every individual is a separate identity and responsible for his own actions. Therefore, the main aim of education is to lead the individual to his self-satisfaction.

Criticism of the Individual Aim of Education

1. The critics of individual aim believe that the individual left to himself will be selfish and indisciplined. The animal instinct of man, if given, a loose region is sure to lead him to the state of primitive barbarism where the law of jungle prevailed.

2. The exaggerated claim of the individual may have an adverse effect in the politics and economy of a country. The policy of *Laissezfaire* is not conducive to national interests in the modern times.

3. Absolute freedom to the individual should not be given. The individual may begin to assert that I must have what I want.

4. According to Raymont, an individual is only a figment of imagination. An individual cannot be conceived in isolation from society.

Supporters of Social Aim in Education

1. Gandhiji formulated the basic scheme with the objective of making people realise that education was not merely for the benefit of the individual but for the needs of a predominantly rural and agrarian population.

2. According to John Dewey, social aim in education is stressed as education should make each individual socially efficient, and this social efficiency must be achieved by the positive use of individual powers and capacities in social occupations. A socially efficient individual is not a drag or parasite on society or any individual. A socially efficient individual is able to earn his livelihood. He also conforms to moral and social standards of conduct.

3. Raymont says that the isolated individual is "a figment of the imagination". The individual being a social animal, will be moulded to the needs of the society. The individual will develop through social contacts.

4. According to the Education Commission 1964-66, "Education cannot be considered in isolation or planned in a vacuum. It has to be used as a powerful instrument of a social, economic and political change and will, therefore, have to be related to the long-term national aspirations, the programmes of National Development in which the country is engaged and the difficult short-term problem it is called upon to face".

Limitations of Social Aims of Education

1. Social aim of education envisages the individual as a non-entity and leaves little scope for his personality development.

2. Extreme form of social aim has led to the concept. "My country! Wrong

or right" This emphasis became responsible for the rise of Nazism in Germany and Fascism in Italy. As a result of this, Second World War took place.

3. Undue stress on social aim of education is against the concept of universal brotherhood.

Synthesis Between Individual and Social Aim of Education

The individual and the society, both be regarded as realities. Neither of the two is absolutely independent of the other. Instead of being regarded as isolated entities, the individual and the society should be considered as functionally related to each other—the individual acting on the society, and the society reacting on the individual. The individual is the product of society which the society in its own turn finds its advancement in the development of its individual members. In the words of John Adam, 'Individuality requires a social medium to grow. Without social contacts we are not human."

According to Ross, "Individuality is of no value and personality is a meaningless term apart from the social environment in which they are developed and made manifest". Self-realisation can be achieved only through social service and social ideas of real value can come into being only through free individuals who have developed valuable individuality. The circle cannot be broken.

PRIORITIES OF AIMS OF EDUCATION IN INDIA

Aims of Education in Accordance with the Nature of Indian Society

The Indian Constitution with its statements contained in the Preamble, Fundamental Rights and Directive Principles form the chief sources of aim of education in India.

The goals placed before the people by the Constitution are those of a democratic society which recognises the dignity and the basic rights of the individual and holds the promise of an order in which social, political and economic justice and equality will prevail.

The salient features of the Indian society as envisaged in the Constitution are:

1. Indian society must be based on the principles of secularism, socialism and democracy.
2. Indian society must be based on justice: social, economic and social.
3. Indian society must provide for liberty of thought, expression, belief, faith and worship.
4. Indian society must be based on equality of status and opportunity.
5. Indian society must be based on fraternity, assuring the dignity of the individual and the unity of the nation.
6. Indian society must provide a reasonable standard of living to its members.

Brief History of Aims of Education in India

As stated from time to time the first attempt to list aims of education in India was made by the University Education Commission (1948-49). The aims were confined to higher education only. Besides, these were formulated before the commencement of Indian Constitution. The second attempt was made by the Secondary Education Commission (1952-53). These related to secondary education only.

The Education Commission (1964-66), popularly known as the Kothari Commission went into reforms of all aspects of education including aims of education.

The Education Commission suggested the following aims of education:

1. Vocational aim for increasing productivity.
2. Character development, i.e., development of moral, social and spiritual values.
3. National and emotional integration aim.
4. Democratic aim.
5. Modernisation of Indian society through awakening of curiosity.

Character Development Aim of Education

A man of character is bound to be liberal, appreciative of his duties and responsibilities towards himself and the society and to remain above the sectarian, regional and religious considerations. He follows the values of secularism, socialism and democracy. Therefore, character formation is the first aim of education in India.

Character has two facets: the one which is personal, and the other which manifests itself in our relationship with society. Both these aspects should be pure and unsullied.

Gandhiji has observed, "All our learning or recitation of the Vedas, correct knowledge of Sanskrit, Latin, Greek and what not will avail us nothing if they do not enable us to cultivate absolute purity of heart. The end of all knowledge must be building up of character". Raymount states, "The teacher's ultimate concern is to cultivate, not wealth of muscle, nor fullness of knowledge, nor refinement of feeling, but strength and purity of character". According to Vivekanand, "The end of all education, all training should be man making". John Dewey has said, "All education forms character–mental and moral". The Secondary Education Commission has observed, "Education is the training of character to fit the students to participate creatively as citizens".

Character is the product of daily, hourly actions and words and thoughts; daily forgiveness, unselfishness, kindness, sympathies, charities; sacrifices for the good of others, struggles against temptations. What is character without elementary personal purity?

In India today we find a lack of character at various levels so much so that the actions of the V.I.P.'s also create doubts in the mind of the common man. State of affairs is very shocking. The present saying is 'As the ruler, so the people'. Perhaps after independence, morality or character has been the greatest causality. Education, therefore, must be devoted to character building activities.

Vocational Aim of Education

Moral or character formation aim of education is also one-sided. An individual must be prepared to earn his livelihood otherwise he will not be a happy man. Of course, values of life must not be sacrificed for "bread and butter".

Gandhiji has also supported the vocational aim. He observed, "True education ought to be for them (boys and girls) a kind of insurance against unemployment". The vocational aim is also called the "bread and butter aim". It can train individuals to become socially efficient. They will, therefore, neither be drags nor parasites on the society. They will contribute to increase production and national wealth. The advocates of the vocational aim argue that all the knowledge a pupil gains in the school, all the culture the pupil acquires in the school will be of no use, if he cannot make both ends meet when he enters life.

Synthesis of Character Formation and Vocational Aim of Education

Vocational aim in education has its own importance but man does not live by bread alone. Education must take into consideration the entire personality of the pupil and not one segment of it. Man has to develop himself aesthetically, intellectually, morally, physically and socially. The University Education Commission 1948-1949 has very rightly observed, "If we wish to bring about a savage upheaval in our society, a *Rakshas Raj*, all that we need to do is to give vocational and technical education to starve the spirit. We will have number of scientists without conscience, technicians without taste, who find a void within themselves a moral vacuum and a desperate need to substitute something, anything for their lost endeavour and purpose".

Pt. Nehru has stated, "Education has mainly two aspects, the cultural aspect which makes a person grow, and the productive aspect which makes a person do things. Both are essential. Everybody should be a producer as well as a good citizen and not a sponge on another person even though the other person may be one's own husband or wife". Gandhiji, it is true, stressed the vocational aspect but at the same time he was very emphatic, "By education, I mean an all-round drawing out of the best in child and man-body, mind and spirit". He was convinced that without character, vocational efficiency had no meaning.

FUNCTIONS AND DIRECTIONS OF EDUCATION IN INDIA

General Functions of Education in Life. Education is expected to perform the following functions:

1. Development of natural abilities of individuals.
2. Development of such capacities in the individuals that help them to harness the natural resources of the country.
3. Development of character.
4. Development of personality.
5. Preparation for living present life.
6. Preparation for adult life and future life.
7. Sublimation of instincts.
8. Creation of socially efficient individuals.
9. Development of community sense.
10. Conservation and promotion of culture and civilisation.
11. Involvement in social welfare.

12. National development.
13. Development of suitable leisure time activities.
14. Developing values of emotional integration.
15. Developing universal brotherhood.

Factors Influencing Functions and Directions of Education in India

As already observed, educational systems is to be transformed in such a way as it fully meets the requirements of a society as envisaged in the Constitution of India. Among the important characteristics of the Indian society are to be (i) Democratic, (ii) Socialist, (iii) Secular, (iv) Modern. Inherent in these are the concept of a welfare state, i.e., raising the standard of living can be improved only with increased production and equitable distribution of wealth. All this demands that education in India should be geared to perform the functions as discussed here.

1. *Social Development*: An individual is social by nature. He always resides and works in society. He has to live and act in the society as a social being. Education, therefore, must aim at social development. The social development finds expression in such concepts as 'education for social service' and 'education for social efficiency'.

2. *Education for Human Resource Development*: The Education Commission 1964-66 has described the situation as "There can be no hope of making the country self- sufficient in food unless the farmer himself is moved out of his age-long conservation through a science-based education, becomes interested in experimentation, and is ready to adopt techniques that increase production. The same is true of industry. The skilled manpower needed for the relevant research and its systematic application to agriculture, industry and other sectors of life can only come from a development of scientific and technological education. Similarly, economic growth is not merely a matter of physical resources or of training skilled workers, it needs the education of the whole population in new ways of life, thought and work".

3. *The Development of Physical Resources of the Country*: This can be made possible through the modernisation of agriculture and rapid industrialisation. This requires the adoption of a science-based technology, heavy capital formation and investment and the provision of the essential infrastructure of transport, credit, marketing and other institutions.

4. *Education for the Development of Skills*: Our principal potential asset is our people. Whether using a plough, driving a truck, designing a steel mill or typing business letters, the human factor is common and vital to all branches of economics activity. Education has an essential role to play in the structure and effectiveness of the country's work force. Education is indispensable in all occupations as it develops proper insight. As economic and productive activities expand there is a greater need for educated people to design, plan, supervise, manufacture, sell and administer. Services of all kinds grow in step with industry. All services need educated personnel for operation and administration.

5. *Education Ensuring Equality of Opportunity*: The National Policy on Education, 1986 has observed, "the New Policy will lay special emphasis on

the removal of disparities and to equalise educational opportunity by attending to the specific needs of those who have been denied equality so far".

6. *Democratisation of Education and the Involvement of People*: Democratising education does not only mean giving more education to more people, but also involving more people in educational management.

7. *Meeting the Needs of an Egalitarian Society*: Education should develop such attitudes and values in the citizens of India so that they contribute to the building of an egalitarian society.

8. *Development of Secular Values*: Education must inculcate such values as are helpful in appreciating the diverse religious points of view and harmonising them.

19

Educational Philosophy

SIGNIFICANCE OF PHILOSOPHY

Philosophy is so deeply involved in human life that Aristotle (384-322 BC), the great Greek Philosopher remarked, "Everyone follows a philosophy, whether he is aware of it or not".

Thousands of years ago, Indian seers and thinkers developed a very comprehensive and well-organised system of philosophy for the guidance of the individual.

Francis Bacon (1561-1626), an English philosopher considered philosophy as the 'great' mother of all sciences.

The subject matter of philosophy is as wide as human experience. It is as old as human life. There is no aspect of life, natural or unnatural, animate or inanimate which falls outsides its domain.

Human beings—primitive or civilised, educated or uneducated, plodding or brilliant cannot escape from philosophy. Aldous Huxley (1894-1963) in his book *Ends and Means* has remarked, "Every human being has a philosophy of his own, good or bad, high or low, purely individual or common with others". He has further observed, "Men live in accordance with their philosophy of life, their concern of the world, this is true even of the most thoughtless".

German Philosopher Schopenhauer (1788-1860) remarks "Every man is a born meta-physician". Different fields of philosophy are: economic philosophy, educational philosophy, moral philosophy, physical philosophy, political philosophy and social philosophy.

MEANING AND DEFINITION OF PHILOSOPHY

Sanskrit word *Darshan* (philosophy) means 'direct perception' of the truth. Seers of ancient India used to see or perceive the truth. The same may be said about Socrates (469-399 B.C.), Plato (427-347 B.C.) and Aristotle (384-322 B.C.)—trio of Greek philosophy.

The word 'philosophy' has a Greek origin. '*Philosophia*' a Greek word consists of two words, i.e. '*phileo*' meaning love and '*sophia*' meaning wisdom. Therefore, the literal meaning of philosophy is 'love of wisdom'.

The following definitions of philosophy help us to understand the true meaning of philosophy.

1. *Aristippus* (435-356 B.C.) thinks that philosophy is "the ability to feel at ease in any society".

2. According to *Plato* (472-347 B.C.) "He who has a taste for every sort of

knowledge and who is curious to learn and is never satisfied may be justly termed as a philosopher". He has also observed, "Philosophy begins in wonder".

3. According to *Aristotle* (384-322 B.C.), "Philosophy is a science which discovers the real nature of supernatural elements".

4. According to *Cicero, Marcus Tullius* (106-43 B.C.) "Philosophy is the mother of all arts and "the true medicine of mind".

5. *Kant* (1724-1804) regards philosophy as "the science and criticism of cognition".

6. *Kant Immanuel* (1724-1804) regards philosophy as "the science and criticism of cognition".

7. In the words of *Fichte*, (1762-1814), "Philosophy is the science of knowledge".

8. *Coleridge, Samuel Taylor* (1772-1834) defined it as the "Science of Science".

9. *Curtis, George William* (1824-1892) states, "During the course of centuries, the meaning attached to philosophy has undergone many changes, and even in the present day, thinkers, are not in complete agreement about the aims and subject-matter of this branch of knowledge".

10. *Russell, Bertrand* (1872-1970) states, "Philosophy is to be studied not for the sake of any definite answers to its question... but rather for the sake of the questions themselves, because these questions enlarge our conception of what is possible... but above all because the mind also is rendered great and becomes capable of that union with the universe which constitutes its highest goal".

11. *Radhakrishnan, Sarvapalli* (1888-1975) considers philosophy as "a logical inquiry into the nature of reality".

12. *Huxley, Aldous* (1894-1963) observes, "Men live in accordance with their Philosophy of Life".

13. *Kabir, Humayun* (1902-1969) states that philosophy "seeks to give knowledge of the whole".

14. *Dumery, H.* in his book '*The Problem of God* (1964)' defines philosophy as a "critical reflection on concrete action".

15. *Prof M. Verma* in book '*The Philosophy of Indian Education* (1969) has explained it as, "(the)... Indian term, *Darshana* as an equivalent to philosophy literally means 'seeing'. The simple physiological act of seeing implies the seen and the 'seer' which is comparatively a good word for the Indian significance of the word philosopher. The 'seeing' is a vision of the entire experienced reality, it is all encompassing, for it is the vision of truth itself". According to Prof. Verma, the term 'philosopher' requires in its derived European sense an intelligent and coherent accounting of the experience of life. It can he arrested at the intellectual level and remain a matter of logical argument. *Darshana* has an extra implication; it includes a 'realisation' an experience of the 'postulated truth' which takes it beyond mere polemics.

16. *Henderson* (1947) thinks that philosophy is a research for "a comprehensive view of nature, an attempt at a universal explanation of the nature of things".

17. In the words of *Bramold*, "Philosophy is a persistent effort of both ordinary and persistent people to make life as intelligible and meaningful as possible".

18. *R.W. Sellers* has defined philosophy in these words, "Philosophy is a persistent attempt to gain insight into the nature of the world and ourselves by systematic reflection".

19. According to *Brightman*, "Philosophy may be defined as the attempt to think truly about human experience".

Summing Up: From above definitions, it may be concluded that philosophy enquires into the nature of life, reality, truth and values. It tries to understand man and his relationship with the universe. Philosophy is rooted in the search for answers to certain types of problems which a man faces in his life. It provides tentative answers to these problems so that life becomes meaningful and intelligible.

CHIEF CHARACTERISTICS OF PHILOSOPHY

From above definitions we conclude that:

1. Philosophy is a search for reality and truth.
2. Philosophy is based on enquiry.
3. Philosophy is local.
4. Philosophy is a dynamic and living force.
5. Philosophy is an art as well as a science.
6. Philosophy is closely related to education.
7. Philosophy is an intellectual attempt to interpret and understand nature.
8. Philosophy is love of knowledge.
9. Philosophy is love of wisdom.
10. Philosophy is a guide to a way of life.

WHY DO WE NEED PHILOSOPHY?

Philosophy gives a direction to life. Philosophy in India emerged as a result of reflection over the experiences and problems of life. Dr. Radhakrishnan, the great Indian philosopher has suggested this meaning of philosophy through the titles of two of his books. "*The Indian View of Life*" and "*The Idealist View of Life*". Human life is always purposeful. The purpose of life is determined by the philosophy of life.

We need philosophy to take decisions wisely and to act consistently. One needs wisdom to distinguish between two extremes—falsehood and truth, ugliness and beauty, right and wrong etc. Philosophy enables us to live by values for we do not live only by bread, vitamins and technological discoveries.

Social Action and Philosophy

Philosophy furnishes the basis for social action as well as for personal conduct. In the words of *A.C. Ewing* (1964), "Unless we suppose that material wealth is the only thing of value, the inability of philosophy to contribute to this would not mean that it was of no practical value. We value material wealth not for itself... but for its contribution to happiness. Now there is no doubt that one of the most important sources of happiness for those who can enjoy it at all is the search for truth and the contemplation of reality and this is the aim of philosophers".

Philosophers have been instrumental in revolutionary political and social reforms. For example, the American constitution is to a very considerable extent an application of the political ideas of the philosopher John Locke. The ideas of Rousseau played an important role in the French Revolution.

It can be materialistic or spiritualist. In ancient Sparta, the philosophy of life was to defend the country from foreign aggression and thus the aim of life was to become a soldier. The ideal Spartan was an ideal soldier. In Nazi Germany, the philosophy of life was determined by racial superiority and an individual was meant for the state. Similar was the case in communist countries. In ancient India attainment of '*Moksha*' or '*Nirvana*' was the guiding philosophy. In theory at least, 'simple living' and 'high thinking' is the philosophy of life in the present day India.

SCOPE OF PHILOSOPHY: DIFFERENT AREAS OF PHILOSOPHY

Scope of philosophy is so vast that *Cicero* (106-43) B.C., a Roman scholar called it as 'the mother of all arts' and "the true medicine of mind".

Francis Bacon, a great English philosopher regarded the philosophy as, "the great mother of the sciences".

Coleridge (1772-1834) a noted poet considered it as the 'Science of sciences'.

Broadly speaking following types of problems come under the scope of philosophy:

1. Problems of reality
2. Problems of knowledge
3. Problems of value

1. *Problems of Reality*: '*Metaphysics*' is the branch of philosophy which deals with this problem. Questions usually discussed are – What is the nature of the universe we live in? What is reality? Such questions have been raised in the *Upanishads*. Mahatma Buddha called the universe '*Maya*'.

2. *Problem of Knowledge*: This area of philosophy is known as '*Epistemology*'. Questions discussed are: How do we get knowledge? How does a man know what is real? Different philosophers have provided different answers.

3. *Problem of Value*: The branch of philosophy which deals with this problem is 'Axiology'. The problem of values include such questions: What are the principles of life? How do they support the view of reality? Problems of values include standards or norms of conduct.

RELATIONSHIP BETWEEN PHILOSOPHY AND EDUCATION: THEIR INTERDEPENDENCE

Education and philosophy are two sides of the same coin of life. *Sir John Adams* said that education is the dynamic side of philosophy. As *Ross* put it, "Education is the active aspect of philosophical belief, the practical means of realising ideals of life".

T.P. Nunn has said, "Educational aims are correlative to ideals of life".

Henderson has expressed similar views, "Educational aims cannot be determined apart from the ends and aims of life itself for educational aims grow out of life's aims. To determine what constitutes worth living has been one of the chief tasks of philosophy".

Spencer is of the view that "true education is practicable only to true philosophies".

Gentile feels that "Education with philosophy would mean a failure to understand the precise nature of education".

Rusk opines, "From every angle of educational problem comes the demands for a philosophical basis of the subject".

Fichte has rightly observed, "The art of education will never attain complete clearness without philosophy".

Dewey said, "Philosophy is the theory of education in its most general phases. Education is a laboratory in which philosophical directions become concrete and are tested". If education is a set of techniques for imparting knowledge, skills and attitudes philosophy is the foundation to vitalise these. Philosophy is the foundation and education is the super-structure.

Max Black in '*A Note on Philosophy of Education*', Harvard Educational Review (Spring 1956) has very aptly described the relationship in these words, "All serious discussion of educational problems, no matter how specific, soon leads to a consideration of educational aims, and becomes a conversation about the good life, the nature of man, the varieties of experience. But these are the perennial themes of philosophical investigation. It might seem a hard thing to expect educators to be philosophers, but can they be anything else?".

From above it is clear that there is a close interrelationship between philosophy and education. Philosophy points out the way, and education follows it. Education thus becomes the best means for the propagation of philosophy. For the good of life, for the good of the individual and for the good of society, we need direction and this direction is provided exclusively by philosophy, which is the mother of all sciences including education. This, however, does not mean that education is enslaved by philosophy. The field of education provides a testing ground to test the truth of wisdom or direction provided by philosophy. Without the testing ground of education, philosophers would remain arm-chair theorists. A constant mutual interaction goes on between the two. It is therefore said that without philosophy education would be a blind effort and without education, philosophy would be crippled. The chief means of testing the wisdom or follies of philosophy is education which has been described as the 'dynamic side of philosophy'.

It is stated that when we define education as the modification of behaviour the direction in which modification is to be carried out is determined by philosophy. This philosophy deals with the end and education with the means.

ALL GREAT PHILOSOPHERS AS GREAT EDUCATORS

A close analysis of the concept of education as given by various philosophers and educators will make it clear that their views on education are based on their various concepts of reality, of knowledge, of wisdom and of values. The great philosophers of all times have also been great educators. Most of the educational movements were the expressions of their philosophical beliefs. Views of great thinkers like Socrates, Plato, Aristotle, Comenius, John Locke, Rousseau, Froebel, Dewey, H.G. Wells, Bertrand Russell, A.N. Whitehead and Aldous Huxley, offer an interesting example of the intimate connection between philosophy and education. The ancient sages in India were all educational philosophers. In recent times, this is fully illustrated in the case of Swami Dayananda, Swami Vivekananda, Sri Aurobindo, Gurudev Tagore, Dr. Radhakrishnan, Gandhiji, etc.

DEPENDENCE OF PHILOSOPHY ON EDUCATION

There is no doubt that almost all philosophers promote their philosophy through education. Following are the reasons on account of which it is said that philosophy depends on education:

1. *Education Serves as the Base*: This implies that an educated person alone is capable of thinking coherently, methodology and systematically.
2. *Education as Transmitter as Promoter of Philosophy*: Education keeps philosophy alive by transmitting philosophy from one generation to another. Teachers through their examples, textbooks and other media promote philosophy.
3. *Education as the Tester of Philosophy*: Education is the testing ground of philosophical ideas and theory. It serves as the laboratory for theory (philosophy).
4. *Education Provides Form and Shape to Philosophical Ideas*: Adams has very rightly observed, "Education is the dynamic side of philosophy. Philosophy is the contemplative side of a theory or problems while education is the active side".
5. *Education as the Translator of Philosophical Principles into Practice*: Philosophy determines the aims of life and education translates these into practice.

DEPENDENCE OF EDUCATION ON PHILOSOPHY

Following are the views of scholars which demonstrate that education depends upon philosophy:

1. *Dewey*: "Philosophy is the theory of education in its most general phase."
2. *Fichte*: "The art of education will never attain complete clearness without philosophy."
3. *Gentile*: "Education without philosophy would mean a failure to understand the precise nature of education."
4. *Ross*: "All educational questions are ultimately the questions of philosophy."
5. *Rusk*: "Philosophy formulates what it conceives to be the end of life, education offers suggestions how this end is to be achieved."
6. *Spencer*: "True education is practicable only by a true philosophy."

SIGNIFICANCE OF STUDYING PHILOSOPHY IN UNDERSTANDING EDUCATIONAL PRACTICES AND TRENDS: CONTRIBUTION OF PHILOSOPHY TO EDUCATION

A study of philosophy is very helpful in understanding the following practices and trends in education. In other words we can say that following is the contribution of philosophy to education.

1. Philosophy and Educational Aims
2. Philosophy and Curriculum
3. Philosophy and Textbooks
4. Philosophy and Methods of Teaching
5. Philosophy and Discipline
6. Philosophy and the Teacher
7. Philosophy and Educational Organisation, Administration and Supervision

1. *Philosophy and Aims in Education*: "No system of education", says *Acharya J.B. Kripalani*, the noted Gandhian philosopher, "can be properly appraised and appreciated, unless it is studied in connection with the ideas and ideals which it represents". The Soviet System of education of the old could properly be understood only in the light of the philosophy of Marxism and Leninism. To gain insight into the British system of education, it is necessary to have the correct perspective of the synthesis between the progressivism and the conservation which the Butler Act tried to achieve.

In Ancient Sparta, the ideal was to defend the country's honour and hence the aim of the Spartan System of education was to prepare citizens to be soldiers and patriots. On the other hand, the Athenian system of education aimed at the cultural development of each individual, in conformity with the Athenian philosophy of that era.

During the British Period, the rulers were guided by their philosophy of imperialism and accordingly formulated the system of education in India.

The aims of education in independent India have been determined by the philosophy underlying our Constitution.

The aim of education has a reference to the ideals or philosophy of a nation. In independent India, philosophy of life is enshrined in the Preamble of its Constitution. Educational aims accordingly draw their inspiration from it. The aims of education in the USA are based on its democratic philosophy. The philosophy of fascism determined the aims of education in Germany during Hitler's time. The philosophy of communism influenced the aims of education in Russia and China.

2. *Philosophy and Curriculum*: The philosophical approach to life is the guiding factor in the determination of the curriculum. Gandhiji's scheme of basic education was an expression of his philosophy. He was against the lopsidedness of the system of education as propounded by Lord Macaulay and was moved by the illiteracy and poverty of the people. His scheme of studies, therefore, emphasised crafts and the environment. He was very keen to make education self-supporting besides developing moral character. The National Policy on Education 1986 lays stress on a Core Curriculum keeping in view the needs of emotional and national integration.

Introduction of self-government in school programme is the outcome of democratic philosophy.

Various philosophies like humanism, idealism, pragmatism and naturalism have influenced curriculum in varying degrees.

Following examples illustrate the influence of philosophy on curriculum formulation:

(a) Individuals, nations and societies have philosophies of life. The aim of life in Ancient Sparta was to live as a soldier. The philosophy of life stressed the development of physical skills and well-trained persons. The philosophy of life was to become an ideal soldier. Content of education, therefore, emphasised physical training and strength.

(b) The Nazi Germany or the Hitler regime believed that the German people were superior to all other races. The system of education in Nazi Germany aimed at producing those Germans who considered themselves superior to all other human beings. Curriculum, text-books, methods of teaching, etc. were geared to this philosophy.

(c) The philosophy of life in a democratic society emphasises the development of individuality. Educational theory and methodology include all processes which enable the individual to develop democratic ideals.

(d) The philosophy of life in our country in ancient times was based upon spiritualism. People believed in simple living and high thinking. The system of education strove hard for attaining salvation by leading a pure and simple life. Accordingly, the scheme of studies was determined.

(e) The Indian sages and seers converted their forest homes into educational institutions in accordance with their philosophy of life. The philosophy of life of Lord Buddha was practised and preached through a well-organised system of monasteries which were also great centres of Buddhist education. Curriculum was formulated accordingly.

(f) Contents of education during the British period were determined by their philosophy which emphasised that Indians should be educated in such a way so as to make them Indian in blood and colour but English in dress, manners and tastes. Also, they wanted to prepare clerks to assist the Britishers to carry out their administration. Thirdly, they were interested in the export of raw materials from India for their manufacturing industries in England. Thus they neglected teaching of Indian culture, philosophy and religion. They also neglected vocational education in the curriculum.

(g) Education in independent India is expected to train the children in accordance with the philosophy as enshrined in our Constitution. Thus the contents of education include material on developing the values of secularism, socialism and democracy.

(h) Recently, far reaching changes have taken place in the erstwhile U.S.S.R. which now comprises a number of Independent States. The philosophy of communism has received a set back and democratic values have gained prominence. Accordingly democratic ideals are also taken note of in the educational system of the Russian Federation.

3. *Philosophy and Textbooks*: The contents of the textbooks must mirror the philosophy or way of life of the people. In a socialist society textbooks

emphasise socialist philosophy. In a state dominated and ruled by religious leaders, textbooks reflect tenets of scriptures. In India, since independence, there has been a great stress on emotional integration and national unity. Accordingly textbooks are being screened from time to time to ensure that they include that matter also which promoters emotional integration and national unity.

4. *Philosophy and Methods of Teaching*: Every school of philosophy has its own methods of teaching. According to the philosophy of idealism, question-answer method, lecture method and discussion method are most suitable methods of education. Naturalism recommends learning by doing, learning by self-experience and direct experience. Pragmatic philosophy advocates project method, problem solving method and socialist techniques. It is through methods that the teacher establishes contact between the child and subject-matter. Rousseau, Fichte and Froebel assume that the child's nature is good and needs perfect freedom in its working. Any intervention with it is wrong. All modern methods are paedo-centric at least in theory. The importance of the educand is stressed in the process of education more than the subject-matter or educator. Under the influence of these philosophic views, the new education holds that the teacher should prepare the environment as best as he can and then leave children alone. Neill's Summer School and the Project Method are the results of these philosophies.

5. *Philosophy and Discipline*: Discipline also, like the curriculum, textbooks and methods of teaching, reflects the philosophy of life accepted at a particular time more directly than any other aspect of school work. In other words, philosophy of an age is reflected in the discipline of its educational institutions. Discipline even reflects the political philosophy prevalent in the country. In a despotic system of government, repression is common. In a democracy, the doctrine of emancipation is advocated as a disciplinary measure.

In a democratic set up, discipline is viewed as inner discipline as well as social discipline based on group work. In the totalitarian state, discipline is regimented and assumes the form of a military discipline, and is based on fear of the teacher and the head. There is little concern for the individuality of the child in a totalitarian type of discipline. The idealists emphasise the impact of impression of the teacher on his students. 'Free discipline' is the slogan of the naturalist.

6. *Philosophy and the Teacher*: A teacher is said to play an important role in shaping and moulding the ideals, habits, manners, tastes and ways of life and above all the character and personality of the students. It is, therefore, very essential that he must have a consistent and sound philosophy in accordance with the philosophy of the nation to which he belongs.

7. *Philosophy and Educational Organisation, Administration and Supervision*: Democratic philosophy lays emphasis on the participation of the staff and the students in running some programmes of the educational institutions. Philosophy of communism provides little scope for such involvement and the head decides everything.

Conclusion: Thus we find that the formation of aims, the choice of a suitable curriculum or even textbooks, the use of proper methods and devices, the decision about the type of discipline to be maintained and how to maintain it, the creation of general tone in the school are ultimately questions of philosophy and a knowledge of all these is very essential to make education purposeful, inspirational and effective.

Idealism has given us an all-inclusive view of education. It has led to the promotion of self-realisation as an aim of education. Naturalism has paved the way for the psychological and scientific trends in education. Realism emphasises the content value and gives an important place to diversified curricula. Pragmatism stresses the practical and social aspects. Humanism extols human values and thoughts and respects human personality. Existentialism stresses the values of free thinking.

SIGNIFICANCE OF PHILOSOPHY TO THE TEACHER

Education is a practical activity. Every educational practice is illuminated with the backdrop of philosophy. The speculative, normative and critical function of philosophy affects not only the direction of moral guidance that the teacher gives but also affects the direction and the emphasis on the curriculum, the teacher's attitudes from day to day, even from hour to hour. No practice is good and scientific unless rooted in philosophical thought which gives logic, rationale, sequence and system to education. Since philosophy speaks the language of analysis and reason, there is hardly any problem of the teacher which is not solved by philosophy.

A basic understanding of philosophical themes on the part of all teachers regarding ancient and contemporary philosophical systems of thought will enable them to reorient their own philosophy and beliefs, help them to understand the problematic situations in the classroom discipline, under-achievement of students and many such other problems, and ultimately enable them to determine the manner in which they will handle these problems.

The naturalists insist that the teacher should never interfere with the free activities of children. He is simply to set the educational environment. The idealists advocate that the teacher's role should be that of the head of a family. Pupils should be inspired by his personality and develop full faith in him. According to pragmatists, the teacher is not to impose anything on the pupils. He is simply to provide opportunity to his pupils for activity and learning. However, a teacher should not be wedded to any of these philosophies. He should derive inspiration from all the philosophies and try to imbibe the best features of every philosophy.

For a teacher working in Indian schools, the philosophic values enshrined in the Constitution should be the guidelines.

Philosophy helps the teacher in the following manner:

1. Philosophy provides direction to the teacher.
2. Philosophy serves as a guide to the teacher for experiments.
3. Philosophy provides clarification of the nature of education to the teacher.
4. Philosophy enables the teacher to think critically, constructively and rationally.
5. Philosophy enables the teacher to handle disciplinary situations satisfactorily.

The following points should help the teacher to understand the relationship between education and philosophy.

1. *Why to Educate*? This is concerned with the aims of education as determined by philosophy. The teacher and the taught must be very clear about the aims of education so that right efforts are made in the right direction. In fact this is the most important aspect of education which is based on philosophies. All other aspects of education i.e. the curriculum, the methods of teaching and the type of discipline etc. are dependent on the aims. The entire educational system is subservient to the fulfilment of these aims. In this sense, it is sometimes stated that the most important contribution of philosophy to education is in the domain of determining aims of education.

2. *Whom to Educate*? The teacher must understand that child is a living being and he is to be enabled to understand the philosophical values enshrined in the Constitution.

3. *What are the Contents of Education*? This leads to the contents of the curriculum. The contents are to be taught in accordance with philosophical thought.

4. *Who is to Educate*? The teacher is to educate and he must understand himself in the context of the philosophy of the society in which he lives.

5. *Where to Educate*? The teacher must understand that school is a place where the principles of philosophy are put into use. Besides, school is not the only agency for this purpose. There are other agencies also to translate philosophical thought into practice. The teacher should keep this aspect in view.

6. *How to Educate*? This involves the techniques of imparting information and knowledge so that children acquire wisdom to make their lives worth living. This also relates to type of discipline needed.

Summing up: As observed by *Gentile*, "The belief that men may continue to educate without concerning themselves with philosophy means a failure to understand the precise nature of education. The process of education cannot go on the right lines without the help of philosophy. Since philosophy speaks the language of analysis and reason, there is hardly any problem of education which is difficult to solve by the teacher who possesses the clear lights of philosophy".

20

Major Philosophies and Their Impact on Education

IDEALISM IN EDUCATION

IDEALISM AS THE OLDEST PHILOSOPHY

Idealism is usually considered as the oldest philosophy. It is on account of the philosophy of idealism that humanity can be saved from the destructive wars and dazzling materialism. Idealism in India is as old as the *Vedas*. The Vedic seers were great idealists. The *Upanishads* and the *Bhagwad Gita* made a very comprehensive analysis of idealism. In the West, Plato—a Greek philosopher (427-347 BC) was a great idealist.

The following views of great thinkers point out the meaning and dimensions of idealism:

1. According to *Kath Upanishad*, an idealist is one who possesses supreme knowledge by concentration of mind.

2. In the words of *Rusk*, "Idealism contends that the material and physical universe known to science is an incomplete expression of reality, that it exists but to subserve, and requires to compliment it a higher type of reality, a spiritual universe." Rusk regards human personality as the 'noblest work of God'.

3. According to *Ross*, "Idealistic philosophy takes many and varied forms, but to postulate underlying all is that mind or spirit in the essential world-stuff, that the true reality is of a mental character."

4. *Horne* defines idealism in these words, "Educational philosophy of idealism is an account of man finding himself as an integral part of a universe of mind."

5. *Brubacher* explains idealism in these words, "Idealists point out that it is mind that is central in understanding the world. To them nothing gives a greater sense of reality than the activity of the mind engaged in trying to comprehend the world."

6. *Harold Titus*. "Idealism asserts that reality consists of ideas, materialism thoughts, minds or and selves rather than materials, objects and force."

Summing up: Idealism contends that spiritual aspects are the chief aspects of human life. Natural or scientific facets of life are subordinate to spiritual ones. When the emphasis is on the spiritual aspect, it is called idealism or philosophy of idealism. The idealist 'idolise' the mind beyond everything. Idealism exalts human personality.

Chief Exponents of Idealism

Eastern Idealists: (i) Vedic seers, (ii) The Upanishads and Gita, (iii) Swami Dayananda, (iv) Swami Vivekananda, (v) Mahatma Gandhi, (vi) Rabindranath Tagore, (vii) Sri Aurobindo.

Western Idealists: (i) Plato—a Greek philosopher (427-347 B.C.), (ii) Kant—a German philosopher (1724-1804 A.D.), (iii) Froebel—a German philosopher (1772-1852 A.D.), (iv) William T. Haris—an American philosopher (1835-1909 A.D.).

FUNDAMENTAL PRINCIPLES OF IDEALISM

The essence of idealism is contained in the Upanishads.

The '*Britharanayaka Upanishad*' states.

Asato ma sad gamaya,
Tamaso me jyotir gamaya,
Mrtyor ma amartam gamaya,

(Lead me from unreal to the real,
Lead me from darkness to light,
Lead me from death to immortality)

According to '*Katha Upanishad*'

Yastu vijnanauan bhauati
Tasyendriyani vasyani
Sadasvaiya saratheh

(He who is possessed of supreme knowledge by concentration of mind must have his senses under control, like spirited steeds controlled by a charioteer)

In brief, following are the main principles of idealism:

1. God is the source of all creation.
2. God is the source of all knowledge.
3. Spirit and mind constitute reality.
4. Material and physical universe is not a complete expression of reality.
5. Material and physical universe is subordinate to a higher type of reality—a spiritual universe, a universe of ideas and values.
6. Spiritual world is more important than the material.
7. Values are eternal, absolute and unchanging.
8. What is ultimately real is not the object itself but the ideal or idea behind it.
9. Man being spiritual is a supreme creation.
10. Man is not the creation of his environment in the sense the term is applied to animals.
11. Man needs some encouragement or light in the face of darkness.
12. There are intrinsic moral and spiritual values.
13. Reality is to be found in man's mind rather than in material nature.
14. Study of man's nature and his mind is more important than the study of material universe.
15. Man has a spiritual nature which expresses itself in the form of intellectual culture, morality and religion.

IDEALISM ON VARIOUS DIMENSIONS OF EDUCATION

1. *Aims of Education according to Idealism*: The most important contribution of idealism to the field of education is that it has provided human life with high aims. It has set out aims of education very clearly. In a world threatened by materialism where technology has taken away much of man's freedom and dignity, the idealist philosophy restores man to his proper place in the universe. The idealists very rightly point out that the aim of education is not merely to enable the individual to produce more material goods but to exalt human personality. Sri Aurobindo, in this regard has observed, "The acquiring of various kinds of information is only one and not the chief aim of education, its central aim is the building of the powers of the human mind and spirit, it is the formation or, as I would prefer to view it, the evoking of knowledge, character and culture—that at least if no more. And the distinction makes an enormous difference." Tagore also believes, "The object of education is the freedom of mind which can only be achieved through the path of freedom" *R.W. Everson* has expressed this very view in the following verses:

Not gold, but only men can make
A people great and strong

The University Education Commission (1948-49) headed by Dr. S. Radhakrishnan has very beautifully stated the aim of education from the view of an idealist, "If we wish to bring about a savage upheaval in our society, a '*Rakshas raj*', all that we need to do is to give vocational and technical education and starve the spirit. We will have a number of scientists without conscience, technicians without taste who find a void within themselves, a moral vacuum."

According to *Froebel*, "The object of education is the realisation of a faithful, pure, inviolable and hence holy life."

In the words of *J.S. Ross*, "The aim of education specially associated with idealism is the exhalation of personality or self-realisation."

According to *Rusk*, "Education must enable mankind through its culture to enter more and more fully into spiritual realm, and also enlarge the boundaries of spiritual realm."

Aims of education according to idealism may be summed up as under:

(i) Exhalation of human personality—unfolding the divine in man.
(ii) Self-realisation by man.
(iii) Development of will power.
(iv) Development of character.
(v) Development of rational attitude.
(vi) Transmission of spiritual and cultural heritage.
(vii) Universal education for universal individual.
(viii) Development of moral values which falls into two categories:
  (a) Duties to self which include physical fitness, self-culture, industriousness, etc.
  (b) Duties to others i.e. respect for and appreciation of the opinion of others, cooperativeness, generosity, liberality, etc.
(ix) Preparation for a holy life.
(x) To cultivate the values of truth, beauty and goodness.

While discussing aims of education, it must be kept in view that idealism does not ignore the vocational aim of education. It simply gives it secondary importance.

2. *Curriculum and Idealism.* Idealism stresses three values of 'truth', 'goodness' and 'beauty'. These three values determine three types of human activities—intellectual, moral and aesthetic. Each type of activity is represented by studies or subjects that should form a part of the curriculum. The following arrangement of the curriculum is recommended by idealism.

Value	*Subject/Activity*
1. Truth	1. It is represented by intellectual subjects or activities. This includes subjects like humanities, languages, social sciences and physical sciences.
2. Goodness	2. This includes subjects like ethics, metaphysics and religion, etc.
3. Beauty	3. Aesthetic subjects or activities like art and poetry etc. relate to this part of the curriculum.

Ross's scheme for a complete curriculum in the light of idealism is as under:

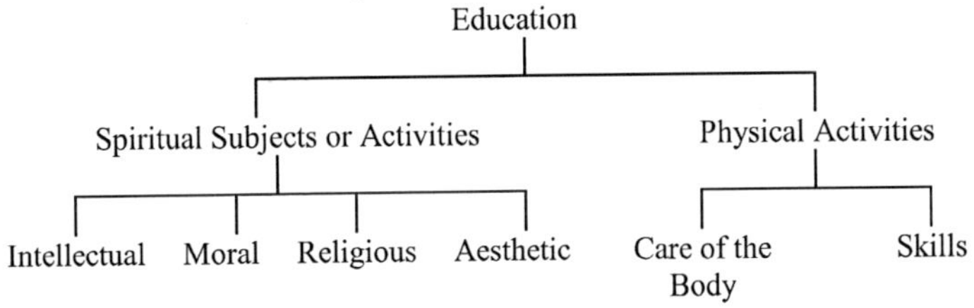

Fig. 17.1: Curriculum

Chief features of curriculum in idealism are:

(i) Curriculum should include those subjects and activities which emphasise higher values of life.
(ii) Curriculum should provide a place of prominence to humanities.
(iii) Ethics and religion should find an important place in the curriculum.

(See also curriculum suggested by Plato)

3. *Idealism and Methods of Teaching*: The idealist suggests the following techniques and methods of teaching:

(i) Narration
(ii) Explanation
(iii) Exposition
(iv) Questioning
(v) Discussion
(vi) Practice and Repetition
(vii) Conversational Method
(viii) Inductive and Deductive
(ix) Contemplation and Reflection

4. *Idealism and Discipline*: While 'freedom' is the slogan of the naturalists, 'discipline' is that of idealists. Disciplining the mind and body of the child are the watchwords of the idealists. An idealist attaches great importance to the

guidance of the teacher to the child for realising his 'self'. Suggested features of discipline according to idealists are:

(i) Idealism believes in inner discipline.

(ii) Inner discipline can be obtained through guidance as well as restrain—inner as well as outer or external.

(iii) There is need for restricting freedom of the child. A child cannot be given a long rope with which he may hang himself.

(iv) The teacher should win over the child through 'impression', i.e., good personal examples of behaviour and conduct. The child especially in the plastic period of his early life considers the teacher to be an ideal person to be emulated by the pupils.

(v) Participation in social service activities develops spirit of sacrifice—an important feature of the life of an ideal person.

5. *Idealism and the Teacher*: Teacher assumes an important place in idealism. He is the key figure in the educative process. His personality is the most vital influence on the education of the child. A child is greatly influenced by his conduct, his way of speech, his etiquette etc.

Idealism considers the teacher a friend, philosopher and guide to his pupils. He guides them in such a way as they may attain 'self-realisation'. Character development and value development are the most important concerns of the teacher.

Froebel's metaphor of the Kindergarten, perhaps, explains best the functions of the educator. The school is regarded as a garden and teacher as the gardener whose function is to tend the little human plants in his charge carefully and to help them to grow to beauty and perfection. The human plant can grow unaided according to the laws of its own nature, yet the gardener is to see that plant attains its finest form; it produces or gives the finest results. Ross has beautifully summed up the place of the teacher in the idealistic school when he says, "The naturalist may be content with briars but the idealist wants fine roses. So the educator by his efforts must assist the educand who is developing according to the laws of his nature, to attain levels that would otherwise be denied to him."

In the words of *Gentile*, "Teacher is a spiritual symbol of right conduct."

According to *Swami Vivekananda*, "What you call the personal magnetism of man—that is what goes out and impresses you."

In the words of *Sri Aurobindo*, "If you wish to be respected by your child, have respect for yourself and be at every moment worthy of respect".

Lauri has said, "If a teacher has not an ideal aim he had better take to shopkeeping".

According to idealism, main functions of a teacher are:

(i) The teacher must assume the role of a Guru.

(ii) The teacher must understand his pupils thoroughly.

(iii) The teacher must be a personal friend and guide to his pupils.

(iv) The teacher should present high standards of behaviour and conduct before his pupils.

(v) The teacher should have a deep knowledge of his subject.

(vi) The teacher should strive hard for providing such a social environment in the classroom that is conducive to imitation by students.

(vii) The teacher should aim at inculcating in the pupils a desire to work hard.

(viii) The teacher should employ thought provoking techniques and thereby encourage his pupils to think for themselves. Just as one cannot teach a subject without a knowledge of it, similarly it is not possible to impart knowledge to a pupil without knowing him. The teacher aims at inculcating in the pupils a desire to work hard by assigning definite tasks to each of the students—the tasks being suited to individual capacity. Questioning and discussion are the main techniques employed by a teacher in the classroom. Classroom environment should encourage constructive thinking.

LIMITATIONS AND WEAKNESSES OF IDEALISM

1. *Subtle Concepts*: Concepts like 'spirit', 'mind', 'soul', 'the cosmos', etc. inherent in idealism have little relevance in classroom teaching.

2. *Nothing Like Spiritual Universe*: The spiritualist theory of spiritual universe as stated by idealists is not considered to be in consonance with the scientific research today.

3. *Over Emphasis on Models*: The idealism in education stresses limitation of models but younger generation prefers invention and originally rather than imitation.

4. *Over Emphasis on Good Manners*: Idealists' too much emphasis on good manners, and modesty may be mistaken for diffidence.

5. *Undue Stress on Information*: Idealism's emphasis on gaining knowledge is likely to turn educational institutions as information-mongers' workshops. School curricula becomes overloaded with obsolete knowledge sometimes.

6. *Ignoring Overall Development of Personality*: Scheme of education based on idealism, by and large, pays less attention to physical, industrial, social and electronic environment of today.

7. *Obsolete Theories*: Obsolete knowledge may create hindrance in infusing new spirit in the contents.

8. *Ignoring ITC*: In general, it is stated that the idealist view in education pays less attention to the present environment dominated by Information Communication Technology (ICT).

9. *Rigorous and Strict Concept of Discipline*: The idealists lay too much emphasis on 'Does' and 'Don'ts'.

10. *Rather Unpsychological*: Idealism parts more emphasis on philosophical concepts and neglects psychological aspects.

11. *Under-rating Science and Technology*: Idealism does not give due place to the development in science and technology.

12. *Less Emphasis on Social Side*: Idealism does not assign proper place to the social aspect of the personality.

CONTRIBUTION OF IDEALISM TO EDUCATIONAL THEORY AND PRACTICE

1. *Right Emphasis on Higher Values*: The present world seems to be plagued with materialism which ignores higher values of life. Idealism aims restoring man to his proper place.

2. *Recognition of Rich Heritage*: Idealism holds that the past culture must be given its due place in any scheme of educational reconstruction.

3. *Due Regard to Human Personality*: The present machine and electronic age treats the human being as a machine. Idealism warns against this type of approach.

4. *Important Place to the Teacher*: Idealism assigns an important place to the teacher in the educative process.

5. *Realisation of Self*: Idealism insists that for the realisation of the 'self', every human being must receive an opportunity to be educated. Thus the goal of the idealist in this context is universal education.

6. *Human Relations*: Emphasis of the idealist on personality development has provided a fresh look at human relations in teaching.

7. *Aims of Education*: Idealism provides clear guidelines for determining aims in education, curricular, discipline, teacher's role and methods of teaching-learning.

8. *Self-Discipline*: Idealism rightly regards self-discipline as the only way for the development of the child.

***Summing Up*:** In a world threatened by materialism, the philosophy of idealism provides light and direction to man for restoring his proper place. The need of the hour is to develop higher values among students. This lead must come from leaders—political, religious and all those who occupy high places in different walks of life. They must set good examples. Educational institutions alone cannot develop higher values of life. Of course, they must take all possible steps to develop higher values in students.

PHILOSOPHY OF NATURALISM IN EDUCATION

MEANING OF NATURALISM

With a view to have a clear perspective, we may take up a few definitions given by eminent philosophers:

1. In the words of *Hocking*, "Naturalism is metaphysics which considers nature as the whole of reality. It excludes what is supernatural or the other world."

2. *James Ward's* view is, "Naturalism is the doctrine which separates nature from God, subordinates spirit to matter and sets up unchangeable laws as supreme."

3. According to *Rusk*, "Naturalism is a philosophical position adopted by those who approach philosophy from purely scientific point of view."

4. *Perry* defines naturalism as, "Naturalism is not science but an assertion about science. More especially, it is the assertion that scientific knowledge is final leaving no room for extra-scientific or philosophical knowledge."

5. *Adams* views naturalism as "Naturalism is a term loosely applied in educational theory to systems of training that are not dependent on school and books but on the actual life of the educand."

6. In the words of *Joyce*, "Naturalism is a system whose salient characteristic is the exclusion of whatever is spiritual or indeed whatever is transcendental of experience from our philosophy of nature and man."

7. *Thomas and Lang* define Naturalism as "Naturalism holds that ultimate reality is material world not spiritual world".

Summing up: 'Return to nature', and break the chains of society' are the watchwords of the naturalists. There is nothing beyond nature.

CHIEF CHARACTERISTICS OF NATURALISM

These are as under:

1. *Supremacy of Nature*: Man is subordinate to nature. There is nothing like 'Supernaturalism'. All values exist in nature.
2. *Belief in Nature*: The naturalists think that everything is nature. Nature alone is the source of all knowledge.
3. *Belief in Science*: According to naturalists, scientific knowledge is final. Science reveals the mysteries of nature.
4. *Materialism is a Reality*: The real world is the material world.
5. *No Faith in Soul*: Naturalism has no faith in soul or spirit. It does not believe in divinity. Human life is interpreted in terms of matter only.
6. *Goodness of the Nature of Man*: A naturalist thinks that everything that comes to us from nature is good but it degenerates in the hands of man.
7. *Equality*: Naturalists regard that in the natural order of things all human beings are equal.
8. *Senses as the Gateways of Knowledge*: Naturalists are very emphatic that all knowledge comes through the senses. The senses are eye, ear, nose, tongue and skin. Knowledge gathered through these is more lasting.
9. *Relative Nature of Values*: Values are created in terms of specific needs.
10. *Creation of Societies*: Man creates societies to meet some of its needs.
11. *Several Illusions*: Moral instinct, innate conscience, providence, power of prayer and freedom of will, etc. are all illusions.
12. *Denial of Supernaturalism*: Naturalism gives little significance to concepts like God, spirit or divine.

Types of Naturalism

(1)	(2)	(3)
Biological Naturalism	Mechanical Naturalism	Physical Sciences Naturalism

Prominent Naturalist Philosophers

1. Bacon, Francis (1561-1626 A.D.), English philosopher
2. Comenius, John (1529-1670 A.D.), Czechslovakian philosopher
3. Rousseau, Jean Jacques (1712-1877), French (Swiss born) philosopher
4. Spencer, Herbert (1820-1903 A.D.), English philosopher
5. Tagore, Rabindranath (1861-1941), Indian philosopher

NATURALISM AND ITS VARIOUS DIMENSIONS OF EDUCATION (IMPLICATIONS OF NATURALISM IN EDUCATION)

1. Principles of Education according to Naturalism

1. Naturalism accords an important place to the child in the educative process.

2. Naturalism advocates education in accordance with the nature of the child.

3. Naturalism considers natural environment as an important source of education.

4. Naturalism gives an important place to the present life of the child and makes it the basis of education.

5. Naturalism states that adequate freedom should be given to the child in the educative process.

6. Naturalism has an insignificant place for acquiring knowledge from books.

2. Naturalism and Educational Aims

1. *Redirection of the Impulses of the Child*: Education should aim at sublimating, redirecting and coordinating the natural impulses of the child for the attainment of natural goals, i.e., the common good of the individual and the society.

2. *Preparing for Struggle for Existence*: The aim of education, should be to equip the individual for the struggle for existence and thus ensure his survival.

3. *Living in Harmony with Nature*: Education should enable an individual to live in harmony with his surroundings and environments by teaching him how to adopt and adjust to those environments.

4. *Conformity with Nature*: Rousseau's aim of education is the development of the child in conformity with nature.

5. *Training for Complete Life*: According to *Herbert Spencer*, education should be a preparation and training for a complete life.

6. *Development According to Natural Ability*: *Rousseau J. Jacques* says that the aim of education should be to develop the child according to his ability.

7. *Development of Individuality*: *T.N. Nunn* thinks that the aim should be to enable the child to develop his individuality and contribute to society.

8. *Struggling Successfully*: *Darwin* states that the aim of education should be to enable the child struggle successfully for his survival.

3. Study of the Child and Child-Centred Education

Naturalism considers a child as the 'Hero' in the drama of education. Naturalists lay emphasis on the nature of the child, his study and the various stages of development through which he passes. The child is born as innocent, simple and pure at heart. His nature is essentially good. Rousseau asserts that the child is not an adult; he is not to be judged from the standards of an adult. Education should be in accordance with the nature of each stage.

4. Naturalism and Curriculum

Although there are divergent views of the naturalists on curriculum contents, they agree on the following points:

1. *Education according to 3 A's*: Curriculum should cater to the age, ability and aptitudes, of the child.

2. *Need Based Curriculum*: Curriculum should be constructed to meet the needs of the child according to the nature of development at each stage.

3. *Emphasis on Self-Preserving Subjects*: It lays stress on the subjects which are helpful in the self-preservation of man.

4. *Basic Sciences*: Naturalism stress basic sciences.

5. *Physical and Health Sciences*: It gives importance to physical and health sciences.

5. The Teacher

Merely an Observer: According to the naturalists, the teacher is not to play the role of a 'giver' of information, ideas and ideals, of a 'moulder' of will-power and character. He is not to interfere with the activities of children. He must not impose himself on them. His duty is to see that their education is the free development of their interests and motives rather than an artificial effort made by him. He should only be an observer of child's development from outside the scene. In fact a teacher should be an 'Observer', 'Protector' and 'Stage setter'.

6. Naturalism and Methods of Teaching

1. *Experience is the Best Teacher*: *Rousseau* advises, "Give your scholar no verbal lessons; he should be taught by experience".

2. *Observation Method*: The child should observe things and discover for himself.

3. *Individualised Instruction*: According to a naturalist, every child has the ability to acquire knowledge and to benefit the individual. Hence the method of class teaching is not useful.

4. *Self-Education*: The naturalist advocates that the child is expected to acquire information, knowledge and, ideas by himself.

5. *Things rather than Words*: *Rousseau* says, "Teach by doing whatever you can, and only fall back upon words when doing is out of question".

6. *Social Learning through Participation*: A child acquires social learning when he takes part in the social activities.

7. Naturalism and Discipline

1. *Discipline by Natural Consequences*: The concept of discipline according to idealists may be expressed in four words, "Discipline by natural consequences". Natural consequences are those experiences which the child receives by following an activity. When the child runs its head against the table, he feels pain. The remembrance of pain makes the child disciplined.

2. *No Punishments*: *Rousseau* states, "Children should never receive punishment as such, it should always come as the natural consequences of his action". If a child is late for a picnic party, let him learn from this experience of being late.

3. *Full Freedom to the Child*: A naturalist starts with the assumption that the nature of child is essentially good. Therefore, he should be given freedom of expression and development.

4. *School Organisation as a Free Society*: According to the naturalists, the school should provide an environment which is conducive to the free development of the growing child. The whole school should be organised into a free, natural society where each child contributes to her or his well-being and where the pupils learn how to lead and how to follow. A system of self-government should, in short, be introduced.

8. Negative Education

Rousseau's curriculum for Emile is based on the principle of negative education. Negative education, according to him, is one that:

(i) tends to perfect the organs that are the instruments of knowledge, before giving this knowledge directly, and

(ii) endeavours to prepare the way for reason by the proper exercise of the senses.

The doctrine of negative education as applied to physical education demands the greatest possible freedom for child in his movement and exercises, simple diet, loose or scanty and light clothing etc. When applied to intellectual education it would amount to absence of verbal lessons, books or any positive studies.

LIMITATIONS OF NATURALISM IN EDUCATION

1. *No Clear Cut Goals*: Naturalism does not offer definite aims of education.
2. *Neglect of Books*: There is a very minor place for books. We cannot neglect the treasure of knowledge contained in the pointed materials.
3. *Negligible Importance to Higher Values*: Naturalism by and large, ignores the higher ends in the process of education.
4. *Undue Emphasis on Education through Nature*: It is certain that physical nature alone cannot be considered adequate for providing all education.
5. *Absolute Freedom a Myth*: Absolute freedom does not exist. It never existed. It will never exist in a civilised society. "Child cannot be given the long rope to hang himself."
6. *Very Little Role for the Teacher*: Naturalism minimises the role of the teacher in the educative process. Even in the electronic age, a teacher occupies an important place in the teaching-learning process.
7. *Neglect of Moral and Spiritual Values*: Naturalism ignores the moral and spiritual development of the child.

CONTRIBUTION OF NATURALISM TO EDUCATION

1. *Child Centred/Learner Centred Education*: Naturalism has brought to the forefront the importance of the recognition of child in the process of education.
2. *Significance of the Study of the Child*: Naturalism has very clearly drawn the attention of the educators to study child carefully and provide education accordingly. It advocates that education, should be 'child centred'.
3. *Enjoyable Process of Education*: Naturalism has stressed that the educative process should be made pleasurable and enjoyable.

4. *Educational Institutions in Natural Surroundings*: Naturalism indicates that educational institutions should be set up in natural surroundings.

5. *Stress or Progressive Methods of Teaching*: Naturalism brings to light the significance, of progressive methods of teaching like 'learning by doing', 'learning by observing' and 'learning by inductive approach'.

6. *New Movements in Education*: Naturalism has given birth to new movements and new types of educational institutions like A.S. Neill's Summer School and Visvabharati.

Summing up: The most important contribution of naturalism is that it has given birth to progressive methods of instruction in accordance with the nature of the child. It is usually said that naturalism has psycholigised education.

PRAGMATISM

Derivative Meaning of Pragmatism

Pragmatism is also known by various names such as 'Practical Philosophy', 'Worldly-wise Philosophy', Utilitarian Philosophy, 'Down to Earth Philosophy' 'Experimental Philosophy', 'Philosophy of Instrumentalism', 'Philosophy of Consequentialism', 'Practical Philosopy' and 'Cash Philosophy' on account of its emphasis on 'utility' aspect.

The word 'pragmatism' is derived from a Greek word '*Pragma*' which means 'to do', 'to make', and 'to accomplish'. Therefore words 'doing', 'making', 'accomplishing' etc. are used while referring to pragmatism. Expressions like 'action', 'practice' and 'activity' have become popular in education on account of pragmatism.

Pragmatism stands between idealism and naturalism.

Origin of Pragmatism

Historically, the Pragmatic approach can be traced to '*Protagorus*, a Sophist philosopher of ancient Greece who said, "Man is the Measure of All Things". In recent times the term first appeared in 1878 in "How to Make our Ideas Clear", an article written by C.S. Pierce. He preferred to use the term "Pragmaticism". He attacked idealism and redefined truth and knowledge in terms of experience and their practical consequences. William James developed this outlook out of the American cultural milieu and became the founder and father of this, what Archie J. Bahm calls, 'down to earth' cash-value philosophy. John Dewey (1859-1952) became its leading and most influential exponent. He practised it in his laboratory school set up in Chicago in 1896. His purpose was to train pupils in cooperation and mutually useful living.

Definition of Pragmatism

1. *Will Durant* sums up the meaning and concept of pragmatism as, "Pragmatism is the doctrine that truth is the practical efficacy of an idea".

2. *William James* defines pragmatism as, "Pragmatism is a temper of mind, an attitude; it is also a theory of the nature of ideas and truth; and finally, it is a theory about reality".

3. *J.B. Prett* states, "Pragmatism offers us a theory of truth of knowledge, and a theory of reality".

4. According to *J.S. Ross*, "Pragmatism is essentially a humanistic philosophy, maintaining that man creates his own values in the course of activity that reality is still in the making and awaits its part of completion from the future, that to an unascertainable extent our truths are manmade products".

5. *Rusk* defines pragmatism as, "Pragmatism is merely a stage in the development of a new idealism—an idealism that will do full justice to reality, reconcile the practical and spiritual values and result as a culture which is the flower of efficiency".

6. *Reid* states, "Pragmatism makes activity, engagement, commitment and encounter its central theme".

***Summing up*:** Pragmatism stands between idealism and materialism—a sort of compromise. Idea or mind is the primary thing in idealism: Matter is at the centre of the universe so far as materialism is concerned. They are in fact the two "antithetical trends" in philosophy. For pragmatism "Experience" is at the centre of the Universe.

Forms of Pragmatism

(1)	(2)	(3)
Humanistic Pragmatism	Experimental Pragmatism	Biological Pragmatism

Humanistic Pragmatism: According to a humanistic pragmatism, "Whatever fulfills our purpose, satisfies our desire, develops our life is true".

Experimental Pragmatism: An experimental pragmatist believes, "Whatever can be experimentally verified is true or that works is true".

Biological Pragmatism: A biologist pragmatist believes, "By this type of pragmatism best is found in the function of thought, in adapting the human organism to its environment".

Chief Promoters of Pragmatism in Modern Times

1. C. B. Pierce (1839-1914 A.D.)
2. William James (1842-1910)
3. John Dewey (1859-1952)

Fundamental Principles of Pragmatism

1. Experience is the central idea in pragmatism. According to *John Dewey*, "Truth is made just as health, wealth and strength are made in the course of experience". It is based on results.

2. William James sees no difference between 'pragmatism' and 'practicalism'. Truth is that which works in institutions. It changes with times.

3. There are no absolute values of life.

4. Action is real and ideas are tools.

5. Man is an active being.

6. Man has the ability to solve his problems.
7. Man solves his problems though the logic of experiments and scientific methods.
8. Knowledge is functional and tentative.
9. Utilitarian aspect is supreme.
10. Past has little value.
11. Present and future are more important.
12. Spiritual character of existence has little significance.
13. Pragmatism rejects all types of authoritarianism whether in government or religion or education.

BROAD FEATURES OF PRAGMATISM IN EDUCATION

1. Education should enable the child to learn new techniques to cope with new situations.
2. Values are created through experimentation.
3. Child learns by doing more than by reflection.
4. Education is a continuous process. Education is a constant reorganising or reconstructing of experience.
5. Educational practices have to be experimental.
6. Curriculum is activity centred.
7. Curriculum is integrated.
8. Moral values cannot be imposed by the elders upon the younger generation.
9. Life situations should be made the basis of education.
10. Education is a social necessity. It is the means by which it renews itself.
11. Suitable environment is needed for the development of the personality of the child.
12. Freedom should be given to the child for the development of his all-round personality.
13. Educational experiments lead to the development of philosophy of education.

Pragmatism and Aims of Education

In the words of *Dewey*, "Education as such has no aim".

According to *Ross*, "The most general aim of education according to pragmatism is just creation of new values; the main task of education is to put the educand into position to develop values for himself". Following are the characteristics of the aims of education according to pragmatism:

1. *No Pre-conceived Aims*: There are no pre-conceived aims of education.
2. *No Fixed Aim*: Aims of education are not final and fixed.
3. *Situations and Aims*: Aims of education arise out of situations.
4. *Adaptation to Environment*: Education should enable an individual to adapt to the environment.
5. *Providing Rich Experiences*: Education should provide more and more purposeful experience.

6. *Social Efficiency*: Dewey lays emphasis on preparing a socially efficient individual.

7. *Making Present Life Rich*: The Pragmatists lay great stress on making the present rich and happy.

Pragmatism and Curriculum

Pragmatism points out the following criteria for curriculum construction.

1. *Principle of Utility*: This is the first concern. The school must provide those experiences that are useful to the child. The utility aspect requires direct training for the later stage of the school.

2. *Principle of Child's Natural Instincts*: The curriculum should be based on the natural instincts of the child.

3. *Principle of Graded Curriculum*: The curriculum should take into account the successive stages of child's development.

4. *Principle of Child's Occupations and Activities*: Curriculum attaches limited importance to book learning. Besides the subjects, the curriculum includes purposive, productive and socialised activities.

5. *Principle of Integration*: Subjects are not treated in water-tight compartments. Subjects are presented as modes of activities. Integration, for the pragmatist is of life, with activity of the learner.

6. *Principle of Social Worth*: A pragmatist also recognises that the subjects and experiences provided to the child must make him socially useful.

7. *Principle of Dynamism*: The pragmatist does not believe in the rigidity of the curriculum. So the curriculum is not static. Curriculum changes according to the needs of the pupils and the society. The main aim of knowledge, i.e., human progress should not be overlooked.

Curriculum includes tools of knowledge as reading, writing, counting, nature study, drawing, handwork, hygiene, physical training, history, geography, science—domestic science for girls and agricultural sciences for boys. Vocational training is an indispensable part of the curriculum.

Pragmatism and Methods of Teaching

The basic principle of education is that child is ever active—doing, doing and doing. While doing, he is learning. While learning, he is doing.

Pragmatism tells us to confront the child with real situations—help him to adjust himself, not by a passive surrender but by a constant, dynamic interaction between himself and the changing situations, himself also changing all the while, for the improvement involves a change in himself. Doing and learning; learning by doing, let him have a perception of 'self'. Let him project himself into a self which he would like to do. Let him strive, struggle, change the situation, change his self and achieve, thus realising his 'self'. All knowledge, all experiences are to be coordinated in human terms. All principles are just pointers.

Child's activities are:

1. Spontaneous activities.
2. Purposeful activities.
3. Socialised activities.

Following are the important principles of pragmatism:

1. Principle of purpose
2. Principle of learning by doing
3. Principle of integration
4. Principle of project or project method

Pragmatism and Discipline

Pragmatism holds that discipline should be social through and through. Free, purposeful and cooperative activities organised in the school lead to social discipline. These activities inculcate attitudes of cooperation and consideration. Besides, these keep the students busy in worthwhile tasks. Moral development taken place through such activities. Students develop a sense of self-control.

Pragmatism and the Teacher

Pragmatism regards the teacher as a helper and guide. The teacher assumes the role of an 'arranger of experience'. According to Dewey, "The teacher is a guide and director, he steers the boat, but the energy that propels it must come from those who are learning".

The teacher's job is to keep the child alive to:

His purposes,
His capacities,
His limitations.

So that he evolves his own discipline.

Develops his own values,
Makes his own adjustment,
And thus realises himself.

Pragmatism and the School

Dewey regarded the school as an 'epitome' of life outside, as the 'miniature of society' and also the 'lengthened arm of the family'.

Dewey sets out the following functions of the school.

1. *Providing a Simplified Environment*: A complex civilisation is too complex to be assimilated in toto. It has to be broken up into portions, and assimilated in a gradual and graded way. The relationships of our present social life are so numerous and so inter-woven that even a child placed in the most favourable position could not readily share in many of the most important of them. The first function of the school, therefore, is to select those features which are fairly fundamental and capable of being responded to by the young.

2. *Eliminating 'the Unworthy Features of the Existing Environment'*: Dewey explains this point, "As a society becomes more enlightened, it realises that it is responsible not to transmit and conserve the whole of its existing achievements but only such as make for a better future society. The school is the chief agency for the accomplishment of this end."

3. *Balancing the Various Elements in the Social Environment*: It is the function of the school to co-ordinate within the disposition of each individual the diverse influences of the various social environments into which he enters.

That education which does not occur through forms of life, forms that are worth living for their own sake, is always a poor substitute for the genuine reality, and tends to cramp and to deaden.

The school, as an institution, should simplify existing social life; should reduce it, as it were, to an embryonic form. Existing life is so complex that the child cannot be brought into contact with it without either confusion or distraction; he is either overwhelmed by the multiplicity of activities which are going on, so that he loses his own power of orderly reaction, or he is so stimulated by these various activities that his powers are prematurely called into play and he becomes either unduly specialised or else disintegrated.

The social life of the child is the basis of concentration or correlation, in all his training or growth. The social life gives the unconscious unity and the background of all his attainments.

The subject-matter of the school curriculum should mark a gradual differentiation out of the primitive unconscious unity of social life.

We violate the child's nature and render difficult the best ethical results by introducing the child too abruptly to a number of special studies, of reading, writing, geography, etc. out of relation to this social life.

The true centre of correlation on the school subject is not science, nor literature, nor history, nor geography but the child's own social activities.

The studies represent the possibilities of development inherent in the child's immediate crude experience.

Following are the important features of a school:

1. School as an enlarged ideal home.
2. School as a society in miniature.
3. School as a child centred institution.
4. School as a place of providing rich experiences.
5. School as a provider of vocational training.
6. School as a place of training socially efficient individuals.
7. School as a place of 'learning by doing'.
8. School as a place where learning takes place through projects.
9. School as a place of discipline through co-curriculum activities and social environment.
10. School as a place where teacher plays the role of a friend, philosopher and guide.

LIMITATIONS OF PRAGMATISM

1. *Ignoring Eternal Values*: Pragmatism, by and large, ignores eternal values.

2. *Ignoring Spiritual Values*: Pragmatism pays little attention to spiritual values.

3. *Over Emphasis on Material Values*: Pragmatism lays too much emphasis on material things.

4. *Utilitarian Approach*: Pragmatism advocates a utilitarian approach only.

5. *Ignoring Cultural Values*: Pragmatism provides very insignificant place to cultural values.

6. *Neglect of Cultural Heritage*: Pragmatism believes that experience is all in all. It ignores the knowledge accumulated through the ages.

7. *Neglect of System*: Pragmatism does not give due importance to regular and systematic instruction.

8. *Limitations of Projects*: The entire knowledge and experience needed by the child cannot be obtained through projects.

9. *Heavy Demand of the Teacher*: Pragmatism places heavy demands on the teacher.

10. *No Fixed Goals*: Pragmatism does not indicate fixed educational goals.

CONTRIBUTION OF PRAGMATISM TO EDUCATION

1. *Freeing the Over Burdened Child*: Pragmatism saves the child from the burden of education which is too much centred on books.

2. *Due Emphasis on Experience*: Pragmatism helps us in realising the value of today's life by experiencing it.

3. *Balanced Approach*: Pragmatism advises us to have a balanced approach towards the past, present and future. The past may be glorious and rich but it must guide for living a glorious and rich life in the present. Thus too much emphasis on cultural heritage should not be laid.

4. *Learning How to Learn*: The focus of the teaching-learning process is to enable the child how to learn.

5. *Inflexible Methods*: Methods of teaching are based on utility and fulfilment the demands of the society.

6. *Group Methods*: Pragmatism advocates that children should get real experience of group life.

7. *Correlated Methods*: Pragmatism stresses that in order to make progressive methods of teaching successful and effective, there is the need of correlation of studies, integration of subjects, use of audio-visual aids, organisation of curriculum activities, learning by doing, direct experience and proper training of senses.

8. *Developing Self-effort*: Pragmatism believes in developing self-effort.

9. *Group Method for Moral Education*: Pragmatism envisages that the method of moral education should be through group life.

10. *Project Method*: Project method is the most important contribution of pragmatism.

11. *Experience and More Experience*: Pragmatism believes in experimenting with new methods.

12. *Pragmatism Against Bookish Knowledge*: Pragmatism lays stress on action rather than reflection. The child does not learn much from books. He learns from his own experiences, new situations and activities. Pragmatism, therefore, enjoins upon the teaching maxim, 'learning by doing'. Practical work is a very important means of instruction. The child should be put in real situations so that he may himself solve the problems arising out of them.

13. *Social Discipline*: Pragmatism accords a special role to activities leading to social discipline.

14. *Balanced Approach to the Role of the Teacher and the Pupil*: Pragmatism accepts that the teacher and the students are the active participants in the educative process.

COMPARATIVE IMPACT OF IDEALISM, NATURALISM AND PRAGMATISM ON EDUCATIONAL THEORY AND PRACTICE

Idealism	*Naturalism*	*Pragmatism*
I. *Basic Philosophical Features*		
1. Idealism believes in the existence of God.	Naturalism has no belief in the existence of God.	Pragmatism has some belief in the existence of God.
2. Universe is God's creation.	Universe is man's creation.	Universe is natural creation.
3. Ultimate reality is spiritual.	Ultimate reality is physical.	Ultimate reality is utility.
4. Eternal spiritual values never change.	Values are not eternal.	Values are changeable.
5. Truth, beauty and goodness are eternal values.	There are no such values.	The nature of these values undergoes changes.
6. Spiritual laws are universal	Physical and natural laws are universal	There are no universal laws
II. *Aims of Education*		
1. Self-realisation aim.	1. Self-expression aim.	1. Self-sufficiency aim.
2. Spiritual development aim.	2. Autonomous development of the indivi - duality aim.	2. Adjustment with present aim.
3. Character development aim.	3. Adjustment to environment aim.	
III. *Curriculum*		
1. Emphasis on ethics and humanities.	1. Emphasis on sciences.	1. Stress on utilitarian subjects and vocational subjects,
2. Study of cultural heritage.	2. Curriculum band on the need, ability and aptitude of the individual nature.	2. Life experiences. 3. Integrated curriculum
IV. *Methods of Teaching*		
1. Lecture method.	1. Direct observation.	1. Learning by doing.
2. Question-answer method.	2. Heuristic method.	2. Project method.

(*Contd.*)

Idealism	Naturalism	Pragmatism
V. *Discipline*		
1. Emphasis on regulated freedom.	Uncontrolled freedom.	Social discipline.
2. Self discipline.	Discipline through natural consequences.	Discipline through group work.
VI. *Teacher's Role*		
1. Important role of the teacher.	Limited role of the teacher.	Teacher as a guide.
2. Importance of teacher's personality.	Very little importance to teacher's personality.	Limited importance.
3. Teacher as an ideal person.	Teacher as an observer.	Teacher as a friend and philosopher.

Rusk explains the difference in these philosophies as "Naturalism reduces everything to life, idealism to mind or spirit and pragmatism sees no necessity for seeking one fundamental principle of explanation. It is quite content to admit several principles and accordingly is pluralistic".

According to *William James*, "For naturalisms reality is ready-made and complete, while for pragmatist, it is still in the making and awaits its part of completion from the future".

Summing up: We cannot remain wedded to a particular philosophy. Each philosophy contributes something to educational theory and practice. We must make a balanced and rational use of each type of philosophy according to needs.

21

Rousseau (1712-1778)

A BRIEF LIFE SKETCH

Rousseau, a great Swiss political thinker and educational reformer lost his father at an early age. His father was a poor watchman and could not provide him regular schooling. He left school at the age of 12 and tried unsuccessfully all sorts of occupations – apprenticeship to an engraver etc. He became a music critic for sometimes at Paris. From the age of twelve to twenty nine years, he remained a vagabond and during his wanderings he met different types of people, learnt to sympathise with the poor. He developed love for nature. He also defied the conventional rules of society.

Rousseau revolted against the established (canons) of society and advocated the doctrine of "Back to nature". He wrote, "Man is born free and every where he is in chains". His ideas were vehemently opposed by the establishment. His books were burnt. He incurred the displeasure of the French authorities and had to live in exile for many years. He was so much disgusted and disappointed that he committed suicide in 1778. However, his greatness was recognised later on and his views had tremendous influence on the outbreak of the French Revolution in 1789.

PUBLICATIONS OF ROUSSEAU AND ESSENCE OF HIS WRITINGS

After wandering for a number of years, he settled down in Paris (France). In 1750, at the age of 38, Rousseau wrote his first book *The Progress of the Art and the Science*. This was followed by *The Origin of Inequality Among Men* (1753), *The New Heloise—A Romance* (1759); *Social Contract* (1762), and *Emile* or *Concerning Education* (1762).

In his publications, he criticised the existing institutions. He attributed the existing oppression and corruption of the society to the advancement of civilisation which according to him was the main cause of the differences and inequalities among men. Regarding the absolute powers of the sovereign, Rousseau wrote, "He cannot impose upon his subjects fetters that are useless to the community".

ROUSSEAU'S VIEWS ON EDUCATIONAL THEORY AND PRACTICES

I. Rousseau's Educational Philosophy

'Return to nature' was the theme of his two educational publications (novels): *The New Heloise* (1761) and '*Emile*' (1762). These books, were among the most widely read of the popular writing of the century.

Rousseau was an arch enemy of child neglect. His *Emile* made Europe child conscious. It is still widely quoted in almost all books on educational philosophy: principles and practices.

II. Sources of Education

According to Rousseau following are the three main sources of education.

1. *Education of Nature*: "The constitutional exertion of our organs and faculties is the education of nature".

(Discussed Separately)

2. *Education given by Men*: "The uses we are taught to make of that exertion, constitute the education given to us by men".

3. *Education from Circumstances*: "And in the acquisition made by our own experience, on the objects that surround us, consists our education from circumstances".

By education from nature, he meant development according to the child's endowments and capacities. By education from men, he emphasised the importance of social environment, teaching how to make use of that development. By education from things, he understood physical environment, helping to gain experience by ourselves. He says that harmonious development of these three factors constitutes an ideal scheme of education.

Such harmony in education is possible by subordinating the education of men and things to that of nature because we have no control over nature. We, must, therefore, direct the other two, to ensure cooperation of these factors for imparting ideal education.

III. Rousseau's Theory of Negative Education

Rousseau believed that everything is good as it comes from nature and it generates in the hands of man, so he advocated that the education of the child should be purely negative. The child should not be taught the principles of truth and virtue but guarded against evil. He wrote, "I call a positive education one that tends to form the mind prematurely and to instruct the child in the duties that belong to him. I call negative education one that tends to perfect the organs that are the instruments of knowledge and endeavours to process the way for reasons, by the proper exercises of senses".

(Discussed separately in another chapter)

IV. Aims of Education

Rousseau's aim of education was the attainment of fullest natural growth of the individual, leading to balanced, harmonious useful and natural life. The real aim of education is to help the child to live his life. He says, "To live is not merely to breathe. It is to act, to make use of our organs, senses, our faculties and of all those parts of ourselves, which give us the feeling of our existence".

This general aim of education was split up by Rousseau, according to the nature, at different stages of human development.

(i) *Infancy*, i.e., from birth to the age of five years, the aim of education is to develop a well-regulated freedom.

(ii) *In childhood*, i.e., between the age of five and twelve, the main aim of education is to provide the child with the strength which he needs for the attainment of well-regulated freedom.

(iii) *In boyhood or pre-adolescent period*, i.e., from twelve years to fifteen years the aim of education is "to acquire such knowledge which may satisfy the wants of the child and must be functionally useful". This is the period for intellectual education—the period of instruction, labour and study.

(iv) *In adolescent period*, i.e., from 15 to 20 years, the aim of education is the training of heart, to make the child loving and tender-hearted so that he may live peacefully in social relationship. In this period, religious, moral and social education is recommended. In the previous periods, the child has already developed physically and intellectually. He must now grow emotionally, aesthetically, socially and morally. The sex instinct, which is sufficiently developed by this time, is to be sublimated by re-directing it to the love of some noble idea and by keeping the young occupied in work and activity.

V. Curriculum

Rousseau recommends curriculum in accordance with the nature of each stage of the child.

Curriculum at the First Stage: Curriculum at the first stage (from one to 5 years) would be such as it develops physical strength. The child should be allowed to wander freely on the country-side. His play-things should be very simple such as branches with fruits and flowers and no expensive toys. 'Let him not be pampered! Let him not be subdued'.

Curriculum at the Second Stage: Curriculum at the second stage (between 5 to 12 years) should lead to the development of senses. Rousseau thinks that if senses are not trained properly, independent reasoning and judgement are impossible. Emile (the hero of the novel Emile) is to be given the greatest freedom of physical movement, simple diet and light clothing. There will be no verbal lessons for him. He will not be instructed in language, history and geography. Emile is to learn from his own experience. No moral instruction is to be given. "Exercise the body, the organs, the senses and powers but keep the soul lying fallow as long as you can." Training for senses means learning to judge, foresee and reason through them. It is more than the mere use of them. All learning must come by play-way. There is no need for the child to learn anything by heart. For Emile there is no curriculum. He has to learn by activity and experience.

Curriculum at the Third Stage: Curriculum at the third stage of pre-adolescence (12 to 15 years) should be built around curiosity which should create an urge for knowledge. Rousseau states that this is the period for developing intellect. Emile is introduced to studies that reveal nature, astronomy, science and the arts and crafts. Rousseau emphasises the learning of manual and industrial arts partly to make Emile independent and partly to overcome the prejudice held against the manual work. Rousseau wanted that the boy must be taken from one workshop to another and he must try his hand at every trade. In this way Rousseau wanted to teach him industrial exchange, banking and transportation. Rousseau does not recommend the study of books. The only book he recommends is *Robinson Crusoe*, a study of life according to nature.

Curriculum at the Fourth Stage: In the fourth stage of the adolescence period (15 to 20 years of age), training of heart should receive attention. In the earlier stages, the boy was an individual working for self-perfection and self-development. Now he has to be social and adapt himself to the conduct and interest of others. The study of society, politics, economics, history and religion are the appropriate studies for the youth to understand complex social relationships. Emile must be provided opportunities for training in moral education about his relations with his fellow men and moral qualities such as benevolence, kindness, service and sympathy. Rousseau recommends that moral education should be given through activities and occupations and not through lectures on ethics. History will be utilised as a means of moral instruction. Travel is recommended for knowing the world and the institutions of the neighbouring countries. At this stage the youth undergoes a new birth on account of the appearance of sex impulse. Sex instruction is to consist of direct moral exhortation on chastity and an explanation of the mysteries of creation in the world of plants, animals and men in a dispassionate manner.

Education of Women: Rousseau maintained that women were the makers of men. They were, "the chaste guardians of our morals, and the sweet security of our place". Their education was to be different from men. Rousseau believed that "Woman is made specially to please man". She has, therefore, to be taught to be soft and sweet and learn to suffer and bear the wrongs of her husband without complaint". The duty of women towards man is "to train him in childhood, to tend him in womanhood, and to counsel him throughout his life". Rousseau, therefore, advocated that her studies, should be practical. Intellectual interests, he believed, destroyed her nature. He stated, "I would a hundred times prefer a simple girl, rudely brought up to a girl of learning".

He remarked, "A woman of literacy education (culture) is the plague of her husband; her children, her family, her servants—everybody". Sophie, therefore, is to learn embroidery, lace making, the art of house decorating and house keeping, sewing etc.

VI. Methods of Teaching

Observation of the Nature of the Child: Rousseau wrote, "I wish some discreet person would give us a treatise on the art of observing children—an art which would be of immense value to us but of which parents and schoolmasters have not yet learnt the very first rudiment".

Art of Teaching: Rousseau further said, "To know how to suggest is the art of teaching".

Rousseau emphasised, "The highest function of the teacher consists not much in imparting knowledge as in stimulating the pupil in its love and pursuit".

He was against the harsh and unsympathetic methods of education which repressed the natural inclinations and tendencies of the child. He advocated simple and direct methods of instruction and urged, "experience before expression" and "objects before words". He said, "Give your scholar no verbal lesson. He should be taught by experience alone. Teach by doing whenever you can and only fall back upon words when doing is out of question. Book knowledge should be as little as possible". Emphasising "object teaching", he remarked, "Let the senses always be the guides. Let there be no books but the world and no other instruction than facts. The child who reads, does not think, he merely reads. He is not receiving instruction but learning words".

Methods of teaching advocated by Rousseau may be summed as:

1. Do not teach books. "I hate books. They only teach us to talk about things that we know nothing about. To conceal their deficiencies, teachers choose the dead languages—words, words, words".

2. Provide opportunities to children from their own experience and not from books.

"Let him (the child) not be taught science, let him discover it".

3. Provide sense training.

4. Never substitute the symbol for the thing unless it is impossible to show the thing itself.

VII. Role of the Teacher

Rousseau assigns a minor place to the teacher in the educative process. He is not called an instructor but only a guide. His main responsibility is to motivate the child to learn. This he can achieve by exploiting the innate tendencies of the child. He must possess a profound understanding of the child's nature and be able to control his emotional reactions. He is not to impose any rules of control upon the child. He is to allow him perfect freedom and guide him properly.

Rousseau wrote, "The highest function of the teacher consists not so much in imparting knowledge as on stimulating the pupil in its love and pursuit". Further he advises, "To know how to suggest is the art of teaching". Rousseau placed stress on developing the reasoning power of the child. He observed, "If ever you (teacher) substitute authority in the place of argument, he (child) will reason no longer, he will ever afterwards be handed like a shuttle cork between the opinion of others".

VIII. Freedom of the Child—Discipline by Natural Consequences

He believes in freedom of the child. It is only in a free atmosphere that the child will be able to develop his inborn and innate capacities. He does not believe in punishing the child so as to correct his future behaviour. The reason behind this assumption according to Rousseau is very simple—the child is not able to link up the punishment administered and the mischief done by him. Children, therefore, should be left alone to experience the consequences of the mischief done by them. Nature, according to Rousseau, is a great teacher. If children commit mistakes and violate the principles of nature, they naturally invite the retribution of nature. This conception in the field of education is known as "Discipline by natural consequences".

Secondly, in the field of education, Rousseau starts with the assumption that the nature of child is essentially good, hence he should have freedom in his actions. Firstly he believes that the child will not commit any immoral act, and secondly even if he commits any, he will learn morality by the natural consequences of the action done.

'EMILE': AN IMPORTANT TREATISE ON EDUCATION

Emile is a treatise on education cast in the form of a novel in which there are three characters; Emile, who may be regarded as 'Rousseau' while a boy, and his tutor, who is obviously Rousseau, as a man, Sophie, who is destined to be the mate of Emile.

Emile consists of five books or parts on training and education.

Book I deals with the infant; Book II with childhood; Book III with the pre-adolescent between the ages of twelve and fifteen; Book IV with adolescence; and Book V with the education of girls.

(Curriculum given in *Emile* has been detailed above)

Lord Morley has described the value of *Emile* in these words, "It touched the deeper things of character. It filled parents with a sense of the dignity of their task. It cleared away the accumulation of clogging prejudices and obscure inveterate usage, which made education one of the dark formalistic arts. It admitted floods of light and air into the tightly closed nurseries and school rooms. It effected the substitution of growth for mechanism... It was the charter of youthful deliverance".

On the other hand, the Parliament of Paris criticised *Emile* very severely. It was ordered to be burnt publicly. Orders for the arrest of Rousseau were issued and he had to run away from France to Switzerland. The reading of *Emile* was forbidden by the Archbishop of Paris. The book was condemned on account of 'Containing an abominable doctrine, ready to subvert natural law and to destroy the foundations of the Christian religion... tending to trouble the peace of States, to cause subjects to revolt against their sovereigns; as containing a large number of prepositions false, scandalous, full of hate against the Church, derogatory to the respect of holy scriptures .... erroneous, impious, blasphemous and heretical".

AN ANALYSIS OF ROUSSEAU'S VIEWS ON EDUCATION

A. Limitations

1. Rousseau has not suggested a formal system of education.
2. Physical nature alone is not sufficient for providing education.
3. Rousseau almost ignores the importance of books and other media. It is difficult to assume that we can neglect the vast intellectual heritage.
4. Absolute freedom as recommended by Rousseau is a myth. It cannot exist. It never existed and will not exist. We cannot allow the child to hang himself from a long rope—punishment by natural consequences. We cannot allow the child to have a taste of poison and suffer the natural consequences of his action.
5. Rousseau does not give due importance to the role of the teacher in the education of the child.
6. It is very difficult to find naturalistic surroundings to locate educational institutions.

7. Rousseau's ideas about the role and education of women are very conservative and do not appeal to the modern mind.

8. Rousseau's educational principles are the outcome of his theorising. These were not put to test in any realistic educational setting.

ROUSSEAU'S CONTRIBUTION TO EDUCATION

Notwithstanding some limitations, Rousseau stands to modern education as Plato to ancient education. His *Emile* made Europe child conscious so much as no writing had done for centuries and it became an inspiring source of reforms. William Boyd in *History of Western Education* has paid glowing tribute to *Emile*. "Judged by effects on thought and action is indeed perhaps the most considerable book ever written on education".

Rousseau's chief contributions may be summarised as:

1. Rousseau was the fore-runner of the modern educational psychology. He ushered in a new movement in education by emphasising the importance of individual differences.

2. He laid stress on the spontaneous unfolding of child's capacities.

3. He pointed out the importance of observing the natural traits of children.

4. He stressed that in the drama of education, child must play the role of the 'hero' and all actors subordinate roles.

5. He propounded the idea of 'learning by doing'.

Opportunistic, unreliable, unscrupulous, at times, a gigolo, at other times a liar, a thief and the unacknowledged father of several illegitimate children by his own confession, Rousseau had the flash of a genius that seemed to attract followers and friends despite his shortcomings. His writings have exercised such an influence on educational theory and practice that they are widely quoted even today. There is no doubt that he is considered one of the great leaders of the world.

22

Dewey, John (1852-1959)

BRIEF LIFE SKETCH OF JOHN DEWEY

Dewey was born in 1859 at Burlington in the USA. He graduated from the University of Vermont in 1879 and started his career as a teacher. Thereafter he joined Hopkins University and obtained his Ph.D. degree in Philosophy in 1884. He worked as a Professor of Philosophy at the University of Minnesota, Michigan and Chicago. His last assignment was his professorship of education and philosophy at the University of Columbia, New York.

Prof. Dewey delivered lectures on education and philosophy at the University of Peking for a period of two years.

The Government of Turkey invited Dewey to draw up a report on the reorganisation of national schools.

Prof. Dewey's philosophy is not simply speculative but based on actual experiences in the classroom. His principles and practices grew out of his experiments in the University Laboratory School, Chicago. He founded this school in 1896, for the chief objective of testing educational theory through experiments.

PUBLICATIONS OF JOHN DEWEY

Perhaps no educator has written such a standard and diverse literature on educational principles and practices as Prof. Dewey. Likewise enormous material has been published on him and his works. His first article entitled 'The Metaphysical Assumption of Materialism' appeared in Journal of Speculative Philosophy in April 1882.

Dewey's important publications are as under:

1. *My Pedagogic Creed* (1897)
2. *Psychology and Philosophic Method* (1899)
3. *Studies in Logical Theory* (1903)
4. *Ethics* (1908)
5. *The Influence of Darwin and Other Essays* (1910)
6. *How We Think* (1910)
7. *Democracy and Education* (1916)
8. *Essays in Experimental Logic* (1916)
9. *Creative Intelligence* (1917)
10. *Lectures at Tokyo Imperial University* (1920)
11. *Reconstruction in Philosophy* (1920)
12. *Human Nature and Conduct* (1922)

13. *Experience and Nature* (1925)
14. *The Public and Its Problem* (1927)
15. *The Quest for Certainty* (1927)
16. *Art as Experience* (1934)
17. *A Common Faith* (1934)
18. *Philosophy and Civilisation* (1934)
19. *Liberalism and Social Action* (1935)
20. *Experience in Education* (1938)
21. *Freedom and Culture* (1939)
22. *Theory of Valuation* (1939)
23. *Problems of Men* (1946)
24. *Knowing and the Known* (1949)
25. *Education Today* (1949)
26. *Interest and Effort in Education* (1953)
27. *Schools of Tomorrow* (1953)
28. *The Child and the Curriculum* (1956)
29. *The School and Society* (1900)
30. *Philosophy of Education* (1958)
31. *Moral Principles in Education* (1959)

PHILOSOPHY OF PRAGMATISM OF DEWEY

(See Chapter 20)

DEWEY'S VIEWS ON VARIOUS ASPECTS OF EDUCATION

1. Dewey's Philosophy of Education

Dewey's philosophy of education is given various names. 'Experimentalism', 'Functionalism', 'Instrumentalism', 'Operationalism', 'Practicalism', 'Pragmatism' and 'Progressivism'. Of course, his philosophy of education is mostly associated with the term 'Pragmatism'. All these terms indicate the dynamic, ever-changing and performing character of life. Dewey suggested the application of experimental logic. He emphasised that as all experiences cannot be educative, the business of the educator is to select an experience or experiences which would enable the individuals to live creatively, constructively, dynamically and fruitfully in the changing environment.

What is a thing for? What is its use? Action must precede knowledge. Whatever knowledge we possess has resulted from our activities, our efforts to survive. Only that which has been organised into our dispositions so as to enable us to adapt our environment to our needs and to adapt our aims and desires to the situations in which we exist is really knowledge.

2. Meaning of Education

Education as a Psychological and Social Process: Dewey does not believe in absolute values. According to Dewey, "Education is the process of reconstruction or reconstitution of experience, giving it a more detailed value through the medium of increased social efficiency". Dewey further observed, "What nutrition and reproduction are to physiological life, education is to social life". He considered education as 'the fundamental method of social progress and reform. In sum, I believe that the individual who is to be educated is a social individual and that society is an organic union of individuals. If we eliminate the social factor from the child, we are left only with an abstraction; if we eliminate the individual factor from society, we are left only with an inert and lifeless mass. Education, therefore, must begin with a psychological insight into the child's capacities, interests, and habits. It must be controlled at every point by reference to these same considerations. These powers, interests, and habits must be continually interpreted—we must know what they mean. They must be translated in terms of their social equivalents in terms of what they are capable of in the way of social service'.

"I believe that all education proceeds by the participation of the individual in the social consciousness of the race. This process begins unconsciously almost at birth, and is continually shaping the individual's powers, saturating his consciousness, forming his habits, training his ideas, and arousing his feelings and emotions. Through this unconscious education the individual gradually comes to share in the intellectual and moral resources which humanity has succeeded in getting together. He becomes an inheritor of the funded capital of civilisation. The most formal and technical education in the world cannot safely depart from this general process. It can only organise it or differentiate it in some particular direction.

I believe that the only true education comes through the stimulation of the child's powers by the demands of the social situations in which he finds himself."

3. Dewey's Concept of Social Efficiency

Social efficiency broadly speaking includes three elements of efficient industrial development and the art of living together. A man must learn to be economically self-sufficient and at the same time acquire qualities and values of an enlightened citizen. An individual must be able to earn his livelihood. An individual who is not able to earn his livelihood, is a parasite. Education must take into account economic aspect. An individual should be trained to make the best use of national resources. A school was considered as a 'society in miniature'.

Dewey was a firm believer in democratic values. He, therefore, insisted that education should provide suitable opportunities to the students to imbibe democratic values.

4. Functions of Education

Dewey explains the functions of education in these words, "It is a common place to say that development of character is the ultimate end of all school work. In general, character means organised capacity of social functioning. It means social interest and responsiveness". He further says, "The function of education is to help the growing of a helpless young animal into a happy, moral and efficient human being".

5. Child's Place in the Educative Process

Dewey observes, "Education must begin with a psychological insight into the child's capacities, interests and habits. These must be continually interpreted, we must know what they mean. They must be translated into their social equivalents—into terms of what they are capable of in the way of social service". In this regard he outlined the function of the teacher as, "The more a teacher is aware of the past experience of students, of their hopes, desires, chief interests, the better will he understand the forces at work that need to be directed and utilised for the formation of reflective habits."

6. Curriculum

The curriculum must grow out of child's interests, experiences, impulses and needs. The curriculum must be child-centred. He stressed that the school subjects should be woven around the child's activities. Lessons should begin with social topics such as food, shelter, modes of communication, speech, reading, drawing, modelling, etc. While laying stress on the needs of the children, Dewey also took into account the needs of the community in which the children live.

Following are the main characteristics and principles of the curriculum:

1. Curriculum should reflect the social life and social activities. It should have utility.
2. It must follow the principle of progressive organisation of knowledge consisting of educative experiences and problems of the learners.
3. The new experiences and problems should grow out of the old ones.
4. The experiences should be flexible and changeable in accordance with the child's interests and should be graded.

7. Methods of Teaching

Dewey said, "All learning must come as a by-product of actions and for its own sake". This reveals his concepts of observation, and direct experience. According to him, a child learns through participation in various activities. He advocated 'learning by doing' and 'learning by living'. He recommended the Project Method which is based on problems, activities, experiments and interests of the learners.

Dewey has explained the problem method of teaching in his books: *How We Think* and *Interest and Effort in Education* as, "the processes by which the mind of the individual comes into relation with the objective world. Interest and self-activity are the characteristic features". It is a method which deals with the intellectual processes that are antecedent to induction and deduction.

Dewey briefly recommended the following methods of instruction:

1. Learning by doing.
2. Learning by integration and correlation.
3. Learning through productive and creative activities.

8. Dewey's Concept of Discipline

Dewey held that the natural impulses of the child ought to be directed and disciplined through the cooperative activities of the school. "Out of doing things that are to produce results, and out of doing in a social and cooperative way, there is born a discipline of its own kind and type". Dewey believed that the child's activities—intellectual, social, moral and physical—are disciplinary in their effect if they are carried out in cooperation with others.

9. John Dewey on the Role of the Teacher

The teacher is engaged not simply in the training of individuals, but in the formation of the proper social life.

Every teacher should realise the dignity of his calling; that he is a social servant set apart for the maintenance of proper social order and the securing of the right social growth.

In this way the teacher always is the 'prophet of the true God' and the usherer in the true kingdom of God. He also said, "The teacher is a guide and director; he steers the boat, but the energy that propels it must come from those who are learning. The more a teacher is aware of the past experiences of students, of their hopes, desires, chief interests, the better will he understand the forces at work that need to be directed and utilised for the formation of reflective habits".

10. Dewey's Concept of Democracy and Democratic Values in Education

Dewey states that democracy is the political and moral philosophy of education. "If education is equivalent to genuine living, then democracy is the moral foundation of education. The essence of education is the extension of shared areas of meaningful action and this is also the essence of democracy".

The school as the 'democratic society in miniature' should provide for the participation of the students in the activities of the school on the one hand and on the other hand it should realise the significance of the experiences, needs and interests of the child as a personality.

Democracy postulates full freedom of enquiry into social and political problems and solving them. Likewise the schools should promote a spirit of enquiry in educational thinking. Discussion should be freely permitted.

The schools should become guardians of academic freedom. Intellectual or moral freedom is the basis of political freedom.

The schools should become living examples of the practices of freedom of enquiry, experimentation and intelligent communication.

Excessive heavy routines and rules are not conducive to self and social disciplines.

Dewey advocates that teacher should be provided opportunities to "participate in the formation of the controlling aims, methods and materials of the school of which he is apart".

To sum up, Dewey wants that education should reflect democratic principles and practices in matters of school organisation, selection of activities and experiences and other matters.

FUNCTIONS OF THE SCHOOL: SCHOOL RELATED TO SOCIAL LIFE

Dewey regarded school as the 'epitome' of life outside, as the 'miniature society' and also the 'lengthened arm of the family'. He said, "The school, now divorced from life, must be reunited with it through activities that will simplify its relations, develop its essential meaning, eliminate its unworthy and obsolescent features, and extend the individual's social environment so that he escapes from the limitations of the group into which he is born".

Dewey sets out the following functions of the school.

1. *Providing a Simplified Environment*: A complex civilisation is too complex to be assimilated in toto. It has to be broken up into portions, and assimilated in a gradual and graded way. The relationships of our present social life are so numerous and so inter-woven that even a child placed in the most favourable position could not readily share in many of the most important of them. The first function of the school, therefore, is to select those features which are fairly fundamental and capable of being responded to by the young.

2. *Eliminating 'the Unworthy Features of the Existing Environment'*: Dewey explains this point, "As a society becomes more enlightened, it realises that it is responsible not to transmit and conserve the whole of its existing achievements but only such as make for a better future society. The school is the chief agency for the accomplishment of this end".

3. *Balancing the Various Elements in the Social Environment*: It is the function of the school to coordinate within the disposition of each individual the diverse influences of the various social environments into which he enters.

That education which does not occur through forms of life, forms that are worth living for their own sake, is always a poor substitute for the genuine reality, and tends to cramp and to deaden.

The school, as an institution, should simplify existing social life; should reduce it, as it were, to an embryonic form. Existing life is so complex that the child cannot be brought into contact with it without either confusion or distraction; he is either overwhelmed by the multiplicity of activities which are going on, so that he loses his own power of orderly reaction, or he is so stimulated by these various activities that his powers are prematurely called into play and he becomes either unduly specialised or else disintegrated.

The social life of the child is the basis of concentration or correlation, in all his training or growth. The social life gives the unconscious unity and the background of all his attainments.

The subject-matter of the school curriculum should mark a gradual differentiation out of the primitive unconscious unity of social life.

We violate the child's nature and render difficult the best ethical results by introducing the child too abruptly to a number of special studies, of reading, writing, geography, etc. out of relation to this social life.

The true centre of correlation on the school subject is not science, nor literature, nor history, nor geography but the child's own social activities.

The studies represent the possibilities of development inherent in the child's immediate crude experience.

LABORATORY SCHOOL, UNIVERSITY OF CHICAGO

Objective: Dewey felt that the changed times demanded that the training of students for a complete living in the society should be provided in the school. For finding out the type of training to be imparted, he carried out his experiments in the school which he established in 1896.

Main Problems: Following were the main educational problems which Dewey wanted to solve:

1. How to bring the school into closer relation with the home and surrounding life.
2. How to introduce subject-matter in various disciplines like history, science and art to impart a positive value and real significance in child's life.
3. How can instructions in different subjects be carried on with everyday experience and occupation, as the background and be correlated with each other.
4. How individual powers and needs be catered to.

Manual Occupations as the Basis: Dewey introduced the following manual occupations related to everyday life for imparting knowledge of various subjects:

(i) Shop work with wood and tools.
(ii) Cooking work.
(iii) Work with textiles (sewing and weaving).

Dewey accorded a central place to occupations and other subjects were treated incidentally as ancillary to practical activities. Dewey observed that the students think out how to make cloth and reinvent the carding frame, tool for spinning and understand the loom. They learn at the same time enough art and science. "Make the construction adequate, make it full, free and flexible, give it a social motive, something to tell and you have a work of art". Likewise the knowledge of various subjects revolves round such occupations.

Graded Curriculum. Development of interests through occupations was to take place in a developing sequence in accordance with the mental development of the child. Elementary school life was divided into the following periods.

1. Play Period (4 to 8 years of age).
2. Period of Spontaneous Attention (8 to 12 years of age).
3. Period of Affective Attention (12 years onwards).

In the elementary school, the curriculum is based on the four-fold interest of the child.

(a) Interest in conversation and communication.
(b) Interest in inquiry.
(c) Interest in making things or construction.
(d) Interest in artistic expression.

ESSENCE OF JOHN DEWEY'S WORK: CONTRIBUTION TO EDUCATION

1. Dewey fused both the psychological and sociological aspects of education.
2. Dewey emphasised democratic values in all dimensions of education.
3. Dewey laid stress on providing rich and varied activities and experiences to students.

4. Dewey's approach to methodology of teaching led to the emergence of the Project Method in education.

5. Dewey advocated that the programmes of the school should be linked with the life of the society. He in this regard, pointed out that the activities should be simplified and that unworthy activities should be discarded.

6. Dewey wanted that the natural interests of the child should be given due attention.

7. Dewey believed in social discipline that could develop through useful activities.

8. Dewey's watchword was social efficiency coupled with individual efficiency.

EVALUATION OF DEWEY'S WORK

Following points of criticism are usually made:

1. Dewey does not suggest any definite aim of education.
2. Dewey attaches more importance to materialism.
3. Dewey does not accept any truth as something permanent.
4. Dewey puts excessive emphasis on individual differences.
5. Dewey lays too much emphasis on experiences.

Prof. V.P. Verma, in *Studies in the Philosophy of Education* (1964) has given the following merits and demerits of Dewey's theory of education.

Merits: (a) It is a 'social' theory of education as opposed to the stress on the isolated self of the individual.

(b) It is a passionate plea for the wide application of the 'experimental' method in education.

(c) It provides the conception of 'democracy' as a social psychological theory of the progressive extension of shared experiences.

Demerits: (a) Dewey's attempt to trace the roots of the dualist approach (two opposed groups of antagonistic interests)—two-fold division of society is a mistake.

(b) Scientific objectivity and veracity may be difficult for being reconciled with democracy, which in practice, means numerical majority.

(c) The neglect of religious education may result in the destruction of the roots of humanistic values and social ethics.

Fredrik Mayor in his *American Ideas in Education* has summed up the contribution of John Dewey in these words, "In Dewey the voice of the pioneer, the stirring energies of the reformer, the patient method of the scientist and the faith of the teacher are united in a search for a new education through which man can survive in a chaotic age."

According to *Rusk*, "In education we cannot but be grateful to Dewey for his great services in challenging the old 'static cold storage ideal of knowledge' and in bringing education more into accord with the activities of present day life."

Regarding the work of Dewey, Irwin Edman (Ed.) in *John Dewey: His Contribution to American Tradition* (1955) has observed, "The breakdown of the violation of school from society, of book learning from vital experience, of the individual from his environment – the extent to which schools and colleges have removed these separations is a measure of the direct impact of refreshing reconstruction of Dewey's thinking".

Prof. Ulich in *History of Educational Thought* has summed up the contribution of John Dewey in these words, "Dewey's work encourages an experimental and scientific attitude. It shows what men can achieve if they rely on their reason and courage instead of clinging to their prejudice".

23

Philosophical Thought in India and Its Contribution to Education

RICH PHILOSOPHICAL HERITAGE

Indian philosophers and seers from the earliest times have thought deeply on the known and unknown and left no aspect of material existence or spiritual projects left untouched. No wherein else in the world did the human mind go deeper into the relationship of soul ('*Atman*') and Supreme Soul, i.e., God '*Brahman*'. In this context, views of some great Western scholars are quoted here.

1. *Francois Marie Voltaire* (1694-1774): French philosopher and writer, "I am convinced that everything has come down to us from the banks of the Ganga – astronomy, astrology, metaphysics, etc. The Vedas are the most precious gift for which the West has been indebted to the East".

2. *FrederichVon Sehlegel* (1772-1829): German critic, philosopher and writer, "there is no language in the world, even Greek, which has the clarity and the philosophical precision of Sanskrit. India is not only the origin of everything, she is superior in everything, intellectually, religiously, politically and even the Greek heritage seems pale in comparison".

3. *Arthur Schopenhauer* (1788-1860): German philosopher and writer, "In the whole world there is no study so beneficial and so elevating as that of the Upanishads. It has been solace of my life, and it will be the solace of my death. They are the product of the highest wisdom.

4. *Ralph Waldo Emerson* (1803-1883): American author, philosopher and essayist, "I owe a magnificent day to the Bhagwad Gita".

5. *Henry David Thoreau* (1817-1962): American philosopher and writer: "I bathe my intellect in the stupendous and cosmogonal philosophy of the Bhagwad Gita in comparison with which our modern world and its literature seems pumy".

6. *Prof. Max Mueller* (1823-1900): German philologist and philosopher, "In the history of the world, the Vedas fill a gap which no literary work in any language would fill. I maintain that to everybody who cares for himself for the ancestors, for his intellectual development, a study of the Vedic literature is indispensable. The Vedic literature opens to us a chapter what has been called the education of the human race, to which we can find no parallel anywhere else".

7. *Mark Twain* (1835-1910): American writer, "India is a land of religions,

cradle of human race, birth place of human speech, grandmother of legend, greater grandmother of tradition".

8. *Alfred Northwhitehead* (1861-1947): British scholar, "The vastness of knowledge of today cannot transcend the *Buddhi* of the *Rishis* in ancient India, and science, in its most advanced stage now, is closer to Vedanta than ever before".

9. *Ella Wheeler Wilcox* (1850-1919): American poet and journalist, "In India, the land of Vedas, the remarkable works contain not only religious ideas for a perfect life but also facts which science has proved true. Electricity, radium, electronics, airship—all are known to the seers who founded the Vedas".

10. *George Bernard Shaw* (1856-1950): English dramatist, Nobel Laureate in literature, "The Indian way of life provides the vision of the natural way of life. We western veil ourselves with unnatural masks. On the face of India are the tender expressions which carry the marks of the creator's hand. This marks Hinduism the most tolerant religion of the world, because its one transcendent God includes all possible Gods".

11. *William Butler Yeats* (1856-1939): Irish dramatist, essayist, poet and Nobel Laureate. "It was my only first meeting with the Indian philosophy that confirmed my vague speculations and seemed at once logical and boundless".

12. *H.G. Wells* (1866-1946): English author, historian and political philosopher, "There is space in its philosophy for everyone, which is one reason why India is a home to every single region of the world. Hinduism is synonymous with humanism. This is the essence in its great liberating quality".

13. *Herman Hesse* (1877-1962): German poet and novelist, noble laureate, "The marvel of the '*Bhagwad Gita*' in the truly beautiful revelation of life's wisdom which enables philosophy to blossom into religion".

14. *Romain Roland* (1894-1963): French Nobel Laureate and historian, "Religious faith in the case of the Hindus has never been allowed to run counter to scientific laws. Such tolerance may be surprising to religious believers in the West, but it is an integral part of Vedantic belief".

CHIEF SOURCES OF INDIAN PHILOSOPHICAL THOUGHT

The following are the chief sources from which Indian philosophical thought derives its inspiration:

1. Four Vedas
2. Six Vedangas
3. Four Upvedas
4. Four Brahamanas
5. One hundred and eight Upanishads (11 are most important)
6. Six systems of philosophy
7. The Bhagwad Gita
8. Three Smritis.

THE VEDIC PHILOSOPHICAL THOUGHT

Four Vedas: The four Vedas are the original and main sources of Vedic philosophy. Subsequent philosophies are based on the analysis and interpretation of the Vedas.

With a view to understand the philosophy of the Vedas, it is very necessary to understand the meaning of the word 'Veda'. Veda is derived from the root of Sanskrit word '*Vid*'. *Vid* means:

1. to know
2. to be
3. to obtain
4. to consider
5. to feel
6. to tell
7. to dwell

Thus the Vedas are concerned with:

1. Knowing God, Soul, Mind and Nature
2. To be one with God
3. To obtain salvation from the cycle of births and deaths
4. To consider various relationships—God and man, Man and nature, etc.
5. To feel oneness with God
6. To tell the glories of God
7. To dwell into the mysteries of universe and all existence

One and the Only One God

According to *Rig Veda* (1.164.46), God is one but the wise call Him by various names. Again *Yajurveda* (2.3.1) says, "He is addressed as Indra, Varuna and Agni". *Atharva Veda* states, "God is one and only one of His kind. He is called neither the second nor the third nor the fourth. He is called neither the fifth, nor the sixth nor yet the seventh. He is called neither the eighth, nor the ninth, nor yet the tenth. He takes care of all those who breathe or who do not breathe". *Rig Veda* (6.45.16) emphasises "One God alone is to be worshipped".

The Vedas declare God to be the essence of joy and bliss and that essence is in every object. All that exists is the abode of God. He is the indwelling spirit of the world. Let us wish for a life of one hundred years, full of activity. To be active is the only way to live well. All we do and have belongs to Him. Those who do not believe in the spiritual basis of life are 'soul killers'. They ruin their future and go to the regions of darkness. Man's mind is powerful, but it is nothing as compared to the universal Soul which pervades and permeates all. When man realises himself in all and in himself, he is free from the trials and tribulations of ignorance, and enjoys peace and bliss.

Threefold Areas of Contents of the Vedas

The contents of the Vedic philosophy may be categorised under the following three heads:

1. The '*Gyan*' or knowledge or wisdom
2. The '*Karma*' or action or code of conduct
3. The '*Upasana*' or dedication and devotion to God

Main Characteristics of the Thought of the Vedas

1. God is one and only one. He is all pervading, Omniscient, Omnipotent and ever present. He is the Supreme Spirit.

2. There are three entities in this universe—God, Soul and Matter.
3. The universe is real. It is not an illusion or dream.
4. This universe is created by God.
5. The soul is immortal.
6. The ultimate aim of life is to obtain salvation (*moksha*) and union with God.
7. Actions are followed by results—the 'Law of *Karma*'. The law of *Karma* is nothing else but the cause and its effect.
8. The theory of 'rebirth' is a necessary corollary of the Law of *Karma* and immortality of the soul.
9. Knowledge of truth should be acquired and dissipated.
10. Justice should be done to all creatures.
11. All human beings should live in peace and harmony.

The Vedas deal with every branch of knowledge and provide the basic knowledge of humanities, social sciences and natural and physical sciences. They deal with every aspect of human life—birth, childhood, youth, old age, death and rebirth. They point out the duties of a learned man, a student, a soldier, a householder, a warrior and an administrator etc. The Vedas have a message for all people of all nations and of all times. They embody the ways of leading a peaceful life.

The Vedas delve deep into the self as well as into the mysteries of God and nature to make life worth living. They are believed to be of divine origin.

The Vedas contain 20,358 verses: *Rig Veda* (10,522); *Atharva Veda* (5,977); *Yajur Veda* (1,984) and *Sama Veda* (1,875).

EDUCATIONAL IMPLICATIONS OF THE VEDIC THOUGHT

1. *Two Types of Education*: The Vedas mention two types of education, namely, '*paravidya*' and '*aparavidya*'. The former relates to spiritual or ecclesiastical knowledge and the latter relating to temporal or worldly matters. Both the types of education are needed.

2. *Objectives of Education*: Knowledge or learning makes one humble, free of ego. (A.V. VI. 41). Education must give due regard to the application of learning. (Y.V. XX. 12) O Lord! Illuminate the learner for a higher and happier life. (A.V. VII. 6.1).

According to R.K. Mukerjee, "Learning in India through the ages had been prized and pursued not for its own sake. It was sought as the means of salvation (*Moksha*) or self-realisation".

3. *Conducive Environment*: According to the Vedic view, through education one creates an environment conducive to attaining accomplishment of mind, intellect of thought, of purpose, of intelligence, of sense and vision. The parents, therefore, must have a selective environment.

4. *Significance of Women Education*: The Vedas give a very honourable and respectable status to women. They were eligible for higher education also. It is of interest to note that as many as 15 women scholars and seers contributed to several verses in the Vedas. Their names are: Angirasi, Shashwati, Apala, Indrani, Lopamudra, Guhu, Romsha, Sarama, Shraddha, Surya, Urvashi, Vagambhrani, Vasukra Patni, Visvasara and Yami. It is stated,

"O Learned Lady! All life is dependent on you, because you impart education to all". (R.V. II 97.17)

The Vedas accord a high position to the status of women and accordingly their education must receive priority.

5. *Education for World Peace and International Understanding*: The Vedas speak of one world and peace all around. Ideas and values of international understanding find their inspirations from the Vedas.

6. *Methods of Instruction*: These were as under:

(i) Lecture method
(ii) Meditation
(iii) Memorisation
(iv) Correct pronunciation
(v) Debates and discussions

8. *Organisation*: There was no state control on education.

9. *Teacher-pupil relations*: These were very close. The students were very respectful to the teachers who regarded them as their own children.

10. *Residential*: The teacher's home was the educational institution.

PHILOSOPHIC THOUGHT AS CONTAINED IN THE UPANISHADS

Major Source of All Indian Philosophical Thought: Different branches of Indian philosophies have been greatly influenced by Upanishads.

In the words of Schopenhaer (1788-1860), a German philosopher, "In the whole world there is no study so beneficial and elevating as that of the Upanishads. It has been the solace of life".

Prof. Max Mueller (1823-1900), another German philosopher endorses these views as, "If these words of Schopenhaer require endorsement, I shall willingly give it as the result of my own experience".

The *Upanishads* are the works of saints and seers. They deal with matter, soul and their relationships. They also point out how to lead a noble life.

Meaning of Upanishad: The word Upanishad consists of Sanskrit word '*Upa*' meaning 'nearby' and '*ni*' meaning 'sitting'. It, therefore, implies the 'sitting' of a disciple (student) in a devoted manner 'near' his spiritual 'Guru' (teacher or preceptor). Thus the term Upanishad means the knowledge received by the student 'sitting' close to the teacher.

Number of Upanishads: Traditionally, the number of Upanishads is given as 108. However, according to the great seer and scholar Swami Sankaracharya (788-820 A.D.), the principal Upanishads are 10 in number: 1. Isha, 2. Kenya, 3. Katha, 4. Prashna, 5. Mundaka, 6. Mandakya, 7. Chandogya, 8. Brihadaranyaka, 9. Aitareya, 10. Taitreya.

Period of Upanishads: Scholars are divided on the date of the composition of the Upanishads. Many of them, however, agree that most of the principal Upanishads belong to the period 7th century B.C.

Subjects Dealt with in the Upanishads: The Upanishads deal with knowledge (*Vidya*) which nullifies or destroys ignorance (*Avidya*) and takes the seeker to salvation (*Moksha*) and to Brahma (God) and help him to understand Him in the true sense and thus liberates him from the bondage of the world. (Freedom from the cycle of births and deaths).

The *Isha Upanishad* embodies in its very opening verse the central theme of all the Upanishads, namely, the spiritual unity and solidarity of all existence.

The second verse of the *Isha Upanishad* states that life is action. "In this world, one should desire to live one hundred years but only by performing actions".

Essence of the Upanishadic Thought

The essence of the Upanishadic thought may be summed up as under:

1. *Main Objective of Life*

   "From the Unreal lead me to the Real;
   From the Darkness lead me to the Light;
   From the Death lead me to Immortality". (*Brihadaranyaka*)

2. *Realisation of the Supreme*: Supreme is realised by truth, austerity, proper knowledge and self-control. (*Mundaka*)

3. *Passion for Truth*: The mental climate as illustrated in the Upanishads is saturated with a passion for truth and a similar passion for human happiness and welfare.

4. *Knowledge*: Knowledge gained through one-pointed determination removes, shatters or destroys avidya (ignorance or spiritual blindness).

5. *Rightful living*: "Do not covet the wealth of anyone". (*Isha*)

6. *Wise man*: "The wise man who realises all beings as not distinct from his own self, does not by virtue of that perception, hate anyone". (*Isha*)

7. *Life is Action*: "In this world, one should desire to live one hundred years, but only by performing actions". (*Isha*)

8. *Constant Effort*: "Arise, awake and stop not till the goal is reached". (*Katha*)

9. *Freedom*: Physical freedom, mental freedom and the spiritual freedom are the watch words of the Upanishads.

10. *Universal Man*: The Upanishads stand in the forefront in proclaiming the concept of 'Universal Man'.

Educational Implications of the Upanishadic Approach

1. *Aims of Education*: The principal aims of education according to Upanishads are:

   1. Self-realisation or spiritual development.
   2. Acquisition of supreme knowledge.
   3. Character development.
   4. Cultural development.
   5. Development of social virtues.

2. *Questioning Approach*: Of the 10 principal Upanishads, the *Prashna*, as its name implies, is an Upanishad of questions. Each of the 6 chapters comprises a question asked by each of a group of 6 inquiring students and the answers given by the teacher.

3. *Most Intimate Teacher-Pupil Relationship*: Education involving the student 'sitting close (near) to' the teacher means the most intimate student-teacher communion.

4. *Earnestness*: The earnestness of the search for truth is one of the important features of the Upanishads.

5. *Inquiring Mind*: The seeker must have an inquiring mind (*Jigyasa*) and the teacher must satisfy the inquiring mind.

6. *Moral Training*: According to the Upanishads, a rigorous moral training is the necessary prelude to spiritual knowledge.

7. *Significant Place of the Teacher in the Upanishadic Approach to Education and Learning*: The Upanishadic approach assigns an important place to the teacher as the communicator of knowledge and wisdom. According to the Upanishadic approach, the truth is not to be comprehended by the mere logical process of argumentation and dialectics. Only the great teacher could impart the Supreme Knowledge. The Katha Upanishad says, "He (the self) of whom many are not even able to hear, whom many even when they hear of him, do not comprehend, wonderful is a man, who found, who is able to teach him (the self), wonderful is he who comprehends him, when taught by an able teacher".

The teacher was expected to possess virtues of affection, humility and truthfulness etc. Plain living, high thinking, disciplined routine, abstinence from pleasures, mental control and above all sincerity were the chief characteristics of an ideal teacher. The Brahmachari or the student was under the direct observation of his teacher all twenty-four hours and was also expected to lead a pious and disciplined life.

8. *Methods of Study*: Listening, practice or recitation, immediate apprehension of the meaning, discourses and disputation were the methods generally followed.

PHILOSOPHICAL THOUGHT OF THE *BHAGWAD GITA*

A Unique Book: *Srimadbhagwad Gita* is considered by several scholars as the epitome of Indian thought.

Sri Aurobindo, the revolutionary turned philosopher and sage has stated the importance of *Gita* in these words "All we need of spiritual truth for the spiritual life is to be found in the *Gita*."

Sri Swami Parmananda describes the essence of *Bhagwad Gita* as "From the simple duty task to the most exhalted state of spiritual consciousness at every step of the soul's evolution, one may turn to this sacred book for inspiration. The *Bhagwad Gita* stands as a summary of all scriptures teaching the essence of the Vedas."

The *Gita* is so popular that it has more than 50 commentaries in Sanskrit and more than 250 commentaries in other Indian and foreign languages. Almost every year we find a new book on the meaning and message of Gita. It is ascribed to seer Veda Vyasa.

In size, the *Gita* is a little book of seven hundred verses. The verses are divided into eighteen chapters. It is in the form of a dialogue between Arjuna, a noted commander and Shri Krishna, an earthly manifestation of God—'*Avatara*'. The setting of the dialogue is highly dramatic. Arjuna is facing the huge army of his cousins with their supporters, many of whom are his elders including his '*guru*' Dronacharya. Arjuna is to strike them for the enforcement of their claim (Five Pandavas) to the part of the ancestral kingdom which is not accepted by Duryodhana, leader of the Kauravas. The sight of his dear ones dissolves his determination to fight and he lays down his arms and thinks of renouncing the world. Shri Krishna, who is acting as his charioteer urges him to fight for his right cause. Krishna succeeds in persuading Arjuna who ultimately wins the struggle.

The wonderful dialogue closes on the note of dedicated activity, promising glory, success and prosperity to the individual who combines physical valour, with divine wisdom and is entitled Moksha or communication with God through liberating dedication.

Principal Teaching of Gita

1. *Immortality of Soul*: The soul is immortal and the body is perishable. The cycle of creation is a hard fact from which there is no escape.

2. *Theory of Incarnations* (*avatars*): The ordered progress of the world at large is so important that God takes on special forms of prophets of incarnations from time to time to ensure its progress by appropriate guidance.

3. *Doing Duty as Dharma*: The essence of the philosophy as contained in the Gita is with inner convictions. We should discharge our duties diligently and honestly irrespective of the consequences and leave the rest to the Almighty. We must fight for justice and the right cause.

4. *Death is Certain*. Death is inevitable to one who is born. One who dies, is bound to take birth. It does not, therefore, behove one to grieve over an inevitable event.

5. *Action or Karma Yoga*: The whole theme of the third chapter is the philosophy of action. This is also known as '*Karma-Yoga*' – communication with God through action.

6. *Two Ways of Liberation*: According to Gita, there are two ways of liberation—those of action and knowledge. However, the order of activity is more important. It combines personal good with social good.

7. *Social Welfare*: To be content with personal perfection is a narrow ideal. The proper ideal is to give to the world the best and the most that one can and to take from it the least. The wise man acts as a source of guidance and inspiration to the ignorant masses.

8. *Attainment of Moksha* (*Liberation*): The wonderful dialogue closes on the note of dedicated activity promising glory, success and prosperity to the individual who combines physical valour, with divine wisdom and is entitled Moksha or communication with God through liberating dedication. One can be united with Him if one transforms one's action into Him. This is real renunciation.

Selected Verses from *Bhagwad* Gita

Soul is Immortal

As the indweller in the body experiences childhood, youth and old age in the body, he also passes on to another body. The serene one is not affected thereby. (*Adhaya* 2.13)

The soul is neither born nor does it die. Coming into being and ceasing to be do not take place in it. Unborn, eternal, constant and ancient, it is not killed when the body is slain. (*Adhaya* 2.20)

As a man, casting off worn-out garments puts on new ones, so the soul, casting off worn-out bodies enters into the other that is new. (*Adhaya* 2.22)

Weapons do not cleave the soul, fire burns it not, water wets it not, wind dries it not. (*Adhaya* 2.23)

Death is Certain

Death is certain of that which is born, birth is certain of that which is dead. You should not lament over the inevitable. (*Adhaya* 2.27)

Action! Action! Action!

Seek to perform your duty; but lay not claim to its fruits. Be you not the producer of the fruits of *Karma*; neither shall you lean towards inaction. (*Adhaya* 2.47)

Perform action, O Dhanajaya, being fixed in yoga, renouncing attachments and even-minded in success and failure; equilibrium is verily yoga. (*Adhaya* 2.48)

Concentration of Mind

When also, like a tortoise its limbs, he can withdraw the senses from sense objects, his wisdom is then set firm. (*Adhaya* 2.57)

The excited senses, O son of Kunti, impetuously carried away the mind of even a wise man, striving for perfection. (*Adhaya* 2.60)

From anger proceeds delusion; from delusion, confused memory; from confused memory the ruin of reason; due to the ruin of reason, an individual perishes. (*Adhaya* 2.63)

Just as a gale pushes away a ship on the water, the mind that yields to the roving senses, carries away his discrimination. (*Adhaya* 2.67)

EDUCATIONAL IMPLICATIONS OF PHILOSOPHIC THOUGHT OF GITA

The greatest lesson for the learner is that he must have complete faith in his teacher who should also be devoted to his work. True knowledge, learning and wisdom are acquired through ceaseless action coupled with devotion. Concentration on studies leads to enlightenment and self-control. The main characteristics of the learner or a devotee are: He is a lover of knowledge and mankind. He is curious to know and has an abiding faith in his teacher. He very politely but with a subtle resolution puts questions to his teacher to solve his problems. The teacher also makes all possible efforts to enlighten his students and guides him in such a way as he attains the ideals of a self-realised individual.

Following are in brief the main implications of the teachings of Gita:

1. Development of virtuous knowledge.
2. Coordination between the individual and social aim.
3. Development of inner consciousness.
4. Establishing the importance of duty in life.
5. Development of logical and intellectual ability.

6. Close spiritual relation between the teacher and the taught.
7. Pursuit of ideas with single minded devotion.

(See also Buddhism and Jainism, Swami Vivekananda, Sri Aurobindo, Tagore and Gandhiji, Constitutional Provisions, Composite Culture of India).

SYSTEMS OF PHILOSOPHY AND THEIR EDUCATIONAL IMPLICATIONS

India has a very rich tradition of philosophical thought. In ancient India, six systems of philosophy emerged as a result of contemplation of six seers.

Chart Showing Six Systems of Philosophy and Their Propounders

(1)	(2)	(3)	(4)	(5)	(6)
Samkhya	*Vaisesika*	*Nyay*	*Yoga*	*Mimamsa*	*Vedanta*
(Kapila)	(Kanada)	(Gautama)	(Patanjali)	(Jamimini)	(Badarayana) Shankara or Sankara of the 8th Century is considered as the greatest exponent of this thought

According to some thinkers, Buddhism and Jainism are the other two in this category.

Vaisesika System of Philosophy

This system of philosophy founded by Sage Kanada attempts to distinguish between the various kinds of ultimate objects and to classify all these under the following five elements:

(i) Earth ('*Prithvi*')
(ii) Water ('*Jal*')
(iii) Air ('*Vayu*')
(iv) Fire ('*Agni*')
(v) Ether ('*Akash*')

These elements exist in the form of Atom, Time, Space, Mind and Self. The creation of the world begins when the atoms of these five elements start to combine. When these elements disintegrate, the world comes to an end.

Salvation, according to Vaisesika depends on when one fully recognises the atomic nature of the universe and its difference with the soul.

Vaisesika seeks to explain the world by reference to original diversity and comes to establish rather a rough view of self and God. It has very little practical value.

Nyaya System of Philosophy

Important features of the Nyaya system of philosophy are:

1. It considers God as the creator of the world.
2. It is a science of reasoning.

3. It makes a detailed study of the sources or testimonies of knowledge (*pramana*).
4. For arriving at some conclusion, it considers the following aspects:
   (i) Perception (*Pratyaksha*)
   (ii) Inference (*Anumana*)
   (iii) Comparison (*Upamana*)
   (iv) Verbal, i.e., words (*Sabda*)

Sankhya System of Philosophy

The Sankhya philosophy is founded by the Sage Kapila who is said to have flourished about the seventh century B.C. It is the oldest philosophy.

According to this philosophy, soul is immortal. The '*Atman*' (soul) pervades all and is indestructible. Only the physical bodies end. The pure soul neither kills nor is killed. Bodies are like garments to be cast off when old and replaced by fresh ones. With the changing states, bodies appear and disappear.

Birth, childhood, youth, old age and death are the various modes of the soul, which owns or casts off the body.

Body's contact with the physical elements brings about pain and pleasure, which should be endured as the sensations are passing phases.

We must keep our body in a state of strength and vigour so as to live well and to discharge our obligations in a satisfying way to ourselves and to society.

Sankhya identifies three principles or qualities ('*Gunas*' in the formation of personalities—*Satva* or goodness, *Rajas* or passion and *Tamas* or darkness. A well-balanced personality is based on the principal of 'Satva'—good contemplation, good thoughts, good understanding and good (pure) food.

The three characteristics are sometimes illustrated as given in the chart.

An ideal personality has *Satva* traits in all his actions.

There is another interpretation of *Sankhya* philosophy. According to this philosophy, there are twenty-five basic principles (*Tatvas*). Of these first is *Prakriti*, i.e. *matter*. It is from matter that all elements like air, water, weather (*akasa*), intelligence (*buddhi*), self-consciousness, sight, touch, hearing, etc. develop. One of the most important *tatvas* is *Purusa* (soul). *Purusa* is not dependent upon *Prakriti*. Likewise *Prakriti* is dependent on *Purusa*. Salvation lies in understanding this difference.

Three Characteristics of Sankhya Doctrine

'*Satva*' trait implies	'*Rajas*' signifies	'*Tamas*' means
(i) Truth	(i) Fierceness	(i) Darkness
(ii) Wisdom	(ii) Violence	(ii) Gloomy
(iii) Goodness	(iii) Passion	(iii) Foolishness
(iv) Beauty		(iv) Undesirable traits

Yoga

Meaning of Yoga: According to sage Patanjali, the author of an ancient book '*Yoga Sastra*' (circa second B.C.), Yoga is a method of controlling the tendencies of mind. Some scholars regard yoga as an attempt of uniting oneself with the Supreme Spirit, i.e. *Paramatma* or God. Yoga is also described as a way of life for the harmonious development of the body, mind and soul. What Yoga is Not! Very often, Yoga is misunderstood and thought of in terms of certain exercises or *asanas* (postures) for training the body. This is a very narrow concept or meaning of Yoga. It is certainly not a physical act or exercise only. It is much more.

Nature of Yoga: The aim of Yoga is to control one's desires and aspirations. Yoga strives to understand the real nature of soul. This can be best understood by controlling one's desires and aspirations. The state of Yoga can be achieved only by controlling one's desires and lusts. Just as we cannot see the true image of a thing in disturbed water, when the mind is unstable and out of control, we cannot perceive God. Yoga meditation is necessary to get a glimpse of God.

Components of Yoga: Yoga has eight components called *Ashtanga*. These are—*Yama, Niyama, Asana, Pranayama, Pratyahara, Dharana, Dhyana* and *Samadhi*. By following these components ignorance is removed and real knowledge is achieved. As the follower (*Sadhak*) proceeds higher and higher, his ignorance is removed and his wisdom is awakened. So the main aim of Yoga is to remove ignorance and to achieve wisdom.

Stages or Branches of Yoga

According to sage Patanjali, following are the eight stages of Yoga:

1. *Yama* (*Self-control*): This refers to the moral discipline for the individual and it includes truth, the practice of *brahmacharya* (celibacy), non-stealing, non-receiving of gifts and observance of the creed of non-violence.

2. *Niyama* (*Observance*): It means self-purification by practising austerity, purity, contentment, studying scriptures and surrendering oneself to God.

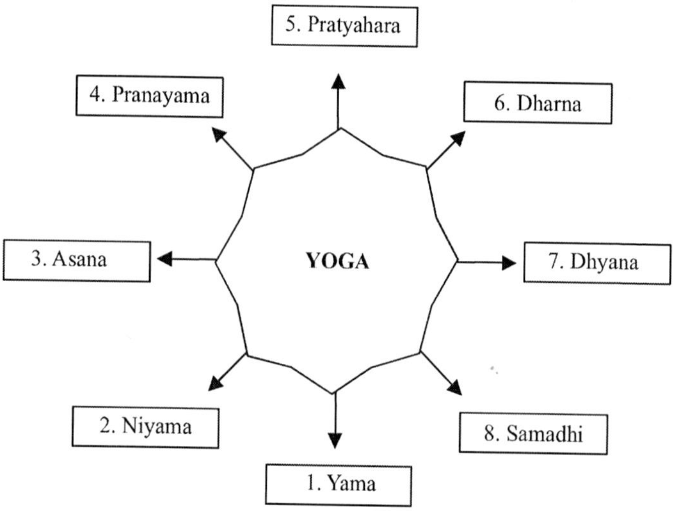

Fig. 23.1: Components of Yoga

3. *Asanas* (*Postures*): This implies practising certain body-postures for acquiring health and developing steadfastness of mind. *Asanas* (exercises or postures) have been developed over the centuries and they help in exercising every muscle, nerve and gland of the body.

4. *Pranayama* (*Control of Breath*): It is the practice of controlling breath for strengthening the respiratory system, purifying blood and soothing the mind.

5. *Pratyahara* (*Restraint*): This is an attempt to free the mind from the domination or control of senses.

6. *Dharana* (*Steadying the Mind*): This is concentration on a single object or point.

7. *Dhyana*: It refers to the concentration on the all-pervading divinity through practice.

8. *Samadhi* (*Meditation*): This is the last stage of Yoga. In this stage, the yogi merges himself with the Divine Spirit, although he is alert and conscious.

Controlling Factors of Mental Processes

Exercise, freedom from worldly desires, and surrender to God are the three main means of control:

(i) *Exercise*: Exercise is necessary to make any state or situation stable. When exercise is continuous and is done with devotion, it becomes fixed strongly.

(ii) *Freedom from Worldly Desires*: To free the mind from worldly desires is Vairagya.

(iii) *Surrender to God*: It is also one of the elements of Yoga. It means to enter into God, that is, to be one with Him or complete surrender to Him. The very aim of prayer is that one should be so near to God that there is no difference between his 'self' and Him.

Relevance of Yoga to Modern Mind

Yoga is an important contribution of ancient India to the world as a means of not only improving health but curing some mental maladies, correcting certain postural defects and removing tension but also uniting with the Supreme. It has assumed all the more significance in the modern times when we are confronted with all kinds of fears, strains, tension and worries. It is now believed in certain quarters of the Western world that Yoga can solve man's several problems and bring peace of mind.

Mimamsa

Sage Jaimini is the originator of this system. It dates back to the fourth century B.C. Jaimini's *Sutras* number two thousand and five hundred. Jaimini stated that due performance of duty as laid down in the Vedas should lead to heaven where there are eternal joys and pleasures. He had an abounding faith in man and his efforts. He laid down ethical purity as the qualifying condition for the performance of the Vedic rituals.

He also enunciated the law of action, holding that every act generates a potency, which comes to surface in its own time.

He propounded *Karma* (Action) as the *Dharma* (Duty). Thus according to him work is the essential duty of man.

This system recognises three paths of salvation. One is concerned with the *Karma Kanda* (ritualism) in accordance with the Vedas. Second is concerned with the *jnanakanda* (pursuit of knowledge) of the Vedas. The third is concerned with the performance of duties in accordance with the teachings of the Vedas.

Vedanta

The literal meaning is end (*anta*) of the Vedas. In this sense, the term is used for the Upanishads. In addition, the Vedanta is one of the six systems of philosophy. According to this school, the highest wisdom of the Vedas is to be found in the Upanishads. Its essence is contained in the phrase '*Tat Twam Asi*' or "That Thou Art". 'That' refers to the Supreme One or *Brahman* and 'Thou', refers to the individual soul or '*Atman*'.

Thus the ultimate goal of life is the realisation of the truth that only Brahman or the Supreme One is real. The material world is '*maya*' or illusion. Spiritual knowledge alone is '*Brahmavidya*'. This knowledge is a means of salvation.

The union of the soul and *Brahma* is salvation. Just as the river loses its identity after falling into the ocean, soul loses its identity after being united with the *Brahman*.

Educational Implications of the Six Systems of Philosophy

All the six systems, by and large, stress the elements of reasoning and critical thinking. There is a great need to emphasise the eight elements of yoga in our educational institutions. It may be noted that 'yoga' is not merely for physical fitness but more importantly for the all-round upliftment of the individual. It should be accepted as a way of life. It develops mental faculty, relieves tension and provides peace of mind and inner solace.

SALIENT FEATURES OF INDIAN THOUGHT AND IMPLICATIONS

Four Pillars of Indian Thought

Indian thought determines the ideals and ways of life that we should adopt. It is focussed on the following four elements:

1. '*Dharma*'. Righteousness.
2. '*Artha*'. Necessities of life.
3. '*Kama*'. Satisfaction of our urges.
4. '*Moksha*'. Liberation.

Dharma (*Righteousness*): It is a spiritual value. '*Dharma*' is not only a central concept of Indian philosophy but also a unique one. It determines what we ought to do in different situations. In fact it regulates one's life. The word '*dharma*' comes from the Sanskrit root '*dhr*' meaning thereby 'to hold' or to 'sustain'. '*Dharma*' denotes right action or right conduct. It has ethical and social values. It includes virtues of control of senses, charity, honesty, love, non-injury, self-restraint, etc. '*Dharma*' puts a check on selfishness. '*Adharma*' is vice.

According to the social concept of ancient Indian thought of '*Dharma*', the ideal life consists of four '*Ashramas*' (stages): '*Brahmacharya*', the period of education and period of celibacy, '*Grihasthya*', the life of the householder, '*Vanaprasthya*', retreat from worldly bonds and finally '*Sanyasa*', the life of a hermit.

Artha: (Wealth or material things). This is only helpful as a means of satisfying one or the other desire of human life.

Kama: Includes physical as well as the psychological satisfaction of the natural urges of a person. Wealth or money is valuable only to the extent it serves, as a means to acquire goods. '*Artha*' thus is an instrument value and it is a means to the realisation of '*Kama*'.

'*Artha*' and '*Kama*' are sought not only by man but also by all living beings.

Moksha (Liberation or salvation). This concept sums up the aim of life in Indian philosophy. It is the realisation of the self. It is spiritual bliss. It is freedom from the cycle of births and deaths. It is becoming 'one' with God. It is the highest attainment man can have. It is the loftiest end. Philosophers and seers have prescribed different ways for the realisation of '*moksha*'. Two of these are most important. One prescribes the practice of '*niskam karma*' (selfless action), leading a pure life. The second prescribes '*dhyana*' (meditation).

A household is expected to earn ('*Artha*') through right ways and spend it rightly for the satisfaction of his needs ('*Kama*') so that he attains '*Moksha*'.

According to some thinkers '*Moksha*' can be realised after death while others think that it can be realised in this very life. In any case the emphasis is on purity and noble deeds.

Is Indian Thought Individualistic? Certainly Not

There are critics who criticise Indian thought as they consider it to be totally individualistic. They sometimes charge that Indian thought disregards social values and is negative and passive. They sum up the Indian thought as making people totally unworldly. According to them it teaches one to become '*Sanyasi*'. They think that '*Dharma*' means individual perfection and running away from the daily pursuits.

While discussing Indian thought it must be stressed that the idealist in India, while talking of the infinite goal does not neglect the immediate objectives of life. Self-realisation or salvation is to be realised in the society. The Indian philosophers very clearly, prescribed four stages of life. Each stage involved certain duties. They believed that the performance of these duties would lead to liberation. Accordingly these duties and values were reflected in the curriculum. Education was considered a means of attaining salvation. Knowledge and wisdom were not gained for their sake but to make man moral and thereby assist him in realising the ultimate objective of life.

Swami Vivekananda, one of the greatest exponents of Indian philosophy observed, "So long as millions live in hunger and ignorance, I hold every man a traitor who, having been educated at their expense, pays not the least heed to them, I call him a '*mahatma*' who feels for the poor. Let these people be your God-think of them, work for them."

Two Paths of Salvation

The Indian way of life or Indian philosophy propounds two paths for self-realisation: *Pravrtimarga* (the path of active life) and *niviritimarga* (the path of renunciation). The main concern of Indian philosophy is *sarvajana sukhino bhavantu* (happiness for all mankind). What is recommended is not 'renunciation of the world but 'self-renunciation'. Unselfishness or 'selfless' is the central point of Indian philosophy.

The *Gayatri Mantra* embodies the essence of Indian thought.

Aum Bhur Bhuvah Svah
Tat Savitur Varenyam
Bhargo Devasya Dhimahi
Dhiyo Yoh Nah Prachodayat

Aum, the celestial sound that resounds in our bodies,
Over the earth and the cosmos up to the gates of heaven,
The effulgence of the rising sun that sets all living things,
To their allotted tasks to strive to achieve their aims in life,
May the dazzling light which is the gift of the gods,
Illuminate our beings,
Let us contemplate on it,
So that our minds gain enlightenment.

Main Elements of Indian Thought

These may be summarised as under:

1. Following the path of truth.
2. Wishing happiness and welfare of the entire humanity.
3. Treating all human beings as friends.
4. Doing one's duty honestly.
5. Eschewing pride.
6. Showing respects to all faiths.
7. Having faith in the freedom of worship.
8. Realising self-being one with the Divine—attaining *Moksha* (Liberation).
9. Earning through righteous means.
10. Following a life of purity and enjoying the pleasures of life according to *Dharma*.
11. Following the spiritual path for salvation.
12. Attaining highest knowledge and wisdom.

Educational Implications of Indian Philosophical Thought

Two Types of Education: The Vedas mention two types of education, namely, *paravidya* and *aparavidya*. The former relates to spiritual or ecclesiastical knowledge and the latter relating to temporal or worldly matters. The intellectual development, moral development and vocational development are the broad aims of education and curriculum should include contents and activities accordingly.

Suitable Environment: According to the Indian thought, through education one creates environment conducive to attain accomplishment of mind, intellect of thought, of purpose, of intelligence, of sense and vision. Education begins in the mother's womb. Preparation has to be made to make the womb a fit receptacle for a worthy promising soul. The mind of the pregnant mother and the environment she is in, have a shaping influence on the child who is yet to be born. The parents, therefore, must have selective environment.

Indian thought stresses close contact between the teacher and the taught for the development of character and personality. Residential educational institutions should be established wherever possible.

Methods of Teaching-Learning: Lectures, meditation, concentration, questions-answers, discussions and debates are the important methods of instruction and learning.

Education of Women: The Vedas accord a high position to the status of women and accordingly their education must receive priority. It would be of interest to note that nearly 20 women seers and scholars are mentioned in the Rig Veda who composed Vedic hymns.

Value Education: The essence of Indian thought is contained in leading a pure and noble life. It is founded on value education and at present is an urgent need to provide value education primarily through personal examples of the elders and value related practical activities.

Free from State Interference: There should be no state interference in the functioning of educational institutions.

24

Swami Vivekananda's Philosophy and Its Impact on Education

BRIEF LIFE SKETCH OF SWAMI VIVEKANANDA

Early Life. Vivekananda's original name was Narendranath Dutt. He acquired the new name in 1886 when he took *Sanyasa*.

He was born in Calcutta in 1863. His father was a practicing lawyer at Calcutta High Court. Under the influence of his mother he made a deep study of Hindu scriptures. At college he was adept in boxing, riding, swimming and wrestling. He was an ardent student of philosophy and poetry. He graduated with honours from Calcutta University.

Education. He had an excellent command over Bengali, English and Sanskrit. He was a voracious reader and had a sharp memory. He could often display a verbatim familiarity with the *Encyclopaedia Britannica*. His principal Rev. W.W. Hastie once remarked, "Narendranath is really a genius. I have travelled far and wide but I have never yet come across a lad of his talents and possibilities, even in German Universities, among philosophical students".

Meeting with Shri Ramakrishna—A Turning Point in Life

He was deeply interested in the study of philosophy and religion. For sometime he was a classroom teacher also. His search for truth led him to Ramakrishna Paramhansa, at Dakshineswar in 1882. Though not literate, Swami Ramakrishna was an enlightened soul. During the next six years of his association with the master, he had a spiritual transformation and emerged as Swami Vivekananda. He left home and travelled all over India. His wandering left him deeply affected by the despair and poverty of the masses of India.

Swami Vivekananda organised the Ramakrishna Mission in 1886, after the passing away of his master.

In 1888, 2 years after his master's death, he set out to the Himalayas. He wandered for 2 years through deserts and forests. In Kanyakumari, after worshipping in the temple, Vivekananda sat on a rock, and meditated for sometime. He went to America in 1893.

Soul-stirring Address at the World Parliament of Religions at Chicago (USA) in 1893. On September 11, 1893, on the opening day of the Parliament, he sat rapt in silent meditation. In the afternoon session he rose to speak. He bowed down to *Saraswati*, the Devi (goddess of learning) and addressed the audience as, "Sisters and brothers of America". Before he could utter another word, people were so much mesmerised that there was applause for full two minutes. When silence was restored, he began his address. His wisdom coupled with universal message of love and tolerance made him a world teacher. In his address, he said that upon the banner of every religion will soon be written, "HELP and not FIGHT', 'ASSIMILATION and not DESTRUCTION', 'HARMONY and PEACE and not DISSENSION'. The Parliament of Religion lasted seventeen days and Swamiji addressed six times.

Message of Spirituality and Social Service. He addressed several meetings in the USA, UK, Sri Lanka and spread the spiritual message.

Swami Vivekananda devoted the rest of his strenuous life in communicating his message of unity and tolerance.

In India, he organised social work also in addition to spiritual pursuits.

MAJOR PUBLICATIONS OF SWAMI VIVEKANANDA

1. *The Complete Works of Swami Vivekananda* – 9 Volumes.
2. *Bhaktiyoga.*
3. *Advaita Vedanta.*
4. *Education.*
5. *Jnana Yoga.*
6. *Lectures from Colombo to Almora.*
7. *Memories of European Travels.*
8. *Philosophical and Religious Lectures of Swami Vivekananda.*
9. *Swami Vivekananda at the Parliament of Religions.*

PRINCIPAL FEATURES OF SWAMI VIVEKANANDA'S PHILOSOPHY

1. God resides in every human heart.
2. The best worship of God is service to mankind.
3. Ethics and morality should be the real basis of life.
4. Love and renunciation should permeate the universe.
5. Religion means self-realisation through self-control.

SWAMI VIVEKANANDA'S PHILOSOPHY OF EDUCATION

Following are the main elements of the philosophy of Swami Vivekananda:

1. All knowledge is in the human mind.
2. Education is the manifestation of the perfection already in man.
3. Knowledge is inherent in man. No knowledge comes from outside.
4. Like fire in a piece of flint, knowledge exists in the mind. Man discovers it.
5. The infinite library of the universe is in our mind.

Swami Vivekananda explains this as, "We say Newton discovered gravitation. The falling of an apple gave the suggestion to Newton and then he studied his own mind. He rearranged all the previous links of thought in his mind and discovered a link among them, which we call the law of gravitation".

SWAMI VIVEKANANDA ON VARIOUS ASPECTS OF EDUCATION

I. Aim of Education. Man-Making

According to Swamiji, education is the manifestation of divinity already existing in man. Education is not the imparting of facts. "If education were identical with information, the libraries would be the greatest sages in the world and encyclopaedias the Rishis". He further observed, "Will you consider a man as educated if only he can pass some examinations and deliver good lectures? The education which does not help the common mass of people to equip themselves for the struggle for life, which does not bring out strength of character, a spirit of philanthropy, and the courage of a lion—is it worth the name?

Swami Vivekananda saw the 'Divine' in the form of the poor whom he called *Daridra Narayan.*

Swami Vivekananda saw the 'Divine' in the form of the poor whom he called *Daridra Narayan*. This denotes the direction of 'Man-making' education. It implies that education should develop a spirit of service and the poor and the needy must be helped to raise themselves.

Man-making education also brings out the significance of the famous words said by Vivekananda at the Parliament of Religions held in 1893 at Chicago. These were: HELP, ASSIMILATION, HARMONY and PEACE. Accordingly education should develop these qualities in man.

Man-making education is inherent in character development as well as vocational development. Man-making education is a very comprehensive concept.

Following are the chief elements of man-making concept for which education should be directed to:

1. Swami Vivekananda believed in the Vedanata philosophy which considers that the ultimate goal of human life is to attain 'Unity with the Creator'. An individual must fully understand this.

2. Service to man is equated with devotion to God. According to Swami Vivekananda, God resides in every human heart. Thus man should develop the spirit of service to his fellow beings.

3. Swami Vivekananda believed in the liberal concept of religion. Essential elements of all religions are the same. No religion is inferior to other religion. Man should follow an attitude of respect for all religions.

4. According to Vivekananda, love is the highest goal of religion. Man should imbibe love for all and hatred for none.

5. Swami Vivekananda developed a synthesis between science and spirituality. Man should attain knowledge of science and spirituality.

6. Swami Vivekananda was a prophet of humanity. His concept of man transcends the cultural boundaries of the East and the West. He was a rationalist and a man must develop rational attitude in life.

II. Role of the Teacher

Vivekananda laid stress on the following qualities that a teacher should have:

1. The first condition is that he should be sinless.
2. The second condition is that he should know the spirit of scriptures.
3. The third condition is the spiritual force of the teacher should be based on love for the students.
4. The fourth condition is that the teacher should think that he is only helping the child to grow. He is the external teacher and he offers the suggestion which arouses the internal teacher, i.e., the mind of the child.

III. Principles of Teaching-learning

Swami Vivekananda emphasised the following:

1. *Self-teaching*: "No one was ever taught by another. Each of us has to teach himself. A child educates itself."
2. *Living Examples of Teacher*: "Words even thoughts, contribute only one-third of the influence in making an impression—the man two-thirds."
3. *Teaching through Positive Suggestions*: "We should give positive ideas. Negative ideas only weaken men. If you speak kind words to them and encourage them, they are bound to improve in time."
4. *Concentration as the Only Method of Education*: "The power of concentration is the only key to the treasure-house of knowledge."
5. *Qualities of the Learner*: "The conditions necessary for the taught are purity, a real thirst after knowledge and perseverance."

IV. Physical and Health Education

"Be strong, my young friends… you will be nearer to Heaven through football than through the study of Gita".

V. Education to be Based on Western Science Coupled with *Vedanta*

"Living with the Guru and a similar system of imparting education are needed. What we want is Western science coupled with *Vedanta*—'*Brahmacharya*' as the guiding motto and also '*Shraddha*' (faith) in one's own self".

VI. Education of the Masses

Vivekananda gave prime importance to the education of the masses. He asserted, "The chief cause of India's ruin has been the monopolising of the whole education of the land, by dint of pride and royal authority, among a handful of men". He further observed, "If we are to rise again, we shall have to do it in the same way, that is, by spreading education among the masses". He considers that "The great national sin is the neglect of the masses, and that is one of the chief causes of our downfall. No amount of politics would be of any avail until the masses in India are once more well-educated, well-fed, and cared for. They pay for our education, they build our temples, but in return they get kicks. They are practically our slaves, if we want to regenerate India, we must work for them".

VII. Women's Education

Vivekananda was an ardent champion of the education of women. He remarked, "Women have many grave problems but none that cannot be solved by that magic word: education!"

VIII. Secular Education

Vivekananda had great regard for all religions. "Let us take in all that has been in the past, enjoy the light of the present and open every window of the heart for all that will come in the future. Salutation to all the prophets of the past, to all the great ones of the present and to all that are to come in the future."

CONTRIBUTION OF SWAMI VIVEKANANDA TO EDUCATION: RELEVANCE OF HIS VIEWS TODAY

1. He laid stress on the character development education.
2. He advocated the education of the masses which implies adult education and free and compulsory education regardless of caste, creed or colour. He said, "I consider that the greatest national sin is the neglect of the masses."
3. He revived the spirit of humanism in education.
4. His clarion call to the educated people was, "So long as the millions live in hunger and ignorance, I hold every man a traitor who, having been educated at their expense, pays not the least heed to them".
5. He considered the education of women as the chief instrument of national regeneration.

***Summing up*:** Educational needs of modern India are reflected in the Preamble to our Constitution. It is clear that educational aims, contents and methods of teaching and in fact the entire process of education must be based on these pillars—Secularism, Socialism and Democracy. From the educational philosophy of Swami Vivekananda as stated above, it is clear that he visualised the needs of independent India and accordingly he set forth his philosophical thought. His views are quite relevant today. He was for a liberal approach to religion and accordingly advocated values of secularism. He believed that ignorance was the most important evil of the society. He advocated mass education, i.e., free and compulsory education as well as, adult education. His advocacy of women education is in accordance with the present day needs. His stress on child-centred education is another remarkable aspect of his educational philosophy. He advocated a system of education that was egalitarian.

Swami Vivekananda's views on education may be summed up in his own words, "We want that education by which character is formed, strength of mind is increased, the intellect is expanded and by which one stands on one's own feet".

25

Rabindranath Tagore (1869-1941): Educational Philosophy and Its Impact

BRIEF LIFE SKETCH

Popularly called Gurudev, Rabindranath Tagore was born in a family known for its progressive views. He was born at Calcutta on May 6, 1861. He wrote his first verse in his eighth year. His schools days was not happy. He studied for sometime in England to become a barrister. Tagore conducted his educational experiments at Shantiniketan. He burst into fame when '*Gitanjali*' won him Nobel Prize for literature in 1913. He utilised the entire amount of award of $8000 for the upkeep of his school at Shantiniketan, which in due course became the Visvabharati University. Tagore visited Europe, Japan, Russia and United States.

Tagore was given the title of 'Knight' in 1915 but he was so pained and stirred by the Jallianwala Bagh Massacre, Amritsar in 1919 that he returned this title. At that time he wrote to the Viceroy of India, "The time has come when badges of honour make our shame, glaring in their incongruous context of humiliation, and I for my part wish to stand, shorn of all special distinctions, by the side of those of my countrymen who, for their so-called insignificance, are liable to suffer a degradation not fit for human beings".

TAGORE'S PUBLICATIONS

1. *Shiksar Herpher* (Our Education and Its Incongruities)
2. *Shiksha Samasya* (The Problem of Education)
3. *Abaran* (Culture or Covering)
4. *Tapovan* (Forest Colony)
5. *Dharmashiksha* (Religious Education)
6. *Hindu Visvavidyalaya* (Hindu University)
7. *Strishiksha* (Women Education)
8. *Shiksar Bahan* (The Vehicle of Education)
9. *My School*
10. *Shiksar Milan* (The Meeting of Cultures)
11. *A Poet's School*
12. *Shiksar Vikiran* (Diffusion of Education)
13. *Ashramer Shiksha* (Education in Ashram)
14. *Bodher Sadhana* (Education of the Feeling)
15. *Several Convocation Addresses*

FACTORS INFLUENCING TAGORE'S PHILOSOPHY OF EDUCATION

Tagore combined the elements of idealism, naturalism and pragmatism. His philosophy of education was influenced by the following factors:

1. Influence of the Home Environment.
2. Influence of the School Environment.
3. Love for Nature.
4. His Extensive Visits.

Influence of the Home Environment: Tagore was born in a family in which the time-honoured ways of Indian life and tradition of the land were strictly adhered to. His father taught him ancient Indian literature. He set before the family the Indian ideals by the example of his own life, by his talks and writings. After leaving the school, Rabindranath Tagore spent a good deal of his time in the company of his father. This constant companionship of his father exerted a great influence on his life.

His Extensive Travels: His wide travels and visits to different countries of the world and his contacts with people of different nations, developed in him a faith in the brotherhood of man and spiritual unity of humanity.

Impact of School Environment: By nature, Tagore had a love for nature. His love for naturalism was strengthened on account of the artificial and unnatural environment of the schools he attended.

Tagore's life in the school was not happy. He felt himself like 'a parrot in the cage'. Tagore was unable to adjust himself to the 'dead routine and the teaching' of the educational institutions. His teachers pronounced that he was 'unfit' for studies. Tagore considered himself 'fortunate to escape' from these 'book learning factories'. He observed later on "The Masters and Pandits who were charged with my education soon abandoned the thankless task... and realised that this boy could never be driven along the beaten track of learning".

Tagore considered school a place of great discomfort, "There was no particular trouble in the school. Yet after all, it was a school. The rooms were pitiless, its walls stood like sentries. There was nothing like a home in it, it was like a big box with many compartments".

Traditional school to him was like a 'prison house'. He observed, "It was more like a pigeon-holed box. The time spent had been thoroughly wasted". About his teachers he wrote, "Of the teachers, I remember only one, whose language was so foul that, out of sheer contempt for him, I steadily refused to answer any one of his questions". Further he said, "I learnt about all the injustice, impatience, anger and partiality underlying the process of instruction, more easily than my lessons". The school according to him was "completely isolated from the surrounding life and beauty". It was a "restless nightmare like a jail... the whole thing was depressed".

All this made him a naturalist.

Impact of Tagore's Extensive Travel: Tagore spent considerable part of his life in travelling several parts of the world. This developed a pragmatic and rational outlook in him.

TAGORE'S VIEWS ON VARIOUS ASPECTS OF EDUCATION IN HIS OWN WORDS

Meaning of Education: Education is nothing short of the highest purpose of man—the fullest growth and freedom of soul.

Tagore's Thought of Education,
'*Visvabharati Quarterly*', Vol. XII, Part I—1946.

Object of Education: The object of education is to give man the unity of truth. We devote our sole attention to giving children information, not knowing that by this emphasis we are accentuating a break between the intellectual, physical and the spiritual life. '*Personality*', p. 126.

Education for Knowing Oneself: The great use of education is not merely to collect facts but to know man and make oneself known to man.

'*Rabindra Rachnavali*', Vol. XII

Freedom of Mind as the Object of Education: I believe that the object of education is the freedom of mind which can be achieved through the path of freedom. '*Personality*', p. 147.

Moral Education: I believe in the hour of meditation, and I must set aside fifteen minutes in the morning and fifteen minutes in the evening for that purpose. I insist on this period of meditation, not however, expecting the boy to be hypocrites and to make believe they are meditating. But I do insist that they remain quiet, that they exert the power of self-control.

'*Personality*' p. 145.

Vision and Reality: Education in all its different forms and channels has its ultimate purpose in the evolving of a luminous sphere of human mind from the nebula that has been rushing round ages to find itself an eternal centre of unity. '*Personality*' p. 80.

Living Contact between the Teacher and the Taught

Communication of life can only be through a living agency. And culture, which is the life of mind, can only be imparted through man to man. Book-learning or scriptural texts may merely make us pedants. They are static and quantitative; they accumulate and are hoarded up under strict guards. Culture grows and moves and multiplies itself in life.

Discipline: For Tagore, an educational institution is "an open house in which students and teachers are one. They must live their compact life together." He observes that an educational institution "must not be a dead cage in which living minds are fed with food artificially prepared." He further remarks that "students are not dancing monkeys or bears." About the discipline of the educational institution he founded, he states, "I never said to them: Don't do this, or don't do that. The boys were encouraged to manage their own affairs."

Curriculum: Tagore was for a curriculum which should satisfy child's aesthetic, creative, spiritual and vocational needs. In his experimental school at Shantiniketan, Science (especially the experimental science) was taught to children in various classes. Shantiniketan school had a very well-equipped laboratory for performing experiments whereas in other schools, people had not even thought of this subject. Nature-study was also taught here, right in the midst of nature.

Methods of Teaching: Tagore strongly criticised the bookish and examination–oriented teaching. He stressed movement of the whole body in various learning activities. He followed the activity principle, and advocated constructive and creative activities. He believed that there should be daily practice by the pupils in expressing immediately what they are learning. The central point in educational activity according to Tagore, is joy which should pervade all types of activities. "Work should be wedded to joy". Tagore also emphasised the principle of curiosity and interest, and the spirit of play. He advocated fullness of experience-physical, mental, aesthetic and emotional. All this truly accords with the modern pedagogy.

Role of the Teacher: Tagore laid great emphasis on the attitude of the teacher. He wrote, "I have found that little children learn more quickly the attitude of the teacher than the knowledge imparted by him."

Tagore felt, "Most teachers do not know that in order to teach boys they have to be boys. Unfortunately, schoolmasters are obsessed with the consciousness of their dignity as grown up persons and as learned men, and therefore they always try to burden the children with their grown up manners and their learned manners, and that hurts the mind of the students unnecessarily." His concept of a good teacher is stated in these words, "A teacher can never truly teach unless he is still learning himself. A lamp can never light another lamp unless it continues to burn its own flame. The teacher who has come to the end of his subject, who has no living traffic with his knowledge, but merely repeats his lesson to his students, can only load their minds; he cannot quicken them. Truth not only must inform but also inspire."

In the final analysis, we must inevitably conclude that education can be imparted only by a teacher and never by a method.

Man can learn only from a man. Just as a water tank can be filled only with water and fire can be kindled only with fire, life can be inspired only with life.... In our social organisation we are searching for a guru who will add meaning and give pace to our life; in our educational system we are searching for a guru who will seek deliverance of our mind from its imprisonment. However, it may be, we want a human being in every sphere of our life. Mere a method shall bring us no salvation. (*Siksa*, 1342, B.S.Ed., p. 286).

CONCEPT OF AN IDEAL SCHOOL

A Poet's School is an important writing showing the place of Nature in life and education. Children have the gift of freshness of senses. They can become natural with Nature and human with the human society. 'For our perfection we have to be vitally savage and mentally civilised.' But the misery is that a child is offered crowded solitude in a city where man is everywhere, with never a gap for the immense non-human, the Nature. The inexpensive power to be happy that the children bring to this world is 'Constantly worn away by friction with the brick-and-mortar arrangement of life.' The city-built education does not take heed of the non-civilised in us, which thirst for colour, for music, for the movement of life. This is why Tagore tried his best to develop in the children of his school 'the freshness of their feeling for nature, a sensitiveness of soul in their relationship with their human surrounding'.

He pointed out the great significance of the school atmosphere in the life of children whose mind, like the tree, has the power to gather food and nourishment from its surroundings. The cultural atmosphere keeps the mind sensitive to rich racial inheritance, glorious traditions and concentrated wisdom of ages. The school atmosphere must also develop sensitiveness of soul and allow freedom to the mind from bondage of ignorance and apathy.

An ideal school, according to Tagore, should have the following characteristics, and he attempted to introduce these elements in his school at Bolpur, located at a distance of about one hundred miles from Calcutta. Later on this school became Shantiniketan and grew into 'Visvabharati'.

1. The school should be situated in natural surroundings. There should prevail the atmosphere of nature's own beauty with her varied gifts of colours and dance, flowers and fruits, with the joy of her mornings and the peace of her starry nights.

2. It should provide an environment after the fashion of ancient '*Tapovans*'—forest schools about which he had read so much in the Upanishads.

3. It should give spiritual training to the students.

4. It should help the children in the cultivation of love of nature and sympathy with all living creatures.

5. It should educate children by providing an atmosphere of freedom.

6. It should educate children by making them alive to their natural surroundings.

7. It should educate children by providing an environment of living aspiration, based upon living contact between the teacher and the taught.

8. It should impart knowledge to children through mother tongue.

9. The school should provide for manual labour.

10. It should provide for close personal contact with the teacher. The number of students in classes should be very small.

11. There should be a well-equipped library.

12. It should be a community school where there is no distinction of caste and creed.

13. It should teach crafts like sewing, book-binding, weaving, carpentry etc.

14. It should include drawing, art and music as an integral part of the curriculum.

15. It should provide students adequate opportunities for choosing their hobbies and occupations.

16. It should be a self-governing institution—has a dairy farm, post office, hospital and workshop. Students hold their own courts.

VISVABHARATI AT SHANTINIKETAN IN NATURAL SURROUNDINGS

Rabindranath Tagore was not a dreamer. He was a great educational practitioner who himself was closely associated with the entire educational practices at Visvabharati.

The word Visvabharati is composed of two words. In Sanskrit, the word *Visva* means 'world' and *bharti* means 'culture'. Thus 'Visvabharati' would mean 'world culture'. The motto of this University is '*Yatra Visvam Bhavati Ekamidam*', i.e., where the world meets in one place. Through the Visvabharati as a whole, the poet and the seer sought "to establish a relationship between East and West, to promote inter-cultural and inter-social amity and understanding and fulfill the highest mission of the present age—the unification of mankind".

The Visvabharati was formally founded on 22nd December 1921. But it was not a new institution. It had grown gradually out of the Shantiniketan Ashrama. Today this 'Visvabharati' is known not only all over the world, but also attracts scholars from different parts of the world.

Tagore has observed, "I have formed the nucleus of an International University, as one of the best means of promoting mutual understanding between the East and the West." It was intended to be, "Treasure of Light" not only for India but also for the world.

Tagore wanted to extend by degrees the scope of this university on simple lines, until it comprehended the whole range of eastern culture—the Aryans, Semitic, Mongolian etc. Its object was to reveal the eastern mind to the world.

Main features of Visvabharati

Tagore describes these as:

1. The institution that bore the name of Visvabharati was founded with the call that man had to be set free not only in the field of Nature but also among mankind.
2. The greatest distinction of our school is the direct and immediate emotional contact of pupils with their teachers and with external nature.
3. A speciality of our institution is that it wants to bring up our pupils in inseparable association with Nature.
4. It wants to hold before the world the ideal of the universality of man.
5. It is intended not only to be the intellectual centre of the intellectual life of India but also the centre of her economic life.
6. It is envisaged to be the nucleus of an international university and as one of the means of promoting mutual understanding between the East and the West.

Natural Environment at Shantiniketan

Education is imparted in the lap of natural surroundings. The influence of green trees, open fields, seasonal skies, songs and chirpings of birds and other natural phenomena, fills the pupils' mind with spiritual elevation. Tagore himself says, "Having in my mind the ideal of a school, which should be a home and a temple in one, where teaching should be a part of worshipful life. I selected this spot far away from all distraction of the town, hallowed by the memory of a pious life, whose days were passed here in communion with God."

Institutions at Visvabharati

Following institutions were started to carry out his experiments in education:

1. Sisu Bhavan (Nursery School)

2. Path Bhavan (School Section—Matriculation Examination)
3. Siksha Bhavan (Higher Secondary)
4. Vidya Bhavan (College of Undergraduate and Post-Graduate Studies and Research)
5. Vinya Bhavan (College of Teaching)
6. Kala Bhavan (College of Fine Arts and Crafts)
7. Sangit Bhavan (College of Dance)
8. Sriniketan (Department of Rural Reconstruction)
9. Siksa Satra (Rural High School)
10. Silpa Sadana (College of Industrial Training)
11. Cheena Bhavan (School of Languages, e.g., Chinese, Tibetan, etc.)

By and large, all formed part of Visvabharati University

TAGORE'S CONTRIBUTION TO EDUCATION

Tagore's concept of education and its practices balance the claims of different schools of educational philosophy, i.e., humanism, idealism, naturalism, pragmatism, realism and supernaturalism. His philosophy is a true blend of the Eastern and Western philosophy.

The Visvabharati is the embodiment of his educational ideals.

Tagore is one of the very few educational philosophers whose philosophy is the outcome of his educational experiments. Simultaneously, he gave a practical shape to his ideology.

Rabindranath was a great educational practitioner. He was not a dreamer only to leave behind a legacy of the principles of life. He worked them out in a constructive way.

Setting up educational institutions in natural surroundings and the environment of freedom from fear—the two principal features of his theory and practice of education bear the mark of his naturalism.

26

Philosophical Thought of Gandhiji (1869-1948)

BRIEF LIFE SKETCH OF GANDHIJI

Mohandas Karam Chand Gandhi (Karam Chand was his father), popularly known as 'Bapu', out of affection and reverence by the people, 'Mahatma', on account of his saintly nature and 'Father of the Nation' for the regeneration of the Indian nation, free from the British rule was a great educator, a nation builder, a political leader, a social worker, a statesman and a writer. Gandhiji had a charismatic appeal and he attracted thousands of devoted workers hailing from all sections of the society. He took up cases which ultimately touched the life of the common man.

Early Life and Education: Gandhiji was born on October 2, 1869 at Porbandar in Gujarat. His father was a Dewan (Chief Administrator and Chief Revenue Officer) of a small state. At school, he was slow, hesitant and shy. He was married to Kasturba at the age of thirteen. His mother was very pious and he was greatly influenced by her.

Education in England: When 18 years old, he was sent to London to study law where he remained for three years. His mother made him promise that in England, he would not take meat and alcohol and indulge in sex. Gandhiji kept his promise.

Work in South Africa: After returning from England, he started his law practice at Bombay. However, he was not very successful.

In April, 1893, he went to South Africa in connection with a civil law case of a firm. In 1893 itself, he was thrown out of a first class compartment in Durban (South Africa) for he was a coloured man. He stayed there for about 20 years. This was a turning point in his life. Gandhiji found that the Indians in South Africa were treated very cruelly and in fact like animals. They had no political rights. Gandhiji took up cases which were not entirely political but touched intimately the life of the people. Gandhiji gave up his legal practice. He completely devoted himself to the service of the people. He put into practice '*Satyagraha*' and '*Ahimsa*'.

GANDHIJI'S PUBLICATIONS ON EDUCATION

Important publications on education and having bearing on education are:

1. *My Experiments with Truth*. (Autobiography)
2. *Basic Education*

3. *Towards New Education*
4. *True Education*
5. *To the Students*
6. *Task Before Indian Students*
7. *India of My Dreams*
8. *Medium of Instruction*
9. *Tasks fore India*

Gandhiji also wrote extensively on education in '*Harijan*'—a paper founded by him.

PRINCIPAL FEATURES OF GANDHIJI'S PHILOSOPHY OF LIFE

1. *Supreme God*: He said, "God pervades everything. God is life, Truth and Light".

2. *Truth and Ahimsa* (*Non-violence*): According to Gandhiji, "Truth and *Ahimsa* are the two sides of a coin. They are intertwined and it is practically impossible to separate them". '*Satyagraha*' implies holding of truth, through love and purity.

3. *Service of Humanity*: Gandhiji observed, "The immediate service of all human beings becomes a necessary part because it is the only way to see Him in His creation".

4. *Self-discipline and Self-purification*: Gandhiji always held the high ideals of purity, sacrifice and service.

5. *Righteousness and Truth as the Highest Religion*: Gandhiji was of the firm view that 'true religion and true morality are inseparably bound up with each other'.

6. *Ram Rajya as the Concept of a Society*: He wanted to establish *Ram Rajya* which he identified with justice, peace, happiness and welfare of all.

According to Gandhiji, man's ultimate aim is the realisation of God and all his endeavour—political, religious and social—must be guided to this end, "The immediate service of all human beings becomes a necessary part of the endeavour, simply because the only way to find God is to see *Him* in *His* creation and be one with it—I am a part and parcel of the whole and I cannot find *Him* apart from the rest of humanity." For Gandhiji, God lives in the temple of humanity and man becomes great exactly in the degree in which he works for the welfare of his fellow men.

FACTORS THAT INFLUENCED GANDHIJI'S PHILOSOPHY OF LIFE AND PHILOSOPHY OF EDUCATION

Following were the chief influences which had a great effect on Gandhiji's philosophy of life and philosophy of education:

1. *Mother's Influence*: Gandhiji's mother taught him the lessons of simplicity and piety.

2. *Three Great Thinkers*.

   (i) Rayachand Bhai Patel who taught Gandhiji the first lesson in non-violence.

   (ii) Ruskin, through his book *Unto the Last* drew his attention to the principle of dignity of labour.

(iii) Leo Tolstoy's *The Kingdom of the God is within You*, greatly influenced his spiritual outlook.

3. *The Phoenix Settlement* (South Africa) where Gandhiji conducted early experiments

4. *The Tolstoy Farm*: In 1911, Gandhiji started an Ashram in Transwal. It was here that Gandhiji helped children in their all-round development. He taught vocations such as cooking, digging and massage work. The medium of instruction was mother-tongue. English was also taught. Children learnt by doing. Textbooks were not used. No punishment was administered. Creed of non-violence was put into practice in letter and spirit.

5. *The Sabarmati Ashram*: After returning to India in 1914, Gandhiji started the Sabarmati Ashram. A school was attached with the Ashram which Gandhiji wanted to make a model school.

THOUGHTS OF GANDHIJI ON VARIOUS DIMENSIONS OF EDUCATION IN HIS OWN WORDS

Meaning of Education

Real Education has to draw out the best from the boys and girls to be educated. This can never be done by packing ill-assorted and unwanted information into the heads of the students. It becomes a dead weight crushing all originality in them and turning them into mere automata.

('*Harijan*', December 1, 1933)

By education I mean an all-round drawing out of the best in child and man—body, mind and spirit. ('*Harijan*', July 31, 1937)

Literacy is not the end of education not even the beginning. It is only one of the means whereby man and women can be educated. Literacy in itself is no education. ('*Harijan*', July 31, 1937)

I would develop in the child his hands, his brain and his soul.

('*Basic Education*', p. 23)

Purity of personal life is the one indispensable condition for building a sound education. ('*Towards New Education*', p. 31)

I hold that true education of the intellect can only come through a proper exercise and training of the bodily organs, e.g., hands, feet, eyes, ears, nose, etc. ('*Basic Education*', p. 123)

True education is that which draws out and stimulates the spiritual, the intellectual and physical faculties of the children.

(Tendulkar, '*Mahatma*', Vol. IV, p. 187)

Education and Character

The end of all knowledge must be building up character. What is education without character and what is character without elementary purity?

('*Towards New Education*', p. 301)

All our learning of recitation of the Vedas, correct knowledge of Sanskrit, Latin and Greek and what not, will avail as nothing if they do not enable us to cultivate purity of heart. The end of all knowledge may be the building of character. ('*True Education*', p. 229)

The Teacher

Woe to the teacher who teaches one thing with the lips and carries another in the heart. ('*To the Students*', p. 16)

The politician may succeed in his purpose even though he lacks character, but a pupils' teacher cannot do without character. If he lacks, he will be like salt without its savour. ('*True Education*', p. 161)

I always felt that the true textbook for the pupils is his teacher.

('*Autobiography*', p. 41)

It is possible for a teacher living miles away to affect the spirit of the pupils by his way of living. ('*Towards New Education*', p. 44)

Education Through Craft

I want the whole process of education to be imparted through some handicraft or industry. ('*Basic Education*', p. 191)

My idea is not to teach a particular profession or occupation to the children, but to develop the full man through teaching that occupation.

(Tendulkar, '*Mahatma*', Vol. IV, p. 200)

The brain must be educated through hand. ('*Basic Education*', p. 190)

The old idea was to add a craft to the ordinary curriculum of education followed in the schools. That is to say, the craft was to be taken in hand wholly separate from education. To me that seems a fatal mistake. The teacher must learn the craft and correlate his knowledge to the craft, so that he will impart all that knowledge to his pupils through the medium of the particular craft that he chooses.

Take the instance of spinning. Unless I know arithmetic I cannot report how many yards of yarn I have produced on the 'takli'. I must learn addition and subtraction and multiplication and division. In dealing with complicated sums, I shall have to use symbols and so I get my algebra. Even here, I would insist on the use of Hindustani letters instead of Roman.

Takli-spinning leads me into the History of East India Company.

There is no limit to the possibilities of knowledge that can be imparted through this medium.

('*Harijan*', February 18, 1939)

Methods of Teaching

It is not by making our brains a store-house for cramming facts that our understanding is opened. An intelligent approach to an industrial training is often a more valuable aid to the intellect than an indifferent reading of literature.

Pupils should know to discriminate between what should be received and what rejected. It is the duty of the teacher to teach his pupils discrimination.

('*Towards New Education*', p. 34)

The utterly false idea that intelligence can be developed only through book-reading should give place to the truth that the quickest development of the mind can be achieved by artisan's work being learnt in a scientific way.

(Bose, Nirmal Kumar, '*Selections from Gandhiji*', p. 288)

The brain must be educated through the hand. ('*Harijan*', Feb. 29, 1939)

The core of my suggestion is that handicrafts are to be taught not merely for production work but for developing the intellect.

('*Basic Education*', p. 44)

I want to teach through hand-work all the subjects like History, Geography, Arithmetic, Science, Language, Painting etc.

(Tendulkar, '*Mahatma*', Vol. IV, p. 196)

Freedom and Discipline

The students mind must not be caged. This does not mean that they are not subject to discipline. No school can be run without it. But discipline has nothing to do with artificial restraint upon students' all-round growth.

('*True Education*', p. 57)

I have always been opposed to corporal punishment.

('*Towards New Education*', p. 19)

GANDHIJI'S DISSATISFACTION WITH THE EXISTING SYSTEM OF EDUCATION AND FORMULATION OF BASIC SYSTEMS OF EDUCATION

Gandhiji realised that the prevailing system of education was unreal and outdated. He observed, "I am convinced that the present system of education is not only wasteful but positively harmful. Most of the boys are lost to the parents and to the occupations to which they were born. They pick up evil habits, effect urban ways and get a smattering of something which may be anything but education".

Gandhiji further observed, "The present system of education does not meet the requirements of the country in any shape or form. English has been made medium of education in all the highest branches of learning, and it has created a permanent bar between the highly educated few and the uneducated many".

Gandhiji went on to criticise the system. "We have up to now concentrated on stuffing children's minds with all kinds of information without even thinking or stimulating or developing them".

Gandhiji accordingly stressed, "Let us now cry a halt and concentrate on educating the child properly through manual work not as a side activity but as a prime means of intellectual activity".

Main Features of the Systems of Education based on Gandhiji's Philosophy

1. Education for a just social order.
2. Education through craft and manual work.
3. Education through mother tongue.
4. Self-sufficient education.
5. Education related to life activities and experiences.
6. Dignity of labour.
7. Correlation.
8. Religious education.
9. Spiritual training.
10. Freedom to children but under discipline.
11. Character development.

12. Mass education.
13. Women education.

ORIGIN OF BASIC EDUCATION/ NAITALEM /WARDHA SCHEME OR SYSTEM OF EDUCATION

The origin of Basic System of Education may be traced back to July 1937 when Gandhiji wrote in '*Harijan*' (a journal started by him), "By education, I mean an all-round development drawing out of the best in child and man—body, mind and spirit. Literacy itself is no education. I would, therefore, begin the child's education by teaching it a useful handicraft and enabling it to produce from the moment it begins its training. Thus every school can be made self-supporting, the condition being that the state takes over the manufacture of these schools".

In October, 1937 a Conference of National Workers was held at Wardha under the chairmanship of Mahatma Gandhi. His ideas were considered and the following resolutions passed:

1. That in the opinion of this Conference free and compulsory education be provided for seven years on a nation-wide scale.
2. That the medium of instruction be the mother-tongue.
3. That the Conference endorses the proposal made by Mahatma Gandhi, that the process of education throughout this period should centre round some productive form of manual labour, and that all other abilities to be developed, or training to be given should, as far as possible, be integrally related to the environment of the child.
4. That the Conference expects that the system of education will gradually be able to cover the remuneration of teachers.

Zakir Hussain Committee on Basic Education: Formulation of the Scheme

The Conference appointed a Committee under the chairmanship of Dr. Zakir Hussain, a renowned educationist. The report of this Committee was published in 1938. The report is known as Wardha Scheme of Education. The scheme was approved by Mahatma Gandhi and accepted by the Indian National Congress.

CURRICULUM OF BASIC EDUCATION AS IT EMERGED IN DUE COURSE

The fundamental features of the scheme that emerged after changes are as follows:

1. A school of say 5½ hours could roughly be divided on the following basis:

Physical activities	20 minutes
Mother Tongue	20 minutes
Social Studies & General Science	60 minutes
Art	40 minutes
Arithmetic	20 minutes
Craft work including study of correlated subjects	2½ hours

2. Free and compulsory education to be given for 8 years (from 6 to 14

years) in two stages. The junior stage to cover five years and the senior 3 years.

3. The medium of instruction is to be the mother tongue.
4. Education is to centre round some form of productive work. The social and physical environment to be used for correlation in addition to craft.
5. The self-supporting aspect not to be over-emphasised. The sale-proceeds of the finished goods to be able to help the school to cover some part of its expenditure.
6. External examinations to be abolished. The day-to-day work of the students to be the determining factor.
7. Text-books to be avoided as far as possible.
8. Cleanliness and health, citizenship, play and recreation to be given sufficient importance.

TENETS/MERITS OF BASIC EDUCATION/CHIEF FEATURES

Following are the tenets of Basic Education:

1. *Craft as the Core of the Basic Plan*: Craft is the medium of education in the basic system. Gandhiji writes, "The core of my suggestion is that handicrafts are not to be taught merely for productive work but for developing the intellect of the pupils". According to his view "stress should be laid on the principles of cooperative activity, planning, accuracy, initiative and individual responsibility in learning". According to him, "the process of education should be imparted through some handicraft or industry".

2. *Self-supporting Aspect*: "Earn while you learn" is another feature of the plan. The idea of a self-sufficient basic school has a special significance in a poor country like India. Without self-sufficient schools it is very doubtful if we could fulfil the obligation to our Constitution of providing free and compulsory education to all the boys and girls of school-going age. In the absence of such schools, we may have to wait for many decades to provide education to such a group.

3. *Integrated Knowledge*: Basic education treats knowledge as an integrated whole. Curriculum is built round three integrally related centres: (i) Physical environment, (ii) Social environment, and (iii) Craft work.

4. *Relationship with Life*: A basic school must become an active environment where teaching is not cut off from the life of the miniature community of the school and the community itself. Education is to be directed to the needs of life. It is not to pursue an idea which has no relation with or is totally isolated from the real situations of life.

5. *Learning by Doing*: Learning by doing sums up the educational methods of basic education. It is absolutely wrong to think that true education is acquired from books alone. There are other methods and sources which are more helpful in acquiring true knowledge. 'Chalk' and 'Talk' lessons are also not very useful. All educationists have condemned bookish knowledge. Gandhiji believed that school must be a 'doing thing'. In basic system of education children acquire the knowledge of the formal school subjects as a by-product of purposeful activities.

6. *Training in Citizenship*: Basic education aims at developing ideas of mutual understanding and habits of cooperative and mutually helpful living

among the students through its various practical and constructive programmes. The new education aims at giving the citizens of the future a keen sense of personal warmth, dignity and efficiency. It is likely to strengthen in them the desire for self-improvement and social service in a cooperative community.

7. *Free and Compulsory Education for Eight Years*. By free and compulsory education, we mean an education for which parents will not have to pay any fee and for which they must send their children to school. Gandhiji writes, "Primary education extending over a period of 7 years or longer, and covering all the subjects up to the matriculation standard except English, plus a vocation used as a vehicle for drawing out the minds of boys and girls in all departments of knowledge should take the place of what passes today under the name of primary, middle and high school education". In due course it was accepted that the duration of free and compulsory education should be for a period of 8 years.

8. *Emphasis on Mother-tongue*: Gandhiji stressed that proper education can only be imparted through the mother-tongue. Foreign language as the medium of instruction makes us unfit for original work. It makes us crammers and imitators. Dr. Zakir Hussain Committee observes, "The proper teaching of mother-tongue is the foundation of all education. Without the capacity to speak effectively and to read and write correctly and lucidly, no one can develop precision of thought or clarity of ideas. Moreover, it is a means of introducing the child to the rich heritage of his people's ideas, emotions and aspirations and can, therefore, be made a valuable means of social education, whilst also instilling right ethical and moral values. Also, it is a natural outlet for the expression of the child's aesthetic sense and application and if the proper approach is adopted the study of literature becomes a source of joy and creative appreciation."

9. *Greater Freedom for the Teacher and the Taught*: In basic education discipline does not mean order and external restraint but an intelligent use of freedom. The teacher gets many opportunities to make experiments, think for himself and put his ideas and plans into practice.

10. *Basic Education as a Means of Social Equality*: The ultimate objective of basic education is to create a social order in which there is no unnatural division between 'haves' and have-nots' and every one is assured of a living wage and the right to freedom.

11. *Basic Education in the Rural as Well as in Urban Area*: It is wrong to assume that basic education is intended to be imparted in the rural area only. "In fact, in one sense there is a greater need for basic education in urban areas than in rural areas. In rural areas the children who participate in the life of the farm or allied occupation of their families have certain types of further education. In performing their jobs the children come into direct contact with actual life, and the experience they get forms the basis of further education. On the other hand, in large towns and big industrial cities the children miss the opportunities for rich experiences and direct contact with life", observed Dr. K.L. Shrimali. Basic education is a plan of national education for the whole country including both rural as well as urban areas. Keeping in view the educative possibilities of a craft in relation to local needs, curriculum may

differ from region to region. There is no rigidity in the curriculum of basic education. It would be wrong to think that rural children should have altogether a different type of education from urban children. Difference will be of a degree and not of kind. Basic principles of life are the same everywhere.

Significance of the Word 'Basic'

The word 'Basic' is derived from the word 'Base' which means the bottom or the foundation of a thing upon which the whole thing rests or is made.

It is basic because it is based on ancient Indian culture.

It is basic because it lays down the minimum educational standards which every Indian child is entitled to receive without any distinction of caste or creed.

It is basic because it is closely related to the basic needs and interests of the child.

It is basic because it makes use of the native potentialities of the child.

It is basic because it is intimately related to the basic occupations of the community.

It is basic because it is for the common man of the country, who is the foundation and the backbone of our national life.

It is basic because it comes first in time, i.e. it is the primary period of one's education.

CRITICISM OF BASIC EDUCATION

1. *Based on Unsound Psychological Foundations*: P.S. Naidu has observed, "The delicate but inexorable laws governing the development of the tender mind of the child have been completely ignored. The child is treated just as a policeman or a soldier, merely as a unit in a homogeneous mass. His individuality is ignored. He is viewed merely as a means to an end—the end being earning capacity and citizenship of sorts". He has further stated, "Play is the only means by which creative energy can be released. Enlightened and informed educational opinion all over the civilised world is decidedly against forcing the child to learn a craft before he is twelve plus. It is nothing short of cruelty to make the child earn an anna or half per hour during the stage when he ought to be playing and enjoying himself."

2. *Deficiency of Craft as the Primary Basis of Correlation*: The critics point out that it is impossible to establish any natural and real correlation between craft and all the subjects. "It is absurd to hang all knowledge from the peg of a single craft."

3. *Basic Education not Suited in an Age of Industrialisation*: As ours is a system of education which claims to produce an integrated individual, the emphasis on craft is out of place in a community which has its face turned towards developing its economy to the full. Basic education failed to relate to the economic policy of the State. But if this point is ignored, we shall find ourselves burdened with an educational system which turns out misfits even more rapidly than the one with which we are so dissatisfied. It is stated that with rapid industrialisation of India, knowledge of science and mathematics may become more desirable than skill in handicrafts.

4. *Ruinous Competition*: This scheme hits the professional artisans hard by creating ruinous competitions.

5. *Deficient Working of Basic Schools*: In the words of J. Lahri, "There is some loss in mechanical arithmetic and spelling lack of sufficient intensive and repetitive drill".

6. *Neglect of the Child*: "In a hurry to pay more attention to craft, it has neglected the child".

"Basic education is looked upon more as a social and economic duty than as a joyful adventure".

7. *Faulty Teaching of Craft*: "Craft is only a slogan, a fiction, which is practised on ceremonial occasions for the benefit of visitors".

8. *Faulty Time-table*: In a basic school nearly half the normal time is given to academic education, the rest being taken up by crafts. And further, since on the time-table academic subjects generally come after the craft work, mostly agriculture, students are sometimes too tired to take to academic work seriously.

9. *No Dexterity in Any Craft*: R.K. Singh has observed, "Students spend one-third or half the time for craft work without acquiring any dexterity worth speaking of in any craft."

10. *Neglect of Religion Education*: There is no place for religious instruction in the curriculum of basic education.

Some Epithets Attached with Basic System of Education

1. *Basic Education is a Fad*: It has no sound psychological and pedagogical basis.

2. *Basic Education is a Fallacy*: The very fundamentals are wrong and not properly conceived.

3. *Basic Education is a Farce*: The scheme is impracticable. Traditional methods are still followed. The craft materials are just stored and a show is put up, whenever there are visitors.

4. *Basic Education is a Fraud*: It is a sort of political stunt to play with the sentiments of the people.

FUTURE OF BASIC EDUCATION AND THE EDUCATION COMMISSION (1964-66)

The Commission believed that the essential elements of basic education were fundamentally sound, but some modifications were needed: The movement of basic education launched by Mahatma Gandhi before independence, proposing a new type of elementary education for the nation which would centre round some form of manual and productive work and have intimate links with the life of the community, was a landmark in the history of education in India. It was a revolt against the sterile, book-centred examination-oriented system of education that had developed along traditional lines during several decades of British rule. It created a national ferment, which may not have transformed the quality of education at the primary stage, but which has certainly left its impact on educational thought and practice on a much wider sphere. "We believe that the essential elements of the system are fundamentally sound, and that with necessary modification these can form part of education, not only at the primary stage but at all stages in our national system. These elements are: (1) productive activity in education; (2) correlation of the curriculum with the productive activity and the physical and social environment; and (3) intimate contact between the school and the local community."

The Commission popularised the concept of "work experience" and saw that two ideas—"work experience" and "basic education"—were essentially similar.

"In the curricula of most contemporary school system, particularly in the socialist countries of Europe, a place is found for what is variously called 'manual work' or 'work experience'. In our country, a revolutionary experiment was launched by Mahatma Gandhi in the form of basic education. The concept of work experience was essentially similar. It may be described as a redefinition of his educational thinking in terms of a society launched on the road to industrialisation".

The Commission gave a call for the reorientation of the basic education programme in view of the changed character and need of the new society. It is not difficult to miss the clear shift of emphasis in terms of a new science-oriented social order in the following words:

"The programme of basic education did involve work-experience for all children in the primary schools, though the activities proposed were concerned with the indigenous crafts and the village employment patterns. If in practice basic education has become largely frozen around certain crafts, there is no denying the fact that it always stressed the vital principle of relating education to productivity. What is now needed is a reorientation of the basic education programme to the needs of a society that has to be transformed with the help of science and technology. In other words, work experience must be forward-looking in keeping with the character of the new social order".

SUMMING UP: THE PHILOSOPHY OF GANDHIJI AND ITS IMPACT ON EDUCATION

It is not quite fair to limit Gandhiji's philosophy and principles of education to basic system of education. His contribution goes far beyond. Basic system of education is just one of his contributions to education. There is no dimension of life and education on which Gandhiji has not expressed his views. His views on the importance of mother tongue as medium of instruction, his emphasis on manual labour, his stress on 'Learning by Earning', his views on the significance of women education and the role of the teacher etc. are quite relevant today.

To Gandhiji, education was an integral part of a comprehensive programme of socio-economic reconstruction of Indian society.

As a political and spiritual leader and an economic and social reformer, Gandhiji was naturally concerned with education. All his constructive programmes, economic, educational, ethical, political, social and spiritual were organically interconnected. Gandhiji wrote, "My life is indivisible whole and all my activities run into one another, and they all have their rise in my insatiable love for mankind."

27

Sri Aurobindo (1872-1950): Integral Education

BRIEF LIFE SKETCH

Revolutionary and freedom fighter turned '*rishi*' (seer), Sri Aurobindo was born in an educated middle class family of Calcutta (Kolkata), West Bengal. Sri Aurobindo was a very brilliant student. At the age of 7, he went to England and spent there about 14 years. He received his education at Cambridge. Besides English, he mastered Latin and Greek, and learnt French, German, Italian and Spanish. At the age of 18, he passed the entrance examination of the coveted I.C.S. [Indian Civil Service (ICS)] – the most coveted service. He, however, did not appear in the riding test, which was also compulsory. This was perhaps on account of his hatred for the foreign rule.

On return to India, he served as a professor of English at Baroda College. He learnt Bengali, Gujarati, Marathi and Sanskrit. He drank deep in the culture and philosophy of India.

Sri Aurobindo took an active part in the freedom struggle and courted arrest. He was a great pioneer in the National Education Movement, launched in the wake of agitation against the 'Partition of Bengal'. He joined as principal of Bengal National College of Calcutta (now Jadavpur University).

In 1910 he left political activities and went to Pondicherry (a French settlement in India at that time). He turned to the study of religious, philosophical and spiritual literature. He propounded the concept of the national system of education.

He set up an international Ashram and International Centre of Education at Pondicherry and started several educational and social activities. He also started a new experiment known as Aurovill as a city of human unity.

Aurobindo's Important Publications on Education and Allied Subjects

1. *A System of National Education.*
2. *Sri Aurobindo and the Mother on Education.*
3. *The Human Cycle.*
4. *Ideal of Human Unity.*
5. *The Life Divine.*
6. *Riddle of the World.*
7. *The Savitri.*
8. *Essays on Geeta.*
9. *On the Vedas.*
10. *Eight Upanishads*

SELECT QUOTES OF SRI AUROBINDO ON EDUCATION

1. "To bring out the real man is the first business of education".
2. "The chief aim of education should be to help the growing soul to draw out which is best and make it perfect for a noble cause".
3. "The best method of moral education is by personal example, daily converse the books read from day-to-day".
4. "Perfect liberty would be desirable for the child".
5. "The teacher is not an instructor or task master, he is a helper and guide".
6. "Indeed if the education is to have its maximum result, it must begin even before birth".
7. "The true basis of education is the study of the human mind".
8. "The idea of hammering the child into the shape desired by the parent or teacher is a barbarous and ignorant superstition".
9. "The education of the intellect divorced from the perfection of the moral and emotional nature is injurious to human nature".

PROMINENT FEATURES OF AUROBINDO'S PHILOSOPHY

1. Everyone has in him something Divine.

2. The task is to find it, develop it and use it.

3. This Divine can be obtained by a spiritual discipline, called yoga.

4. Aurobindo's concept of yoga is not that of a *sanyasi* who turns away from life in order to turn towards God.

5. Yoga is for the ordinary man, while he carries on his worldly pursuits.

6. If a merchant wishes to follow yoga, he regards his work as Divine he does not use unfair practices to earn money.

7. If a student, looks for higher values, he must observe *Brahmacharya* (self-control).

SRI AUROBINDO'S MAIN IDEAS ON EDUCATION

1. Aims of Education

1. According to Sri Aurobindo, "The chief aim of education should be to help the growing soul to draw out which is best and make it perfect for a noble cause".

2. The education should enable an individual to realise his inner self which is a part of the universal consciousness. The individual has to enter into right relationships not only within himself but also with the people of his country and with the universal society to which he belongs.

The human race is composed of people or nations and a nation is composed of individuals. The nations make the universal humanity.

2. Functions of Education

Following are the chief functions of education:

(i) To bring out the real man.

(ii) To build the powers of the human mind and spirit, i.e., the evoking of knowledge, character and culture.

(iii) To enable the individual to establish a clear continuity between the past, present and the future.
(iv) To enable the individual to establish right relations with life.

3. Nature of the Child and Principles of Teaching

Sri Aurobindo attaches great importance to the divine gift inherent in the children. Accordingly he has stated the following three principles of teaching:

The first principle of true teaching is that nothing can be taught. The teacher is not an instructor or task master, he is a helper and guide.

The teacher's work is to suggest and not to impose on the mind of the students. He does not actually train the mind of his student but helps him to perfect his mind and encourages him in every way in this process. Thus he does not impart knowledge, but shows the way how knowledge can be acquired. Knowledge is within the pupil and the pupil has to help himself to bring it out, but he needs help. Somebody must tell him where it is and how it can be 'habituated to rise to the surface'. Teacher alone can do this work.

The second principle is that the mind has to be consulted in its growth. The idea of hammering the child into the shape desired by the parent or teacher is a barbarous and ignorant superstition. Sri Aurobindo wrote, "It is wrong and rather immoral to force adult will on the child. The divine in the child should not be ignored and mutilated. To force the nature of the child to abandon its own '*Dharma*' is to do permanent harm".

The third principle of teaching is to work from the near to the far, from the known to the unknown. Man's nature is moulded by his soul's past, his heredity and his environment. The past is the foundation, the present is the material and future is the aim and each must find its due and natural place in any national system of education.

4. Main Principles of Learning

(i) Concentration is the first principle of learning.
(ii) '*Abhyasa*' or steady natural practice is the second principle of learning.

5. Moral Education

This should be on the following methods:

(i) Personal examples of the teachers and elders.
(ii) Study of books having lofty examples.
(iii) '*Satsanga*' i.e., good company.
(iv) Suggesting and not commanding and imposing.

6. Discipline

'*Chitta Shuddhi*' i.e., purification of the mental and moral habits should be the basis of discipline. This means to discriminate between right and wrong impressions and to absorb right ones in the mind.

Sri Aurobindo advises teachers not to be arbitrary, despotic, impatient and ill tempered.

7. Physical Education

Perfection is the true aim of education and physical development is an integral part of perfection. Moreover without physical development, '*Dharma*' cannot be performed. Only a healthy body can contain a healthy mind. As the Sanskrit saying goes, '*Shariram khalu dharmasadhanam*' (the body is the means of fulfillment of *dharma*).

8. Curriculum

It should include the following:

(i) Physical development studies
(ii) Mental development studies
(iii) Cultural development studies
(iv) Vital sciences relating to preservation of body etc.
(v) Vocational development studies
(vi) International understanding programmes

9. Teacher—A Guide and Helper

Sri Aurobindo observes, "The teacher is not an instructor or task-master; he is a helper and guide. His business is to suggest and not to impose. He does not actually train the pupil's mind, he only shows him how to perfect his instruments of knowledge and helps and encourages him in the process. He does not impart knowledge to him; he shows him how to acquire knowledge for himself. He does not call forth the knowledge for himself. He does not call forth the knowledge that is within. He only shows him where it lies and how it can be habituated to rise to the surface".

NATIONAL SYSTEM OF EDUCATION

Prevailing Defects in Education: Shri Aurobindo found the following defects in the prevailing system of education:

1. It was denationalising.
2. It was degrading.
3. It was impoverishing the mind; soul and character.
4. It was bad in kind.

Main Characteristics of the National System of Education: Aurobindo pointed out the following elements:

(i) Human and spiritual values are complementary and supplementary.
(ii) Education does not become national by tagging the word 'national' to the system.
(iii) Education should pay due attention to modern knowledge and scientific progress.
(iv) Mere knowledge of science does not make us educated in the true sense. This must be related to powers of the human mind and spirit.
(v) There should be a balanced understanding of the national and international relationships of universal humanity.

INTEGRAL EDUCATION

Meaning of Integral Education

According to Sri Aurobindo, "Integral education is that which helps to bring out to full advantage, makes ready for the full purpose of life and scope of all that is in the individual man, which at the same time helps him to enter into his right relation with life, mind and soul of the people to which he belongs and with the great total life, mind and soul of humanity of which he himself is a unit and his people or nation, a separate and yet inseparable member".

The human body, mind and intellect combine together to form a magnificent machine; we call it a machine for want of a better world but it is superior to any other equipment built by man. Education must integrate these elements to serve its real purpose.

TWO-FOLD BASES OF INTEGRATED EDUCATION

1. Individuality is one whole.
2. Humanity is one. There are no inconsistencies in the East and the West.

1. Individuality is One Whole

(a) *Harmonious Development of Three Dimensions of Individuality*: Body, mind and soul have their significance when they are harmoniously developed as they constitute the whole individuality. Likewise individual's intellectual development must develop in relation to his moral, emotional and spiritual nature and vice versa. In other words integral education must develop all the dimensions of the individuality of the person. According to Sri Aurobindo, there should be a balanced and harmonious development of all the aspects of human personality-cognitive (knowledge), conative (skills) and affective (attitudes and values). An individual thus becomes an integrated individual.

(b) *Socio-economico-politico Integration*: Neither man has been regarded as a pre-eminently reasoning animal so that education should aim at developing only his mental capacities, nor has he been seen as an economic, political and social being only so that education should train him as a productive and disciplined member of the society. These, no doubt, are aspects and characteristics of human being but they do not define the whole of the real man. The real man is not only a bundle of selfish interests, nor alone an intellectual entity, nor merely a social being. He is something more. Beyond the physical and mental bounds there is spiritual existence. Sri Aurobindo said, "India has seen always in man the individual a soul, a portion of the divinity enwrapped in mind and body".

(c) *Different Aspects of the 'Self' but 'Self' is One*: Man is the conscious manifestation of the universal spirit. We may distinguish in man different aspects of his being, mental, intellectual, ethical, practical, aesthetic, physical and the like but all these have been as powers of a 'self' that manifests through them and yet they are not all the 'self'.

(d) *No Concentration on Academic Perfection Alone*: The study of mind is fundamental in education. Any system of education which concentrates on academic perfection of the child with disregard to his mind is destined to fail. It would rather hamper the intellectual growth than producing an integrated mind.

2. Oneness of Humanity

Sri Aurobindo immersed himself in Vedanta and Yoga. Instead of seeing conflict or finding inconsistencies between the East and the West, he evolved a synthesis of both. He also synthesised 'Spirit' and 'Matter', 'Science' and 'Vedanta'.

3. Multiple Cells

Sri Aurobindo considers all forms in the universe as multiple cells of one consciousness and the Yoga as the means through which one may come into contact with the true 'self' and unite the separate parts of oneself and also can see the divine in others.

4. Inner as Well as Outer Realisation

Aurobindo says that we must aim not only at an inner realisation but an outer realisation also—the establishment of the Kingdom of God not only within the heart but also in the world of human affairs.

TASK OF INTEGRAL EDUCATION

What really is the task of integral education? Sri Aurobindo said that there are three that education must take into account:

1. The man
2. The nation or people
3. Universal humanity

Education must enable us to understand the interrelationship among these three.

Stages or Phases of Integral Education

According to Aurobindo, education to be integral must have the following aspects relating to the five principal activities of the human being:

1. The physical
2. The vital
3. The mental
4. The psychic
5. The spiritual

Sri Aurobindo stated that usually these stages or phases of education succeed each other in a chronological order following the growth of the individual. This, however, does not mean that one stage should replace another until another is complete but that all must continue, complementing each other, till the end of life.

Five Stages or Phases of Integral Education

(1)	(2)	(3)	(4)	(5)
Physical Education	Vital Education	Mental Education	Psychic Education	Spiritual Education

1. *Physical Stage of Education*: It includes:
   (1) Total harmonious and integrated development of the body.
   (2) Physical discipline, i.e., control of various part of the body.
   (3) Freedom from diseases.
2. *Vital Stage of Education*: The vital education has two elements:
   (1) Development and utilisation of senses.
   (2) Becoming conscious and gradually controlling them.

Thus vital education is very important in training senses.

3. *Psychic Stage of Education*: The word 'psychic' implies sensitiveness relating to non-material. Psychic education, therefore, implies education which includes development of non-material values. In the words of Mother, an outstanding disciple of Sri Aurobindo, "One thing is absolutely indispensable, the will to discover". Psychic is related to Yoga.

4. *Mental Stage of Education*. Mental education has the following aspects:
   (1) Development of power of attention and concentration.
   (2) Development of the capacity to expand mental horizon.
   (3) Development of the capacity to enrich mental horizon.
   (4) Development of the capacity to organise ideas around a central theme.
   (5) Development of reasoning power so as to accept desirable thoughts and reject undesirable ones.
   (6) Development of the power to accept or reject ideas coming from different quarters.
   (7) Development of the power to get inspiration from the higher regions of the being.

5. *Spiritual Stage of Education*: This is the highest level of education. It is also called 'super-mental education'. This stage is reached after one develops physical, vital, mental and psychic elements. According to Mother, "It will, by its all powerful action, work not only upon the very substance of which they are built and upon the environment in which they live". This requires deep and intensive insight and persistent efforts. This leads to 'eternal bliss'.

MEASURES FOR ACHIEVING THE ENDS OF INTEGRAL EDUCATION

Following are the measures suggested by Sri Aurobindo:

1. Role of the Teacher: According to Aurobindo, "The teacher is not an instructor or task master; he is a helper and a guide. His business is to suggest".

2. Principles of Education: Sri Aurobindo enumerated the three principles:
   (1) The teacher's work is to suggest and not to impose principles on the minds of the students.
   (2) The second principle is that the child has to be consulted in the growth.
   (3) The third principle is to work from the near to the far.

3. Discipline: Aurobindo wrote, "If education is to bring out to full advantage all that is in the individual child, we should first generate a safe custody of all that is in the individual. The divinity in man is not to be insulted".

4. Moral Training:
   (1) It should be through personal example of the teacher,
   (2) '*Sadhna*' should be the basis of moral training,
   (3) It should be based on practical opportunities,
   (4) It should come through Yoga.

5. Immense Faith in the Potentialities of the Child: Teacher must have an immense faith in the capacity of the child.

6. Physical Education: Perfection or integral development is the true aim of all culture. Therefore, the physical part of it cannot be left aside. Sri Aurobindo refers to the old Sanskrit adage '*Sariram Khalu Dharma – Sadhanam*' – the body is the means of fulfilment of '*dharma*'.

7. Curriculum at the International Centre, Pondicherry: It includes:

(1) Psychic and spiritual studies
(2) Academic subjects
(3) Physical and health education
(4) Cultural activities like art, music, drama
(5) Vocational training
(6) Education for international understanding

8. Basic Principles of Integral Teaching-Learning: Integral teaching-learning process involves the following elements:

1. ***Sense Training*:** Sense training is developed through observation of natural phenomenon under the guidance of the teacher.
2. ***Developing Power of Investigation*:** Observation plays an important role in developing power of investigation.
3. ***Training of Memory and Mind*:** Training of memory and mind is done by equipping the students to note similarities and dissimilarities.
4. ***Training in Making Judgements*:** The above factors provide suitable training in making judgements.
5. ***Training of Logical Faculty*:** This depends upon:
   (i) Ascertaining correctness of facts.
   (ii) Collecting accurate data.
   (iii) Sifting facts by eliminating false elements.
6. ***Training of Imagination*:** Training of imagination depends upon the following three elements:
   (a) Forming correct images.
   (b) Developing power of creative thinking.
   (c) Training in appreciating the existence of truth, goodness and beauty of soul in all existing things.
7. ***Training of Language*:** This is done through appropriate methods of teaching and also through concrete things.
8. ***Free Environment*:** Sri Aurobindo has stressed the significance of free environment under the guidance of the teacher.

CONTRIBUTION OF SRI AUROBINDO TO EDUCATION

The Ashram School: The school was originally started in 1943 for the children of Sri Aurobindo's disciples. It expanded gradually from a Primary School to a full-fledged High School. There are resident as well as day-students.

The International Centre of Education: The objectives underlying the centre are:

1. To evolve a system of education for making it dynamic, ideal for society.
2. To organise an environment which may provide inspiration and facilities

for the exercise and development of the five aspects of personality—the physical, the vital, the mental, the psychic and the spiritual.

3. To emphasise the unity of all knowledge.

4. To develop the sense of oneness of mankind.

5. To discover and prepare for the role India has to play in the formation of the new international harmony.

***Summing up*:** To understand the concept of integral education as propounded by Sri Aurobindo, we must understand the interrelationship among the different elements within the man, the nation and the universal humanity. We must see the synthesis among these.

UNIT III : SOCIOLOGICAL FOUNDATIONS OF EDUCATION

28

Educational Sociology

MEANING AND DEFINITION OF SOCIOLOGY

Sociology is the study of social relationships. It studies the human behaviour in groups. It relates to the social structure and social phenomenon. In its study, different forms of human interrelations are involved.

The term 'Sociology' was coined in 1838 by August Comte (1798-1857) of France who is considered to be the 'Father of Sociology'. It is formed by joining the Greek word 'Soclus' meaning 'Society' and the Latin word 'Logos' meaning 'Science of Study'. Thus Sociology implies a scientific discipline or science of society.

Comte was followed by an English philosopher, Herbert Spencer (1820-1903) who wrote his book "*Principles of Sociology*" in 1876. Spencer believed that the human individual was like the "Cell" and the society was like an "Organism" composed of different cells.

Emile Durkheim (1857-1917) of France also made valuable contribution to Sociology.

Although Sociology as a discipline is the product of the 19th century, concepts related to sociology are as old as Manu, Yajanvalkia, Kautilya, Confucious, Aristotle and Plato.

Some of the important definitions of Sociology are:

Duncan defined sociology as "the scientific study of the processes of interactions of persons."

In the words of *E. Durkheim*, "Sociology is the science of collective representation."

Gillin and Gillin state, "Sociology in its broadest sense may be said to be the study of interaction arising from the association of living beings."

Green states, "Sociology is the synthesising and generalising science of man in all his social relationships."

MacIver and Page define Sociology as "Sociology is about social relationships, the network of relationships we call society."

Max Weber, a well-known German sociologist considers Sociology to be a "science which attempts the interpretative understanding of social action."

From the above definitions of Sociology, it is clear that the central theme in Sociology is 'social interaction'. Social interaction includes interaction with cultural and other institutions, such as the family, the play and peer group, religious, economic and educational institution—in fact every form of group living. It studies the customs and traditions that grow out of these interactions, the institutions that crystallise these basic human interests and the changes that occur in these institutions. Sociology also studies the possibility of 'directing' these changes in the ultimate interest of human welfare. It helps to understand the force that 'bring changes' and also the 'effect' of these changes on behaviour and personality development in individuals. It throws light on man as a social being. It examines social changes and social control.

Sociology is subdivided into different branches of specialisation. Each branch has specialised methods of investigation and research. Important branches are:

1. Criminal Sociology.
2. Educational Sociology.
3. Industrial Sociology.
4. Medical Sociology.
5. Occupational Sociology.
6. Rural Sociology.
7. Social Stratification Sociology.
8. Urban Sociology.

MEANING OF SOCIOLOGICAL BASIS OF EDUCATION: EDUCATIONAL SOCIOLOGY

Sociological basis implies that Sociology plays an important role in determining educational issues just as philosophical, psychological, religious and scientific basis influence education, the same way sociological basis. The sociological basis of education has led to the emergence of sociology of Education or Educational Sociology. Some scholars distinguish between Educational Sociology and Sociology of Education.

E. George Payne (USA) often called the '*Father of Educational Sociology*' has given the meaning of Educational Sociology as "Educational Sociology is the science which describes and explains institutions, groups and social processes in relation to the educational system in its evolution and changing function."

Ottaway explains the meaning of Educational Sociology as "Educational Sociology starts with the assumption that education is an activity which goes on in a society, and its aims and methods depend on the nature of the society, in which it takes place."

According to *Dan W. Dodson*, "Educational Sociology is particularly interested in finding out how to manipulate the educational process to achieve better personality development."

In the words of *Brown*, "Educational Sociology is the study of interaction of the individual and his cultural environment including other individuals, social groups and patterns of behaviour."

In the words of *Good*, "Educational Sociology is the scientific study of how people live in social groups."

In the words of *Cook and Cook* "Educational Sociology is the study of human factors in the educative process, with the aim to improve teaching and learning in all types of educational systems."

Carte's view is "Educational Sociology is the study of those processes of Sociology that are significant for the educative process."

From above, it is clear that social interaction is the key problem of Educational Sociology.

Educational Sociology is the applied side of Sociology which is the study of social relationships. Social relationships are of various types and Educational Sociology covers educational relationships.

BRIEF HISTORY OF THE DEVELOPMENT OF EDUCATIONAL SOCIOLOGY

George Payne explained the various dimensions of Educational Sociology in his book '*The Principles of Educational Sociology*', published in 1928. In this book he explained the effects of learning on group life and that of the group life on learning. He further explained how education as a social process may eliminate social defects. He also described how education as a social process may strengthen desirable ideals and standards that a society aims to achieve.

John Dewey, a great American educational thinker did a lot of work to popularise the ideas of Educational Sociology through his books "Experience and Education" (1938), "Schools of Tomorrow" (1942) and "Education To-day" (1949). Dewey greatly emphasised the social function of education. He considered school as a social institution which 'purifies' and 'idealises' the existing social institutions.

SCOPE OF EDUCATIONAL SOCIOLOGY

The scope of Educational Sociology is very vast. It has constantly extended its domain. Its scope now includes as stated below:

1. It includes the relation of education to various social forces, particularly culture.
2. It includes how culture is handed over to coming generations through agencies like the school, the home, the religious organisations, the play-groups etc.
3. It includes how socialisation, especially of the child takes place as a result of social interaction.
4. It includes the role of these agencies in the educational process: (a) the school, (b) the press, (c) the radio, (d) the T.V., (e) the cinema.
5. It includes education as a means of social change and social control.
6. It deals with the impact of sociological thinking on the meaning, aims and functions of education, the curriculum including co-curricular activities, social organisation and methodology of teaching.

Important Issues of Study in Educational Sociology

1. Interrelation of education and sociology.
2. Education as an instrument of social progress.
3. Place of school in society.
4. Place of a teacher in society.
5. Mutual relations of students and teachers.

6. Social life in the school.
7. School and the community.
8. School and its relations with social institutions.
9. Promotion of social feeling in the students.
10. Social aspirations, needs and problems and educational system.
11. Curriculum and the needs of the society.
12. Promotion of critical and constructive approach.
13. Social advancements.
14. Equalisation of educational opportunities.
15. Role of the mass media in education and social progress.
16. Use of group and cooperative methods of teaching.

Aims of Studying Educational Sociology

Harington has suggested the following aims of studying Educational Sociology:

1. To acquire knowledge about school work and the work of teachers in relation to society and social progress.
2. To study the impact of social elements on the school.
3. To acquire knowledge of the effects of social elements on the individual.
4. To construct curriculum with comprehensive understanding of the economic and cultural tendencies of society.
5. To gain knowledge about the democratic ideals.
6. To employ research techniques for achieving the aims of Educational Sociology.

Broad Sociological Perspective or Basis of Education

Sociological perspective of education implies the following:

1. Education is essentially a social process.
2. Education takes place only in society.
3. Social milieu (environment) itself educates the child.
4. Education has an important social role to play.
5. Education is a life-long process.
6. School is just one but the most important of all the social institutions.

IMPORTANCE OF EDUCATIONAL SOCIOLOGY: CONTRIBUTION OF EDUCATIONAL SOCIOLOGY TO EDUCATION

Educational Sociology has a great bearing on education. As a matter of fact, there is no dimension of education which has remained unaffected by Educational Sociology. It is rightly stated by Zelong, "Educational Sociology today stands at the head of a great road of high promise, the road to practical technology that may contribute vitally to the development of a new kind of education—an education that actually develops citizens who know how to take part and delight in social participation and who have developed a truly sympathetic understanding of the emotional feeling of divergent groups, from those of the social community to those of the world."

In the opinion of educational sociologists, the school is the focal point around which revolves the life of the growing child. Man is a social being. He is a member of the society. The influence of society on education is imperative. Education involves several interrelations. Education must be a social activity. Education influences the society and is also influenced by the society. Educational reforms cannot be discussed in a vacuum. Social movements make changes in educational aims, contents, methods of teaching and its organisational set up. In fact the functions of education undergo radical changes. Clarke has very rightly observed, "No writer on education can wholly shake himself free from the influence of time and place." Dewey explains how the changing society affects education in his book "The School and Society" in these words, "Whenever we have in mind the discussion of a new movement in education, it is especially necessary to take the broader social view. Otherwise, changes in the social institutions and traditions will be looked at as the arbitrary invention of particular teachers. It is only by connecting education with the general march of events that the school can lose its isolated character."

Sociology discharges five different types of functions as far as education is concerned:

1. *Technical Function*: The study of Sociology helps to determine the functions of educational institutions and also suggests why they should be improved.

2. *Introductory Function*: Sociology acquaints the people with the nature of the educational system and its processes and also indicates the directions which it should follow.

3. *Informative Function*: A scientific study of Sociology helps to get various functional information about the problems of society and provides guidelines to education for solving problems relating to it.

4. *Cultural Function*: The study of Sociology helps to develop a cosmopolitan outlook, universal brotherhood and tolerance towards other societies and outlines the role of education in this task.

5. *Democratic Function*: The most important function discharged by Sociology is the democratic function. This democratic function of Sociology becomes the most dominant basis of education. Education is expected to provide great help in understanding the democratic structure and developing democratic skills and values in the students as well as the masses.

From above we conclude that the sociological bases of education are:

1. Education takes place in society.
2. Education is essentially a social process.
3. Social environment itself educates the child.
4. Education has a social role to play.
5. Education is a lifelong process.
6. Education is not schooling. It is more than that.
7. Education is formal, non-formal and informal.
8. School is not the only social institution of education. There are several other social institutions that impart education.
9. Economic and political factors of the society play a dominant role in educational reforms.
10. Education must be social in nature, i.e., it must develop democratic skills and values in the students.

Some of the important influences of Sociology are given below.

1. *Sociological Basis and the Meaning of Education*: In this regard, Brown's views have great significance. In his words, "Education is the consciously controlled process whereby changes in behaviour are produced in the person and through the person within the group."

2. *Sociological Basis and the Aims of Education*: The development of sociological tendency in education has put special emphasis as regards aims of education.

(i) Development of social attitudes, feelings and qualities.
(ii) Development of a socially efficient individual.
(iii) Improvement in vocational efficiency.
(iv) Effective use of leisure time and development of healthy recreational pursuits.

The social aims in education finds expression in such concepts—'education for social services', 'education for citizenship', 'education for social efficiency', 'education for emotional integration', 'education for national unity', 'education for nationalism' and 'education for patriotism' etc.

Why Social Aim in Education? An individual is regarded as endowed with a social nature. He is social by nature. He resides in an intricate web of social relations. Without social relations a new born baby would almost perish. An individual cannot live and develop in isolation from society. An isolated individual is a figment of imagination. A socially efficient individual is an asset to the society. He is not a drag or parasite on any individual and society. He is able to earn his livelihood. Education, therefore, should aim at the development of the individual in such a way that he becomes a useful member of the society. He should be made aware of his rights, responsibilities and relationships while living in a group.

3. *Sociological Basis and Functions of Education*: Monroe lays down the following main functions of education.

(a) Diffusion of more and more knowledge.
(b) Education as a means of social control.
(c) Education as a means of transmission of social heritage.
(d) Education as a means of social progress.
(e) Education as a means of developing constructive and creative outlook of the individuals.

4. *Sociological Basis and the Curriculum*: The primary concern of the curriculum is the development of "We feeling—a feeling that the student belongs to the society and has a spirit of social interaction."

Brown, More and Cole point out the following principles of constructing school curriculum from the view point of sociology:

1. Curriculum should be based on the conditions, problems and needs of society.
2. It should be based on the real concerns and problems of pupils.
3. It should reflect the basic cultural values of the society it serves.
4. It should be an agent in the transmission of the highest values of the culture.
5. It should provide educational programmes and activities that give them

wholesome participating roles in society. This participation is conducive to the development of responsible citizenship.

6. The curriculum must be functional in its relation to adult living and concurrently be adapted to the level of development of the child.

7. The school programme should treat with dignity all worthwhile vocations and services in community life.

8. The curriculum should develop healthy attitudes regarding human relations.

9. It should prepare the child for the world society.

10. It should prepare socially efficient individuals.

11. It should be flexible and changeable for the effective realisation of socially determined objectives.

12. It should lead to the development of genuine 'We feeling'—"a feeling that the student belongs to the group and has a spirit of social interaction."

5. *Sociological Basis and Methods of Teaching*: The following are the sociological basis of the methods of teaching:

1. The methods of teaching should enable the pupil to acquire those skills and knowledge in the classroom which are helpful to him in his adjustment to social situations.

2. The methods of teaching must seek to utilise the social forces operating in the social life with a view of developing a capacity for social adjustment.

3. The methods should develop problem-solving and constructive thinking.

4. The socialised techniques, the project and group methods, by and large should replace the lecture and recitation method.

6. *Sociological Basis and the Role of the Teacher*: It is said that the destiny of a nation is shaped in its classroom and it is the teacher who is a very important instrument in moulding that destiny. To be able to discharge such a high responsibility, it is very necessary that the teacher must become conscious of his role towards society. His behaviour should indicate his attempt to do his job properly. His personality must reflect characteristics of good citizenship. The teacher himself must be exposed to the concept of freedom, egalitarianism, dignity of the individual, rights and duties etc. so that he may transmit the same to the younger generation.

The educational sociologists consider teacher as a 'social engineer'—an engineer who can play an important role in social reconstruction. The Educational Commission (1964-66) observed that the "destiny of India is being shaped in its classroom." It is therefore, the teacher who is an important instrument in shaping the destiny through his influence on the children. A teacher is expected to:

1. Possess right attitude of social behaviour.
2. Remain above casteism, regionalism, etc.
3. Give due regard to the dignity of the pupils.

7. *Sociological Basis and the School*: Dewey's ideal school is expected to perform the following functions:

1. Reflecting and epitomising the larger society outside its walls.
2. Purifying the activities of the society in its environment.
3. Simplifying the activities of the society in its environment.
4. Balancing the activities of the society in its environment.

8. *Sociological Basis and the Discipline*: Discipline is social through and through. It should come through participation in group activities and social service activities.

Summing up. Sociology shapes education and forms a vital force in the entire framework of education. The whole superstructure of education has depended upon social forces, needs and demands. The expectations and aspiration of a changing society are reflected through the educational system of a country or a nation. Thus, we can hardly afford to think of education in isolation today. Clarke has rightly stated, "No writer on education, however much he strive for after universal thought can wholly shake himself free from the influence of time and place."

Society is dynamic, it grows and changes and as such these social changes must not only be reflected in education but also must affect it. It is only by connecting education with the general march of events that the school can lose its isolated character. As Dewey has stated, "School must become the child's habitat to be a miniature community, an embryonic society."

29

Education as an Instrument of Social Change: Role of the School

In simple words, social change implies change in the social structure and functions of the various units which form society. Social structure includes social institutions like the family, the marriage system, caste system, educational institutions, customs, manners, literacy forms, language, dress and food habits etc.

The following definitions of social change explain the various dimensions of social change:

1. *Prof. R.B. Mathur* explained the concept of social change in "*The Third India Year book of Education—Educational Research* (1964)" in these words, "Social change refers to the modifications in the organisation and behaviour of the group as expressed in its laws, institutions, customs, modes and beliefs. The change may be gradual or sudden, evolutionary or revolutionary. When change is supposedly for the better, it becomes 'progress' which is essentially an evolutionary concept."

2. According to *B. Kuppaswami*, "When we speak of social change we might assert that there is some change in social behaviour and in the social structure."

3. *Herry Johnson* would like to include five kinds of changes under social change: (a) change in social values; (b) institutional changes; (c) change in distribution of possessions and rewards; (d) change in personnel; and (e) change in abilities or attitudes of personnel.

4. *Kingslay Davis* defines social change as, "Only such alterations as occur in social organisation, i.e., in the structure and functions of society."

5. *Prof. S.P. Ruhela* views social change as "The term social change might imply changes in social attitudes, behaviour, customs, habits, manners, relations and values of people, in social institutions and structures, in the ways or styles of living."

6. According to *MacIver and Page*, "Social change is a process responsive to many types of changes, to changes in the man-made condition of living, to changes in the attitude of man and changes that go beyond human control to the biological and physical nature."

7. *Delbert C. Miller* observes, "Social change refers to a pattern of social relationship in a given social setting, which exhibits changes over some definite period of time."

8. *Sir Jones* states, "Social change is a term used to describe variation in or modification of any aspect of social processes, social interactions or social organisation."

9. *Fairchild* has stated, "Social change means variations or modifications in any aspect of social process, patterns or forms."

10. *Dawson and Getlys* observe, "Cultural change is social change since culture is social in its origin."

11. *Merril and Eldredge* have defined social change as, "Social change means that large number of persons are engaged in activities that differ from those which they or their immediate forefathers engaged in sometime before. When human behaviour is in the process of modification, that is only another way of indicating that social change is occurring."

12. *Gillen and Gillen* observe, "Social changes are variations from the accepted modes of life whether due to alterations in geographical conditions, in cultural equipment, composition of the population or ideologies and whether brought about by diffusion or intervention within the group."

SIGNIFICANT FEATURES OF SOCIAL CHANGE AND ELEMENTS

1. Social change may mean discarding some old elements or old things.
2. Social change may mean addition of new elements or things.
3. Social change may be sudden or slow.
4. All aspects or elements may not change at the same rate.
5. Social change may be brought about by violent or non-violent means.
6. Social change may be planned or unplanned.
7. Social change is fairly lasting.
8. Social change sets a trend.
9. Social change is revealed in the social relations and values.
10. Social change affects a sizeable population of the society.
11. Social change may be caused by internal factors, i.e., factors inside the society and external factors, i.e., factors outside the society.
12. Social change may be complex.

Chief Elements of Social Change

(1) *Changes in Social Structures*

This includes changes in

(i) Class structure
(ii) Caste systems
(iii) System of land tenure, e.g., changes in the Zamindar system
(iv) Labour conditions
(vi) Institutional structure in the school

(2) *Changes in Social Behaviour*

(i) Customs
(ii) Food habits
(iii) Intermingling
(iv) Speech habits
(v) Openness and broadmindedness

(*Note*: The list is not exhaustive. Only some examples of various areas of social life are mentioned.)

Patterns of Social Change

MacIver and Page list three patterns of social change as shown below:

Patterns of Social Change

(1) *Cumulative Change*	(2) *Social Change in Reverse Direction*	(3) *Wave-like Social Change*
Later social changes based on earlier social changes	Change in upward direction but afterwards reversal of direction	Alternating ups and down in social change

Some Examples of Factors Affecting Social Change

1. Disappearance of the Indus Valley Civilisation/Society probably on account of natural factors like floods.
2. Changes in Indian Society as a result of religious and social movements, influence of Buddhism etc.
3. Social changes in India on account of political domination of the British over India and India's independence.
4. Social changes in India on account of the impact of ICT.

PROCESS OF SOCIAL CHANGE

Process of social change may be classified in a number of ways:

Process of Social Change: Classification I

- Planned Process of Social Change
- Unplanned Process of Social Changes

Process of Social Change: Classification II

- Non-violent Process of Social Change
- Violent Process of Social Change

Process of Social Change: Classification III

- Evolutionary Process of Social Change
- Revolutionary Process of Social Change

Process of Social Change: Classification IV

- Man-made Process of Social Change
- Natural or Geographical Process of Social Change (The Indus Valley Civilization Vanished Perhaps on Account of Floods or some Natural Calamity)

CAUSES/FACTORS OF SOCIAL CHANGE

There are a large number of causes or factors that bring about social change. Sometimes even one cause may become responsible for social change. At other times, some factors or causes jointly act in such a way that social change becomes inevitable. Again it is stressed that the processes, causes and effects of social change work simultaneously.

Ideas and ideologies of great leaders have played an important role in social change. The influence of prominent personalities like Marx and Lenin in Russia, Mao Tse Tung in China and Gandhiji in India are some of the well-known examples of modern history which led to social changes.

Ideas like 'Liberty', 'Equality' and 'Fraternity' were great forces in giving birth to French Revolution which in turn immensely changed the French society.

The Important Factors of Social Change with Special Reference to India

1. Demographic
2. Geographical/National
3. Globalisation
4. Hinduisation
5. Indianisation
6. Information and Communication Technology
7. Industrialisation
8. Liberalisation
9. Modernisation
10. Nationalisation
11. Politicalisation
12. Privatisation
13. Sanskritisation
14. Secularisation
15. Social mobility or socialisation
16. Spiritualisation
17. Urbanisation
18. Westernisation

Note: Some factors may be more prominent in playing their role in social change. Some may come into conflict. Some may play their role in an invisible manner. Parson has very rightly observed, "There is the plurality of possible origin of social change."

A brief analysis of some factors of social change is given here:

1. *Demographic Factors*: Increase or decrease in population has an immediate effect upon social change. Partition of India leading to unprecedented migration led to several changes in Indian society.

2. *Geographical Factors*: It is said that on account of floods or some other natural phenomenon, Indus Valley Civilisation came to an end.

3. *Hinduisation*: This process of social change consists of the attempts of many tribal communities in India to enter the broad field of Hindu social structure. Also attempts are made to popularise Hindu beliefs and customs etc.

4. *Indianisation*: This is the process of social change in which several people belonging to different faiths, tend to identify themselves with Indian culture. In several catholic churches in South India and elsewhere, it is observed that many nuns wear Indian dresses—sarees and blouses. Worship is also done in Indian style. Lamps, candles, incense, 'prasad' etc. are used in the Indian style. Instead of English, regional languages are used in religious songs and prayers.

5. *Industrialisation*: Industrialisation has also given rise to social changes like, drinking, trade union activities, growth of slums, educational institutions, banks, roads etc.

6. *Modernisation*: Modernisation is a process of social change which emphasises rational, secular and scientific approach.

7. *Politicisation*: It is the process of social change through the spread of knowledge about political ideologies, parties and leaders. In this process of social change, people become aware of their rights and responsibilities.

8. *Sanskritisation*: In this process, low caste Hindu or tribe or other group attempts to change its customs, ideologies, rituals and ways of life in the direction of a high caste.

9. *Secularisation*: Movements like Arya Samaj and Brahmo Samaj have promoted the process of secularisation. It is a process of change which views events, things and ideals from a rational point of view.

10. *Social Mobility*: Social mobility is the process of change in status.

11. *Urbanisation*: This is the process of social change which has led to continuous migration from rural areas to towns. This results in the same social problems as industrialisation.

12. *Westernisation*: This is the process of social change in India which has influenced culture, living styles, values etc. of the Indian people as a result of western impact, especially during the British rule.

13 to 17. *Globalisation, Nationalisation, Privatisation and Spiritualisation*: The influence of these factors is discussed separately.

BARRIERS TO SOCIAL CHANGE

(1) Conservative Nature of Society
(2) Cultural Barriers
(3) Economic Barriers
(4) Illiteracy
(5) Lack of Means of Communication
(6) Political Barriers
(7) Psychological Barriers
(8) Religious Barriers

EDUCATION AND SOCIAL CHANGE

INTER-RELATIONSHIP BETWEEN EDUCATION AND SOCIAL CHANGE

Education is an Agent of Social Change

At the same time it is influenced by social change. This relationship functions in three ways.

1. Education as a condition of social change.
2. Education as an instrument of social change.
3. Education as a result of social change.

Education is Both Retrospective and Prospective

Education is both a creation and creator of social change. It is both conservative and progressive. Education transmits the culture of one generation to another. The rising generation has not only to be conveyed the activities and experiences of the past generation and asked to carry on those activities but it has also to be asked to make necessary changes in these activities and experiences to meet the new situations which it will meet. An integration of the old must take place with the new ones. It must be remembered that the communities live in the present, on the past and for the future. This means that activities and experiences in the present have to be built on the past and the present will guide the activities of the future. Thus, education is continuous, reorganisation and integration of activities and experiences. Education is a constructive agency for improving our society. Brown has stated, "Education brings changes in behaviour, and if its main functions are to remain mere transmission or enrichment of culture, it will fall short of its role in a dynamic society. Education must also provide situations at all age levels but within the maturity and ability of the individual to stimulate a creativeness of mind, which can explore new horizons and bring the vision of the future into a living reality."

Impact of Social Change on Education

Social change exercises a great influence on all the dimensions of education—aims, curriculum, methods of teaching, discipline etc. For instance under the British rule, the society was geared to meet the requirements of the colonial powers and accordingly education system became subservient to social changes. Likewise, after independence, an altogether a new social system emerged. This led to far-reaching changes in the educational system.

EDUCATIONAL IMPLICATIONS FOR BRINGING ABOUT SOCIAL CHANGE IN A DEMOCRATIC SET UP

1. Promotion of Democratic Values.
2. Development of Human Resources.
3. Development of Physical Resources.
4. Ensuring Equality of Opportunity.
5. Ensuring Dignity of Labour.
6. Developing Values of National Unity and Emotional Integration.
7. Fostering Scientific Values.
9. Promoting Secular Values.
9. Balancing Material, Scientific and Spiritual Values.
10. Developing World Outlook.
11. Providing Education for All, i.e., Universal Elementary Education and Adult Education.

EDUCATION AS AN INSTRUMENT OF SOCIAL CHANGE

Gandhiji wanted to bring about a silent social revolution in India through the basic system of education. In his words, "The Basic school should be the spearhead of a non-violent social revolution."

The role of education in the process of social change has been envisaged by J.S. Brubacher in these words, "If the lamp of reason is not lit or if the light is blown out, but it remains to struggle. When rational processes are put aside, it is only too likely that clubs and machine guns will become the social arbiters. Bullets will replace ballots. What a confession of intellectual and moral bankruptcy? And at what a cost?"

According to *H.C. Dent*, "A national system of education has two vital functions to perform—a traditional preservation function and a growth facilitating function. In a time of social flux both these functions become overwhelmingly important."

It is not without reason that the report of the Education Commission 1964-66 begins with these words, "The destiny of India is now being shaped in her classrooms. This, we believe, is no mere rhetoric." Education Commission has further observed that realisation of country's aspiration involves changes in the knowledge, skills, interests and values of the people as a whole. This is basic to every programme of social and economic betterment of which India stands in need. It has pointed out this fact as "If this change on a grand scale is to be achieved without violent revolution (and even then it would still be necessary) there is one instrument, and one instrument only that can be used, Education. Other agencies may help, and can indeed sometimes have a more apparent impact. But the national system of education is the only instrument that can reach all the people. It is a difficult instrument whose effective use requires strength of will, 'dedicated' work and sacrifice. But it is a sure and tried instrument, which has served other countries well in their struggle for development. It can, given the will and the skill, do so for India."

The International Commission on the Development of Education (1972) expressed its views, "Education must recognise itself for what it is: it may be the product of history and society, but it is not their passive play thing. It is an essential factor in shaping the future, particularly at the present moment, since in the last resort education has to prepare mankind to adapt the change, the predominant characteristic of our time... It has to prepare for change, show people how to accept them and benefit for them, create a dynamic, non-conformist, non-conservative frame of mind. Concurrently, it has to play the part of an antidote to the many discussions within man and society."

Education is the fulcrum upon which hangs the peaceful and evolutionary transition of society. It can ensure that the gap between reality and ideas does not become so great that it can be bridged only by revolutions which make a clean break with the past. Hence, education is not to be thought of merely as the passing on of the cumulative wisdom of society to the next generation. This will necessarily imply far-reaching changes in education and educational techniques.

The National Policy of Education in India (1986 and amended in 1992), in its introductory remarks highlighted the role of education in these words, "Education has continued to evolve, diversify and extend its reach and coverage since the dawn of human history. Every country develops its system of education to express and promote its unique socio-cultural identity and also to meet the challenges of the times. There are moments in history when a new direction has to be given to an age-old process. That moment is today."

Two-fold Functions of Education in Social Change

The problem of education in relation to social change is two-fold:

1. Adjustment to the changing situation.
2. Creation of a new order through change in knowledge, new ideas and or in other words education for social progress.

AGENCIES OF EDUCATION AND SOCIAL CHANGE

In the words of Dewey, "By various agencies, unintentional and designed, a society transforms of its own resources and ideals. Education is thus a fostering, a venturing and a cultivated process. All these words mean that it implies attention to the conditions of growth. When we have the outcome of the process in mind we speak of education as shaping, forming, moulding activity—that is a shaping into the standard form of social activity."

Types of Agencies of Education Contributing to School Change

(1) *Formal Agencies of Education*	(2) *Informal Agencies of Education*	(3) *Non-formal Agencies of Education*
1. Schools	1. Home	1. Correspondence Course
2. Colleges	2. Peer Group	2. Adult Education Centres
3. Institutions of Higher Education	3. Library	3. Open Schools
	4. Reading Room	4. Open University
	5. Social Clubs	5. Distance Education
	6. Press	6. Continuing Classes
	7. Films	7. Church
	8. Radio	
	9. T.V.	
	10. Internet etc.	
	11. Play Groups	
	12. Youth Organizations	
	13. Telephone (Mass Media includes telegraphy, telephone, radio, movies, T.V. etc.)	

SCHOOL AS A SOCIAL INSTITUTION AND AN AGENT OF SOCIAL CHANGE AND THE ROLE OF THE TEACHER

Mere conservation of the culture is not enough. Ryburn feels, "The progressive school can never be content that the present generation should simply remain where their forefathers were."

Dewey observes, "The school is primarily a social institution."

The future of mankind depends upon the education imparted in schools, "A world whose schools are unreformed is an unreformed world," writes *H.G. Wells*. This shows to what extent proper organisation of a school is necessary.

According to *K.G. Saiyidain*, the school is a centre of vigorous life. It is in direct intimate contact with the realities of the life around, reflecting the best and worthiest of its features which are simple enough to appeal to the child.

The Secondary Education Commission (1952-53) outlines the functions of the school as, "The secondary school must make itself responsible for equipping its students adequately with civic as well as vocational efficiency—and the qualities of character that go with it—so that they may be able to play their part worthily and competently in the improvement of national life. They should no longer emerge as helpless, shiftless individuals who do not know what to do themselves."

The Education Commission (1964-66) observed, "The destiny of India is now being shaped in her classroom." This clearly explains the significant role of the school in social change.

P.C. Nunn describes the role of the school in these words, "A nation's school... are an organ of its life, whose special function is to consolidate its spiritual strength, to maintain its historical continuity, to secure its past achievements, to guarantee its future. Through its schools a nation should become conscious of the abiding sources from which the best movements in its life have always taken their aspiration, should come to share the dreams of its nobler sons, should constantly submit itself to self-criticism, should purge its ideals, should reinform and redirect impulses."

S. Balakrishna Joshi sums up the concept of a school as, "A well-conducted school is a happy home, a sacred shrine, a social centre, and a society in miniature and a bewitching *Brindavan*, all beautifully blended into a synthetic structure."

P.C. Wren describes the functions of a school as "Organise the school to benefit the scholar, to train his faculties, to widen his outlook, cultivate his mind, to form and strengthen his character, to develop and cultivate his aesthetic sense, to build up his body, give his health and strength, to teach him his duty to himself, to the community and the state, in short to make an honest, capable and healthy man of him—organise the school for this and not to prepare him for the matriculation examination."

Elements in the School Contributing to Social Change

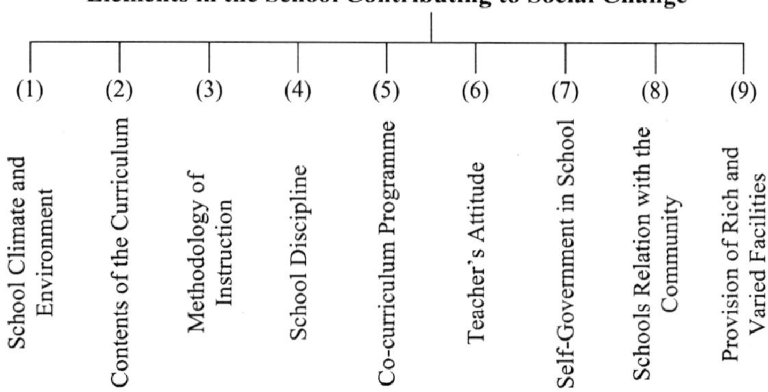

The school is a social institution set up by the society to train and discipline its future citizens in certain forms of activities. It must play a major role in moulding the ideas, habits and attitudes of children with a view to producing well-balanced personalities, physically strong, mentally alert, emotionally stable, culturally sound and socially efficient.

Programmes of the School in Social Change

1. *Providing Balanced, Purified and Simplified Environment.* According to Prof. Dewey, the function of the school is to simplify, purify and balance the activities of the society. The school curriculum should reflect all this.

2. *Training in Art of Living Together.* The school activities should provide training in the art of living together.

3. *Making Provision for Experimentation*: The school laboratory will not be a toy-affair, where a few simple and carefully planned experiments are performed under vigilant eye of the teacher who sees that the prescribed routine is followed. It will endeavour to give them something of the thrill and joy of discovery and the educative experience of learning through trial and error.

4. *Developing Opportunities for Self-Discipline*: Discipline in the school will not be a matter of arbitrary rules and regulations enforced through the authority of the teachers helped by the lure of reward or the fear of punishment. The students will be given full freedom to organise functions, to conduct many of the school activities through their own committees and even to deal with certain types of disciplinary cases. In this way, discipline will be maintained through the influence of the social group and it will gradually lead to the development of self-discipline.

5. *Developing Child's Entire Personality*: School should provide a richly varied pattern of activities to cater to the development of its children's entire personality. It has to formulate a scheme of hobbies, occupations and projects that will appeal to draw out hidden powers of children of varying temperaments and aptitudes.

6. *Providing a Stimulating Environment*: The primary concern of the school should be to provide for its pupils a rich, pleasant and stimulating environment which will evoke their manifold interests and make life a matter of joyful experience.

7. *Transforming itself into an Activity School*: The school must be transformed into an "activity school" because activity has an irresistible appeal for every normal child and is his natural path to the goal of knowledge and culture.

8. *Training in Democratic Living*: We have embarked upon a new way of life, i.e., democratic way of life. So for bringing about social change (commensurate with this) schools should incorporate such activities as 'student self-government'.

9. *Developing Scientific Outlook*: Emphasis on all school programmes should be laid in the development of scientific temper in the minds of the students.

10. *School as a Centre of Community Service*: School must provide opportunities to the community to use its resources.

11. *School and Social Service*: From time to time, the students should be provided opportunities to undertake social service activities.

TEACHER AS A SOCIAL ENGINEER AND AN AGENT OF SOCIAL CHANGE

1. *Prof. Ottaway* thinks that teachers in the school can have a very powerful influence in the community they choose. Teachers' professional organisations and unions are among the orthodox pressure groups and they can bring their views before public opinion and government.

2. *The McNair Report on the Training of Teachers in England* states, "It is a truism to say that every teacher, in however humble a capacity he or she may be serving, is directly and vocationally involved in moulding the shape of things to come." "If that truism be true", observes Prof. W.O. Lester Smith of the London University; "the unsettled times in which our young citizens are going to live their lives make it necessary that those who aspire to teach should have thought and should continue to think about the problems of society with all the intelligence at their work."

3. An American educationist, *Edmund W. Gordon* has pointed out, "It is the task of the teacher to educate—to educate for change—to educate through change—to educate for orderly planned revolution. If necessary, to educate through more disruptive revolutionary action."

4. In the words of *H.G. Wells* (1886-1946), the noted historian and thinker "The teacher is the real maker of history."

5. According to *Dr. S. Radhakrishnan*, "He acts as the pivot for the transmission of intellectual erudite and technical skills from generation to generation, and helps to keep the lamp of civilisation burning. He not only guides the individuals, but also to say shapes the destiny of the nation."

6. *The National Commission on School Teachers* (1983-85) states, "We underscore that the prime task of the teacher is concerned with man-making namely the making of the India of tomorrow."

7. *The National Commission on Teachers for Higher Education* (1983-85) writes, "Teacher is an agent of change."

Ways of Playing the Role of Social Engineer by the Teacher

A teacher can convey and disseminate attitudes and values to the students through the following ways:

(i) Direct teaching.
(ii) Providing opportunities to the students for living and practising the virtues of secularism, socialism and democracy.
(iii) Teacher himself becoming models embodying the desired attitudes and values.
(iv) Undertaking social awakening programmes.

Desired Competency in the Teacher to Play the Role in Social Change

It is said that the destiny of a nation is shaped in its classroom and it is the teacher who is a very important instrument in moulding that destiny. To be able to discharge such a big responsibility, it is very necessary that the teacher must become conscious of his role towards society. His behaviour must indicate his attempt to do his job properly. His personality must reflect characteristics of good citizenship. The teacher himself must be exposed to the concepts of freedom, equalitarianism, dignity of the individual, rights and duties etc. so that he may transmit the same to the younger generation.

Constraints on the Teachers to Play Their Role in Social Change

Prof. S.P. Ruhela and K.C. Vyas pose this question in the context of Indian situation, "How can they be so when the occupation of school teachers has so far not been able to emerge as a profession in the strict sense of the term due to their effective unenlightened and uncommitted professional organisations, and when many teachers' training institutions still continue to be disgusting educational slums, concentration camps, factionalism and inaction, in which teachers are very poorly socialised, trained and motivated to think and act creatively or innovate."

LIMITATIONS OF EDUCATION IN BRINGING ABOUT CHANGES

1. *Limited Resources*: Adequate funds are needed for providing educational facilities on a large scale. Besides funds are needed for qualitative improvement of education. Ill-equipped individuals cannot bring about social changes in the society.
2. *Attitude of 'No Change'*: People in general and even educated people are reluctant to follow new paths.
3. *Poverty and Ignorance of the Masses*: Percentage of literacy remained very low in India for a number of years. It is only recently that considerable improvement has become visible. Likewise a substantial percentage of people are still below the poverty line. In such a situation, social reforms take place very slowly.
4. *Lack of 'Political Will'*: Revolutionary constructive educational reforms could not be carried out on account of the non-availability of necessary political support. Thus education remained ineffective to a considerable extent in playing its role in social change.

Summing Up: We may sum up the role of education and the school with the views of two great thinkers. *M.V. Jeffreys* has observed, "It is hard to realise, in our own day, the magnitude of the revolution of which the schools were the instrument. It is not only that the mass of people have been taught to read and write and that the universities are open to talent. What has happened in a social revolution, in which cultural authority has shifted from family and social tradition to school... the agency of social revolution was education."

There are educationists and thinkers like Philip Coombs who think otherwise. They think that the notion that education can change the society is an illusion. To quote *Philip Coombs*, "Education is not a cure for all the ills of the world anymore than it is responsible for causing them. Education at best has at its disposal only limited time and means for satisfying all the expectations that individuals and society bring to the educational process."

SOCIAL CHANGE AND EDUCATION OF THE MASSES

Stressing the importance of the poor, *Swami Vivekananda* said, "If the poor boy cannot come to the education, education must go to him." Swami Vivekananda realised the importance of the education of neglected sections of the society and their contribution to national welfare. He wrote, "There are thousands of single minded, self-sacrificing sanyasins in our own country, going from village to village, teaching religion. If some of them can be organised as teachers of secular things also, they will go from place to place, from door to door, not only preaching but teaching also. Suppose two of these may go to a village in the evening with a camera, a globe, some maps, etc. They can teach a great deal of astronomy and geography to the ignorant. By telling stories about different nations, they can give the poor a hundred times more information throughout the year than they can get in life time through books. Kindle their knowledge with the help of modern science. Teach them history, geography, science, literature and along with these the profound truths of religion through these." All this implies in the present situation, a programme of functional social education. Such a programme is likely to develop new approach to understand the issues of national development. It is also likely to develop their capacity to produce more. They will learn the use of new implements—agricultural and industrial. They will have a better standard of life and living. Thus they will contribute to national welfare.

EDUCATION OF THE DEPRIVED SECTIONS OF THE SOCIETY

A society is composed of several sections. There are some sections of the society which come under the category of deprived sections. Without their welfare, national welfare cannot be imagined. Education is considered as an important instrument of their welfare.

The National Policy on Education has observed, "In our national perception, education is essentially for all. This is fundamental to our all-round development, material and spiritual." PART IV of the National Policy on Education, titled 'Education for Equality', includes several programmes for removing disparities and to equate educational opportunities by attending to the specific needs of those who have been denied equality so far. It lists special measures for the speedy promotion of education of the following categories:

1. Education for Women's Equality.
2. The Education of Scheduled Castes.
3. The Education of the Scheduled Tribes.
4. Other Educationally Backward Sections and Areas.
5. The Minorities.
6. The Handicapped.

30

Education and National Development

MEANING OF NATIONAL DEVELOPMENT

The term national development is very comprehensive. It includes all aspects of the life of an individual and the nation—cultural, democratic, economic, educational, emotional, material, moral, physical, spiritual and social. All aspects of development are very important and interrelated also. If one aspect remains undeveloped, others are also affected. National development is not synonymous with economic development though economic development is an important facet of national development.

The United Nation Decade Report has defined it as, "National Development is growth plus change. Change in turn is social and cultural as well as economic and qualitative as well as quantitative."

It is truism to say that is hardly a dimension of national life which is not influenced by education in one form or the other.

Problems of National Development in India

Although India has made a tremendous progress in all areas of national life since independence, still much remains to be done. Industrialised and several developed countries are far ahead of India in national development. Nearly 26 per cent population is below the poverty line. About one-third population is literate. Life expectancy is also quite lower. Infant mortality under one year is high. Net primary enrolment attendance is below average. It is, therefore, important that deficiencies in the planning process need to overcome as speedily as possible. Increase in growth rate of economy has little significance when a substantial percentage of population does not get the benefit of development of economy. On the whole it can be said that strenuous efforts are needed to achieve the desired objectives of national development.

CHIEF CHARACTERISTICS OF A DEVELOPING (EMERGING) AND A DEVELOPED (INDUSTRIALISED) SOCIETY

The chief characteristics of a developed and a developing society are broadly as under:

	Developed Society		*Developing Society*
1.	Very high gross national net product (GNP) per capita.	1.	Low GNP per capita.
2.	Very low infant mortality rate (number of deaths of infants).	2.	High infant mortality rate.
3.	High adult literacy.	3.	Low adult literacy.
4.	High life expectancy.	4.	Low life expectancy.
5.	High percentage of schooling (completing primary and secondary state).	5.	Low percentage of schooling.
6.	Very low drop-out rates.	6.	High drop-out rates.
7.	Industry dominated economy.	7.	Agriculture dominated economy.
8.	High percentage of urban population.	8.	High percentage of rural population.
9.	Population growth rate is low.	9.	Population growth rate is high.
10.	Most of the population can afford items of comfort.	10.	Most of the people cannot afford such items.
11.	Distribution of income is fairly even.	11.	Most people are poor.
12.	People are engaged in gainful employment.	12.	Relatively there is more unemployment and under employment.
13.	Production in the farms and factories is done by the latest modern techniques.	13.	The techniques of agricultural and production are primitive in general.
14.	People in general are not superstitious.	14.	People in general are ignorant and superstitious.

INDIA'S NATIONAL DEVELOPMENT VIS-À-VIS WORLD (AROUND 2007)

Indicator	*India*	*Developing Countries*	*World*	*Industrialised Countries*
(1)	(2)	(3)	(4)	(5)
1. Under 5 (years) Mortality Rate	76	83	72	09
2. Infant Mortality Rate Under 1 Year	43	57	52	05
3. GNI Per Capita (US$)	820	1900	750	37,000
4. Life Expectancy at Birth (Years)	64	66	68	79
5. Total Adult Literacy Rate	61	76	78	99%
6. Net Primary Enrolment Attendance	76	84	82	96
7. Percentage of Population Below $1 a Day 1995-2005	34	19	20	NA

Source: The State of the World's Children 2008.

Observations on National Development

Although India has made a tremendous progress in all areas of national life, still much remains to be done.

PROBLEMS OF NATIONAL DEVELOPMENT.

1. Low production.
2. Low per capita income.
3. Low standards of life of the people.
4. Conservative society.
5. Danger to emotional and national integration.
6. Slow progress in universalisation of elementary education.
7. Low adult literacy rate.
8. Low standard of education
9. Population explosion
10. Decline in democratic, secular and social values.
11. Bringing about a synthesis between moral and scientific values.
12. Lack of equality of opportunity.
13. Wide gap between the rich and the poor.

SIGNIFICANT ROLE OF EDUCATION IN NATIONAL DEVELOPMENT

It is not without significance that the report of the Education Commission 1964-66 has been titled as *Education and National Development*. The Education Commission has observed, "If the pace of national development is to be accelerated, there is need for a well-defined, bold and imaginative educational policy and for determined and vigorous action to vitalise, improve and expand education."

The Commission further observed that education cannot be considered in isolation or planned in a vacuum. It has to be used as a powerful instrument of social, economic and political change and will, therefore, have to be related to the long-term national aspirations and the programmes of national development on which the country is engaged and the difficult short-term problems it is called upon to face.

The Commission has rightly observed, "In a world based on science and technology it is education that determines the level of prosperity, welfare and security of the people. On the quality and number of persons coming out of our schools and colleges will depend our success in the great enterprise of national reconstruction whose principal objective is to raise the standard of living of our people."

The National Policy on Education (NPE) 1986 has observed, "The country has reached a stage in its economic and technical development when a major effort must be made to derive the maximum benefit from the assets already created and to ensure that the fruits of change reach all sections. Education is the highway to that goal." The modified NPE 1992 also endorsed the above statement.

Regarding the special role of higher education in national development, NPE has observed, "Higher education provides people with an opportunity to reflect on the critical social, cultural, moral and spiritual issues facing humanity. It contributes to national development through dissemination of specialised knowledge and skills."

ROLE OF EDUCATION IN SOLVING PROBLEMS OF NATIONAL DEVELOPMENT

1. To develop such skills which lead to increased production.
2. To modernise Indian society.
3. To promote values of emotional and social integration.
4. To promote democratic ideals.
5. To promote socialism.
6. To strengthen secular values.
7. To inculcate ideas of international understanding.
8. To promote the small family norm.
9. To develop environmental awareness.
10. To bring about a synthesis between cultural values and scientific values.
11. To prepare individuals for self-employment.
12. To prepare manpower needed for different areas of national life.
13. To develop spirit of service.
14. To develop sensitivity towards performing one's duties as stated in the Constitution.
15. To provide equality of opportunity for the optimum development of one's personality.

It may be emphasised that problems of national development are interrelated and areas overlap.

ROLE OF EDUCATION IN INCREASING PRODUCTION

Following recommendations are made for making education to fulfil this task:

(i) Making science as a basic component to education and culture.
(ii) Introducing socially useful productive work as an integral part of general education.
(iii) Vocationalising education, especially at the Senior Secondary School level to meet the needs of industry, agriculture and trade.
(iv) Improving scientific and technological education and research at the university stage with special emphasis on agriculture and allied science.

ROLE OF EDUCATION IN THE MODERNISATION OF INDIAN SOCIETY

Education should perform the following:

(i) Adopting new methods of teaching.
(ii) Awakening of curiosity, the development of proper interest, attitudes and values and the building up of such essential skills as independent study and capacity to think and judge for oneself.
(iii) Changing the composition of the intelligentsia; educating people of all strata of society.
(iv) Emphasising vocational subjects, science education and research.
(v) Establishing major universities of the excellence in the country.

ROLE OF EDUCATION IN PROMOTING SOCIAL AND NATIONAL INTEGRATION

The following steps are recommended:

(i) Introducing a common school system of public education.

(ii) Making social and national service an integral part of education at all stages.

(iii) Developing all modern Indian languages.

(iv) Taking necessary steps to enrich Hindi as quickly as possible so that it is able to function effectively as the official language of the Union.

(v) Encouraging and enabling students to participate in community living on the school or college campus.

ROLE OF EDUCATION IN DEVELOPING DEMOCRATIC VALUES

Education should aim at the development of democratic values through the following:

1. Organising student self-government in schools.
2. Decentralising educational management

ROLE OF EDUCATION IN ESTABLISHING A SOCIALISTIC PATTERN OF SOCIETY

The educational system should provide for:

(i) Equality of opportunity in education.

(ii) Common school system.

(iii) Compulsory social and national service.

(iv) Liberal provision of scholarships.

ROLE OF EDUCATION IN DEVELOPING SECULAR OUTLOOK

Following steps are needed:

(i) Introducing instruction in moral, social and spiritual values.

(ii) Providing syllabus giving well-chosen information about each of the major religions of the world.

(iii) Encouraging students to meet in groups for silent meditation.

(iv) Presenting before students high ideals of social justice and social service.

ROLE OF EDUCATION IN PROMOTING INTERNATIONAL UNDERSTANDING

This could be done by taking the following steps:

(i) Revising of textbooks and elimination of hostile material about other communities.

(ii) Organising inter-country student exchange programme.

(iii) Celebrating UN days.

31

Social Justice, Equality: Role of Education (Empowerment of SCs, STs, OBCs and Education)

MEANING OF SOCIAL JUSTICE AND EQUALITY

Social justice and equality have vast social justice dimensions and cover almost everything which promotes the welfare of all the members of the society in general and in particular the welfare of the weaker or backward sections of the society. It implies the following:

(i) Equality of opportunity.
(ii) Economic security.
(iii) Abolition of special privileges of upper sections of society.
(iv) Abolition of social inequality.
(v) Abolition of social evils.
(vi) Protective discrimination, i.e., providing special benefits to backward classes or sections.
(vii) Minimising gaps in wealth.
(viii) Protection of the interest of the workers.
(ix) Fulfilment of basic needs of all the members of society.

SIGNIFICANCE OF SOCIAL JUSTICE AND EQUALITY

Dr. B.R. Ambedkar, the chairman of the drafting committee of the Constitution of India; in his final address to the Constituent Assembly on November 25, 1949, very rightly stressed the importance of social and economic equality in these words:

"On the social plane, we have in India a society based on the principles of graded inequality which means elevation of some and degradation of other, on the economic plane we have a society in which there are some who have immense wealth as against many who live in abject poverty. On the 26th January 1950, we are going to enter into a life of contradictions. In politics we will have equality and in social and economic life, we will have inequality. In politics, we will be recognising the principle of one man one vote and one vote one value. In our social and economic life, we shall by reason of our social and economic structure, continue to deny the principle of one man one value. How long shall we continue to live this life of contradiction? How long shall we continue to deny equality in our social and economic life? If we continue to deny it for long, we will do so by putting our political democracy in peril. We must remove this contradiction at the earliest possible moment or else those who suffer from inequality will blow up the structure of political democracy."

Social Justice and Equality: Safeguards in the Indian Constitution

Social justice and equality call for a social order in which each member is provided with the maximum opportunities for his optimum development.

Following are the provisions in the Constitution which relate to social justice and equality:

1. Preamble: It *inter alia* mentions

Justice, social, economic and political

Equality of status and opportunity.

2. Fundamental Rights: *Right to Equality*

Article 14: Equality before law.

Article 15: Prohibition of discrimination on grounds of religion, race, caste, sex or place of birth.

Article 16: Equality of opportunity in matters of public appointment.

Article 17: Abolition of untouchability.

Article 29 relates to the protection of the language, script and culture of minorities. It also eliminates discrimination in matters of admission to educational institutions.

3. Directive Principles of State Polity:

Article 38 specifically relates to secure a social order for the promotion of welfare of the people.

Article 38(2) states, "The State shall, in particular, strive to minimise the inequalities in income and endeavour to eliminate inequalities of status, facilities and opportunities."

Article 39 relates to the following:

(a) Right to an adequate means of livelihood.

(b) Checking concentration of wealth in a few hands.

Article 43 and *43(a)* relate to the participation of workers in the management of industries and living wages.

Article 46 relates to the educational and economic interests of SCs, STs and OBCs.

Article 330 relates to reservation of seats for SCs and STs in the Lok Sabha.

Article 331 is concerned with the representation of the Anglo-Indian community in the Lok Sabha.

Article 332 makes reservation of seats for SCs and STs in the Legislative Assemblies of the States.

Article 338 to *342* relate to the appointment of National Commission for SCs, STs and OBCs. Posts have been reserved for various categories.

While discussing the various aspects of equality, it must be remembered that there cannot be 'absolute equality'. Equality implies that the impact of inequality should not result in permanent subordination of some sections of society to others in any of the sphere of socio-economic life.

IMPACT OF SOCIO-ECONOMIC INEQUALITY ON THE INDIAN DEMOCRACY

1. Socio-economic inequality develops social tension which encourages forces of disintegration and thus poses a threat to democracy.

2. On account of socio-economic inequalities, the poor and the weaker sections of the society do not have enough resources to match the resources of the rich, and in this way, financial difficulties create hurdles to contest elections.

3. On account of large resources, the upper classes are able to get more representation in the legislatures.

4. On account of inequalities, the poor and the backward sections tend to lose faith in democratic values.

5. Inequalities tend to turn democracy into autocracy. It negates the principle of equity and justice.

6. Socio-economic inequalities provide handle to the upper classes or the landlords to offer temptations to the backward sections to vote for them.

7. Socio-economic inequalities create discontent and hated among the downtrodden and their fury seeks outlets in riots and violence which vitiate smooth election procedure.

Types of Social and Economic Inequality in India

- Caste inequality *Jati Pratha* Untouchability
- Poverty and income inequality
- Inequality between the rural and urban population
- Gender inequality
- Regional inequality
- Inequality between SCs, STs and other sections
- Inequality in literacy and education

CAUSES OF SOCIAL AND ECONOMIC INEQUALITY

- Untouchability
- Caste system
- Conservative attitude
- Unequal distribution of resources of the community
- Illiteracy
- Colonial legacy
- Gender bias

THREE-FOLD STRATEGY FOR THE EMPOWERMENT OF SCs, STs AND OBCs: MINIMISING INEQUALITY

- Social Empowerment
- Economic Empowerment
- Social Justice

Social Empowerment (Specially Through Education)

Creating an enabling environment for the welfare and development of the socially disadvantaged groups by removing the existing inequalities, disparities and other persisting problems besides providing easy and equal access to basic minimum services through—

- Education being the most effective instrument of empowering the socially disadvantaged groups, all-out efforts to be made to improve the educational status of these groups, especially of women and the girl child.

- Universalisation of primary education by 2007 and at elementary stage by 2010 with a special focus on low literacy pockets, and educationally backward communities, viz. SCs, STs, OBCs, minorities and women with a special focus on the girl child.
- Improving enrolment/retention rates of these groups in schools and thus reducing school drop-out rates through special incentives/support services like hostels, financial assistance, scholarships, free books and food, uniforms, etc. and thus improving the educational status of these groups, especially that of their women and girl children.
- Vocational training/education to improve the technical and productive capabilities of these groups, suiting local needs and market demands.
- Supplementing primary health care services through the Pradhan Mantri Gramodaya Yojana (PMGY) so as to fill the critical gaps, both in the infrastructure and services in the SC/OBC/Minority concentrated areas.
- 'Reaching the Un-reached', viz. SC/OBC/Minority groups, those living in the most backward and neglected areas, in general and their women and the girl children, in particular through the Universalised/Expanded programmes of ICDS, Supplementary Nutrition Programme, Mid-Day Meals, etc.
- Encouraging the participation of the socially disadvantaged groups in the planning and developmental processes at every level through ensuring their adequate representation in various democratic decision-making institutions like Panchayati Raj/Local Bodies, State Assemblies/Parliament, etc.

Economic Empowerment

The socially disadvantaged groups economically, promotion of employment-cum-income generation activities with an ultimate objective of making them economically independent and self-reliant through:

- Optimising the traditional ability of SCs/OBCs in agricultural production and maximising their productive capacity through endowing a piece of land, upgradation of skills, modern technology, equipment and ensured irrigation facilities.
- Enacting special legislative measures to ensure payment of minimum wages and equal wages with no gender discrimination to the SCs, especially in the informal sector.
- Re-orienting the employment opportunities for the disadvantaged to enable them to face the challenges of economic reforms and expanding private sector through equipping them suitably with the technical skills and emerging trades.
- Encouraging development of small entrepreneurship through formation of Self-Help Groups and with the support credit and markets through the corporations, exclusively set-up for these Groups.
- Modernisation of technologies and upgradation of skills in traditional arts and crafts sectors such as handlooms, handicrafts, lace making, glass work, metal work, etc. and thus ensuring value addition to the products to compete with the quality of the products of modern markets.

- Motivating the private and corporate sectors to invest in the welfare and development of weaker sections and thus fulfil their social obligations/responsibilities.

Social Justice

Eliminating all types of discrimination against the socially disadvantaged groups with the strength of legislative support, affirmative action, awareness generation/conscientiousness of the target groups, and change in the mind-set of the people through:

Reservation Policy: Strict implementation of reservation policy in education and services for SCs and in services for OBCs.

Eradication of Manual Scavenging: Total eradication of the most inhuman practice of manual scavenging continuing still in the present-day civilised world on a time-bound basis and with a Mission Mode Approach by 2007, by conversion of dry latrines into wet and weaning away the manual scavengers from this profession and rehabilitate them with alternative attractive and sustainable jobs.

Safeguards Against Atrocities: To uphold civil rights and prevent/curb social discrimination, exploitation, untouchability and atrocities against the disadvantaged groups through effective legislations.

Establishment of Mobile Courts: To set-up adequate number of special/mobile Courts in each District for speedy settlement/redressal of grievances for these groups and extend timely and adequate financial support as a measure of social justice to compensate/rehabilitate the victims.

Strengthening the Working of Commissions: Revitalising the four already existing Statutory Commissions, viz. for SCs and STs, for OBCs, for minorities, and for safai karamcharis and thus make them effective instruments to safeguard the rights and interests of these groups and thus ensure social justice to them.

Organising Awareness Programmes: Special 3-pronged strategy of 'Awareness Generation'—through changing the mindset and attitudes of the people towards these groups; 'Conscientiousness of the Target Groups'—to make them conscious of their own rights, privileges and governmental support available for them; 'Sensitising both officials and non-officials'—with special training programmes so that they can work with right perspective to meet the special needs of these groups.

SCHEDULED CASTES AND SCHEDULED TRIBES: SOCIAL JUSTICE AND EQUALITY

Meaning of Scheduled Castes and Scheduled Tribes

There is no set definition of SCs and STs but under Article 341 and Article 342 of the Constitution, certain classes are declared as SCs and STs.

Population of Scheduled Castes

In 2001, the population of Scheduled castes was 166.6 million, which accounted for 16.2 per cent of the total population.

Almost half of the total population of SC is concentrated in the states of Bihar, Haryana, Madhya Pradesh, Punjab, Rajasthan and U.P.—popularly known as Hindi belt in the north.

In the south, SCs are concentrated mainly in Andhra Pradesh and Tamil Nadu.

In the east, they are in Bengal and in the west in Maharashtra.

Traditionally Considered Characteristics of STs

1. Very little education.
2. Livelihood dependent upon land.
3. Very poor.

Social Life: Tribal people at different places have different cultures, faiths, traditions and values.

Scheduled Tribes

Origin of the Term Scheduled Tribes (*ST*): As distinct from the so-called mainstream population, the British used this term with respect to groups living in forests and hills, etc. It was also used with the prefix like indigenous people, etc. The term Scheduled Tribe denotes people belonging to these groups. Traditionally they have had very little contact with the main culture.

Traditionally Considered Characteristics of the Tribal People

1. The tribal people live in rather inaccessible parts of the country.
2. The tribal people live away from the civilised world.
3. They belong to these races—Australoid or Mongoloids or Negrito.
4. They speak tribal dialects.
5. They believe in ghosts and spirits and worship them.
6. They profess primitive religion known as 'Animism'.
7. Their chief occupations are gathering forest products, hunting, etc.
8. They are, by and large, meat eaters.

Total Tribal Population

The population of tribal people in 2001 was estimated to have reached 84.3 million. This represented 8.19 per cent of country's total population.

Population Profile of the Tribal People

1. The largest concentration of ST population is found in the North-Eastern States: Mizoram (94.8%); Nagaland (87.7%); Meghalaya (85.5%); and Arunachal Pradesh (63.7%).
2. Union Territories: Lakshadweep (93.2%); Dadra and Nagar Haveli (79%); Andaman and Nicobar Islands (5.5%).
3. Madhya Pradesh (23.3%); Orissa (22.2%); Rajasthan (12.4%); Maharashtra (9.3%); Bihar (7.7%).
4. Almost nil in Haryana, Punjab, Chandigarh, Delhi and Pondicherry.

Table 31.1: Total Population, Sex-wise and Residence-wise (2001) of SC, ST

	Total Population of India	*SC*	*ST*
	1,028,610,328	166,635,700	84,326,240
Males	532,156,772	86,088,760	42,640,829
Females	496,453,556	80,546,940	41,685,411

Note: India (Excluding the population of Mao-Maram, Paomata and Purural Sub-division of Senapati District of Manipur.
('Census of India 2001': Final Population Totals) (Registrar General & Census Commissioner India, 2004)

Table 31.2: Specific Articles in the Constitution for SCs and STs

Sl. No.	*Article*	*Main Provisions*
1.	Article 15(2)	Removal of any disability, liability, restriction or conditions with regard to access to shops, public restaurants, hotels and places of public entertainment or use of wells, tanks, bathing ghats, roads and places of public resort maintained wholly or partially out of state funds or dedicated to the use of general public.
2.	Article 16 (4 and 4A) and 335	Permitting the State to make reservation for backward classes in public services in case of inadequate representations and requiring the State to consider claims of the Scheduled Castes and Scheduled Tribes in the making of appointments to public services.
3.	Article 17	Abolition of untouchability and forbidding its practice in any form.
4.	Article 19 (e)	General right of all citizens to move freely, settle in and acquire property in any part of the country.
5.	Article 25 (b)	Providing for social welfare and throwing open by law of Hindu religious institutions of public character to all classes and sections of Hindus.
6.	Article 46	It enjoins upon the state to promote with special care the educational and economic interests of the weaker sections of the society and in particular of the SCs and the STs and promises to protect them from social injustice and all forms of exploitation.
7.	Article 164 (1)	It provides for the appointment of Special Minister in some States for looking after the work of SCs and STs.
8.	Article 244, 244A, and 275 (1)	Special provision for administration and control of scheduled and tribal areas in some states.

(*Contd.*)

Sl. No.	*Article*	*Main Provisions*
9.	Article 275 (1)	It promises grant-in-aid for promoting the welfare of STs and raising the level of administration of the Scheduled Areas.
10.	Article 338	It relates to the appointment of National Commission for Scheduled Castes and Scheduled Tribes.
11.	Article 340	It empowers the State to appoint a Commission to investigate the conditions of the Society and Educationally Backward Classes.
12.	Article 341 and 342	It relates to specify those Tribes or tribal communities to be as SCs and STs.
13.	Fifth Schedule of the Constitution	It relates to the administration and control of Scheduled Areas and Scheduled Tribes.
14.	Sixth Schedule	It provides for administration of tribal areas in the States of Assam, Meghalaya, Tripura and Mizoram.

MEASURES FOR THE DEVELOPMENT OF SCs AND STs

1. Acts Passed for the Protection of SCs and STs

A. *Legislation Against Untouchability (1955) and Protection of Civil Rights Act (1976)*

For enlarging the scope and making penal provisions more stringent, the Untouchability (Offences) Act, 1955 has been comprehensively amended and renamed as the Protection of Civil Rights Act, 1955 which came into force with effect from November 19, 1976. This Act provides for penalties for preventing any person on grounds of untouchability, from enjoying the rights accruing on account of abolition of untouchability.

B. *Legislation to Check Atrocities Against SCs and STs*

Scheduled Castes and Scheduled Tribes (Prevention of Atrocities) Act, 1989, which came into force on January 30, 1990, specifies offences which are considered as atrocities and provides for deterrent punishments for commission of the same. It also envisages preventive measures, and states to evolve schemes, among others, for economic and social rehabilitation of such victims. All States and Union Territories except Arunachal Pradesh and Nagaland have specified special courts for trial of offences under this Act. Exclusive special courts have been set up in Andhra Pradesh, Madhya Pradesh, Rajasthan, Gujarat and Karnataka.

2. National Commission for SCs and STs

In 1990, by the 65th Amendment of the Constitution, the Special Officer's post under Article 338 has been substituted by the National Commission for Scheduled Castes and Scheduled Tribes. The Commission suggests measures for the upliftment of SCs and STs.

3. Parliamentary Committees

Government had set up three Parliamentary Committees, first in 1966, second in 1971 and third in 1973 to examine the implementation of the constitutional safeguards for welfare of Scheduled Castes and Scheduled Tribes. The Committee has since then constituted as a Standing Committee of Parliament on Labour and Welfare.

APPROACH FOR EMPOWERING TRIBALS

- *Resolving the Un-resolved Issues through*:
  - Taking effective steps to prevent the serious problem of displacement of tribals and ensuring their effective rehabilitation through a laid down Rehabilitation Policy.
  - Involving tribals, especially those engaged in shifting cultivation, closely and gainfully in joint forest management, social forestry, agro forestry, etc. and facilitate rightful collection and gainful disposal of minor forest produce (MFP) and other produce.
  - Strengthening the grassroot democratic institutions, viz. Gram Sabhas, etc.
- *Solving the Persisting Problems through*:
  - Providing basic minimum services, viz. food, nutrition, safe drinking water, primary health care, education, safe environment, productive assets at least at the level of survival and sustenance with a special focus on women and children.
  - Promoting educational development among the tribals especially through reducing dropout rates and encouraging enrolment/ retention with a special focus on women and the girl child.
  - Making education relevant and suitable to their milieu, local situations and functional needs besides vocationalisation of education to equip the tribal youth with the most wanted technical knowledge and upgradation of skills.
  - Developing Forest Villages, on priority basis, by ensuring basic infrastructure and with basic minimum services for those tribals living therein.
  - Review and reform of the working of the financial and other support mechanisms.
  - Effective implementation of the Indian Penal Code.
- *Enactment of the Scheduled Tribes and Other Traditional Forest Dwellers (Recognition of Forest Rights) Act, 2006*
  - Aims to improve the lives of the tribals and other traditional forest dwellers living in forest by vesting the right to self-cultivation of forest land for livelihood, right of ownership, collection, use and disposal of minor forest produce, traditional and customary rights; Rules for carrying out the provisions of the Act are being framed and shall be notified shortly.
- *New Scheme of "Top Class Education for ST Students" introduced from 2007-08*
  - To encourage meritorious ST students for pursuing studies at

degree and post degree level in any selected Government or private institutes covering fields of management, medicine, engineering, law and commercial courses.

- 635 scholarship per year to be awarded to cover full tuition fee and other non-refundable dues in respect of Government/ Government funded institution; for private institution with a ceiling of Rs.2 lakh per annum per student,; and Rs.3.72 lakh per student for the private sector flying clubs for Commercial Training.

National Commission For Safai Karamcharis Act, 1993

Composition of the Commission: Under this Act, the Commission shall consist of:

(a) a Chairperson
(b) a Vice-chairperson
(c) Five members

One of the members to be a woman.

Functions and Powers of the Commission

The Commission shall perform all or any of the following functions, namely:

(a) recommend to the Central Government specific programmes of action toward elimination of inequalities in status, facilities and opportunities for Safai Karamcharis under a time-bound action plan;

(b) study and evaluate the implementation of the programmes and schemes relating to the social and economic rehabilitation of Safai Karamcharis and make recommendations to the Central Government and State Governments for better coordination and implementation of such programmes and schemes;

(c) investigate specific grievances and take *suo motu* notice of matters relating to non-implementation of—

(i) programmes or schemes in respect of any group of Safai Karamcharis;
(ii) decisions, guidelines or instructions, aimed at mitigating the hardship of Safai Karamcharis;
(iii) measures for the social and economic upliftment of Safai Karamcharis;
(iv) the provisions of any law in it application to Safai Karamcharis.

OVERALL STRATEGIES FOR THE DEVELOPMENT AND WELFARE OF THE SCs AND STs

The Government has adopted the following fourteen-fold strategy for the development of the Scheduled Castes and Scheduled Tribes:

1. Specific provisions in the Constitution for the advancement of SCs and STs.

2. Special Component Plans formed by the Central and State Government for the development of SCs and STs.

3. Special Central Assistance to the States for the projects taken up by the State Governments for the welfare of the SCs and STs.

4. Setting up Scheduled Caste Development Corporation (SCDCs) and ST Development Corporation.

5. Legislative measures.
6. Reservation of seats in the Parliament and State Legislatures.
7. Reservation in services.
8. Constitution of National Commission.
9. Assistance to voluntary organisations for Scheduled Castes and Scheduled Tribes.

DIRECTIONS CONTAINED IN NATIONAL POLICY ON EDUCATION (1986 AND 1992) ON THE EDUCATION OF THE SCHEDULED CASTES

4.4 The central focus in the SCs' educational development is their equalisation with the non-SC population at all stages and levels of education, in all areas and in all the four dimensions – rural male, rural female, urban male and urban female.

4.5 The measures contemplated for this purpose include:

(i) Incentives to indigent families to send their children to school regularly till they reach the age of 14;

(ii) Pre-matric Scholarship scheme for children of families engaged in occupations, such as, scavenging etc. to be made applicable from Class I onwards. All children of such families, regardless of incomes, will be covered by this scheme and time-bound programmes targeted on them will be undertaken;

(iii) Constant micro-planning and verification to ensure that the enrolment, retention and successful completion of courses by SC, and provision of remedial courses to improve their prospects for further education and in employment;

(iv) The recruitment of teachers from Scheduled Castes;

(v) Provision of facilities for SC students in hostels at district headquarters, according to a phased programme;

(vi) Location of school buildings, balwadis and Adult Education Centres in such a way as to facilitate full participation of the Scheduled Castes.

4.5 *Revised Para* of Education Policy, 1992 (vii) The utilisation of Jawahar Rozgar Yojana resources so as to make substantial educational facilities available to the Scheduled Castes; and

4.5 *NPE 1986 Para* (vii) the utilisation of N.R.E.P. and R.L.E.G.P. resources so as to make substantial educational facilities available to the Scheduled Castes;

(viii) Constant innovation in finding new methods to increase the participation of the Scheduled Castes in the educational process.

The Education of Scheduled Tribes

4.6 The following measures will be taken urgently to bring the Scheduled Tribes on par with others:

4.6 [*Revised Para* (i)] Priority will be accorded to opening primary schools in tribal areas. The construction of school buildings will be undertaken in these areas on a priority basis under the normal funds for education, as well as under the Jawahar Rozgar Yojana, Tribal Welfare Schemes, etc.

4.6 [*NPE 1986 Para* (i)] Priority will be accorded to opening primary schools in tribal areas. The construction of school buildings will be undertaken in these areas on a priority basis under the normal funds for education, as well as under the N.R.E.P., R.L.E.G.P., Tribal Welfare Schemes, etc.

(ii) The socio-cultural milieu of the ST has its distinctive characteristics including, in many cases, their own spoken languages. This underlines the need to develop the curricula and devise institutional materials in tribal languages at the initial stages, with arrangements for switching over to the regional languages.

(iii) Educated and promising Scheduled Tribe youths are encouraged and trained to take up teaching in tribal areas.

(iv) Residential schools, including Ashram Schools will be established on a large scale.

(v) Incentive schemes will be formulated for the Scheduled Tribes, keeping in view their special needs and life styles. Scholarships for higher education will emphasise technical, professional and para-professional courses. Special remedial courses and other programmes to remove psycho-social impediments will be provided to improve their performance in various courses.

(vi) Anganwadis, Non-formal and Adult Education Centres will be opened on a priority basis in areas predominantly inhabited by the Scheduled Tribes.

(vii) The curriculum at all stages of education will be designed to create an awareness of the rich cultural identity of the tribal people as also of their enormous creative talent.

MEASURES BEING TAKEN TO PROMOTE EDUCATION AMONG SCs: EQUALISATION WITH NON SCs

The central focus in the SCs' educational development is their equalisation with the non-SC population at all stages and levels of education, in all areas and in all the four dimensions-rural male, rural female, urban male and urban female. The measures being taken as per directions given in NPE (*see* page 308).

Promotion of Education Among STs

The measures are being taken to bring the Scheduled Tribes on par with others as per directions in NPE (*see* page 308 and 309)

Preparatory Classes and Compensatory Instruction for SCs and STs

Many children belonging to the Scheduled Castes, Scheduled Tribes and economically weaker sections come from a comparatively poor environment. They may not be neat or smart. Their usage of standard language may be poor. Their vocabulary is underdeveloped as compared to their peers. They may not have formed the initial mathematical concepts. On the other hand they may be more enthusiastic to learn. Because of the lack of a congenial home environment, these children may not be in a position to complete their home assignments. Their parents are usually employed as landless labour or in other manual or agrarian activities. Therefore, such children are not able to conceptualise their future as educated persons.

There is the need to conduct some preparatory classes for children coming from the Scheduled Castes and Scheduled Tribes. The primary objective of conducting such classes is to raise the school entry ability level of such children. This is also helpful in having a somewhat homogeneous grouping in the class. The classes may be conducted two to three weeks in advance of the general admissions. Classes may be conducted on healthy habits, personal and environmental cleanliness, eating habits etc. The children may also be helped in improving the pronunciation of the words and picking up standard language. For this, they may be motivated to participate in discussions, recitation and story-telling etc. Initial concepts of mathematics may also be introduced.

Remedial Instruction

Students coming from Scheduled Castes and Scheduled Tribes are also likely to be deficient in the scholastic areas. The school may provide some remedial education programmes. Adoption of instructional strategies, such as peer group learning, monitorial assistance, diagnostic testing and tutoring would help to improve the educational levels of these learners.

Provision of outdoor games and activities, co-curricular and work experience activities will also help in the retention of such children in the schools and create an interest in them for continuing schooling.

ROLE OF THE TEACHERS

The teachers can play an important role in developing a favourable school climate conducive to the educational progress of Scheduled Castes and Scheduled Tribes. Some suggestions in this regard are given here.

1. The teacher's own example in his behaviour towards students belonging to these castes is the most effective and powerful way to build up a congenial climate.

2. The school staff should ensure non-discrimination between the children of Scheduled Castes, Scheduled Tribes and other communities.

3. The school staff should avoid the use of the caste names or derogatory words while calling roll calls or naming children.

4. Teachers should provide equal opportunities to all the children to participate in the curricular and co-curricular activities of the school, including games.

5. Frequent meetings between the staff, school teachers and parents of Scheduled Castes and Scheduled Tribes children should be arranged. The details of the schemes for promoting education amongst Scheduled Castes and Scheduled Tribes should be explained to the parents at these meetings. It should be impressed upon them that they must continue the education of their children.

6. Special attention should be paid to motivating parents to educate girls.

7. Teachers should suggest to illiterate parents the advantages gained by attending functional literacy classes in the centre.

OTHER BACKWARD CLASSES (OBCs)

Constitutional Provisions

1. *Article 15(4) of the Constitution*: It enjoins upon the state the creation of special provisions for the advancement of any socially and educationally backward classes of citizens or for the Scheduled Castes and Scheduled Tribes.

2. *Article 16(4)*: It enables the State for making provisions for the reservation of appointments or posts in favour of any backward class of citizens which in the opinion of the state is not adequately represented in the services under the state.

3. *Article 38*: It makes it obligatory for the state to "strive to promote the welfare of the people by securing and protecting as effectively as it may a social order, in which Justice, Social, Economic and Political shall form all the institutions of the national life."

4. *Article 46*: It contains a very significant directive regarding promotion of educational and economic interests of other weaker sections and protecting them from social injustice and all forms of exploitation.

5. *Part XVI of the Constitution*: It contains "special provisions relating to certain classes" and under this part, Article 340 envisages the appointment of a Commission to investigate the conditions of Backward Classes.

Mandal Commission (1978-1980)

Appointment of the Mandal Commission

In pursuance of the Article 340 of the Constitution of India regarding the appointment of a Commission for the promotion of the Backward Classes, the President of India appointed a Commission under the Chairmanship of B.P. Mandal in 1978.

Major Recommendations

The Commission in its report, submitted in 1980, made the following recommendations:

1. Twenty-seven per cent of the posts in public services should be reserved for Other Backward Classes (OBCs).
2. Welfare programmes specially for the OBCs should be started by the Government of India in the same manner and to the same extent already done in the case of Scheduled Castes and Scheduled Tribes.
3. Special educational schemes with emphasis on vocational training should be started for OBCs.
4. Seats should be reserved for OBC students in all scientific, technical and professional institutions run by the Centre as well as the State Governments.

By and large, all the recommendations have been accepted. Only the 'creamy layer' (upper section of OBCs) has been excluded from the benefits.

National Commission for Backward Classes

The process of identifying the OBC is an unending process and is kept open. The government also set up on August 14, 1993, a National Commission for Backward Classes as a permanent body for entertaining, examining and recommending upon requests for inclusion and complaints of under-inclusion in the lists of OBC class citizens.

National Backward Classes Finance and Development Corporation

This body was set up by the Government of India in January 1992 as a company with the objective of providing concessional loans to the members of backward classes living below the poverty line. The Corporation has also launched a special scheme for eligible women beneficiaries of backward classes under the name of SWARNIMA.

Educational Schemes for the Welfare of OBCs

From 1998-99, following schemes have been launched for the welfare of OBCs:

(a) Pre-examination coaching; to coach candidates belonging to OBCs whose parent's/guardian's annual income is less than Rs. one lakh,

(b) Hostels for OBC Boys and Girls,

(c) Pre-matric Scholarships,

(d) Post-matric Scholarships,

(e) Assistance to voluntary organisations: The scheme involves the voluntary sector to improve educational and socio-economic conditions of the OBCs to get them gainfully employed.

Summing up: Educational Provisions for the Deprived Sections: Equality of Educational Opportunity

It is observed that well-planned, sustained and vigorous efforts as stated below would go a long way in promoting education among the deprived sections.

1. Promotion of mother-tongue as the medium of instruction.
2. Need based curriculum.
3. Special training of teachers.
4. Provision of suitable school building/accommodation.
5. Extension of Ashram schools.
6. Provision of extensive facilities.
7. Encouragement of tribal parents.
8. Flexibility in school hours.
9. Popularisation of tribal dialects.
10. Economic incentives to parents.
11. Special training for talented tribal students.
12. Provision of audio-visual aids.
13. Improvement of teacher-community relations.
14. Relaxation of prescribed norms for the opening of schools in tribal areas.
15. Opening of non-formal education centres.
16. Incentive programme for adult education.
17. Relaxation of prescribed pupil-teacher ratio.
18. Guidance facilities.
19. Incentives for students.
20. Provision of scholarships.
21. Organisation of study camps.
22. New initiatives for universalisation of elementary education.
23. Facilities for teachers – incentives like reservation of seats for their wards in Public Schools, Sainik Schools, etc.
24. Conducive environment in educational institutions.
25. Educational provisions – teaching-learning material.
26. Preparatory classes.
27. Compensatory and remedial teaching.

28. Relaxation of qualifications for tribal people in teacher training.
29. Effective monitoring programme.
30. Special role of the teachers.

For the successful working of Indian democracy and the achievement of national objectives as contained in the Constitution, it is very important to take speedy measures for the promotion of education among the children of the weaker sections.

GRADUAL INCREASE IN LITERACY RATES AMONG SCs AND STs

The literacy percentage of Scheduled Castes increased from 10.7 in 1961 to 54.69 in 2001. The literacy among males was 16.96% in 1961, which increased by 49.68 percentage points and reached 66.64% in 2001. The literacy of Scheduled Caste females was as low as 3.29% during 1961, which was now increased to 41.90% thereby registering in increase of 38.61 percentage points during 1961-2001. The literacy of Scheduled Tribes was 8.53% during 1961, which has increased to 47.10% in 2001. In the year 1961 the literacy percentage of Scheduled Tribe Males was 13.83%, which increased to 59.17% in the year 2001. The literacy percentage of Scheduled Tribe females, which was as low as 3.16% during 1961, increased to 34.76% in the year 2001. A comparative position of literacy percentages of Scheduled Castes and Scheduled Tribes in Rural-Urban areas is given below in Statement.

Literacy Rates of SC/ST by Sex and Urban/Rural, 1961 to 2001

Year/Region	*Scheduled Castes*			*Scheduled Tribes*		
	Male	*Female*	*Persons*	*Male*	*Female*	*Persons*
1961						
Rural	15.06	2.52	8.89	13.37	2.90	8.16
Urban	32.21	10.04	21.81	30.43	13.45	22.41
Total	**16.96**	**3.29**	**10.27**	**13.83**	**3.16**	**8.53**
1971						
Rural	20.04	5.06	12.77	16.92	4.36	10.68
Urban	38.93	16.99	28.65	37.09	19.64	28.84
Total	**22.36**	**6.44**	**14.67**	**17.63**	**4.85**	**11.30**
1981						
Rural	27.91	8.45	18.48	22.94	6.81	14.92
Urban	47.54	24.34	36.60	47.60	27.32	37.93
Total	**31.12**	**10.93**	**21.38**	**24.52**	**8.04**	**16.35**
1991						
Rural	45.95	19.45	33.25	38.45	16.02	27.38
Urban	66.60	42.29	55.11	66.56	45.66	56.60
Total	**49.91**	**23.76**	**37.41**	**40.65**	**18.19**	**29.60**
2001						
Rural	63.66	37.84	51.16	57.39	32.44	45.02
Urban	77.93	57.49	68.12	77.77	59.87	69.09
Total	**66.64**	**41.90**	**54.69**	**59.17**	**34.76**	**47.10**

Dropout Rates 2004-05 (Provisional)

	Overall	*SCs*	*STs*
Classes I to V			
Boys	31.81	32.7	42.6
Girls	25.42	36.1	42.0
Total	**29.0**	**34.2**	**42.3**
Classes VI to VIII			
Boys	50.49	55.2	65.0
Girls	51.28	60.0	67.1
Total	**50.84**	**57.3**	**65.9**
Classes I-X			
Boys	60.41	69.1	77.8
Girls	63.88	74.2	80.7
Total	**61.92**	**71.3**	**79.0**

Source: *Educational Statistics 2005-2006*, Department of Education, Government of India.

32

Education for Secularism, Democracy and Socialism

ORIGIN AND MEANING OF THE TERM SECULARISM

The word 'Secularism' was first used in 1846 by a British thinker George Holydake (1817-1906). In his book '*English Secularism*', he defined secularism as, "Secularism is a code of duty pertaining to this life, founded on considerations purely human and intended mainly for those who find theology, indefinite or inadequate, unreliable or unbelievable."

Holydake based secularism as a social and ethical system, on the following principles:

1. Principle of material and cultural improvement of human beings.
2. Principle of respect and research of all truth, whatever be its source.
3. Principle of concern for 'this present age' or world and its improvement.
4. Principle of independent rational morality, which does not base itself on faith in divine order commandment.

The meaning attached to secularism tends to minimise the importance of the spirit and the DIVINE power. It also tends to ignore the spiritual side. Both the elements are considered basic to Indian thinkers. The definition lays stress on material improvement only.

The word 'Secularism' is derived from the Latin word '*Saeculum*' meaning 'this present age'. Accordingly Holydake also emphasised the word 'this age'.

The Dictionary meaning of 'Secularism' are as under:

(1) '*Chamber's Dictionary*': "The belief that the state, moral education, etc. should be independent of religion."

(2) '*Oxford Dictionary*': "The doctrine that morality should be based solely in regard to the well-being of mankind in the present life, to the exclusion of all considerations drawn from belief in God."

(3) '*Webster's Dictionary*': "A system of doctrines and practices that rejects any form of religious faith and worship."

(4) As explained in *Wikipedia*, the term connotes;... 'that certain practices or institutions should exist separately from religion or religious belief'; '... it asserts the right to be free from religious rule and teachings, and freedom from government imposition of religion upon the people, within a state that is neutral on matters of belief, and gives no state privileges or subsidies to religions'; '... it refers to a belief that human activities and decisions, especially political ones, should be based on evidence and fact rather than religious

influence'; '... in European laicism, it has been argued that secularism is a movement towards modernisation, and away from traditional religious values'; '.... In United States, some argue that state secularism has served to a greater extent to protect religion from governmental interference, while secularism on a social scale is less prevalent'; '... within countries as well, differing political movements support secularism for varying reasons'; '... in political terms, secularism is a movement towards the separation of religion and government'; '... secularism can also be the social ideology in which religion and supernatural beliefs are not seen as the key to understanding the world and are instead segregated from matters of governance and reasoning... and in this sense, secularism can be involved in the promotion of science, reason, and naturalistic thinking'.

SECULARISM IN THE INDIAN CONSTITUTION

The term 'Secularism' did not occur in the Constitution of India when it was adopted in 1950. It was inserted in the Constitution of India in 1976 as it was feared that religious fundamentalism was on the increase and it was posing a great threat to national unity and integrity.

Following are the provisions on Secularism in the Constitution:

1. *Article 15: Prohibition of Discrimination on Grounds of Religion, Race, Caste, Sex or Place of Birth.* (i) The State shall not discriminate against any citizen on grounds only of religion, race, caste, sex, place of birth or any of them, (ii) No citizen on grounds only of religion, race, sex, place of birth shall be denied access to shops, wells, tanks, etc.

2. *Article 25(1): Freedom of Conscience*: According to this Article, all citizens are equally entitled to freedom of conscience and the right to profess, practice and propagate religion. However, while the freedom of conscience is absolute, i.e., without any restriction, the exercise of freedom of propagation of religion is subject to restrictions in the interest of harmony, public morality and order.

3. *Article 27: Exemption from the Payment of Taxes.* As per this Article, no person shall be compelled to pay any taxes, the proceeds of which are specifically appropriated in payment of expenses for the promotion or maintenance of any particular religion or religious denomination.

Views of Great Thinkers on Secularism

1. *H.V. Kamat*, a veteran Parliamentarian expanded the concept of secularism in the Constituent Assembly as "When I say that State should not identify itself with any particular religion, I do not mean to say that a State should be anti-religious or irreligious. We have certainly declared India to be a secular state. But to my mind, a secular state is neither a Godless state, nor an irreligious or an anti-religious State. In short, by a secular State is meant that the State shall not make any discrimination whatsoever on the ground of religion or community against a person professing any particular form of religious faith. This means that no particular religion in the State will receive any patronage or protection."

2. *Dr. B.R. Ambedkar*, the principal architect of our Constitution explains secularism in the following words, "Secular State does not mean that it shall not take into consideration the religious sentiments of the people. All that Secular State means is, that this Parliament shall not be competent to impose any particular religion upon the rest of the people. This is the only limitation that the Constitution recognises. (Parliamentary Debates, 1951 Vol. III, Part-II)."

3. *Dr. Rajendra Prasad, the first President of India* has very clearly observed that becoming secular, India has not been anti-religious or irreligious. He stated, "There are some who think that because we are a Secular State, we do not believe in religion or spiritual values. Far from being so, it really means that in this country all are free to profess or preach the faith of their liking and that we wish well of all religions and want than to develop in their own way without any hindrance."

4. *Dr. Radhakrishnan, the second President of India* explained secularism as follows:

"When India is said to be a secular state, it does not mean that we reject the reality of an unseen spirit or the relevance of religion to life or that we exalt irreligion. It does not mean that secularism itself becomes a positive religion or that the State assumes divine prerogatives. Though faith in the Supreme is the basic principle of the Indian traditions, the Indian state will not identify itself with or controlled by any particular religion. We hold that no one religion should be given preferential status, or unique distinction, that no one religion would be accorded special privileges in national life or international relations for that would be a violation of the basic principles of democracy and contrary to the best interest of religion and government. This view of religious impartiality, or comprehension and forbearance, has a prophetic role to play within the national and the international life."

5. *Jawaharlal Nehru, the first Prime Minister of India* has explained the secular nature of our State. "It means while religion is completely free, the state including in its wide fold various religions and cultures, gives protection and opportunities to all and thus, brings about an atmosphere of tolerance and cooperation."

6. On the concept of a 'Secular State', *Justice M.H. Beg*, in his judgement in *Ziyauddin Burhamudin Bukhari vs. Brijmohan Ramdass Mehra and Bros.* (1975 Suppl. S.C.R. 281) said:

"The secular state, rising above all differences of religion, attempts to secure the good of all its citizens irrespective of their religious beliefs and practices. It is neutral or impartial in extending its benefits to citizens of all castes and creeds. Maitland has pointed out that such a state has to ensure, through its laws that the existence or exercise of political or civil right or the right or capacity to occupy any office or position under it or to perform any public duty connected with it does not depend upon the profession or practice of any particular religion.

Our Constitution and the laws framed thereunder leave citizens free to work out happy and harmonious relationships between their religious and the quite separable secular fields of law and politics. But they do not permit an unjustifiable invasion of what belongs to one sphere by what pertains really to another. It is for courts to determine, in a case of dispute, whether any sphere was or was not properly interfered with, in accordance with the Constitution, even by a purported law."

In the *Kesvananda Bharti case* (AIR 1973 SC 1461), secularism was held to be a purported law."

7. In the *Ayodhya case* (AIR 1995 SC 605), the Supreme Court explained secularism thus:

"It is clear from the constitutional scheme that it guarantees equality in the matter of religion to all individuals and groups irrespective of their faith emphasising that there is no religion of the State itself. The Preamble of the Constitution read in particular with articles 25 to 28 emphasises this aspect and indicates that it is in this manner the concept of secularism embodied in the constitutional scheme as a creed adopted by the Indian people has to be understood while examining the constitutional validity of any legislation on the touch-stone of the Constitution. The concept of secularism is one facet of the right to equality woven as the central golden thread in the fabric depicting the pattern of the scheme in our Constitution."

INDIAN CONCEPT OF SECULARISM AND A SECULAR STATE

The Indian concept of secularism is expressed in the following often quoted principles:

1. '*Sarva-dharma-samantva*' or '*Sarva-dharma-sambhava*'—equal regard for all faiths and creeds.
2. '*Ekam Brahma Vipra Bahuda Vadanti*'—God is one, wise men call Him by different names.

Although the word secularism was introduced only in 1976 in our Constitution, our secularism is historical. We have had great breadth of vision as expressed above.

Ashoka's secular outlook is one of the landmarks not only of Indian civilisation but also of the human civilisation. He made a passionate appeal for developing a spirit of reverence and tolerance for all faiths.

India as a Secular State. Ours is a secular State. It means that the State shall not discriminate against the followers of a particular religion. All Indians—Hindus, Muslims, Sikhs, Christians and others have the freedom to practise their religion.

Characteristics of the Secular State of India

1. Indian State treats all religions on equal footing.
2. Indian State neither interferes with nor promotes any religion.
3. It permits individual and collective freedom of religion to all citizens.
4. It views all individuals as citizens with equal rights and not as members of any particular religious group.
5. It is not against any religion.
6. It functions in a way independent of religion.
7. It allows religious education in some educational institutions run and managed by minorities subject to certain conditions.

Secular Outlook or Characteristics of a Secular-Minded Individual

Following salient features of secularism emerge from the above stated views:

1. Secular outlook treats all religion on an equal footing.
2. Secular outlook accepts freedom of religion.
3. Secular outlook implies freedom of worship.
4. Secular outlook implies tolerance.
5. Secular outlook encourages rational thinking.
6. Secular outlook views all citizens with equal rights.
7. Secular outlook encourages moral and spiritual values.
8. Secular outlook believes in co-existence.
9. Secular outlook stresses free inquiry.
10. Secular outlook means freedom of mind from dogmatic ideas.
11. Secular outlook is not a negation of religion.

EDUCATIONAL IMPLICATIONS OF SECULARISM

Secular education should be imparted in educational institutions for the following reasons:

1. Secular education develops a moral outlook.
2. Secular education helps in the development of liberal attitudes and values.
3. Secular education develops wider-vision.
4. Secular education develops an attitude of appreciation and understanding of others' point of view.
5. Secular education develops democratic values.
6. Secular education develops scientific temper of mind.
7. Secular education develops humanistic outlook.
8. Secular education synthesises materialism and spiritualism.
9. Secular education serves as an antidote to religious fanaticism and hatred.

Secularism and Different Dimensions of Education

Educational Aims: These include development of a wider outlook, moral outlook, rational attitude, scientific temper and love for humanity.

Curriculum: Curriculum to include contents, values and experiences conducive to the above mentioned aim. Lives of great personalities to be included. Celebration of festivals of different faiths to be organised.

Recognition of Educational Institutions: Only those educational institutions to be recognised which follow secular values.

Limitations of Secularism

One of the most glaring limitations is that the word secular has different interpretation. Its meaning are not clarified in the Constitution. It means different things to different people.

Summing up: Secularism accords an important places to ethical, moral and spiritual values. These must be inculcated in the students through education.

Secular outlook should be given in the contents of textbooks.

The teacher should not discriminate students on the basis of religion or belief.

Admission should be given to students irrespective of religious belief.

DEMOCRACY AND EDUCATION

Meaning of Democracy

At the outset, it may be emphasised that democracy is a way of life and not only a political system.

In view of the respect for the dignity of the individual and his full development, it is felt that democracy is the only instrument for the achievement of this objective.

The word democracy is derived from two Greek words, *demos* or *demose* meaning 'people' and *Kratein* or *kratia* meaning 'rule'. Thus it implies the 'rule of the people'.

Definitions of Democracy

There is no exaggeration when it is stated that there are as many definitions as there are thinkers.

E.B. Burns in his *Ideas in Conflict* (1960) observed, "Few words have been more loosely and variously defined than democracy. It has almost literally meant all things to all men."

Here some of the most acceptable definitions of democracy are given.

1. The Greek philosopher *Cleon* defined democracy in 422 B.C. in these words, "That shall be democracy which shall be of the people, by the people, for the people."

2. *Aristotle* (384-322 B.C.) defined democracy as 'a government of many'.

3. *U.S. President, Abraham Lincoln* (1809-65) defined democracy "as the government of the people, by the people and for the people."

4. *Lord Bryce* (1832-1932), a British jurist, historian and diplomat gave a functional definition of democracy in these words. "The word democracy denotes that form of government in which the ruling power of the state is legally vested, not in any particular class or classes, but in the members of the community as a whole. This means, in communities which act by voting, that rule belongs to the majority as no other method has been found for determining peacefully and legally which is deemed to be the will of the community."

5. *Bassett* defines democracy as, "It is a political system by which every citizen has an opportunity of participating through discussion in an attempt to reach voluntary agreement as to what shall be done for the good of the community as a whole."

6. *Sir John Seeley* defines democracy as "government in which everyone has a share."

7. According to *Barker*, "Democracy is a mode of spirit and an attitude of the mind."

8. *Gattell* writes, "Democracy is that form of government in which the mass of the population possesses the right to share in the exercise of sovereign power."

9. According to former U.S. President, *F.D. Roosevelt* (1882-1945), "Democracy is not a mere matter of universal suffrage and unhampered expression of the people's will. It must be a positive and constructive force in the daily lives of the people and provide not merely for political but economic needs also. If men were forced to choose between liberty and bread, they would choose bread."

10. A very suitable definition of democracy is also found in the words of the University Education Commission (1948-49). "Democracy is a way of life and not merely a political arrangement. It is based on the principle of equal freedom and equal right for its members, regardless of race, religion, sex, occupation or economic status."

Factors Leading to the Development of Modern Democracy

Modern democracy got an impetus from five events which are termed as 'great revolutions'. These are:

(i) The Glorious Revolution, 1688 (England).
(ii) The American Revolution, 1776.
(iii) The French Revolution, 1789.
(iv) The Industrial Revolution, (eighteenth and nineteenth centuries).
(v) The Russian Revolution, 1917. However, this was confined to the supremacy and involvement of the working class. It was basically a form of economic democracy.

SIGNIFICANCE OF EACH LETTER IN THE TERM DEMOCRACY: VALUES OF DEMOCRACY

The spirit of democracy as a way of life and a form of government may be explained by assigning ideals and values to each letter of the word democracy.

D stands for — Division of authority and power
— Dignity and worth of the individual
— Duty-Consciousness
E stands for — Equality
— Ethical values
M stands for — Mutual understanding
— Mass education
O stands for — Objective attitude
— Open mindedness
C stands for — Cooperation
— Classless society
R stands for — Rational approach or thinking
— Respect for others' point of view
— Right relationship between rights and responsibilities
A stands for — 'Appreciation of others' culture, beliefs and point of view
— Adult franchise
C stands for — Cooperative attitude
— Caring and concern for others
— Constructive and creative attitude
Y stands for — Yearning for peace and living together

Chief Characteristics of Democracy in a Broader Sense

From the definitions given above, following characteristics of democracy emerge:

1. Democracy is a way of life. It is an approach to various problems.
2. Democracy as a form of government is based on the consent of the people.
3. Equality, liberty, tolerance, justice and decentralisation are the watch words of democracy.
4. Democracy represents the will of the people. People are sovereign.
5. People elect those representatives who represent their needs and aspirations.
6. These representatives form laws for the people.
7. It is based on the principle of universal adult franchise.
8. Elections are held at regular intervals.
9. There is an election machinery to conduct elections in a fair manner.
10. Citizens enjoy fundamental rights.
11. Citizens have the right to change the government through election.
12. Usually there are several political parties representing various views that participate in elections.
13. All the three organs of the government, i.e., the legislature, the executive and the judiciary are independent and they are supposed to function according to the law of the land.
14. It has faith in the goodness and rationality of man.
15. It recognises the importance of the dignity of man.
16. Every citizen of the prescribed age has the right to contest election.
17. Every citizen possessing the requisite qualifications has the right to contest and hold political post.

DIMENSIONS OF DEMOCRACY

1 *Economic Dimension*	2 *Educational Dimension*	3 *Ethical Dimension*	4 *Political Dimension*	5 *Social Dimension*
This implies 1. Economic equality as far as possible	This denotes 1. Equal opportunities in obtaining education	This means faith that an individual is entitled to enjoy full respect for his individuality.	This includes 1. Participation of the people in government.	This incorporates equality of all, irrespective of caste, class, colour, creed, sex and wealth etc.
2. Satisfaction of the basic needs of the people.	2. Maximum development of the individual.		2. Election and Adult franchise.	
3. Equality of opportunity in undertaking economic activities.	3. Sharing of responsibility in running the educational system.		3. Division of authority among the Central Government, State Government and Local Bodies.	
4. Freedom from want.	4. Education for all.			

MOST ESSENTIAL ELEMENTS OF DEMOCRACY

1. Equality
2. Liberty
3. Secularism
4. Adult Franchise

Conditions/Requisites for the Successful Working of Democracy

1. Well-knit and well-organised political parties.
2. Social equality.
3. Strong and effective leadership.
4. Universal adult franchise.
5. Economic equality.
6. Literate population.
7. Sound traditions.
8. Decentralisation of power.
9. Spirit of tolerance and mutual goodwill.
10. Rule of the law.
11. No privileges and no discretionary powers at any level.
12. Civic values among the citizens.
13. Belief in non-violence and absence of violence.
14. Eternal vigilance.
15. National, state and regional planning.
16. Periodical elections.
17. Effective election machinery.

RELATIONSHIP BETWEEN DEMOCRACY AND EDUCATION

Democracy and Education

The University Education Commission has explained the relationship of democracy and education in these words, "Democracy affirms that each individual has a unique adventure of life. The function of education is guidance of this adventure for the realisation of the potentialities of each individual."

Prof. Dewey in his book "*Democracy and Education*" has explained very clearly the relationship between education and democracy in these words, "A society which makes provisions for participation in its good of all its members on equal terms and which secures flexible adjustment of its institutions through the interaction of the different forms of associated life is a democratic society. Such a society must have a type of education which gives individuals a personal interest in social changes without introducing disorder."

Prof. K.G. Saiyidain explains the functions of education and democracy in his book *Education, Culture and Social Order* in these words, "Education must be so oriented that it will develop the basic qualities of character which are necessary for the functioning of the democratic life." He lists the following qualities to be developed by education for the democratic life:

(i) Passion for social justice.
(ii) Quickening of social conscience.
(iii) Tolerance for cultural and intellectual differences in others.

(iv) Development of love for work.
(v) Deep and true love for the country.

Significant Implications of Democracy in Education

1. Education is essential to a citizen to function as a voter and a legislator.
2. Education is essential to a citizen to understand and discern intelligently the programmes of political parties.
3. Education is necessary to enable the citizens to prepare themselves for securing the means of livelihood without which a democracy is meaningless.
4. Education is essential to develop such attitudes, skills and knowledge which enable the citizens to participate intelligently in the social and other processes.
5. Education enables an individual to understand the laws of the land and their implications.
6. The right to education becomes a fundamental right in a genuine democracy.
7. The right to vote and the right to participate intelligently in shaping the policies of the State demands not merely the right to education but the right to education in the language of the people.
8. Education for all is a natural corollary of a democratic set-up.

IMPACT OF DEMOCRACY IN EDUCATION

1 Democracy and Aims of Education
2 Democracy and Curriculum
3 Democracy and Teaching-Learning Process
4 Democracy and Discipline
5 Democracy and the Teacher
6 Democracy and Educational Administration, Organisation and Supervision

I. Democracy and Aims of Education

Following are the aims of education in a democracy.

1. Training students in the art of living together.
2. Development of the capacity to think clearly.
3. Development of the capacity to receive new ideas.
4. Development of the ability to think rationally and scientifically.
5. Development of tolerance.
6. Development of true patriotism.
7. Development of the qualities of leadership.
8. Development of the qualities of followership.
9. Improvement of vocational efficiency.
10. Development of the creative energy of the students.

II. Democracy and Educational Administration. This implies:

1. Principle of sharing responsibility.
2. Principle of equality.
3. Principle of freedom.

4. Principle of cooperation.
5. Principle of justice.
6. Principle of recognising the individual worth.
7. Principle of leadership.

III. Democracy and Curriculum. This means:

1. Education according to 4 A's, i.e., age, ability, aptitude and aim of the students.
2. Emphasis on flexibility.
3. Reconciliation to the needs of the society and the pupils.
4. Provision of core-curriculum.
5. Group activities and group work.

IV. Democracy and the Methods of Teaching

1. Principle of sharing in planning.
2. Use of a variety of methods.
3. Group and project work.

V. Democracy and Discipline

1. Discipline becomes self-discipline.
2. No place for 'flogging'.
3. Student participation in running some of the affairs of the students.
4. Student self-government.

VI. Democracy and the Teacher

1. Teacher as a guide and helper.
2. Teacher as a friend.
3. Creation of a healthy environment.
4. Student-centred teaching-learning process.
5. Very few 'do's' and 'don'ts'.
6. Teacher as a believer in the theory of 'Impression rather than repression'.

VII. Democracy and Mass Education

Education is the birth right of every individual. It implies:

1. Universalisation of elementary education.
2. Adult literacy/education.
3. Continuing education.

FUNCTIONING OF THE SCHOOL ON DEMOCRATIC PRINCIPLES AND PROMOTION OF DEMOCRATIC VALUES IN THE STUDENTS

Following are the important principles and considerations for the realisation of democratic values:

1. *Development of Individuality*: It recognises that the child can develop his individuality only when his native power and capacities are given free play to interact fruitfully with his environment.

2. *Many-sided Development of Personality*: It aims at the many-sided development of the personality of the child.

3. *Individual Differences of Children*: It takes into consideration the individual differences of children.

4. *Provision for Diversified Courses*: It provides for diversified courses.

5. *Respect for the Individuality of the Child*: It respects the individuality of the child.

6. *Freedom of the Child*: The progressive school attaches great value to the freedom of the child.

7. *Rich Environment*: It aims at providing rich and active environment to the child.

8. *Constructive and Creative Activities*: It provides constructive and creative activities. Group work is encouraged.

9. *Social Activities*: It provides activities for social participation.

10. *Development of Curiosity*: It develops lively curiosity and hunger for the acquisition of knowledge.

11. *Manual Work*: It provides opportunities for manual work.

12. *Learning by Experience*: It replaces information by experience.

13. *Atmosphere of Love*. It emphasises atmosphere of love and affection.

14. *No Place for Corporal Punishment*. It gives no place to corporal punishment.

15. *Curriculum in Terms of Activities*. Its curriculum is in terms of different activities and experiences besides school subjects.

16. *Stress on Co-operation*: It stresses co-operative attitude at every stage and in all its activities.

17. *Self-government*: Student self-government on a balanced scale may be introduced under the guidance and supervision of the teachers.

18. *Role of the Teacher*: The teacher plays the role of a friend, philosopher and guide.

19. *Centre of Community Service*: The school serves as centre of community service and is closely linked with community.

20. *International Understanding*: It imparts training in International brotherhood and peace.

33

Empowerment of Women: Role of Education

GENDER BIAS IN GENERAL

Usually gender bias consists of inferior views and prejudices about girls and women. Traditionally people in India seem to have been orthodox in thinking that girls and women are fit for the household jobs only. According to them, a woman's primary duty was to look after the welfare of the family within the confines of her husband's house. For long, they were not considered suitable for administrative and political work. However with the concerted efforts of social reformers, like Raja Rammohan Roy, Swami Dayanand, Swami Vivekananda, Mahatma Gandhi and others, the need to pay more attention to their education and status has been gradually appreciated and several steps in this direction taken. The impact of Western thought has also been quite appreciable.

Here a few illustrations of gender bias are given.

1. Political Institutions in the World

(1) Out of about 200 member countries of the UNO, just about half dozen women occupy the office of the State. In the USA, considered to be one of the most progressive countries there has been no women head of the State. Similar is the case in all European countries, except Germany (2005). Even in Communist countries like the erstwhile USSR (now Russian Federation) and China, no women has occupied the highest office.

Most of the UN Organisations are headed by men.

(2) Women's participation in national parliaments (Fig. 33.1) is very small.

(3) *Right of Vote in Elections to Women.* The USA and Sweden extended adult franchise to women in 1920, France in 1945, Italy in 1948 and Switzerland, popularly known as the home of democracy as late as 1973. India provided this in the first general elections in 1951.

(4) *Literacy Rates.* Only about 80 per cent of women as compared with men are literate in the world.

(5) *Gross Secondary School Enrolment Ratio.* In several regions of the world, secondary school enrolment rates of girls are lower than boys.

GENDER DISPARITY IN INDIA

1. Political Institutions

(i) One women President out of 15.

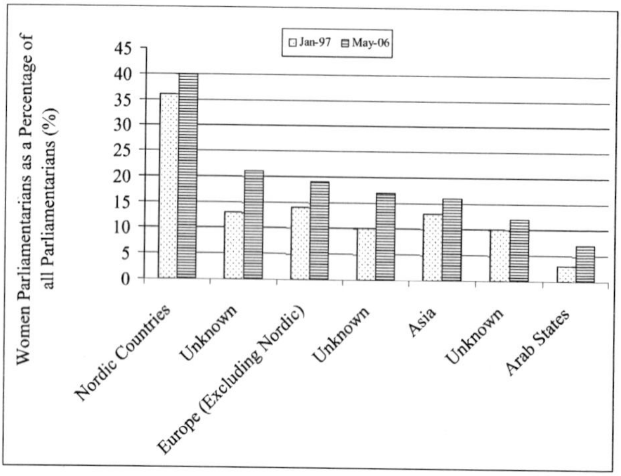

Fig. 33.1: Women's Participation in National Parliaments Across Regions

Source: Data are drawn from the Inter-Parliamentary Union Databases on 'Women in National Parliaments', June 2006.

(ii) One women Prime Minister out of 17.
(iii) No women Vice President out of 12.
(iv) Only about 10% women representation.
(v) Very few Governors.
(vi) Very few Chief Ministers.

2. Administration

1. No women Chief Justice so far.
2. No Head of the Defence Forces.
3. Only about 10 per cent representation in senior administrative services like IAS.

3. Education

1. Not more than dozen Vice-Chancellors out of more than 300 Universities/Deemed Universities etc.
2. No head of NCERT, NIEPA (now NUEPA), CBSE etc.

Gender Disparities in Literacy Rate

There are gender disparities in literacy at all-India level, as also within individual States. The gap was narrowest in Mizoram where male literacy was recorded at 90.69 per cent and female literacy at 86.13 per cent in 2001. In Kerala, the rates were 94.2 and 87.86 per cent respectively in 2001. The gap is widest in the low literacy states. In Bihar, 60.32 per cent males are recorded to be literate in 2001 as against 33.57 per cent females. The rates are 70.23 and 42.98 per cent respectively in Uttar Pradesh and 76.46 and 44.34 per cent in Rajasthan. At the same time, it should be recognised that these States, as also Jammu and Kashmir and Madhya Pradesh, have come a long way since 1961, when female literacy rates were in single digits. The exception is Meghalaya where in spite of low overall literacy rate, the difference between male and female rate is small.

Table 33.1: Gap in Male/Female Literacy Rate (1981-2001)

(*in per cent*)

Census	*Females*	*Males*	*Literates*	*Male-Female Gap in Literacy Rate*
1981	29.76	56.38	43.57	26.62
1991	39.29	64.13	52.21	24.84
2001	54.16	75.85	65.38	21.69

Note: (i) The literacy rate relate to the population aged seven years and above, (ii) The 1981 Census Literacy rates exclude Assam. The 1991 Census Literacy Rates exclude Jammu and Kashmir.

Table 33.2: Girls Enrolment Per Hundred Boys in 1950-51 and 2004-05

Year	*Primary*	*Upper Primary*	*Secondary*
1950-51	39	18	16
2004-05	88	80	71

Table 33.3: Percentage of Girls to Total Enrolment

Year	*Primary*	*Upper Primary*	*Secondary*	*Higher Education*
1950-51	28.1	16.1	13.3	10.0
2004-05	46.7	44.4	41.5	38.9

Sex Ratio

Sex ratio, measured in terms of the number of women per 1000 men, is representative of women per 1000 men, is representative of gender inequality in India. Biologically, the sex ratio should be in favour of women, and it is so, in almost all countries of the world. However, a pronounced skew in sex ratio in favour of men has been a feature of most states in India. This is largely attributed to lower status of women in Indian society, which contributes to early marriages, lower literacy levels, higher fertility and mortality levels, and affects adverse progress in human development. It is 933 in India.

WOMEN'S WELFARE IN INDEPENDENT INDIA

Constitutional Provisions (Specific Provisions for Women)

Part III - Fundamental Rights

Article 15: Prohibition of discrimination on grounds of religion, race, caste, sex or place of birth.

1. The State shall not discriminate against any citizen on grounds only of religion, race, caste, sex, place of birth or any of them.

2. No citizen shall, on grounds only of religion, race, caste, sex, place of birth or any of them, be subject to any disability, liability, restriction or condition with regard to—

(a) Access to shops, public restaurants, hotels and places of public entertainment; or

(b) The use of wells, tanks, bathing ghats, roads and places of public resort maintained wholly or partly out of state funds or dedicated to the use of the general public.

3. Nothing in this article shall prevent the state from making any special provision for women and children.

Article 16: Equality of opportunity in matters of public employment

(2) No citizen shall, on grounds only of religion, race, caste, sex, descent, place of birth, residence or any of them, be ineligible for, or discriminated against in respect of, any employment or office under the State.

Right Against Exploitation

Article 23: Prohibition of traffic in human beings and forced labour

(1) Traffic in human beings and *begar* and other similar forms of forced labour are prohibited and any contravention of this provision shall be an offence punishable in accordance with law.

Part IV – Directive Principles of State Policy

Article 39: Certain principles of policy to be followed by the State

The State shall, in particular, direct its policy towards securing:

(a) That the citizens, men and women equally have the right to an adequate means of livelihood;

(b) That there is equal pay for equal work for both men and women;

(c) That health and strength of workers, men and women, and the tender age children are not abused and that citizens are not forced by economic necessity to enter a vocations unsuited to their age or strength.

Article 42: Provision for just and humane conditions of work and maternity relief

The state shall make provision for securing just and humane conditions for work and maternity relief.

Article 44: Union civil code for citizens

The State shall endeavour to secure for all citizens a uniform civil code throughout the territory of India.

Part XV – Elections

Article 325: *No person to be ineligible for inclusion in, or to claim to be included in a special, electoral roll on grounds of religion, race, caste or sex.*

There shall be one general electoral roll for every territorial constituency for election to either House of Parliament or to the either House of the Legislature of State and no person shall be ineligible for inclusion in any such roll or claim to be included in any special electoral roll for any such constituency on grounds only of religion, race, caste, sex or any of them.

WOMEN'S WELFARE: SOME MILESTONES

I. Milestones Towards Women Welfare During British Rule

S. No.	*Year*	*Act/Effort*	*Details*
1.	1815	Women's Education	The Amitya Sabha, founded by Raja Rammohun Roy, emphasised the importance of education of women.
2.	1815	Attack on 'Sati System'	The noted social reformer Raja Rammohun Roy (1774-1833) wrote the first book in Bengali in which he attacked Sati – the practice of burning widows on the funeral pyres of their husbands.
3.	1829	Sati Abolition Act	William Bentinck, the Governor-General of India passed the Sati Abolition Act.
4.	1956	Widow Remarriage Act	Widows were allowed to remarry.
5.	1872	Civil Marriage Act	Some changes were introduced in marriage rules.
6.	1917	Franchise for women	A delegation of women met the Secretary of India and pleaded for franchise for women.
7.	1927	Women's Conference	All India Women's Conference was set-up.

II. Acts Passed in Independent India

Sl. No.	*Year*	*Act/Effort*	*Details*
1.	1951	Farm Labour Act	Providing break to working women for nursing children.
2.	1952	Employee's State Regulations Act	Providing maternity facilities to women.
3.	1956	Beedi and Cigarette Employees Act	Providing child care system at the place of work.
4.	1961	Pre-maternity Care Act	Providing for abortion and maternity leave.
5.	1976	Contract Labour Act	Regulating working hours and maximum 9 hour's work.
6.	1976	Equal Wages Act	Providing for equal wages for man and woman.
7.	1976	Child Marriage Prohibition Act	Providing for abolition of child marriage.
8.	1979	Inter State Migrant Workers Act	Providing for separate public toilet facilities for women.
9.	1986	Women Vulgarity Prohibition Act	Providing for prevention of vulgar exhibition of womanhood.

(*Contd.*)

Sl. No.	Year	Act	Details
10.	1961	Dowry Prohibition Act (Amendment Act 1986)	Prohibition of dowry, providing for strengthening enforcement.
11.	1987	Sati Prohibition Act, 1987	Providing for banning Sati practice.
12.	1993	73rd and 74th Constitutional Amendment Act	Providing for 30 per cent reservation for women in Panchayats.
13.	1994	Pre-Natal Diagnostic Technique (Regulation and Prevention of Misuse Act)	Providing for prevention of determination of female foetus in the womb of the mother as illegal.
14.	2004	Equal Rights for Daughters to Ancestral Property.	The Government of India decided on December 15, 2004, to provide by law equal share of ancestral property to daughters along with sons. This is to amend Hindu Succession Act, 1956 which granted unfair benefits to male heirs of a Hindu who died without a will and deprived women the right to seek share in ancestral property.
15.	2006	Protection of Women from Domestic Violence Act	Providing safeguards for women.

Department of Women and Child Development

A separate Department for Women and Child Development was set up at the Centre in 1985 to give a distinct identity and provide a nodal point on matters relating to women's development.

National Institute of Public Cooperation and Child Development

The National Institute of Public Cooperation and Child Development (NIPCCD) is an autonomous organisation functioning under the aegis of the Department of Women and Child Development as its technical arm. The objectives of NIPCCD are to develop and promote voluntary action in social development, conduct a comprehensive review of child development and development and promote programmes in pursuance of the National Policy for Children. It also seeks to develop measures for coordination of government and voluntary action in social development and evolve a common framework for organising children's programmes by government and voluntary welfare action.

Central Social Welfare Board

The Central Social Welfare Board (CSWB) was set up in 1953 with the objective of promoting social welfare activities and implementing welfare programmes for women, children and the handicapped through voluntary organisations. The CSWB is unique in the sense that it was the first organisation in post-Independence era to achieve people's participation for implementation of welfare programmes for women and children through non-governmental organisations (NGOs). Presently more than 18,000 NGOs are receiving financial assistance and guidance from the Board. The programmes implemented by the Board include: socio-economic programme for needy/destitute women, condensed courses of education and vocational training courses for women and girls, awareness generation projects for rural and poor women, family counselling centres/voluntary action bureaux, holiday camps for children, welfare extension projects in border areas, and balwadis, crèches and hostels for working women, etc.

EMPOWERMENT OF WOMEN

Meaning of Empowerment of Women

The term 'Empowerment of Women' became popular in India in the 1990s. It implies involving women in decision-making and implementing processes in all areas of national life, including political and administration.

In the 1970s, the term 'welfare' with respect to women was used. In the 1980s, the term 'development' replaced the term 'welfare'. The 1990s replaced the term 'development' with 'empowerment'.

The Tenth Plan aimed at empowering women through the National Policy for Empowerment of Women (2001).

Important Features of the National Policy for Empowerment of Women (2001)

(i) To create an environment through positive economic and social policies for full development of women to enable them to realise their full potential.

(ii) To enable women to enjoy all human rights and fundamental freedoms on equal basis with men in all spheres—civil, cultural, economic, political and social.

(iii) To provide equal access to women to health care, quality education at all levels, career and vocational guidance, employment, equal remuneration, occupational health and safety, social security and public office, etc.

(iv) To strengthen legal systems aimed at elimination of all forms of discrimination against women.

The policy envisages that all Central and State Ministries would drew up time bound Action Plans for women empowerment. They would also consult National/State Commission for Women.

For the realisation of goals, the National Policy lays emphasis on:

1. Strengthening institutional mechanisms.
2. Resource management.
3. Legislation.
4. Gender awareness.
5. Partnership with voluntary Organisation.
6. International cooperation.

Special Initiatives/Achievements for the Empowerment of Women during the Ninth Plan (1997-2002)

- Adoption of Women's Component Plan (WCP) to ensure that benefits from other developmental sectors do not by-pass women and not less than 30 per cent of funds/benefits flow to them from all the women-related sectors. Review of the progress of WCP during the Ninth Plan reveals that funds flowing from one of the women-related Departments (viz. Family Welfare) was as high as 70 per cent of its Gross Budgetary Support of the Ninth Plan; (1997).

- Launching of *Swa-Shakti* to create an enabling environment for empowerment of women through setting up of self-reliant Self-Help Groups (SHGs) and developing linkages with lending institutions to ensure women's access to credit facilities for income-generation activities; (1998)
- *Stree Shakti Puraskars* instituted for the first time in the history of women's development to honour 5 distinguished women annually for their outstanding contribution to the upliftment and empowerment of women; (1999)
- Adoption of a National Policy for Empowerment of Women to eliminate all types of discrimination against women and to ensure gender justice, besides empowering women both socially and economically; (2001)
- Celebration of the Year 2001 as 'Women's Empowerment Year' for awareness generation to remove negative thinking, besides building up confidence in women through the processes of conscientisation so that they can take their rightful place in the mainstream of the nation's social, political and economic life; (2001)
- Launching of *Swadhar* to extend rehabilitation services for 'Women in Difficult Circumstances'; (2001)

Rashtriya Mahila Kosh (RMK)

The *Rashtriya Mahila Kosh* (RMK), since its registration in 1993, has established its credentials as the premier micro-credit agency with its focus on women and their economic empowerment through the provision of credit to poor and assetless women in the informal sector. RMK mainly channels its support through Voluntary Organisations, Women's Development Corporation, Women's Cooperative Societies, Block Samitis under the *Swayamsidha* programme.

Economic, Gender Rights and Social Empowerment of Women

Economic Empowerment

Ensuring provision of training, employment and income generation activities with both 'forward' and 'backward' linkages with the ultimate objective of making all women economically independent and self-reliant through:

- Organising women into Self-Help Groups under various poverty alleviation programmes, viz. Swarna Jayanti Gram Swarozgar Yojana (SGSY), Swarna Jayanti Shahari Rozgar Yojana (SJSRY), Rashtriya Mahila Kosh (RMK), Support for Training and Employment Programme (STEP), Training-cum-Production Centres for Women (NORAD), etc. and offering them a range of economic options along with necessary support measures to enhance their capabilities and earning capacities with an ultimate objective of making them economically independent and self-reliant.

- Ensuring that women in the Informal Sector who account for more than 90 per cent are given special attention with regard to improving their working conditions as the same continued to be very precarious without even minimum or equal wages, leave aside other legislative safeguards.
- Ensuring that the employers fulfil their legal obligations towards their women workers in extending child care facilities, maternity benefits, special leave, protection from occupational hazards, allowing formation of women workers, associations/unions, legal protection/aid, etc.
- Re-training/upgrading the skills of women displaced from traditional sectors due to advancement of technology so that they can take up jobs in the new and expanding areas of employment and formulating appropriate policies and programmes to promote alternative opportunities for wage/ self-employment in traditional sectors like khadi and village industries, handicrafts, handlooms, sericulture, small-scale and cottage industries.
- Increasing access to credit for women.

Gender Justice

Eliminating all forms of gender discrimination and, thus, enabling women to enjoy not only *de-jure* but also *de-facto* rights and fundamental freedom at par with men in all spheres, viz. political, economic, social, civil, cultural, etc. through:

- Complete eradication of female foetus and female infanticide through effective enforcement of both the Indian Penal Code, 1860 and the Pre-Natal Diagnostic Technique (Regulation and Prevention of Misuse) Act, 1994 with most stringent measures of punishment so that a very harsh path is set for the illegal practitioners.
- Working out strategies, in close collaboration with the Ministry of Labour, to ensure extension of employment opportunities and thus, remove inequalities in employment—both in work and accessibility.
- Expediting action to legislate reservation of not less than 1/3 seats for women in the Parliament and in the State Legislative Assemblies and thus ensure women in proportion to their numbers reach decision-making bodies so that their voices are heard.
- Arresting the ever-increasing violence against women and the Girl Child including the adolescent girls on top priority with the strength and support of a well-planned Programme of Action.
- Initiating/accelerating the process of societal reorientation towards creating a gender-just society.

Social Empowerment

Creating an enabling environment by adopting various affirmative developmental policies and programmes for development of women.

EDUCATION FOR WOMEN'S EQUALITY AND EMPOWERMENT

The NPE 1986 stipulates that "Education will be used as an agent of basic change in the status of women. In order to neutralise the accumulated distortion of the past, there will be a well-conceived edge in favour of women." For achieving this, "The National Education System will play a positive, interventionist role in the empowerment of women." The NPE's programme includes the following dimensions:

1. Redesigning of courses to develop new values.
2. Redesigning of textbooks to eliminate all sex bias.
3. Training and orientation of teachers for developing sensitiveness to women's issues and their empowerment.
4. Orientation of decision makers and administrators to women issues.
5. Active involvement of educational institutions in enabling women in the process of empowerment of women.
6. According priority to the removal of illiteracy among women through provision of special support services, setting of time-bound targets and effective monitoring.
7. Increasing participation of women in vocational, technical and progressional education at all levels.
8. Following policy of non-discrimination to eliminate stereotyping in vocational and professional courses.
9. Promoting women's participation in non-traditional as well as in existing and emergent technologies.

Mahila Samakhya (MS) Programme

The Programme launched in support of Women's education as envisaged in NPE revolves around the *Sangha* (Village Level Women's Collective) which is considered as the nodal point. The process of mobilising women and creating an environment for women participation in learning is facilitated by a *Sahayogni* (a cluster coordinator in-charge of 10 villages). She is a crucial link between the village *Sangha* and the district implementation unit of the programme. The district implementation unit provides resource support and inputs to meet the needs of women. The district units in turn are supported by a state office.

Mahila Samakkya has expanded its coverage to 40 districts and over 7000 villages.

The *Sangha*, the nodal point of the programme, addresses a wide range of issues relating to the livelihood of women, their education, health, etc. It has taken an active lead in enrolling children, primarily girls, in the village schools.

Achievements Since 1950-51

Table 33.4: Percentage of Girls Enrolment to Total Enrolment by Stages

Year	*Primary (Classes I-V)*	*Upper Primary (Classes VI to VIII)*	*Secondary/ Sr. Secondary/ Intermediate (Classes IX-XII)*	*Higher Secondary (Degree or Above)*
1950-51	28.1	16.1	13.3	10.0
2004-2005	46.7	44.4	41.5	39.4

Table 33.5: Gross Enrolment Ratio (GER) Since 1950-51

	1950-51			*2004-05*		
	Boys	*Girls*	*Total*	*Boys*	*Girls*	*Total*
I. Primary (I-V)	60.6	24.8	42.6	110.7	104.7	107.8
II. Upper Primary (VI to VIII)	20.6	4.6	12.7	74.3	65.1	69.9
III. Elementary (I-VIII)	46.4	17.7	32.1	96.9	89.9	93.5

Table 33.6: Drop-out Rates Since 1960-61

	1960-61			*2004-05*		
	Boys	*Girls*	*Total*	*Boys*	*Girls*	*Total*
I. Primary (I-V)	61.7	70.9	64.9	31.80	15.42	29.00
II. Elementary (I to VIII)	75.0	85.0	78.3	50.49	51.28	50.84
III. Secondary (I-IX)	NA	NA	NA	60.41	63.88	61.92

Observations

- The gap in male-female rate has decreased from 24.84 per cent in 1991 to 21.60 per cent in 2001.
- Female literacy increased by 14.41 per cent, i.e., from 39.29 per cent to 53.7 per cent whereas male literacy increased by 11.17 per cent, i.e., from 64.13 per cent to 75.30 per cent during the last decade.
- Gender equity and women's empowerment is also visible as about 60 per cent of participants and beneficiaries are women.

34

Value Education

VALUE EDUCATION—THE ONLY BASIS OF ESTABLISHING A TRULY DEMOCRATIC, SECULAR AND SOCIALIST SOCIETY

Inculcation of desirable values in the pupils of all ages is absolutely essential for meeting out the crisis of character. In the situation that is rapidly developing, it is equally important for us to give a proper value-orientation to our educational system.

Addressing the one of the most inspiring gatherings ever held at the U.N. in August-September 2000, the U.N. Secretary General called upon the religious and spiritual leaders to 'look within' and to consider what they could do to promote "justice, equality, reconciliation and peace."

There is no doubt that some sort of 'spiritual therapy' is needed for having a value-based society.

MEANING OF A 'VALUE'

In the words of Wuchohn, "Value is a conception, emplicit or implicit, distinctive of an individual or characteristics which influence the selection, from available modes and ends of action."

Rokeach defines values, "as an enduring belief, a specific mode of conduct or end along a continuum of relative importance.

John Dewey views a value as, "The value means primarily to prize, to esteem, to appraise, to estimate. It means the act of cherishing something, holding it dear and also the act of passing judgement upon the nature and amounts of values as compared with something else."

W.H. Kilpatrick has explained the concept of values as, "That out of man's capacity for goal seeking behaviour arise his wants and efforts and out of these come in consciously chosen ends (goals) a mean. Because ends conflict, man is led to weigh his goals against each other, when this is done critically enough values emerge."

Henderson in this context observes, "It has been pointed out that man acts to satisfy his wants, anything which satisfies a human want becomes thereby a value. To say that our conduct is motivated by our value is another way of saying that we act to satisfy our wants."

A value stands for ideals men live for. Values are the part and parcel of the philosophy of a nation. They are guiding principles of life which are conducive to one's mental, physical and social health.

CLASSIFICATION OF VALUES

Values have been classified in a number of ways and their meanings also sometimes differ.

(i) 1. Instrumental Values. 2. Intrinsic or Cultural Values.
(ii) 1. Global Values. 2. Individual Values.
(iii) 1. Essential Values. 2. Personal Values. 3. Social Values. 4. Cultural Values. 5. Institutional Values.
(iv) 1. Disciplinary Values. 2. Cultural Values.
(v) 1. Liberalising Values. 2. Sentimental Values.
(vi) 1. Preparatory Values. 2. Introductory Values. 3. Practical or Utilitarian Values. 4. Conventional Values.
(vii) 1. Traditional Values. 2. Modern Values.
(viii) 1. Material Values. 2. Non-material Values.
(ix) 1. Religious Values. 2. Spiritual Values.
(x) 1. Secular Values. 2. Scientific Values.
(xi) 1. Individual Values. 2. National Values.
(xii) 1. Ethical Values. 2. Spiritual Values.
(xiii) 1. National Values. 2. Global Values.

Instrumental Value: A subject is said to have instrumental value when it is pursued, not for its own sake, but for some ends beyond itself. Instrumental values include preparatory or introductory, practical or utilitarian, socialising and conventional values.

A subject is said to have a *Preparatory* value when it prepares the way for other studies. Arithmetic prepares the way for Algebra. When a particular study introduces us to a number of subjects, it has an *introductory* value. It is identical with the preparatory value. To illustrate we may select Physical Geography which introduces us to a little of Botany, Zoology, Physics and Chemistry. The *practical or utilitarian* value lies in a study of subject whose pursuit is useful inasmuch as it satisfies many wants and needs. The subject is individually and directly practical when the knowledge of the subject is applied directly by the person himself. A person may use his knowledge of hygiene to escape small pox. The same knowledge can, however, be used through other agencies, through society, for example. A subject is said to possess a socialising value when it creates socially desirable habits and reactions, or when it enables us to understand society in its complexities. The socialising value includes moral values too. These moral values refer to certain moral traits that society wants individuals to develop. The *conventional value* implies a value which is conventionally desirable in a subject. Certain subjects may be studied because their knowledge is expected of people of a certain class. Their knowledge is indeed for proper social intercourse and social enjoyment. In the times of Locke, a gentleman was expected to learn Latin, Greek and Grammar because they were necessary in that social set up.

Intrinsic values are inherent in the subjects that we may describe as cultural studies. These have been described by Dewey as the appreciative studies. The resulting experiences in these subjects are worthwhile on their own account. These values that accrue from their studies are in the form of aesthetic pleasures or intellectual joys.

The cultural values have been subdivided into the liberalising and the *sentimental values*. The liberalising value consists in the pleasure that accompanies intellectual insight. The sentimental value, on the other hand, refers to pleasure that emerges when our feelings are exercised. Our feelings may be aroused by the aesthetic, the comic, the social and the moral situation. Drama, Literature, Music, Painting, Sculpture and Religion have, in varying degrees, these values.

Professor Cunningham lays stress on the disciplinary values of the subjects. Their pursuit is important because it gives rise to mental activity and forms sound habits and skills. Each subject, he says, causes certain type of mental operation or discipline. For example, natural sciences produce an attitude of mind characterised by precision which results from observation and reflective thinking. The humanistic sciences produce the discipline of tolerance. Metaphysical sciences, theology and philosophy produce the discipline of unification because in all these the ultimate aim is to achieve harmony and unity in life. The discipline of appreciation is produced by such subjects as painting, music, sculpture and others. The language arts will produce the discipline of expression which consists not only in the training to express oneself but also in being able to understand what others say and write.

Essential Values: These values involve the basic nature of man himself and include elementary physical skills, basic social skills, ability to use symbols such as language and numbers.

Personal Values: These values make a person good for himself.

Social Values: These values are good for the society and form the basis of the relationship of an individual with other people in society.

Institutional Values: These include values established by institutions, political etc.

Global Values: These values pertain to the entire humanity.

ALPHABETICAL CLASSIFICATION OF VALUES

We shall base our discussion regarding traditional and modern values on the basis of the classification of values as compiled by NCERT in its publication entitled '*Documents on Social, Moral and Spiritual Values in Education*' (1979). These values for the sake of convenience are classified here alphabetically.

1. Abstinence
2. Appreciation of cultural values of others
3. Anti-Untouchability
4. Citizenship
5. Consideration for others
6. Concern for others
7. Cooperation
8. Cleanliness
9. Compassion
10. Common cause
11. Common Good
12. Courage
13. Courtesy
14. Curiosity
15. Democratic Decision Making
16. Devotion
17. Dignity of the individual
18. Dignity of Manual Work
19. Duty
20. Discipline
21. Endurance
22. Equality

23. Friendship
24. Faithfulness
25. Fellow-feeling
26. Freedom
27. Forward look
28. Good Manners
29. Gentlemanliness
30. Gratitude
31. Honesty
32. Helpfulness
33. Humanism
34. Hygienic Living
35. Initiative
36. Integrity
37. Justice
38. Kindness
39. Kindness to Animals
40. Loyalty
41. Leadership
42. National Consciousness
43. National Integration
44. National Unity
45. Non-Violence
46. Obedience
47. Patriotism
48. Peace
49. Proper Utilisation of Time
50. Punctuality
51. Purity
52. Quest for Knowledge
53. Regularity
54. Resourcefulness
55. Respect for Others
56. Reference for Old Age
57. Secularism and Respect for All Religions
58. Self-Confidence
59. Self-Control
60. Self-Discipline
61. Self-Duty
62. Self-Help
63. Self-Reliance
64. Self-Respect
65. Self-Restraint
66. Self-Support
67. Sense of Discrimination between Good and Bad
68. Sense of Social Responsibility
69. Simple Living
70. Sincerity
71. Socialism
72. Social Justice
73. Social Service
74. Solidarity of Mankind
75. Spirit of Enquiry
76. Sympathy
77. Team Work
78. Tolerance
79. Truthfulness
80. Universal Love
81. Universal Truth
82. Value for National and Civil Property

TRADITIONAL AND MODERN VALUES

Strictly Speaking, there is no water-tight compartment between the traditional values and modern values. It is also true that there is difference in emphasis on some values with the change of time. However, there are some values like personal purity—self-control, self-discipline, truth, universal love etc. which are of a universal nature.

The following ancient values contained in an ancient Indian invocation are equally relevant even today.

Sarve bhavantu sukhinah
Sarve santu niramayah
Sarve bhadrani pashyantu
Ma kaschit dukha bhag bhavet!

(May all live happily
May all enjoy good health
May all see auspiciousness
May none experience distress
May peace prevail everywhere!)

There is no dividing line between values. However an attempt is made here to distinguish between the traditional values and the modern values in view of the following factors:

1. Modern emphasis on Democratic Values as against traditional Colonial Values.
2. Modern emphasis on Socialist Values as against the traditional emphasis on Capitalist Values.
3. Modern emphasis on Secular Values as against traditional emphasis on Religious Values.
4. Modern emphasis on Scientific Values as against traditional emphasis on Superstitious Values.
5. Modern emphasis on Global Values as against Traditional emphasis on Nationist Values.
6. Modern emphasis on Emotional Integration and National Unity as against the traditional emphasis on Local/Regional Values.

EDUCATION AND NEED FOR INCULCATION OF VALUES

The Kothari Commission has rightly observed, "The expanding knowledge and the growing power (science) which it places at the disposal of modern society must, therefore, be combined with the strengthening and deepening of the sense of responsibility and a keener appreciation of moral and spiritual values."

The National Policy on Education 1986 has very aptly stressed the need for the inclusion of values in the curriculum: "The growing concern over the erosion of essential values and an increasing cynicism has brought to focus the need for readjustments in curriculum in order to make education a forceful tool for the cultivation of social and moral values." The policy has described these values as, "In our culturally plural society, education should foster universal and eternal values, oriented towards the unity and integration of our people. Such value education should help eliminate obscurantism, religious fanaticism, violence, superstition and fatalism." The National Policy further envisaged that "apart from this combative role, value education has a profound positive content, based on our cultural heritage, national goals and universal perceptions. It should lay primary emphasis on this aspect."

VALUE-BASED CURRICULUM IN INDIA

Value-based curriculum is the paramount need of the hour on account of the following facets of life.

- Pluralist nature of our society comprising multi-linguistic, multi-racial and multi-religious groups.
- Existence of a sizeable section of the society below the poverty line.
- Deep-rooted superstitions in people.

- Fatalistic attitude.
- Increased use of 'money power' in democratic elections.
- Widespread prevalence of corruption.
- Consumer culture or materialistic outlook.
- Growth of favouritism.

SCHOOL PROGRAMME FOR DEVELOPING VALUES OF VARIOUS KINDS

Following are the important activities to be undertaken in the school in this regard:

1. Celebration of national festivals.
2. Social service programmes.
3. Emphasis on the unity of all religions, harmony among communities and national integration.
4. Development of scientific temper.
5. Community prayer in the school.
6. Health and cleanliness programmes.
7. Socially useful productive programmes.
8. Citizenship training programmes.
9. Cultural and recreational programmes.
10. Student self-government in schools.
11. Introduction of Information Technology.
12. International understanding.
13. Appropriate teaching-learning situations.

ROLE OF THE TEACHER

The teachers must play an important role in such programmes. The most important aspect is that they should set good examples of conduct and behaviour which the students may imbibe in themselves.

Lastly, it may be stressed that the teachers, the educational workers, the educators, the supervisors, the administrators and above all the parents must try their best to promote value-oriented education.

SYNTHESIS BETWEEN THE TRADITIONAL VALUES AND MODERN VALUES: SYNTHESIS BETWEEN SCIENTIFIC, SECULAR AND SPIRITUAL VALUES

In the attempt to inculcate values through education, we should draw freely upon our own traditions as well as the traditions of other countries and cultures of the world. There are strands within Indian thought itself which can lead to the new outlook appropriate for a modern society, and which can prepare the people for a willing acceptance of life with all its joys and sorrows, its challenges and triumphs. In them, too, we can find inspiration for social service and faith in the future. Mahatma Gandhi, for instance—and some other great leaders of thought—discovered the inspiration for their idealism and their passionate striving for social justice and social reconstruction largely from these sources. It is such re-interpretations and re-evaluations of the past that are now most needed. It is, however, specially important in the world of today that this effort should not be restricted to the national sources only. It would be necessary to draw upon liberalising forces that have arisen in the western nations and which have emphasised among other things, the dignity of the individual, equality and social justice.

India is on the move again with the promise of new renaissance in the making. The most powerful tool in the process of this renaissance and modernisation is education based on secular values on the one hand and on the other on science and technology. In this context we cannot do better than to quote Pt. Jawahar Lal Nehru, "Can we combine the progress of science and technology with the progress of mind and spirit also? We cannot be untrue to science because that represents the basic fact of life today. Still less can we be untrue to those essential principles for which India has stood in the past throughout the ages. Let us then pursue our path to industrial progress with our strength and vigour and at the same time remember that material riches without toleration and compassion and wisdom may well turn to dust and ashes."

The Education Commission 1964-66 has observed, "We believe that India should strive to bring science and the values of the spirit together in harmony and thereby pave their way for the eventual emergence of a society which would cater to the needs of the whole man and not only to a particular fragment of his personality."

Remarks made by Albert Einstein in '*Ideas and Opinions*' in this regard are very enlightening: "It is not enough to teach man a speciality. Through it he may become a useful machine but not a harmoniously developed personality. It is essential that the students require an understanding of and a lively feeling for values. He must require a vivid sense of the beautiful and of the morally good. Otherwise he with his specialised knowledge resembles a well-trained dog rather than a harmoniously developed person."

35

Futurology: Education for the Future Society

MEANING AND ORIGIN OF THE TERM FUTUROLOGY

The term 'futurology' was coined by a German Professor Ossip K. Flechthein in the mid 1940s. He proposed it as a new branch of knowledge dealing with a 'new science of probability'. It implies a detailed critical analysis and reasoning of the states of things which would develop in the future.

The literal meaning of the term futurology is the study of the future.

The discipline of futurology is referred to by the following terms:

(i) Foresight
(ii) Futurism
(iii) Prospective (Latin America)
(iv) *Futuribles* (The name of a Journal also published in France)
(v) Future Studies (Common term used in English-speaking world)

CHIEF CHARACTERISTICS OF FUTUROLOGY

1. It often examines possible as well as probable state of future things from current trends.

2. It attempts to provide a systematic and holistic view based on insights from a wide range of different disciplines.

3. It relies on 'backcasting' i.e., seeking what changes in the present would be required to arrive at envisioned alternative future state of things on the basis of past and present.

Futurists: Foresight practitioners are called futurists.

Future Studies: This discipline emerged in mid-1960s. It reflects on how today's changes or the lack these of become tomorrow's reality. Among the futurists of the 1960's, important scholars were: Olaf Helmer, Bertrand de Jouvenel, Dennis Gabor, Oliver Markley, Burt Nanus and Wendell Bell.

SUBJECTS AND METHODS OF STUDY OF FUTUROLOGY

The subjects and methods include possible, probable and desirable alternative variations or transformation of the present.

EDUCATION AS A FIELD OF STUDY IN FUTUROLOGY

The USA is a pioneer in taking up education as a field of study in futurology. The studies in the subject began in the 1960s. Since then several countries have developed theories in the area of future education. Several tools have also been developed.

KEY FACTORS IN THE PARADIGM SHIFT IN THE FUTURE EDUCATION

Factor	*Development*
Time	The time factor will no longer be a constraint. Asynchronous education frees the student from the demands of time.
Space	The distance factor will no longer be a constraint. The student can take part in education without being physically present at the teaching institution.
Cost	The pedagogical investment for modern distance education is certainly greater than that of the traditional model, whether in terms of initial outlay or the investment connected with delivering the education. There are two factors, however, which will reduce the overall cost in factors of scale: 1. The reduction of needs in terms of area and premises; and 2. The appreciable increase in the size of the virtual class.
Relationships	The traditionally vertical teacher-student relationship will evolve towards a more *horizontal* model, in which the teacher becomes a facilitator, expert or colleague and the learner becomes active. In this evolution of roles the group will gain importance as a source for consultation, dialogue and collaboration. Through this mechanism the education is 'received' by the individual in interaction with a group, of which the teachers constitute only one element. Roles are thus completely redefined, and the dynamism of the new roles requires a new student.
Information/ knowledge	The transfer of knowledge is no longer the primary object of education. The student must learn to gather information as the need arises, to evaluate it, and to transform it into knowledge through the relational process.
Market	By easing the constraints of space and time, education will open up to the *global market*, where language will become one of the main constraints on expansion.
Competition/ collaboration	The internationalisation of the education market and the emergence of new entities placed deliberately in the commercial area will intensify competition between educational establishments. In parallel collaboration and strategic alliances on the part of universities will become imperative as the appropriate response to change.
Assessment	The traditional concepts of student assessment based on (examination) results will have to be adapted to new methods in which the assessment of the process will gain more importance so that the measuring of assimilated knowledge can be circumvented and factor more sensitive to the equation of the new *professional* can be integrated: ability to carry out research, to adapt, to communicate, to collaborate, etc.
Type	The distinctions drawn between the various types of education (primary, secondary, technical, university, vocational) will become less important, and the emphasis will be placed on *continuing* education.

(Didier Oilo, *From Traditional to Virtual: The New Information Technologies: Thematic Debate*, UNESCO, 1998)

CHIEF CHARACTERISTICS OF THE FUTURE EDUCATION

1. *Technological Use in Schools*: Schools are likely to go High Tech. They will increasingly make use of laptops, and computers for learning aids. Some of the schools may become virtual institutions.

2. *Domination of Private Schools*: The State school system may see its decline if not demise. An increasing number of parents would prefer privately financed schools. There is likely to be a wide gap in the infrastructure and fee structure of different types of private schools.

3. *Individualised Instruction or Self-Learning*: Internet is likely to be used in general by students to gain knowledge. Schools would offer more opportunities for individualised learning.

4. *Merger of Several Categories of Students: Adult Students with Secondary/ High Classes Students*: There may be a merger of some categories of adult students with high school students if technology accelerates enough.

5. *Online Learning*: Teachers will follow online checking method of student's assignments.

6. *Increasing Use of Computers*: As more and more assignments are transferred from paper-borne to an electronic borne media. The students' need for computers will become more pressing.

7. *Chatting*: More students will begin chatting among themselves.

8. *E-mail*: E-mail will become means of storing homework and other information and therefore greater use of computers.

9. *Quality and Quantity of Information*: Quality and quantity of information will increase with a spectacular increase in the use of internet.

10. *Dependence of the Students on the Online Reference Material*: As online reference study guides which cover almost every subject in the school curriculum, will become more and more effective in their coverage of material learned in the classroom, students' dependence on this material will increase.

11. *Freedom to Choose Subjects*: Students would be able to choose any subject at will. They will also be able to decide on what their future career will be and therefore concentrate on its pre-requisites rather than on anything else.

UNESCO AND REFORMS IN EDUCATION

Since its birth, UNESCO has been playing a leading role in stimulating and promoting the reflections and debates on the future of education. Its major reports in this area are:

1. *'Learning to Be' (1972)*: Report published by the International Commission on the Development of Education.

2. International Symposium on the Evolution of the Content of General Education Over the Next Two Decades (1980).

3. '*The Contents of Education: A World View of Their Developments from the Present to the Year 2000 (1987)*' – a publication.

4. International Symposium and Round Table on Education (1989).

5. International Conference on Education (1994).

6. Planning of Higher Education in the Twenty First Century: Role of Management: Report of a Workshop (1995).

7. International Commission on Education for the Twenty-First Century (1993-1996).

The Commission was established at the beginning of 1993. Jacques Delors of France was the Chairman of the Commission. It had 15 members including the Chairman. Dr. Karan Singh, of India's who has been a diplomat and several times Minister *inter-alia* Health and Education, author of several books was one of the members.

The Commission gave its report, in 1996. The report entitled '*Learning the Treasure Within*'.

In the words of the Chairman of the Commission, "The Commission affirms its belief that education has a fundamental role to play in personal and social development."

Four Pillars of Education: According to the Commission, educational structure stands on four pillars:

1. Learning to Know
2. Learning to Do
3. Learning to Live
4. Learning to Be

Accordingly the Commission suggested future reforms in education.

FUTURE SCENARIO OF TENSIONS AND THE ROLE OF EDUCATION

Jacques Delores, Chairman of the International Commission on Education for the Twenty First Century (1993-96) studied the role of future education in the context of the following tensions, although not new, but becoming the central to the problems of the twenty-first century.

The Tension between the Global and the Local: People need gradually to become world citizens without losing their roots and while continuing to play an active part in the life of their nation and their local community.

The Tension between the Universal and the Individual: Culture is steadily being globalised but as yet only partially. We cannot ignore the promises of globalisation nor its risks, not the least of which is the risk of forgetting the unique character of individual human beings; it is for them to choose their own future and achieve their full potential within the carefully tended wealth of their traditions and their own cultures which, unless we are careful, can be endangered by contemporary developments.

The Tension between Tradition and Modernity, which is Part of the Same Problem: How is it possible to adapt to change without turning one's back on the past, how can autonomy be acquired in complementarily with the free development of others and how can scientific progress be assimilated? This is the spirit in which the challenges of the new information technologies must be met.

The Tension between Long-term and Short-term Considerations: This has always existed but today it is sustained by the predominance of the ephemeral and the instantaneous, in a world where an over-abundance of transient information and emotions continually keeps the spotlight on immediate problems. Public opinion cries out for quick answers and ready solutions, whereas many problems call for a patient, concerted, negotiated strategy of reform. This is precisely the case where education policies are concerned.

The Tension between, on the One Hand, the Need for Competition, and on the Other the Concern for Equality of Opportunity: This is a classic issue, which has been facing both economic and social policy-makers and educational policy-makers since the beginning of the century. Solutions have sometimes been proposed but they have never stood the test of time. Today, the Commission ventures to claim that the pressures of competition have caused many of those in position of authority to lose sight of their mission, which is to give each human being the means to take full advantage of every opportunity. This has led us, within the terms of reference of the report, to rethink and update the concept of lifelong education so as to reconcile three forces: competition, which provides incentives; cooperation, which gives strength; and solidarity, which unites.

The Tension between the Extraordinary Expansion of Knowledge and Human Beings' Capacity to Assimilate it: the Commission was unable to resist the temptation to add some new subjects for study, such as self-knowledge, ways to ensure physical and psychological well-being or ways to an improved understanding of the natural environment and to preserving it better. Since there is already increasing pressure on curricula, any clear-sighted reform strategy must involve making choices, providing always that the essential features of a basic education that teaches pupils how to improve their lives through knowledge, through experiment and through the development of their own personal cultures are preserved.

Lastly—Another Perennial Factor—The Tension between the Spiritual and the Material: Often without realising it, the world has a longing, often unexpressed, for an ideal and for values that we shall term 'moral'. It is thus education's noble task to encourage each and every one, acting in accordance with their traditions and convictions and paying full respect to pluralism, to lift their minds and spirits to the plane of the universal and, in some measure, to transcend themselves. It is no exaggeration on the Commission's part to say that the survival of humanity depends thereon.

Education and Points of Emphasis

(1) *Aim of Education*: Education has to face up to this problem now more than ever as a world society struggles painfully to be born: Education is at the heart of both personal and community development; its mission is to enable each of us, without exception, to develop all our talents to the full and to realise our creative potential, including responsibility for our own lives and achievement of our personal aims.

This aim transcends all others. Its achievement, though long and difficult, will be an essential contribution to the search for a more just world, a better world to live in.

(2) *Moral and Cultural Dimensions of Education*: There is, therefore, every reason to place renewed emphasis on the moral and cultural dimensions of education, enabling each person to grasp the individuality of other people and to understand the world's erratic progression towards a certain unity; but this process must begin with self-understanding through an inner voyage whose milestones are knowledge, meditation and the practice of self-criticism.

This message should guide educational thinking, in conjunction with the establishment of wider and more far-reaching forms of international cooperation.

Seen in this context everything falls into place, whether it be the requirements of science and technology, knowledge of self and of the environment, or the development of skills enabling each person to function effectively in a family, as a citizen or as a productive member of society.

(3) *Flexible System of Education*: Education must make its contribution to economic and social development. The education system is all too often blamed for unemployment. This observation is only partly true; above all it should not obscure the other political, economic and social prerequisites for achieving full employment or enabling the economies of underdeveloped countries to take off. As for education, the Commission believes that valid responses to the problems of mismatch between supply and demand on the labour market can come from a more flexible system that allows greater curricular diversity and builds bridges between different types of education, or between working life and further training. Such flexibility would also help to reduce school failure and the tremendous wastage of human potential resulting from it.

Such improvements, desirable and feasible as they are, do not, however, obviate the need for intellectual innovation and the implementation of a model of sustainable development based on the specific characteristics of each county. Given the present and foreseeable advances in science and technology, and the growing importance of knowledge and other intangibles in the production of goods and services, we need to rethink the place of work and its changing status in tomorrow's society. To create tomorrow's society, imagination will have to keep ahead of technological progress in order to avoid further increases in unemployment and social exclusion or inequalities in development.

(4) *Life Long Education and Learning Society*: For all these reasons, it seems to us that the concept of an education pursued throughout life, with all its advantages in terms of flexibility, diversity and availability at different times and in different places, should command wide support. There is a need to rethink and broaden the notion of lifelong education. Not only must it adapt to changes in the nature of work, but it must also constitute a continuous process of forming whole human beings - their knowledge and aptitudes, as well as the critical faculty and the ability to act. It should enable people to develop awareness of themselves and their environment and encourage them to play their social role at work and in the community.

(5) *Increasing the Ability to Learn How to Learn*: Every aspect of life, at both the individual and the social level, offer opportunities for both learning and doing. It is thus very tempting to focus too much on this side of the question, stressing the educational potential of the modern media, the world of work or cultural and leisure pursuits, even to the extent of overlooking a number of fundamental truths: although people need to take every opportunity for learning and self-improvement, they will not be able to make good use of all these potential resources unless they have received a sound basic education. Better still, school should impart both the desire for, and pleasure in, learning the ability to learn how to learn, and intellectual curiosity. One might even imagine a society in which each individual would be in turn both teacher and learner.

SECONDARY EDUCATION/SCHOOL FOR THE FUTURE

Delors Report (1993-1996) or Report of the International Commission on Education for the Twenty-first Century had observed that Secondary education is a "crucial point in the lives of individuals, it is at this stage that young people should be able to decide their own future, in the light of their tastes and aptitudes, and they can acquire the abilities that will make for a successful adult life." The report continued that secondary education "should thus be adapted to take account both of different processes whereby adolescents attain maturity and of economy and social needs."

The Dakar Framework for Action (*UNESCO 2000*) stated, "Education is a fundamental human right. It is the key to sustainable development and peace and stability within and among countries, and thus an indispensable means for effective participation in the societies and economies of the twenty-first century, which are affected by rapid globalisation."

It is in the above context, that UNESCO International Expert Meeting on "General Secondary Education in the Twenty-first century: Trends, Challenges and Priorities" was held in Beijing, People's Republic of China, from 21 to 25 May 2001.

The meeting focused on the following three dilemmas of secondary education.

- In respect of mass and selective schooling.
- In respect of general and selective (vocational) education.
- In respect of cognitive and behavioural outcomes.

These recommendations are valid for India also.

Main Recommendations

Mass and Selective Schooling

- Countries should continue to be committed to the goal of mass Secondary Education as a minimum in terms of policy and provision.
- Commitment to universal access to Secondary Education as an aspiration should be maintained with efforts to remove barriers and obstacles as well as build on strengths and opportunities especially for girls.
- Serious attention be given to making adequate provision for those not selected into Secondary Education, those who drop out or leave before completing the cycle and those denied access to their preferred streams.
- Where there is not full transition from Primary to Secondary and/or from lower Secondary to upper Secondary, efforts must be made to accommodate all those who are eligible through alternative provisions. Where this is not possible, available places should be allocated equitably and transparently.
- Mass access to Secondary Education will require partnership between governments and other providers (private, NGOs, etc.), but governments should seek to safeguard the interests of learners by ensuring that quality standards are maintained by all providers.
- The structure of programmes and streaming practices should be

reviewed to offer greater flexibility and choice to learners in the selection process, including the option to return to a preferred stream.

- Future orientation at Secondary Education should be towards greater quality and diversity of what is provided, more flexibility in the organisation of learning and greater responsiveness to the needs and circumstances of learners.

General and Selective (Vocational) Education

- The Secondary Education system should focus on links between academic and vocational subjects and their interdependence in the overall education of adolescent learners of both genders.
- Secondary Education is about preparation for life and should reflect the reality of life in the twenty-first century that encompasses a seamless to-and-fro between continued learning and the world of work.
- The nature of vocational subjects, the way in which they are organised and taught, as well as the recognition given to them determine their status in the Secondary school curriculum.
- Secondary Education including Vocational Education needs to address not only the human resource needs of the society but also the development needs and aspirations of the individual.
- There is a strong trend in Secondary Education in most countries to include some element of Vocational Education for all learners. Some countries are experimenting with ways of providing such joint education to different population groups, including migrants, isolated rural populations and learners in regular secondary schools.
- Incorporating Vocational Education into Secondary Education can be expensive resulting in poor quality teaching and a lowering of status of these subjects. Innovative and cost-effective strategies to overcome this problem have included contracting out the teaching of subjects to nearby specialist schools and centres or creating different ways of teaching Vocational disciplines that are less demanding in terms of equipment, materials and practically trained instructors.
- As the trend of life-long learning is becoming clear, Secondary Education is adjusting to this reality by developing flexible structures and varied options in their programmes, as well as having stronger links to the world of work.

Cognitive and Behavioural Outcomes

- There is recognition that academically based education does not adequately address students' needs in terms of realising their full potential, especially in a context of rapid economic, cultural and social change and gender based discrimination.
- Given the declining role of other socialising agencies. Schools should take greater responsibility for helping learners acquire life-skills.
- The emerging role of teachers (notably as facilitators), their status, integrity and commitment are essential for implementing life-skills education successfully. The quality of pre-service and in-service teacher training is critical in this regard.

- Teaching methods, school facilities and services should be developed and adapted to provide life-skills/behavioural education.
- The role of Secondary school principals needs to be consistent with this new reality.
- Education decision-makers need to be sensitised to the consequences of their choices based on evidence of such factors as the links between academic success and personal and community well-being.
- A multi-sectoral approach involving government ministries, NGOs local communities, etc. is essential for successful implementation of this kind of education.

36

Future Education in India

BRIEF HISTORY OF ATTEMPTS FOR EDUCATIONAL REFORMS IN INDIA FOR THE FUTURE

The first attempt in India for educational reforms was made on January 5, 1985 when the then Prime Minister Rajiv Gandhi declared that a new education policy would be formulated that would equip the country both scientifically and economically to enter the twenty-first century. This statement resulted in the National Policy on Education (1986). With a view to implementing the NPE, a Programme of Action (1986) was prepared and followed.

In 1992, the Policy was reviewed and slightly revised in the light of the experience gained in the implementation of the Policy. Accordingly a new Programme of Action (1992) was planned.

The National Council of Educational Research and Training, New Delhi, usually called the academic wing of the Ministry of Human Resource Development, Department of Education, Government of India, published in 1986 a book entitled *School Education in India: Present Status and Future Needs*, which contained the views of the eminent educators of the country.

POINTERS TOWARDS FUTURE REFORMS IN EDUCATION: SUGGESTIVE MODELS

Notwithstanding the time gap, these views are still relevant and provide useful pointers. Here, three models are briefly reviewed.

A. PROF. MALCOLM S. ADISESHIAH'S MODEL

Prof. Malcolm S. Adiseshiah, a great scholar and educationist in an article '*Educational Perspectives*' described the position in the beginning of the 21st century as "Education of the future will be life-long—a glimpse of a great and revolutionary truth will emerge that education is not a spatial monopoly of something called the school and college; that it is not a time-bound learning experience; that there is no such thing as childhood education, adolescent education, youth education, or adult education. There is just education which is a way of life, a life-long way of life. Every year, every month, everyday, from the cradle to the grave, a person will be learning, open to learning and given the opportunity to learn in the home, school, university, factory, farm, hospital, office, cooperative, temple, trade union, political party, cinema and club. Education will be open. Schools without walls, polyvalent classes, integrated schools, universities of the air, will be juxtaposed with firms, farms, factories and business houses as education extension agents with their survey documentation and research facilities. The whole wide-open area of self-instruction, similar to what is taking place in our rural areas, will be operative. Let us not forget that for the farmer and his wife the farm is the school, what they do in their daily life is their curriculum of learning. Their experience in dealing with their daily survival problem is the substance of their evaluation. Life-long education will be a fact of life".

Prof. Adiseshiah suggested the following educational model for meeting the future needs:

1. *Non-formal Education System*: Launching the non-formal education sub-system for the two priority groups—school drop-outs in the age group 6-14 and working adult illiterates in the age group 15-40, evolving, devising functional curricula, producing learning materials, mobilising teaching resources from trained teachers as well as progressive farmers, engineers, musicians, dramatists and sportsmen and using existing buildings, labs and workshops for running the concentrated courses.

2. *Multiple Entry Points*: Reorganising the existing formal education sub-system into multiple entry and exit points at its different levels so that students could enter, leave and re-enter the school and university system at anyone of several points to answer the call of work in the home, farm, factory or office, continue their education through organised non-formal programmes.

3. *Establishing Relationships*: Establishing the relationship between the two sub-systems involving the nexus between their educational content, methods and technologies of teaching and learning.

4. *Vocationalisation of Secondary Education*: Vocationalising the second level of education.

5. *Important Components of Education*: Things like computerised instruction, open learning systems undifferentiated curricula for rural-urban and male-female populations, inter-disciplinary approaches to teaching, integration of education and work and establishment of a value system which would promote international understanding, peace and harmony will become some of the important components of education in the beginning of the 21st century.

B. PROF. S.V.C. AIYA'S MODEL

S.V.C. Aiya, a former Director of NCERT in an article 'School Science Curriculum Dynamics' incorporated in the same book visualised the scenario for 2000 A.D. as, "Inadequate control of population will create serious problems on the food and health fronts, requiring a specific orientation of school science towards agriculture and preventive medicine.

"Even in agriculture, the demand for unskilled and illiterate labour will decrease. Skilled workers must be mentally prepared to learn, even on their own, new jobs and move to them. Apart from similar qualities, technicians must have proficiency in an international language like English and must be capable of innovating to fill gaps between old and new techniques, etc. Technologists including management personnel, must be familiar with the use of computers, statistical methods, etc. It is their responsibility to reduce pollution, prevent upsetting of the ecological balance and more generally, everything that harms society. They have to instil in society a sense of duty and of social purpose. They have to persuade those concerned to move to new technologies and guard against obsolescence.

"Capacity for logical, orderly and exact expression, ability to properly comprehend technical literature, often in a language other than their mother tongue, and proper realisation of social responsibilities appear to be pre-requisites for skilled workers, and to a much greater extent for technicians and technologists. These qualities have to grow from education at the school level. Hence the humanities and social sciences will go together with science. So far as science is concerned, the forecast indicates that much greater attention has to be paid to application. In addition there is need to move children at school even directly into technology."

C. FUTURE SCENARIO AND KIRPAL'S MODEL OF FUTURE EDUCATION

Dr. P.N. Kirpal, a former Secretary, Ministry of Education, Government of India (now known as Ministry of Human Resource Development, Government of India) in an article published in a book '*School Education in India: Present Status and Future Needs*', NCERT, 1986, visualised the future scenario in terms of 12 problems. He referred to the three great explosions of accelerated development, three crucial issues contending for mastery, three deep conflicts requiring peaceful resolution and balanced synthesis and three poignant gaps portending grave dangers and fateful challenges. Dr. Kirpal further observed, "Some of these twelve problems have plagued several civilisations of the past, but in the 21st century they can threaten the entire humanity and consequently call for global efforts to overcome the evil and nurture the good implicit in the choices and solutions that may be offered and taken."

Three Explosions: (1) Explosion of Population; (2) Explosion of Knowledge, and (3) Explosion of Expectations.

Three Issues: (1) Issues of War and Peace; (2) Issues of Man and Environment; and (3) Issues of Culture and Technology

Three Conflicts: (1) Conflict between the Inner Man and the Outer Man; (2) Conflict between Freedom and Social Organisation; and (3) Conflict between Tradition and Modernity.

Three Gaps: (1) Gap between Developed and Developing Countries; (2) Gap between Knowledge and Wisdom; and (3) Gap between Power and Love.

Ten Principles for the Transformation of Education for Future Needs

Dr. Kirpal suggests ten principles for a profound renewal and transformation of education:

1. Our thinking should be hard and without rhetoric.
2. Education is synonymous with life.
3. Education is a comprehensive national task involving all people and all society.
4. Integrated education should serve man and social development.
5. Value-oriented education is essential for balanced personality and harmonious society.

6. Indian education should draw upon the growing corpus of international education and enrich it by its own contributions.

7. Education should support and strengthen a great cultural renaissance.

8. Education should help development by cooperative enterprise.

9. The defences of peace are best built in the minds of men.

10. The use of new technology calls for great care and discrimination to absorb it into the national ethos and safeguard moral and cultural values.

FUTURE SCHOOLS AND CLASSROOMS OF INDIA

Following are the characteristics of new schools:

I. Philosophy or Objectives of Future Schools

The Delors Commission Report or the Report of the International Commission on Education (1993-1996) has outlined the philosophy of education on four pillars and the schools must base their programmes accordingly.

1. Learning to Know
2. Learning to Do
3. Learning to Live Together
4. Learning to Be.

1. *Learning to Know.* Learning to know implies:
   (i) Concentrating on a small number of concepts.
   (ii) Combining a sufficiently broad general knowledge with the opportunity to work in depth on a small number of objects.
   (iii) Learning to learn so as to benefit from the opportunity education provides throughout life.

2. *Learning to Do*: Learning to do means:
   (i) Acquiring not only occupational skill but also move broadly the competence to deal with many situations and work in teams.
   (ii) Learning to do in the context of students' various social and work experiences which may be informal.

3. *Learning to Live Together.* This means:
   (i) Developing an understanding of other people.
   (ii) Appreciating the spirit of interdependence.
   (iii) Managing conflicts in a spirit of respect for the values of pluralism, mutual understanding and peace.

4. *Learning to Be*: It implies:
   (i) Bettering development of one's personality.
   (ii) Enabling the student to act with greater autonomy.
   (iii) Developing power of judgment.
   (iv) Developing personal responsibility.
   (v) Paying due regard to all aspects of person's potential, i.e., memory, reasoning, aesthetic sense, physical capacities and communication skills.

II. Structuring of the School

Schools, as social institutions, may need to rethink the way they are structured. At present they tend to be based on a nineteenth century hierarchical scientific management model: the superintendent is the manager, the teacher is the worker and the student is the product. Other organisational models for schools may need to be considered if students' development as whole persons is to be enhanced. Rather than considering how to prepare young people for the future, we need to think about preparing for the future with the help of young people through their active participation in and involvement with constructive and cooperative educational environments.

III. Classrooms as Mini Social Realities

In the classroom a "pedagogy of democratic fellowship" can be created in which children collaborate and support each other in their learning. Such classrooms can be mini social realities in which students assume different roles including those of leadership. Teachers are facilitators, organisers and managers of the learning—in this way, they focus not so much on what they are to teach but on supporting their students' learning. In this way, values are imparted through action and interpersonal behaviour in the classroom.

IV. Teaching of Science

A number of issues for the teaching and learning of science will need consideration:

(1) *Science Based on Daily Life Activities*: All students at school should have exposure to science education. However, school science is often divorced from people's everyday understandings. As a result, what is learnt in school is forgotten once examinations have been taken—the learning does not carry over to people's daily lives. If the contexts chosen for science work can draw more on people's daily life experience and their own ideas, then it is more likely that this gap can be bridged. Teaching the science involved in the working of everyday devices, such as farm tools may be helpful in this respect as well as not requiring expensive laboratory provision. However, low-cost science equipment will still be required to meet the needs of developing countries.

(2) *Science as an Enquiry*: In school science courses more emphasis will need to be placed on science as enquiry, as an exciting way of finding out about the world, rather than as a body of knowledge. We need to teach less but teach it more effectively. The local environment should become the laboratory of education, not only in the study of science, but in other areas, such as history and the social sciences.

(3) *Humanistic View of Science*: Science courses should give students the opportunity to consider the social, economic and ecological impact of scientific and technological innovations. The flavour of science as a human pursuit can be given through student's own enquiries. By developing testing and comparing ideas within a group, students can realise that others may have different ideas of their own and can appreciate the way science itself proceeds. Studies of the way scientific ideas have changed over the times, how different societies have developed different theories, and how scientific controversies have occurred in scientific knowledge.

(4) *Environmental Science*: Environmental science will have an important place in helping young people appreciate the interdependence of living things and the fragile balance in the biosphere. For this locally based case studies would be appropriate and are most likely to stimulate the interest of students.

V. Equality of Opportunity

Equality of opportunity is central to our concerns. It is well-known that in most countries present curricula and teaching methods result in girls achieving less well on physical science courses than boys. The orientation towards the science taught, the way it is presented and the methods of teaching will need to be reviewed to address this problem. The teaching of science to girls as well as boys should be seen in the context of career guidance and counselling in order that equality of opportunity between men and women can be realised in education and training.

VI. Refraining Our View of Technology

Our view of technology may also require reframing. There is a tendency for technologies to be viewed as ways of exploiting and controlling the environment to specific ends. In the future, technologies will continue to be developed which meet basic human needs in ways which are appropriate to each culture. Now, with our recognition of factors, such as, the limited physical resource of the earth and the delicate balance that needs to be maintained in the biosphere, we can no longer afford to neglect the various side effects that a technological innovation may have. There will always bc costs as well as benefits to be considered as a result of any new technological innovation. Additionally, the role of technology in helping to solve environmental problems needs to be studied.

In a sustainable world there will be need for technological developments and enterprise, not only of a high technology nature, but low cost intermediate technologies will be required. Technology teaching tends to be undervalued compared with science teaching. We suggest that, if we are to develop enterprising students, there may be a case for technology to have a more prominent place in the curriculum.

Technology courses are being implemented in schools in a number of countries. These give students the opportunity to design, construct and evaluate devices or systems which can be chosen to address needs in the students' own environment. In developing and evaluating products in this way, students can also be given the opportunity to consider the costs and benefits of the innovation and hence see the activity in social and environmental terms.

VII. Languages and Language Teaching

A policy for the teaching of languages is needed both to enable people with different mother tongues within a country to communicate and participate in that society and to provide for foreign language teaching to be a high priority in the progressively interconnected world of the twenty-first century. With mass communication now operating on a global scale, there is a real possibility of the English language becoming progressively dominant. However, the importance of preserving the rich cultural heritages embodied in the world's variety of languages was recognised as being essential.

In considering language education for the twenty-first century, the following points were made:

(a) Mother tongue, or the language of the home should be used in the beginning years of schooling where possible. Reading and writing skills in the mother tongue can later be built on in the context of lifelong education.

(b) Foreign languages in schools will require greater attention.

VIII. Communication of Better Quality

Increased communication is needed between teacher, other professional personnel in the school and peer groups. Social learning, human relationship skills values, attitudes, etc. can be stimulated and facilitated in peer groups, provided that teachers and other professionals can offer support and supervision.

IX. Social Sciences in the Curriculum

At a more fundamental level, it is a question of helping pupils to acquire, as they embark on life, the ability to interpret those things that mainly affect their personal future and the future of society as a whole. From this point of view support from the social and human sciences is essential, insofar as they relate both to life itself and to social phenomena. Needless to say, history and philosophy should also occupy an important place in such multidisciplinary research: philosophy because of its role in forming that critical outlook which is indispensable to the functioning of democracy and history because of its irreplaceable role in broadening the individuals horizons and raising awareness of collective identities. The teaching of history should, however, transcend the national context and should encompass a social and cultural dimension, in order that knowledge about the past may lead to a better understanding and a truer appreciation of the present. There is new strategy to be worked both by those who decide the main lines of emphasis of education policy and by those who draw up curricula. The aim would be to integrate the achievements of the social sciences into a global approach whereby a broad understanding of past and present could be attained.

X. Democratic Functioning of the School

With the emerging new democracies, an increasing number of countries are adopting democratic principles of political organisation. This involves a wide range of actors in the decision-making process, including various experts and diverse members of civil society. The challenges occasioned by this new political context go far beyond the establishment of formal democratic mechanisms to include the transformation of the daily life of the citizenry itself. This results in a greater emphasis on shared responsibility in decision-making. This movement involves an increasing emphasis on critical thinking, freedom of expression, the free flow of information and on a philosophy of human rights, with particular to the rights of the individual.

Education in tolerance and respect for other people, a prerequisite for democracy, should be regarded as a general and ongoing enterprise. Values in general and tolerance in particular cannot be taught in the strict sense: the desire to impose from the outside predetermined values comes down in the end to negating them, since values only have meaning when they are freely chosen by the individual. At the very most, therefore, schools may facilitate the daily practice of tolerance by helping pupils to allow for the point of view of others and by encouraging the discussion of moral dilemmas or cases involving ethical choices, for example.

(This aspect of democracy has been taken up in an earlier chapter).

XI. Teaching of Life Skills

Given the declining role of other socialising agencies schools should take greater responsibility for helping learners acquire life-skills. The emerging role of teachers (notably as facilitators), their status, integrity and commitment are essential for implementing life-skills education successfully. The quality of pre-service and in-service teacher training is critical in this regard.

XII. Teaching Methods

Teaching methods, school facilities and services should be developed and adapted to provide life-skills/behavioural education.

XIII. New Role of the Heads of Schools

The role of heads of school needs to be consistent with this new reality. Education decision-makers need to be sensitised to the consequences of their choices based on evidence of such factors as the links between academic success and personal and community well-being. A multi-sectoral approach involving government ministries, NGOs local communities, etc. is essential for successful implementation of this kind of education.

XIV. Broad Based Work Places

Education for the workplace of the future will need to be broadly based during the early years. One way of creating a flexible workforce for the twenty-first century will be to continue the broad general education currently characteristic of primary school education in most countries. This should be continued and general education should extend at least into the early years of secondary education. Primary school students need to be introduced to the concepts related to the world of work at an early age so that they can understand the role of work in our socio-economic system. The point of time when vocational education should be introduced into the educational system will depend greatly on the stage of development and the economic structure of the country or region involved.

XV. Use of New Technology

ICT (Information and Communication Technology will be used widely in educational institutions.

XVI. Teachers for Future Education in India: Radical Change in the Role.

The role of the teachers of the future would go a radical change in the future. They would in the real sense would play the role of facilitators of information and knowledge. They would guide the students as 'how to learn'. Emphasis will be on guiding the students. They would be well-versed in the use of ICT in education. A variety of teaching-learning methods would be used.

XVII. Parental Education

Support by society for the careers of children and counselling during their early years. This may include parent education and enabling parents or those with the primary care for young children to have adequate time to spend building sound relationships with them. In societies where parents, due to work obligations, have less time at home, schools are being expected to shoulder the responsibility for children's moral development. However, development of this kind occurs through experience within an environment and formal teaching cannot succeed by itself. There will need to be a partnership with other agencies in society including politicians and the media to address this issue.

XVIII. Non-Military National Service

Some developing countries have introduced a concept of non-military national service. This encourages young people to provide services to their communities and nations at several stages during and after their formal education. This process is also a very effective introduction to the world of work, the development of work ethics and encourages the commitment to public service.

XVIX. Other Programmes

Other programmes include:

(i) Provision of inclusive education.
(ii) Provision of compensatory education.
(iii) Elimination of gender bias.
(iv) Strengthening equity.

37

Agencies of Education: School as an Agency of Education

MEANING AND SIGNIFICANCE OF AGENCIES OF EDUCATION

It is rightly observed by Counts that "The school is but one among many educational agencies." The common belief that education is confined to schools and colleges is not entirely true. No doubt schools and colleges do occupy the most predominant place in the society as educational institutions. But when we use the word 'education' to denote the idea of the all-round development of the personality of the individual, we must recognise the role of other agencies of the society besides the schools and the colleges. Schools function for a short time daily. They function for nearly seven months only during the year. The rest of the time of the students is spent outside the school premises—in the family, in the neighbourhood and with the peer groups. They are influenced by mass communication, media and other agencies like social education centres, libraries etc.

According to some educators, of all the education we receive, we learn one-fourth from our teachers, one-fourth from books, one-fourth from our colleagues and one-fourth from the overall environment. This indicates the type of education and the multitude of agencies of education.

Education in a wider sense takes place from the womb to the tomb, i.e., from the conception to cremation. Education is a life-long process. Education goes on whether we are aware of it or unaware of it. Thus there are several types of social institutions that impart education. There are active as well as passive agencies of education. Likewise there are formal, non-formal and informal agencies of education. They are agencies of education run and managed by the Government. Private agencies are also involved in running different types of educational institutions.

Education imparted in formal agencies is called formal education. Education given in non-formal agencies is called non-formal education. Education received in informal ways is called informal education.

While discussing different types of agencies, it may be borne in mind that teachers are not the only educators. As observed by T. Ramount, "Let us agree to recognise explicitly that in a real sense teachers are not the only educators. In other words it is life that educates, the school provides a part of life's experience."

The agencies of education, we mean various sources, i.e., the institutions and organisations that play their role in varying degrees in the process of education.

BROAD CLASSIFICATION OF AGENCIES OF EDUCATION – I

	1. Formal agencies of Education		*2. Informal Agencies of Education*		*3. Non-formal Agencies of Education*
1.	School	1.	Art Gallery	1.	Adult and Social Education Centres
2.	College	2.	Cinema	2.	Play ground (when regular physical education is organised)
3.	Home or Family (in the Past)	3.	Home/Family	3.	Radio (Educational Programmes)
4.	Church (in the past)	4.	Library	4.	T.V. (Educational Programmes)
5.	Adult school (on regular basis)	5.	Museum	5.	Professional Organisations like Teachers' Associations when they organise seminars, workshops etc.
6.	Open school (when contact classes are also arranged)	6.	Peer group	6.	Clubs when educational talks etc. are organised.
7.	T.V. (When used as an integral part of the curriculum and pre-telecast and post-telecast lessons are organised)	7.	Play ground (when not supervised by the teacher)	7.	Cinema (When educational pictures are organised)
8.	Radio (When used as an integral part of the curriculum and pre-broadcast and post-broadcast lessons are organised)	8.	Press	8.	Internet (When some educational course is organised)
9.	State	9.	Reading Room	9.	Correspondence Institutions
		10.	Radio (Normal Programme)	10.	Open Learning Institutions
		11.	Television (Normal)	11.	Distance Learning Institutions
		12.	Voluntary Organisations like Bharat Sewak Samaj, Boy Scouts etc.		
		13.	Internet		

AGENCIES OF EDUCATION: CLASSIFICATION NO. II

Active Agencies of Education	*Passive Agencies of Education*
1. The Family	1. Cinema
2. The School	2. Radio
3. The Community	3. T.V.
4. The Religion	4. Internet
5. The State	5. Library
6. Social Clubs	6. Magazines
7. Peers	7. Newspapers
8. Neighbourhood	8. Market places
	9. Reading Room

AGENCIES OF EDUCATION: CLASSIFICATION NO. III

Formal	*Informal*	*Commercial*	*Non-Commercial*
(1)	(2)	(3)	(4)
1. School	1. The Family	1. Cinema	1. Dramatic Clubs
2. Religious Institution	2. General Games	2. Radio	2. Social Welfare Centres
3. Library	3. The State	3. T.V.	3. Sports Club
4. Art Galleries	4. The Peer Group	4. Clubs	4. Scouting and Guiding
5. Museum	5. The Community	5. Newspaper	5. Youth Welfare Clubs
6. Zoo	6. The Society	6. The Press	6. Adult Education Centres
7. Organised Games			

AGENCIES OF EDUCATION: CLASSIFICATION NO. IV

(1)	(2)	(3)	(4)
Government Run	Government Aided	Government Unaided	Semi Government

Note: There are several ways of classification

Formal Agencies of Education and Formal Education

Formal agencies of education like schools and colleges impart formal education. These agencies are consciously and deliberately planned to bring about specific influences on the educand. They have regular working hours. They prepare students for taking public examinations on regular basis. Usually they employ full time staff. They follow prescribed curriculum and textbooks. They have to conform to rigid departmental rules and regulations.

Informal Agencies of Education and Informal Education

The informal agencies do not follow any set pattern of instruction or education. In fact they impart education incidentally. Education is not organised deliberately in these institutions. These are informal groups. Education is indirect. One may learn without being conscious of it. Nevertheless influence of informal agencies of education is quite significant.

Non-Formal Agencies of Education

'Flexibility' is the key-word in the case of non-formal agencies of education. The system is an 'open one' with regard to: (1) Admission (2) Curricular work, (3) Place of instruction, (4) Mode of instruction, (5) Time and duration of instruction (6) Regular/temporary/part time staff. Open School, Open University, Open Learning Institutions and agencies imparting correspondence education come under non-formal agencies of education. Adult education agencies are usually placed under this category.

NO WATERTIGHT DIVISION OF AGENCIES OF EDUCATION

There is no clear-cut dividing line in classifying educational agencies into formal, non-formal and informal agencies. Even a school can take the form of a non-formal agency of education when it organises adult education classes and programmes. Students in the school acquire a good deal of education through informal contacts with the peers and the teachers. The press, the radio and the T.V. are normally termed as informal agencies of education. However, when they take up occasional programmes of formal education, they assume the form of non-formal agencies of education. Regular school broadcasts and T.V. lessons based on the school curriculum may be considered as programmes of formal education and radio and T.V. as agencies of formal education.

The entire programme of correspondence/distance education/open education may be classified both formal as well as non-formal, depending upon the type and mode of educational activity.

An adult school which follows a regular programme of education comes under the category of formal agency of education. However, when it is used for educational work, for sometime only it is placed under the category of non- formal agency of education. Recreational programme of an adult school may be placed under the category of informal education and this comes under the category of an informal agency of education.

With the increasing use of new educational technology and science and especially information communication technology (ICT), it has become very difficult to divide educational agencies into water tight compartments.

BROAD COMPARISON BETWEEN FORMAL AND NON-FORMAL EDUCATION

		Formal Education Agency	*Non-Formal Education Agency*
1.	Learners	It caters to learners who are in a position to attend full time	It caters to learners who cannot go to school or have dropped. It also includes learners who want to improve their qualifications by studying at home
2.	Aims	To get a certificate or degree needed for a job or self-employment	(i) To increase knowledge and skills

(*Contd.*)

		Formal Education Agency	*Non-Formal Education Agency*
			(ii) To better qualifications (iii) To pursue studies for self-satisfaction
3.	Place	An educational institution—school or college—full time	No specific place—can be home, factory, farm, library, open space etc.
4.	Age	Usually prescribed ages	Any age
5.	Grade	Students are grouped into classes	Usually no grouping
6.	Curriculum	Rigid and fixed	Curriculum not fixed
7.	Textbooks	Prescribed textbooks	Usually no prescribed textbooks
8.	Examination	Examination at regular intervals. Written tests. Essay and short answer	Normally no examination Assign-ments
9.	Teachers	Teachers usually on full time basis	Usually part time teachers
10.	Methods of Teaching	Direct teaching methods. Face to face teaching. Lecturing	Contact programmes, radio, T.V. Correspondence lesson, very little face to face teaching
11.	Status	Usually high status	Usually not considered at par with formal agency of education

SCHOOL AS AN AGENCY OF EDUCATION

IMPORTANCE OF SCHOOL AS A SOCIAL INSTITUTION AND A FORMAL AGENCY OF EDUCATION: SELECT VIEWS

A school is one of the most important formal agencies of education. It plays a very significant role in discovering, and moulding the innate capacities, attitudes, habits and ideas of the children with a view to producing well-balanced personalities: aesthetically rich, culturally refined, emotionally stable, mentally alert, morally sound, physically strong, socially efficient and spiritually enlightened.

Following quotations of the eminent thinkers illustrate suitably the importance of the school:

1. In the words of *Kandel*, "The school exists to accelerate the impact of the essential aspects of culture which prevails in the society".

2. *J.S. Ross* observes, "Schools ought to stress the duties and responsibilities of individual citizen. They ought to train their pupils on the spirit of cheerful willing and effective service".

3. *H.G. Wells* has remarked, "A world whose schools are unreformed is an unreformed world".

4. According to *Dewey*, "The school is primarily a social institution—an

effective agency in bringing the child to share in the inherited resources of the race, and to use his own powers for social ends".

5. According to *K.G. Saiyidain*, the school is a centre of vigorous life. It is in direct intimate contact with the realities of the life around, reflecting the best and worthiest of its features which are simple enough to appeal to the child.

6. *The Secondary Education Commission* (*1952-53*) outlines the functions of the school as, "The secondary school must make itself responsible for equipping its students adequately with civic as well as vocational efficiency—and the qualities of character that go with it—so that they may be able to play their part worthily and competently in the improvement of national life. They should no longer emerge as helpless, shiftless individuals who do not know what to do themselves".

7. *The Education Commission* (*1964-66*) observed, "The destiny of India is now being shaped in her classroom". This clearly explains the significant role of the school in social change.

8. *P.C. Nunn* describes the role of the school in these words, "A nation's school ... are an organ of its life, whose special function is to consolidate its spiritual strength, to maintain its historical continuity, to secure its past achievements, to guarantee its future. Through its schools a nation should become conscious of the abiding sources from which the best movements in its life have always taken their aspiration, should come to share the dreams of its nobler sons, should constantly submit itself to self-criticism, should purge its ideals, should reinform and redirect impulses".

9. *S. Balakrishna Joshi* sums up the concept of a school as, "A well-conducted school is a happy home, a sacred shrine, a social centre, and a society in miniature and a bewitching Brindavan, all beautifully blended into a synthetic structure."

10. *P.C. Wren* describes the functions of a school as "Organise the school to benefit the scholar, to train his faculties, to widen his outlook, cultivate his mind, to form and strengthen his character, to develop and cultivate his aesthetic sense, to build up his body, his health and strength, to teach him his duty to himself, to the community and the state, in short to make an honest, capable and healthy man of him—organise the school for this and not to prepare him for the matriculation examination".

11. *Harold Rugg* thinks of school as an "enterprise in living, both social and personal".

FUNCTIONS AND ROLES OF THE SCHOOL IN THE SOCIETY

The school is expected to perform the following functions and roles:

1. transmitter of cultural heritage of the society.
2. conserver of cultural heritage of the society.
3. promoter of cultural heritage of the society.
4. connecting link between home and the community.
5. provider of special environment for the all-round development of the child.
6. provider of a planned scheme of things for the child.

7. promoter of cultural pluralism, i.e., tolerance of all cultures.
8. promoter of ideals of the State.
9. promoter of social development of the child.
10. promoter of democratic values in the child.
11. promoter of secular values in the child.
12. promoter of ethical, moral and spiritual values of the child.
14. promoter of professional and vocational skills and values in the child.
15. promoter of egalitarian values in the child.
16. promoter of innate abilities of the child.
17. promoter of values of international understanding and peace.
18. centre of community.
19. trainer in the art of living together.

Summing up: In the words of S. Balakrishna Joshi, "In a word, a well-conducted school is a happy home, a sacred shrine, a social centre, a State in miniature and bewitching Brindavan—all beautifully blended into a synthetic structure".

MEASURES TO BE TAKEN BY THE SCHOOL TO PERFORM ITS FUNCTIONS

1. *Balanced and Simplified Environment*: The school discharges its several functions through curriculum. The school is envisaged to become an 'idealised miniature community'.

2. *Art of Living Together*: The school provides a number of group activities through which students get a lot of training in the art of living together.

3. *Training in Democratic Living*: School incorporates activities like student self-government.

4. *Opportunities for Vocational Training*: School includes several programmes and activities like work experience and vocational subjects.

5. *Development of Child's Entire Personality*: The school makes all possible efforts to provide a pleasant and stimulating intellectual, physical and spiritual environment which will evoke the manifold interests of the students and develop them creatively and constructively. It formulates a programme of hobbies, occupations and projects that cater to the varying aptitudes and temperaments of the students.

The school library, laboratory and workshop become the hub of stimulating activities.

6. *Spirit of Cooperation*: The head of school should develop an environment of cooperation and harmony among staff members so that the students also imbibe this attitude.

7. *Cooperation with Several Agencies of Education*: School enlists the cooperation of the various formal, non-formal and informal agencies wherever considered necessary.

8. *School as a Centre of Community Service*: School can organise adult education classes. It can take up community service programmes.

9. *Provision for School Experimentation*: The school laboratory will not be a toy-affair, where a few simple and carefully planned experiments are performed under vigilant eye of the teacher who sees that the prescribed routine

is followed. It will endeavour to give them something of the thrill and joy of discovery and the educative experience of learning through trial and error.

10. *Opportunities for Self-Discipline*: Discipline in the school will not be a matter of arbitrary rules and regulations enforced through the authority of the teachers helped by the lure of reward or the fear of punishment. The students will be given full freedom to organise functions, to conduct many of the school activities through their own committees and even to deal with certain types of disciplinary cases. In this way, discipline will be maintained through the influence of the social group and it will gradually lead to the development of self-discipline.

11. *Development of Child's Entire Personality*: School should provide a richly varied pattern of activities to cater to the development of its children's entire personality. It has to formulate a scheme of hobbies, occupations and projects that will appeal to draw out hidden powers of children of varying temperaments and aptitudes.

12. *Provision of a Stimulating Environment*: The primary concern of the school should be to provide for its pupils a rich, pleasant and stimulating environment which will evoke their manifold interests and make life a matter of joyful experience.

13. *Transformation into Activity School*: The school must be transformed into an "activity school" because activity has an irresistible appeal for every normal child and is his natural path to the goal of knowledge and culture.

14. *Development of Scientific Outlook*: Emphasis on all school programmes should be laid in the development of scientific temper in the minds of the students. Needless to state that scientific temper is very conductive to social change.

FUNCTIONS OF THE SCHOOL IN BEHAVIOURAL TERMS: HISTORICAL LETTER OF ABRAHAM LINCOLN TO THE HEADMASTER OF HIS SON'S SCHOOL

The word of wisdom stated more than one hundred years ago are still valid today. (extracts)

He will have to learn, I know that all men are not just, all men are not true. But teach him also that for every scoundrel, there is hero, that for every selfish politician, there is a dedicated leader.

It will take time, I know; but teach him if you can, that a dollar earned is of more than five thousand.

Teach him to learn to lose and also to enjoy winning.

Steer him away from envy if you can.

Teach him to learn that the bullies are the easiest to lick.

Teach him if you can, the wonder of books but also give him quiet time to ponder over the eternal mystery of birds in the sky, bees in the sun and flowers on a green hillside.

Teach him it is far more honourable to fail than to cheat.

Teach him to have faith in his own ideas, even if anybody tells him they are wrong.

Teach him to be gentle with gentle people and tough with the tough.

Try to give my son the strength not to follow the crowd when everyone is getting on the band-wagon.

Teach him to listen to all men. Teach him also to filter all he hears on a screen of truth and take on the good that comes through.

Teach him, if you can how to laugh when he is sad.

Teach him there is no shame in tears.

Teach him to scoff at cynics and to beware of too much sweetness.

Teach him to sell his brawn and brain to the highest bidders, but never to put a price tag on his heart and soul.

Teach him to close his ears to a howling mob.

Teach him to stand and fight if he thinks he's right.

Teach him gently but do not cuddle him because only the tests of fire make fine steel.

Let him have the courage to be impatient. Let him have the patience to be brave.

Teach him always to have sublime faith in himself because then he will always have sublime faith in mankind.

Summing Up

In the words of *S. Bala Krishna Joshi*, "A school is not a mere brick and mortar structure housing a miscellany of pupils and teachers; a school is not a market place where knowledge is doled out to unwilling consumers of varying capacities; a school is not a railway platform where a heterogeneous crowd gathers with diverse objects; a school is not a vigorous reformatory where juvenile suspects are kept under vigilant watch; a school is a spiritual organism with a distinctive personality of its own, a school is a vibrant community centre, radiating life and energy all-round, a school is a wonderful edifice, resting on the foundation of goodwill—goodwill of the public, goodwill of the parents, goodwill of the pupils. In a word, a well-conducted school is a happy home, a sacred shrine, a social centre, a state in miniature and bewitching Brindavan, all beautifully blended into a synthetic structure."

(*See also Chapter 2*)